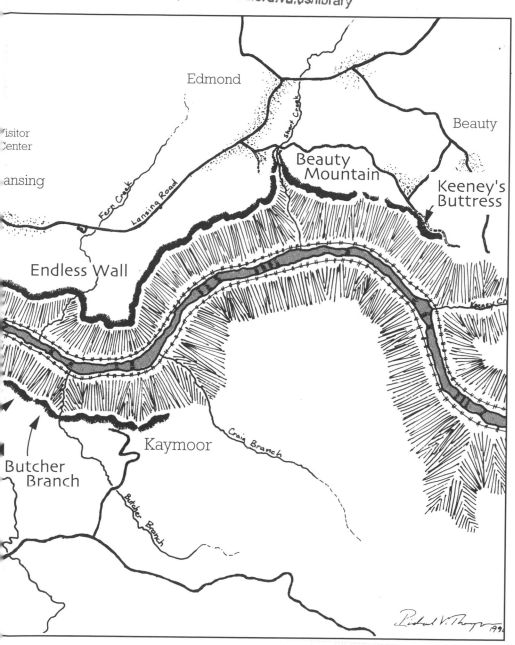

Edmond

Beauty

Visitor
Center

Beauty
Mountain

Keeney's
Buttress

ansing

Fern Creek

Lansing Road

Sheet Creek

Keeney Cr.

Endless Wall

Kaymoor

Craig Branch

Butcher
Branch

Butcher Branch

Fern Point Cirque with climbers on *The Prowesse.*

NEW RIVER ROCK

by Rick Thompson

Chockstone Press
Conifer, Colorado
1997

ISBN: 1-57540-015-4

FRONT COVER: Doug Reed on the first ascent of *Harbinger Scarab,* Endless Wall. Photo by Carl Samples.
BACK COVER: Fern Point, Endless Wall. Photo by Rick Thompson.

All maps by the author.

PUBLISHED AND DISTRIBUTED BY

Chockstone Press, Inc.
Post Office Box 1269
Conifer, CO 80433-1269

DEDICATION

In loving memory of my mother, June Corace Thompson and my grandfather, Frank Corace. Early in my youth you both inspired me with your passion for life, something I've carried with me since.

With each passing year I miss you both a little more.

WARNING: CLIMBING IS A SPORT WHERE YOU MAY BE SERIOUSLY INJURED OR DIE. READ THIS BEFORE YOU USE THIS BOOK.

This guidebook is a compilation of unverified information gathered from many different climbers. The author cannot assure the accuracy of any of the information in this book, including the topos and route descriptions, the difficulty ratings, and the protection ratings. These may be incorrect or misleading and it is impossible for any one author to climb all the routes to confirm the information about each route. Also, ratings of climbing difficulty and danger are always subjective and depend on the physical characteristics (for example, height), experience, technical ability, confidence and physical fitness of the climber who supplied the rating. Additionally, climbers who achieve first ascents sometimes underrate the difficulty or danger of the climbing route out of fear of being ridiculed if a climb is later down-rated by subsequent ascents. Therefore, be warned that you must exercise your own judgment on where a climbing route goes, its difficulty and your ability to safely protect yourself from the risks of rock climbing. Examples of some of these risks are: falling due to technical difficulty or due to natural hazards such as holds breaking, falling rock, climbing equipment dropped by other climbers, hazards of weather and lightning, your own equipment failure, and failure or absence of fixed protection.

You should not depend on any information gleaned from this book for your personal safety; your safety depends on your own good judgment, based on experience and a realistic assessment of your climbing ability. If you have any doubt as to your ability to safely climb a route described in this book, do not attempt it.

The following are some ways to make your use of this book safer:

1. **CONSULTATION:** You should consult with other climbers about the difficulty and danger of a particular climb prior to attempting it. Most local climbers are glad to give advice on routes in their area and we suggest that you contact locals to confirm ratings and safety of particular routes and to obtain first-hand information about a route chosen from this book.

2. **INSTRUCTION:** Most climbing areas have local climbing instructors and guides available. We recommend that you engage an instructor or guide to learn safety techniques and to become familiar with the routes and hazards of the areas described in this book. Even after you are proficient in climbing safely, occasional use of a guide is a safe way to raise your climbing standard and learn advanced techniques.

3. **FIXED PROTECTION:** Many of the routes in this book use bolts and pitons which are permanently placed in the rock. Because of variances in the manner of placement, weathering, metal fatigue, the quality of the metal used, and many other factors, these fixed protection pieces should always be considered suspect and should always be backed up by equipment that you place yourself. Never depend for your safety on a single piece of fixed protection because you never can tell whether it will hold weight, and in some cases, fixed protection may have been removed or is now absent.

Be aware of the following specific potential hazards which could arise in using this book:

1. **MISDESCRIPTIONS OF ROUTES:** If you climb a route and you have a doubt as to where the route may go, you should not go on unless you are sure that you can go that way safely. Route descriptions and topos in this book may be inaccurate or misleading.

2. **INCORRECT DIFFICULTY RATING:** A route may, in fact, be more difficult than the rating indicates. Do not be lulled into a false sense of security by the difficulty rating.

3. **INCORRECT PROTECTION RATING:** If you climb a route and you are unable to arrange adequate protection from the risk of falling through the use of fixed pitons or bolts and by placing your own protection devices, do not assume that there is adequate protection available higher just because the route protection rating indicates the route is not an "X" or an "R" rating. Every route is potentially an "X" (a fall may be deadly), due to the inherent hazards of climbing – including, for example, failure or absence of fixed protection, your own equipment's failure, or improper use of climbing equipment.

THERE ARE NO WARRANTIES, WHETHER EXPRESS OR IMPLIED, THAT THIS GUIDEBOOK IS ACCURATE OR THAT THE INFORMATION CONTAINED IN IT IS RELIABLE. THERE ARE NO WARRANTIES OF FITNESS FOR A PARTICULAR PURPOSE OR THAT THIS GUIDE IS MERCHANTABLE. YOUR USE OF THIS BOOK INDICATES YOUR ASSUMPTION OF THE RISK THAT IT MAY CONTAIN ERRORS AND IS AN ACKNOWLEDGEMENT OF YOUR OWN SOLE RESPONSIBILITY FOR YOUR CLIMBING SAFETY.

TABLE OF
CONTENTS

ACKNOWLEDGMENTS

It's been nearly a decade since I published the first edition of *New River Rock*. To the many climbers and friends who helped with that first-ever guide to the magical cliffs of the New River, I again extend my deepest gratitude. A very special thanks to my beloved friends Mike Artz and Carl Samples for their dedicated assistance in compiling that edition.

The following people have contributed to making this edition possible; Andrew Barry, Eddie Begoon, Roxanna Brock, Bruce Burgin, John Burcham, Tom Clancy, Steve Erskine, Rick Fairtrace, Scott Garso, John Harlin, Tom Howard, Peter Lewis, Rich Pleiss, Bob Rentka, Rick Skidmore, Ray Snead, Cal Swoager, Glenn Thomas, and Mark Van Cura

Thanks to *Leave No Trace* for allowing me to present their Minimum Impact Climbing message.

I extend my genuine thanks to Doug Cosby, Tom Isaacson, Gene Kistler, Kenny Parker, Greg Phillips, Stuart Pregnall and Bob Value for the enormous amount of time they each spent assisting with this edition.

To my close friends and partners in climbs Eric Hörst, Ron Kampas, Doug Reed and Carl Samples; I'm forever grateful to each of you for your dedicated commitment to bettering this book. Without your help it would certainly be something far less than it is.

Many kudos to my friends who, for the last six years, kept encouraging me (read prodding) to finish this edition. Life got crazy for a while. Thanks for your unwavering support. It's with the greatest pleasure that I send this one to press.

And finally to my family; Dad, Holly, Frank, Carol, and my sons RT and Chris. Thanks for believing.

Rick Thompson, Boulder, Colorado
March, 1997

SUPERINTENDENT'S FOREWORD

Since my early park service jobs as a climbing ranger at Mt. Rainier and Grand Teton, I have viewed climbing as one of the great opportunities that visitors to national parks have available to them. Climbing encompasses a sense of exploration, challenge and discovery that is an integral part of the park experience. Whether standing on the summit of the Grand Teton, hanging in a hammock a thousand feet off the deck in Yosemite, or contemplating the next move on a route at the New, climbing is an incredible way to visit and enjoy the national parks.

New River Gorge National River offers some of the best and most diverse climbing in the United States. Though your focus may be on the walls of sandstone that provide so many great routes, this park contains a variety of visitor uses and a diversity of resources. Each year, over 1.6 million people visit the three park sites administered here. They come to Bluestone National Scenic River, Gauley River National Recreation Area, and New River Gorge National River for the spectacular scenery and rich history, as well as to go fishing, hiking, boating, mountain biking, camping, and climbing. Among the many resources are the scenery, plant and animal life, streams and rivers, historic and archeological sites, and cliffs. Enabling this great variety of people to visit and enjoy the park, and protecting the diversity of resources contained within, are the primary goals of the National Park Service.

The rapid growth of climbing activity in this park over the past ten years has put substantial pressure on the climbing resources. Increased use of trails and climbing sites has damaged soils and vegetation, often with a negative result. Maintaining positive relationships with private property owners and park neighbors is critically important. Areas with significant historical or natural resources may require special techniques to protect them, and the incredible increase in commercial climbing use needs to be addressed. All of these issues require your help, cooperation, and involvement to solve.

Climbing is a welcome and historic use of national park lands, and continued access is a high priority. This park has acquired over 40,000 acres of land that is now open to the climbing community, and hopefully more will be added in the future. Come and climb, experience New River Gorge, and share with us the responsibility for preserving the resources of the New for future generations of climbers!

Pete Hart
Superintendent, New River Gorge National River

Endless Wall's Kaymoor Slab. Climbers can be seen on the second pitch of *Riding the Wave* and *Fool Effect*.

photo: Rick Thompson

The bridge from nearly a mile downstream.

INTRODUCTION

WELCOME TO THE NEW

Welcome to West Virginia's New River Gorge, the East Coast's one pitch paradise. In the land where Nuttall Sandstone, not coal, reigns king, lies a spectacular collection of classic routes. Textbook examples of every imaginable rock geometry can be found on these expansive cliffs which tower high above the river. After you've climbed just a sampling of the climbs, you'll be wondering whether there isn't something magical about this place.

From its name, one would gather the area to be a recent geologic occurrence, but fact is, 'bout the only thing really new at the gorge is the bridge, the park, and its renown as a recreational mecca. In contrast to the name, the New River is considered to be one of the oldest rivers in North America. It occupies the 100-million-year-old stream bed of the prehistoric Teays River, which was once the master river of the eastern North American continent. The Teays was destroyed by the most recent Ice Age, except for the portion now known as the New River Gorge.

Originating high in North Carolina's Blue Ridge Mountains, it winds its way along a north-westerly course, cutting across the grain of the Appalachian Mountains of Virginia and the Allegheny Plateau of West Virginia. It finally ends at its confluence with the Gauley River, not far downstream from Bubba City. Along the 60-mile stretch between that confluence and Hinton, West Virginia, it has carved a spectacular gorge. Reaching depths of 1,200 feet, and featuring mile after mile of precipitous cliffs capping the sheer gorge slopes, it's easy to understand why it's been called "the Grand Canyon of the East."

In the past two decades, the New has experienced a continual rise in popularity thanks to its diverse recreational resources. But the 100 years that preceded marked an age of industrialism, a time when whitewater, rockclimbing and mountain biking were unheard of. In 1873, the Chesapeake and Ohio Railway completed its tracks through the gorge, opening miles of otherwise inaccessible terrain to development. The 60 years that followed brought the glory days of the coal mining and coke-making industries to this region. The rich supply of low-sulfur, or "smoke-less," coal was easily mined from the slopes of the gorge. As mines were opened, small communities sprouted nearby, and by the turn of the century, more than a dozen towns prospered along the fifteen-mile stretch between Thurmond and Fayette Station.

When viewed from the Bridge Buttress the massive scale of the bridge is domineering.
photo: Glenn Thomas

The boom continued until the early 1930s when the coal market crashed. Some of the villages turned to ghost towns almost overnight. And though mining continues on a small scale, the golden age of coal is long over for the New River Gorge. Today we're reminded of this bygone era by the architectural skeletons of these once-thriving communities.

Recreational notoriety began in the mid-60s when a small group of whitewater enthusiasts first recognized the potential of this area. Word of the whitewater opportunities on the New and the nearby Gauley spread amongst their inner circle. By the mid-70s, five commercial rafting companies were operating here. It was at this time that climbers also took notice of the escarpment that rims the gorge. Initially, a tiny group of local climbers began to explore the most accessible outcrops. They found the outcrops, though not excessively tall, to be of superb quality. But as with the whitewater, the good word initially stayed with the local group.

In the late 70s, two landmark developments occurred that forever altered the area's socio-economic status and at the same time brought the New into the recreational limelight. The first was the 1977 completion of the renowned New River Gorge Bridge. At 3000 feet in length this towering structure is the longest single-span arch bridge on the planet. Soaring nearly 900 feet above the river, it's also the highest bridge east of the Mississippi. There are many other impressive statistics, like the 22,000 tons of maintenance free, Cor-Ten steel that it's built with, or the 17,000 cubic yards of concrete buried in the abutments that support each end. That's enough concrete to build nearly five miles of two-lane highway. But more important than these engineering statistics, the bridge completed the final link of the Appalachian Corridor L Expressway (Route 19). For the first time ever this mountainous region was readily accessible.

The second development occurred in November of '78 when Congress designated the 50-mile stretch of river between Hinton and Fayetteville, as the New River Gorge National River. The area encompasses more than 63,000 acres, comprised primarily of steep gorge slopes and tributary watersheds. The river corridor is managed by the National Park Service. Their mission is preserving and protecting the outstanding natural, scenic and historic resources in and around the gorge, while providing balanced recreational opportunities.

Situated at the north end of the bridge is the Canyon Rim Visitor Center, operated by the National Park Service. This beautifully designed facility is adjacent to Route 19, providing a convenient stop for travelers. Without a doubt it's the area's single best place to learn more about the gorge. A number of intriguing displays and a most excellent slide show provide an overview of the gorge including its history. Also worth taking in is the unique vantage of the bridge from the Overlook Platform, an airy perch situated atop a 75 foot buttress. Other National Park Service sites of interest include the recently completed Thurmond Depot, the river put-in facility at Cunard, and the Kaymoor historic site.

The 80s and 90s have brought a new era to the gorge; the age of human powered outdoor recreation. Although whitewater is still the most popular of these venues, climbing, hiking and mountain biking aren't far behind. As a result of these opportunities the New River Gorge has emerged as one of the East Coast's recreational meccas.

CLIMBING HISTORY

BY CARL SAMPLES

The climbing history of the New River Gorge spans little more than two decades, making it a youngster among the venerable climbing areas of the eastern U.S. such as the Shawangunks, Seneca Rocks, and the White Mountains of New Hampshire. This late blooming was largely due to its relative isolation, there being no nearby urban population center, and until 1977, when the New River Gorge Bridge was completed, no highway system connecting it to the recreating public. The New River had been known to insider rafting and kayaking enthusiasts as a hidden white water gem in the early '70s, and indeed a small group of local climbers first tasted the delights of its Nuttall sandstone as early as '74. *The Bridge Buttress*, which practically overhangs old route 82, then the main route across the gorge, was the most eye-catching piece of rock around. The

T.A. Horton on a 1979 free attempt on *High Times.*

photo: Steve Erskine

initial forays were toproping adventures by a circle of southern West Virginia climbers which included Nick Brash, Bruce Burgin, Steve Erskine, T. A. Horton, Hobart Parks, and Rick Skidmore. The first known lead was Skidmore's ascent of *Zag* (8) in 1975, today an area standard that one can get in line for on any given weekend. He led *The Mayfly* (9) later that same season, and like *Zag*, it was originally given the rating of 5.7, a precedent that would lead to many sandbaggings in future years.

The standards rose, although unknowingly, with Skidmore's lead of *Chockstone* (9) in '76, as the "5.7 syndrome" claimed another route. Whether the undergrading was a correlation with the notoriously stiff grades of nearby Seneca Rocks, or simply an underestimation of their abilities, these pioneering Gorge climbers continued the trend with ascents of other "5.7 classics" at the Bridge Buttress such as *The Tree Route* (10a),*The Layback* (9), and *Jaws* (9) in 1978. In retrospect, Greg Anderson's *Tree Route* has become known as the New River's first 5.10.

Other trends of the late '70s included aid ascents of several of the more intimidating crack lines as training for road trips to Yosemite. The first of these was *Blood and Guts*, which became known as *Handsome* and *Well Hung*, by Erskine, Skidmore, and Parks, and perhaps the most interesting was an overnight bivy on the first ascent of *The Butler Done It* (*Welcome to Beauty*). The locals also began to explore the miles of cliffline running in either direction from the Bridge Buttress, putting up the first routes at the North Bridge Wall in '77, the Junkyard Wall and Beauty Mountain in '78, and Endless Wall in '79. Landmarks of this era of discovery were Erskine's *Climbing Under the Influence*, now known as *New Yosemite* (9), at the Junkyard, Brash and Burgin's *Screamer Crack* (8) at Beauty Mountain, and Skidmore's *Anal Clenching Adventures* (5.9 A1) at Fern Buttress. A lull in new route activity set in during the 1980 season and into '81 when many harder climbs were top-roped but few lead attempts were made on them. Brash's lead of the spectacular *Supercrack* (9+) at Beauty Mountain is certainly an exception, and marked a new level of confidence in local climbers to seek out harder-looking lines.

The year 1981 brought the first spark of outside influence to touch the New. Later it would slowly fan into flames as word wafted through the climbing community. For years the small circle of local climbers, on their frequent trips to other areas such as Seneca Rocks, Stone Mountain, and Linville Gorge had tried to convince people to come and sample the New River sandstone. In '79, Burgin and Brash had even placed a photo album complete with maps in the Gendarme, the climbing shop and social center of Seneca Rocks, but no one ventured to the New. In May of '81 they met Tom Howard on a climbing trip to his home state of North Carolina and convinced him to plan a trip north. That September, Howard and his partner Bill Newman were given the grand tour of Beauty Mountain where they established the exemplary offwidth *Momma's Squeeze Box* (8), the first route done by an out-of-state climber. The next day they hiked to the rim of Endless Wall on Burgin's advice, and after rappelling in, did the first ascent of the striking dihedral *New Fangled Dangle,* which they graded 5.10a. Years later it was realized that the loose chockstone wedged in the initial roof crack had been placed there by none other than Brash and Burgin on a previous attempt. Two years had passed before Howard had used the chockstone to pull the 5.10 overhang, but today the stone is gone and the desperate start is given a solid 5.11 grade. The two Carolinians wrapped up their initial trip at Beauty Mountain where they bagged *Fat Man's Folly* (9), *Mononuclear Knows It* (8), and the Brain centerpiece *Brain Teasers* (10a).

The fall of '81 continued with several top-notch climbs being established at Endless Wall and Beauty Mountain. Burgin and Brash, perhaps inspired by the enthusiasm of new visitors to the Gorge, climbed *Springboard* (10a) at Fern Buttress, Brash's first 5.10 lead. Howard returned in October with Jim Okel and Dan Perry, and they pulled off the amazing *Rod Serling Crack* (10b) at Beauty, *Underfling* (10b) at the Bridge, and *Night Gallery* (10b) at Endless. Howard, always with an eye for a great line, culminated the most productive season at the Gorge yet with ascents of *The Undeserved* (10b) and *Roy's Lament* (9), two of the best crack lines on Endless Wall.

Strangely, this late-season flurry did not carry its momentum into '82. Howard was busy in North Carolina and did not visit that year, and the local climbers were also quiet. The most notable ascents were done on the Overlook Buttress by Rich Pleiss (early Seneca Rocks guidebook author) and company, which included the Bridge Area's 3rd 5.10, *The Sandman* (10a). The calm of '82 was soon to give way to the storm of '83.

In early March, Cal Swoager and Phil Wilt, two climbers from Pittsburgh, were returning from North Carolina's Crowder's Mountain, where they had heard tales of clean cracks and miles of cliff, and so decided to stop and see for themselves. After parking below the bridge and carrying their gear past classic line after classic line, they finally stopped beneath an exceptional finger crack. Naming it *First Strike* (10a), they began a season in which the list of players grew into a who's who list of the top climbers from the states surrounding West Virginia, a season characterized by choice hard crack climbing.

Swoager returned a few weeks later, this time with Ed McCarthy, and led three previously toproped routes at the Bridge: the twin *Gemini Cracks* (10 a &c) and *Sundowner* (10d). In May, Doug Reed climbed *Englishman's Crack* (11b), the first 5.11 lead at the New, and the first of his many landmark routes. May also brought climbers back to Beauty where Reed and Howard did *Burning Calves* (10b), while Wilt and McCarthy plucked such plums as *Happy Hands* (9), *Mushrooms* (10a), and *Wham Bam Thanks for the Jam* (10b).

Summer brought a steady rise in standards when Pleiss freed *Handsome and Well Hung* (11a), and the aid was eliminated on the intimidating *Welcome to Beauty* (11b) by Seneca Rocks climber Pete Absolon, the New River's second and third 5.11's. The list grew rapidly as Wilt, along with another Seneca climber Mike Artz, added *Genocide* (11c) from a hanging belay at the lip of a roof, and Swoager flashed the right-hand variation to *Welcome to Beauty* (11c/d). Kris Kline, yet another Seneca hardman, led the superb *Marionette* (11c) and Artz kicked off a long list of first ascents with the tremendous *Agent Orange* (11d). The eighth and final 5.11 of '83 was *The Force* (11c) added by Reed. Although not at the cutting edge of difficulty, the ascent of *Four Sheets to the Wind* (9) by Wilt and Carl Samples represented the first visit to the Junkyard by climbers outside the small circle of locals.

After a particularly rainy spring in '84, the Junkyard again became the focus of visiting climber's attention when Reed and Howard snatched a number of good lines including *Rapscallion's Blues* (10c) and *Enteruptus* (10a). Howard then teamed up with Wes Love to add *The Entertainer* (10a). New route activity waned later in the year however, as the Seneca Rocks faction were busy filling in the remaining lines there in anticipation of a new guidebook release, and the Pittsburgh contingent spent the season exploring new crags on the Chestnut Ridge in northern West Virginia. In August, Climbing magazine featured an article on the *New* written by Bruce Burgin, including a spectacular cover photo of Tom Howard hanging it out over the river on a variation finish to *Supercrack* at Beauty Mountain. The crowds weren't immediately flocking to the Gorge but the seed had been planted for the new route explosion of '85. Several quality routes were completed in the fall of '84, mainly at Endless Wall. Pleiss and Tim Mein added a variation to *The Undeserved* called *Mig Squadron* (11a) and the 5.8 classic *Fantasy* a short distance downstream. Howard and Reed were also busy there with such high caliber routes as *Mud and Guts* (10b), *Bisect* (10c), and *Triple Treat* (10a). At the Junkyard, Swoager became the first climber to venture beyond the wooden ladders where he found the stunning finger crack *Zealous* (10d). This route characterizes the '84 season, in which climbers showed a diversity of interest through a willingness to explore further to find the highest quality lines.

The '85 season stands out as the first of several boom years at the New River Gorge. The stage had been set: now some eighty established routes were scattered over seven miles of cliff along the northern rim of the Gorge, with heaviest concentrations at the Bridge, the Junkyard, and Beauty Mountain. There were a handful of dedicated climbers poised to fill in the gaps: from the south came Mike Artz and Andrew Barry, an Australian climber temporarily living in Blacksburg, Virginia, while the northern contingent was led by Cal Swoager and another Pittsburgher, Rick Thompson.

New River pioneer Bruce Burgin in 1985 at the top of *The Undeserved* after the second ascent.

photo: Rick Thompson

The spring began with consolidation at the Bridge Buttress, as Swoager added a number of significant routes including *Blunder and Frightening* (10b), *Maranatha* (10c), *Two Edged Sword* (10d), and the celestial *Angel's Arête* (10b). Barry boldly finished *High Times* (11a) through the tiered roofs to the top, although today few climbers venture beyond the anchor at the end of the finger crack. Swoager also returned to Beauty Mountain where he climbed the exciting *Broken Sling* (10b) and *Hallaluah Crack*, which he conservatively rated 5.11d, thinking perhaps it was harder than that. Subsequent repeats by nimble fingered climbers have established the consensus grade at 5.11c, though Swoager's notorious sausages probably made the tips crux considerably harder. The time was not ripe yet for 5.12.

Consolidation continued at the Junkyard where McCarthy led *New River Gunks* (7) and Swoager added *Team Jesus* (10b), *Faith Crack* (10c), and *Realignment* (10d), as well as what may be the first true face climb at the *New, Recreation* (9), a gripping adventure which he protected with two pairs of opposed skyhooks. Thompson was also active at the Junkyard, along with Salt Lake native Scott Garso, establishing *Lapping the Sap* (10a) and *Danger in Paradise* (10b) among others, while Barry grappled with the daunting roof crack of *Stuck In Another Dimension* (11a). Activity progressed downstream with 5.11's by Barry (*Childbirth*), Swoager (*Five-eight*), and Thompson (*Commuter Flight*), the last in conjunction with the visiting John Harlin. The swarming effect was most noticeable a bit further downstream at the Dog Wall where a dozen routes were done in a couple of weekends.

Late in the summer, Swoager kicked off a flurry of activity at Beauty Mountain by doing both the *Right* (11c) and *Left Sons of Thunder* (11d) in a single day, demonstrating his vision for the bold and dramatic. Barry led *Trancendence* (11d), audacious in its own right, and later followed up with the improbable *Steve Martin's Face* (11d). Artz and Swoager bagged the incredible finger crack *Chasin' the Wind* (11b), the only route in the gorge that offers two pitches of 5.11.

October of '85 was perhaps the single most impressive month of new route activity in the area history, as the prominent activists focused their energy on the four mile expanse of Endless Wall. Burgin established the standard Central Endless rappel on the final weekend in September, which, in conjunction with the Jacob's Ladder climb-out, provided effective access all the way downstream to Diamond Point. On the first weekend in October Artz and Barry started the flood with ascents of *Oystercracker* (10a), *Tuna Fish Roof* (11d), *Celibate Mallard* (10c), and *The Orgasmatron* (10d), while Thompson and Garso did *Imperial Strut* (10b), and what they later learned were the second ascents of *The Undeserved* and *Roy's Lament*, adding a 10b direct finish to the latter. The next weekend found the core group aimed at Diamond Point, where in two days most of the classic lines were climbed. Artz, Thompson, and Mike Cote did *Nestle Crunch Roof* (10b), *Remission* (10b), *Can I Do It Till I Need Glasses* (10c), and *The Diving Swan* (11a) the first day, then Thompson returned with Tom Howard to add the stellar *Raging Waters* (11a) while simultaneously Doug and Maurice Reed climbed *Zygomatic* (11c). Their day continued upstream where Barry led another of his trademark bold face climbs, *Recondite* (11b), and Howard and Thompson established *Lobster In Cleavage Probe* (10a) and the ever popular *Grafenberg Crack* (9) on what would become known as Dr. Ruth's Big Buttress. The Reed brothers wrapped up this milestone weekend with *Wire Train* (10c). More than a dozen of the best lines Endless Wall had to offer were completed over a span of ten days.

But it was Swoager who pulled the 'coup de grace' at Diamond Point two weeks later by cranking the awesome finger crack *Leave it to Jesus* (11d), his last and arguably best effort at the New. Meanwhile, activity was heating up further downstream as Rick Fairtrace and Scott Jones, both Pennsylvania climbers, found the exemplary *Ritz Cracker* (9) at Fern Buttress, and then on an exploratory trip to Fern Point established the first route there with S*mooth Operator* (9+), a supreme fist and hand crack. The end of October found Thompson and partner Bob Value at Fern Point where they grabbed the first ascent of *Mellifluus* (11a), then he returned a week later with Glenn Thomas, Dave Sippel and Mark Van Cura to do *Autumn Fire* (10b), *Premarital Bliss* (9+), and the unlikely *Biohazard* (10a). Artz' lead of the sensational *Linear Encounters* (11a) in November wrapped up activity there for the season.

During this period of rapid growth at Diamond and Fern Points, Phil Heller had been busy establishing several hard lines at Fern Buttress. Routes such as *Berserker* (11c), *The Sun Viking* (11d), and *The Monolith* (11d A1), stand as tribute to his talent and vision. The final route of '85 was done there when Howard and Thompson climbed *Crescenta* (10a) on a snowy December day, bringing to a close a season in which not only did the total number of routes in the Gorge practically triple, but the New came into its own as one of the major cragging areas of the eastern U.S. It had been the year of Endless Wall, beginning its transformation from remote outlying cliff to what many were coming to consider the heart of New River climbing.

The honemaster himself, Eddie Begoon.

photo: Peter Noebels

Several quality routes were done in 1986 at both ends of the difficulty range. Heller, Alex Karr, and Mike Kehoe did several 5.11 testpieces at Fern Buttress including *Grand Space* (11b) and *Fern Creek Direct* (11a), then Barry and Artz ticked *Pleasure and Pain* (11b) and *Surge Complex* (11a). The first routes to be given the 5.12 rating were done a month later when Karr pulled the double-tiered roof on *The Old Duffer's Route* (12b) at Central Endless and Barry negotiated *Strongly Stationary* (12a), the thin face left of Artz' sweet and spicy arête *Welcome To Huecool* (11d R) at the South Bridge Wall. Rick Fairtrace and Scott Jones established three moderate gems on the Star Trek Wall which have proven immensely popular, while at Fern Point Glenn Thomas, along with Thompson, climbed the Gorge's most uniquely positioned 5.9, the sweeping arête of *The Prowesse*. Thompson, this time with Scott Garso, found *Riding the Crest of a Wave* (9), one of the New's longest routes, offering two pitches of stimulating 5.9 climbing. In May, Barry again pushed the envelope with another technical 5.12 face climb, this time at Beauty Mountain. *The Beast In Me* (12a) was one of the early routes at the New to require fixed protection, though the hand-drilled, Australian-style bolt (no hanger-use a wired nut), placed high up in the crux, reflected a strong commitment to the spirit of adventure.

Summer brought a resurgence of interest at the Bridge Area Crags, from The Rostrum on the upstream end to the North Bridge Wall downstream. Routes such as Scott Garso's *Mounting Madness* (8 R), Thompson's *You Snooze, You Lose* (10d R/X) and *The Vertex* (10d R), Samples' *Dr. Rosenbud's Nose* (10c), and Artz' *Ook Ook Kachook* (11a) all contain a level of commitment inherent in straying away from vertical crack systems, an element which New River climbers were increasingly coming to grips with. Perhaps the prime example is Barry and Artz' *Destination Unknown* (11a) on the back side of The Pinnacle at the North Bridge Wall, a bold and entirely improbable steep 5.11 face. Riding the confidence gained from this success, they tackled two of the premier lines at Beauty Mountain, *The Will To Power* (11c) and *Chorus Line* (12b), both requiring a willingness to risk long falls in order to solve difficult cruxes.

Thompson, Garso and Samples after a day in the bush in 1986.

photo: Ron Kampas

Once again Endless Wall became the late season destination, as the lines around Dr. Ruth's Big Buttress were cleaned up by Thompson and friends, including *Technarete* (10b), *Insertum Outcome* (10b), and the popular face climb *The Diddler* (10a). Artz and fellow Virginian Eddie Begoon added *Crystal Vision* (10a) and then did two classic offwidths, *Lunar Debris* (9) and *Crescent Moon* (7), the latter being perhaps the best of its grade at the New. The final obvious crack line at Diamond Point was completed when Begoon, along with Glenn Thomas, nabbed *Crack a Smile* (10a). Fall also produced the first three routes to snake their way up Kaymoor Slab, where Barry ran it out on *New Wave* (11a R) and *Paralleling* (11a R), and Thompson quivered through *The Upheaval* (10b R). Away from Endless, standards were advanced at the Junkyard when, on his first visit to the New, Eric Hörst prevailed on *Pilots of Bekaa* (12a), a prelude to his accomplishments the following year.

The first edition of New River Rock was released in the spring of '87 containing 465 routes and variations at the four established cliffs: The Bridge Area Crags, The Junkyard, Beauty Mountain and Endless Wall. The New had taken the first turn towards becoming a destination climbing area, and the average number of climbers on any given weekend was slowly rising. Many of the classics began to see frequent ascents as climbers, armed with the fresh guidebook, were finding one of the interesting downclimbs or a rappel point to get a sampling of Endless Wall. Yet the Gorge still harbored undiscovered cliffs, so as the crags that were now so familiar to the local activists became more popular, they simply focused their energies on something new.

For a brief period the Ambassador Buttress held their interest, a crag first visited by climbers in '83, when Eric Anderson, Doug Chapman, and Paul Goesling climbed the obvious dihedral now known as *Kidspeak* (10a) and a perfect handcrack around the corner, opting to rappel from pins at its abrupt end on the wall. In March and April a rediscovery of the crag produced several excellent routes including Howard's *Lunar Tunes* (10a), Artz' *Consenting Clips* (10b), and the complete ascent of *Clumsy Club Crack* (10b) by Samples, adding an 'R' rated direct finish. Begoon clawed his way up the first sport climb at the New, naming it *The Bolting Blowfish* (12a), its all-fixed protection consisting of two tied-off knifeblades and two bolts. Other noteworthy routes added on return trips to the Ambassador Buttress were *Newveau Reach* (11c) by Artz, *Chasing Rainbows* (10a) by Begoon, *Pleasure Principals* (11a) by Thompson, and *Dragon In Your Dreams* (11c) by Kenny Parker.

It was Parker who spearheaded an early season push downstream beyond the Dog Wall and Cat Cliff, to discover a discontinuous two mile stretch of sandstone that would become known as Bubba City. Comprised of ten individual crags, the first action centered around the easy access point at Bubba Buttress, then quickly spread downstream to Central Bubba and the Head Wall. While the Ambassador Buttress had diverted attention, Parker and company were busy systematically bagging many of the obvious plums such as *Face It Bubba* (11a), *Basic Bubba Crack* (9), and *Dumbolt County* (10b). It didn't take long for word to spread among the inner circle and by May the feeding frenzy was on. Artz and Begoon teamed up to establish a number of fine routes including *Shear Strength* (11c) and *Burnin' Down the House* (12a). Parker took on *The Raging Tiger* (10d), Artz jammed the outstanding *Little Creatures* (10d), and Thompson managed *Tworgasminimum* (10d).

As Bubba City became the center of activity, Rick Fairtrace chose instead to explore the untouched miles of cliff so plainly visible across the Gorge from Endless. His initial visit in March produced *Raiders of the Lost Crag* (10b), and Kaymoor had its first route. On return trips he added many fine crack climbs including *Searching For Sanctuary* (9+) and the stellar *Fairtracer* (10d), but persistent tendonitis kept him from following up these efforts, so while the north rim areas were rapidly gaining popularity with the number of new visitors increasing weekly, Kaymoor would quietly slip back into obscurity until the '90s.

Paralleling the early season exploration was a sharp rise in top-end difficulty routes at the Junkyard and elsewhere. In the spring, Hörst returned to the Junkyard to do *Brother Sun* (12c), a steep, multiple-roofed corner system that suited his Gunks-bred style of power climbing. A serious training-oriented approach to the sport put him in position to attempt desperate-looking lines with confidence, as evidenced by *Fearful Symmetry* (12b), a thin crack done in May at Central Endless, and his first effort at Bubba, *Regatta de Blank* (12a).

The summer brought heated action to Bubba City, and while good routes in the more moderate grades were still being found, the impetus was towards difficult face and arete climbs, often requiring an increased use of fixed anchors for protection. Leading the push was Hörst, as he added a hit list of 5.12's including *Bubbacide* (12b), *Desperate But Not Serious* (12b), and *Incredarete* (12c), solidly establishing the grade at Bubba. Other treasures found during this exhilarating time were Artz' *Tour de Bubba* (11b), Bob Rentka's *Bubbatism By Fire* (12a R), and Reed's *Head With No Hands* (11b). Other climbers were coincidentally pushing the limits of known cliff line steadily in a downstream direction beyond the Ames and Head Walls, climbing many routes, including an occasional classic, along the increasingly broken series of walls . Doug Chapman, Kenny and Kevin Parker, and John Trautwein found dozens of lines on the Little Head Wall, the Ameless Wall, Kingfish Buttress, Sandstonia, and the far flung Rubble Rock. Perhaps the best route along these remote and still today relatively untraveled crags is Parker's *King of Swing* (11a) at Kingfish, a steep hand crack rivaling any in the Gorge for its aesthetic appeal.

Bubba City's easily accessible, sheer faces and particularly compact sandstone provided the ideal arena in which to transform the style of route conception at the Gorge. Thompson's *The Raptilian* (10d) became the second sport climb at the New in October, although the standard practice was to use only the bare minimum of fixed gear, and most of the new routes required placing protection in addition to the occasional pin or bolt. The highlight of the fall was the introduction of 5.13 to the New with Hörst's ascent of the steep and thinly pocketed *Diamond Life* (13a) at Central Bubba. The results of tests done on the Bubba City proving grounds were about to be played out on the other major crags in the Gorge, as climbers warmed to the sport climbing concept already catching fire at other major U.S. climbing areas such as Smith Rock and Shelf Road.

The first of the major crags to be scrutinized for lines previously considered too thin on protection was the Bridge Buttress where March brought its first 5.12's, Hörst's *Team Machine* (12a) and *Mega Magic* (12c), and Stuart Pregnall's *Frenzyed* (12a). 1988 brought full maturity to the Bridge Area with the addition of such sterling routes as Thompson's *The Stratagem* (12a) and *Little Head Logic* (12a), Hörst's *Pirouette* (12d), and John Bercaw's *Are You Experienced?* (12c) and *Locked On Target* (13a). This last route, which Bercaw completed in May, was actually the fourth 5.13 at the New, following Hörst's spring effort on *Welcome to Conditioning* (12d/13a) and Reed's superb *Dissonance* (13a), both on Endless Wall. Other select lines climbed in early '88 at Endless were the futuristic *Jesus and Tequila* (12b) by John Scott and Dave Groth, and on a return visit from his new residence in California, Andrew Barry added *Back With My Kind* (11c/d).

Bubba City experienced consolidation in '88, when many of the classic 5.12's were climbed, and the trend toward more fixed gear was unfolding. Hörst was far and away the most prolific, and best among his many accomplishments were *Masterpiece Theater* (12d/13a), *Pump and Circumstance* (12b), *Likme* (12a), *Michelin Man* (12a), and *The Cutting Edge* (12b). Two of the best 5.11's at Bubba City were done by visiting Bob D'Antonio along with Thompson, *Boschtardized* (11c), the first 5.11 sport climb at the New, and the popular *Tongulation* (11c/d), both at the Ames Wall.

In August, Reed established *Sacrilege* (12b) and Thompson added *Hold the Dog* (11d), the first and second sport climbs on Endless Wall. Then in October, Reed climbed *Freaky Stylee* (12a) with Porter Jarrard at Fern Point, the first climb at the New to be equipped with cold shut anchors at the top, and the doorway was open to sport climbing expansion along the four mile Endless Wall. Before the season ended Reed and Thompson had added a number of sport routes to the Fern Point

Carl Samples at the office.

photo: Rick Thompson

repertoire including *Le Futuriste* (12b) and *Modern Primitive* (12c/d). Further upstream, Artz, with Begoon and Don Wood, established *Sugar Bubbas* (11a), Reed and Thompson inaugurated the classic *Aesthetica* (11c), and Parker added the testy Bubbas at *Arapiles* (12b). Sport climbing was introduced at Beauty Mountain in the fall of '88, strangely enough by some visiting French climbers, who put up a couple of short, steep routes, but whose most notable ascent was Beauty's first 5.13 and the New's hardest route to date, Pierre Deliage's *Stabat Mater* (13b). All was not sport climbing at the Gorge however, as Samples found *Party In My Mind* (10b) at Fern Point, and though the lone bolt appeared two weeks later, placed by an unknowing would-be first ascensionist, it now prevents a groundfall from the first crux. In general, 1988 can be characterized as a turning point in climbers' approaches to establishing new routes; the core group of activists had now largely embraced the use of fixed anchors as the sole means of protection on many of the new breed of harder, steeper routes. The stage was set for a sport climbing revolution at the New River.

Spring of '89 marks the second wave of explosive new route activity along Endless Wall. At Fern Point, Thompson established a number of classic routes such as *New Age Equippers* (11c), *Dangerous Liaisons* (12b), and the slab testpiece *Dead Painters Society* (12a). This was also the scene of Hörst's *Standing Up In the Big Tent* (12c), *Civilizing Mission* (12b), and the descriptive *Whip It* (12b). The addition of the Honeymooner's ladders during the previous winter spurred a burst of activity from Central Endless to the Wall of Points. Hörst climbed *Bullet the New Sky* (12a), a supreme arete, while upstream Begoon and Artz were cleaning up with *Kline the Billy Goat* (11b) and *Man-O-War* (12b). Doug Reed ranged the Endless herding up exemplary routes such as *Sparks* (12c) and *Martini Face* (12c), then capped it off by redpointing *The Racist* (13c) in May, which would stand as the New's hardest route for two years. Central Endless remained the spotlight for new route activity through the summer and into fall with additions like Hörst's *Gift of Grace* (12b) and *This Sport Needs an Enema* (12b), Thompson's *How Hard is That Thang?* (12b), Reed's *Harlequin* (12b), and Jarrard's *Caption* (12b/c). Thompson also spotted a few more plums at Fern Point including *Stealth and Magic* (12c/d) and the dynamic *Pocket Pussy* (12b), while Hörst added the immensely popular *Smore Energy* (11b).

The long stretch of rock between Jacob's Ladder and Beauty Mountain, known as Upper Endless, also became the scene of concentrated attention. Artz and Begoon struck first with *White Powderete* (11a), *Spurtin' Fer Certain* (12a), and *Lactic Weekend* (11c). Reed countered with the first routes at the cave-like Cirque, *Hourglass* (12a/b), and the testpiece *Superstition* (12d), featuring two pitches of 5.12d. Visiting climber Scott Franklin left his mark with the short but intense *Super Mario* (13b) on a boulder at the upstream terminus of Upper Endless. Beauty Mountain received attention from the sport climbing collective in '89 as well, first by another visiting climber, Brooke Sandahl, who established the prominent *Gun Club* (12c). Jarrard conquered the improbable with *Ad Lib* (12d), and Reed chimed in with *Grace Note* (12b) and *Loud Noise* (12b/c). The final blows of the year were landed at Fern Point by Hörst on *Mental Wings* (12c) and Thompson on *Eurobics* (12d/13a). The '89 season was one of maturation for the birthplace of New River sport climbing, Bubba City, but more importantly, it marked the blossoming of sport climbing at all the other major crags in the Gorge.

In 1990 Beauty Mountain and Endless would yield a bumper crop of choice routes. March brought Thompson and Samples back to the Wall of Points to send a pair of lines spotted the previous November, *Euro Nation* (10a/b) and *Flashpoint* (11d), and by April all the heavy hitters were in full swing at Endless. Reed knocked out two of the best hard sport climbs around with *Quinsana Plus* (13a) and *Pudd's Pretty Dress* (12c), while Porter Jarrard succeeded on the twin crimpfests *Libertine* (13a) and *Oblivion* (12d). D.C. area regular Doug Cosby added *Hellbound For Glory* (12a) and *Maximum Leader* (12c), while Hörst persevered on *Sweetest Taboo* (13b), redpointing this Fern Point testpiece in May.

By late spring Beauty Mountain bore precious fruit as Dekker plucked *Chunky Monkey* (12b), while Reed reaped *Disturbance* (11d) and *Green Envy* 12b), then mastered the thin and powerful *Sportster* (13b). Summer didn't slow the pace as he added *Concertina* (12a), Cosby cranked *Smokin' Guns* (12a) and *It's a Fine Line* (12d), and Thompson redpointed the archetypal slab route *Ewe Can't Touch This* (12c/d).

At Central Endless, Reed established what has become a trade route with *The Legacy* (12a), and followed up with the physical *Titan's Dice* (13b), an unlikely line through a giant roof system. As the prime autumn season ensued, Thompson dialed in *What Will People Think?* (12c/d) on the Kaymoor Slab and Jarrard mastered the desperate roof on *Idols of the Tribe* (13a) at Fern Point, but the season clincher was managed by Dekker at Upper Endless when he redpointed *Tubin' Dudes* (13c). The '90 season was studded with brilliant successes on a wide variety of projects, as eyes were opened to the abundant sport climbing potential of Endless and Beauty Mountain.

Returning to the New in the spring of '91 hungry for new rock after a season of scooping the cream of the routes along the north rim crags, Doug Reed went straight to the apparently virgin cliff capping the southern slope of the Gorge. Establishing *Magnitude* (11d) on the first day, he then began work on a route through a wide band of cave-like roofs which would become *Lactic Acid Bath* (12d), the first route in the Glory Hole of Kaymoor. The first month of the season produced a battery of excellent sport routes on the steep, well-featured walls including *The World's Hardest Five Twelve* (12a) and *Out of the Bag* (11d) by Reed, *The Haulage* (12c/d) and *Sanctified* (13a) by Jarrard, and the ever popular *Rico Suave Arête* (10a) by Thompson.

By May, Kaymoor was indeed 'out of the bag', as new routes came from many different parties. Joe Crocker blazed the excellent *Carolina Crocker and the Tipple of Doom* (12a), Cosby grabbed gold on *Thunder Struck* (12b), and Jarrard devoured *Dining At the Altar* (12a). Steve Cater added two popular lines with *Moon Child Posse* (11c) and *Lost Souls* (12a), as activity crept further downstream from the Rico Suave Buttress and White Wall toward Butcher's Branch. Gary Beil grabbed the truly classic *Flight of the Gumbie* (9) while Reed pushed on to the Seven-Eleven Wall to find the amazing *Slash and Burn* (12d). In June, Reed returned to the shade of The Hole, where he completed *Burning Cross* (13a) and *Blood Raid* (13a). The summer brought rapid consolidation to Butcher's Branch and the Seven-Eleven Wall, where many outstanding 5.11's were found, highlighted by Shannon Langely's *Sancho Belige* (11c), and Reed's *Mo' Betta Holds* (11c/d) and *Scenic Adult* (11d). As the ferocious pace of new route activity at Kaymoor slowed and the chalk dust settled, the final tally registered some eighty new routes in less than six months, placing the New solidly at the top of the Eastern sport climber's list.

Eric Hörst at Bubba City in 1988.

photo: Rick Thompson

This collective focus on Kaymoor, combined with a late season flux of climbers to the crags around Summersville Lake, effectively halted new route activity on the north rim, with one notable exception at Beauty Mountain. Harrison Dekker had begun working on a controversial abandoned project which had suffered an unfortunate hold fabrication at the crux. The damage had been repaired by Porter Jarrard, but then he had been unable to complete the route. In October of '91 Dekker succeeded on what still stands as the New's hardest route, *The Travisty* (13d).

Climbing at the New River Gorge had matured by the end of the '91 season; following seven years of rapid growth, the senior crags of The Bridge, Junkyard, and Beauty Mountain were all but climbed out, and many of the area's great lines had been done along the now well-traveled Endless Wall. Traditional climbing had climaxed from '85 to '88, while the majority of routes done after '89 were sport climbs, culminating with the Kaymoor explosion. The New was drawing the attention of climbers from across the country, and the number of 'regulars' spending weekends there grew into the hundreds.

Persistent scrutiny over the next couple of years by the familiar activists revealed several outstanding climbs, the best enhancing the palette at the top end of the difficulty scale. In the spring of '92, Reed, at the forefront, probed Endless, finding *Dial 911* (13a) beside his testpiece The Racist, then over the summer established *The Pocket Route* (13a), *Bloodshot* (13a), and *Shovel Jerk* (13b) on what has become known as the Reed Wall. The next year he continued with Endless masterpieces like *Blackhappy* (12b) and the outrageous *Satanic Verses* (13b/c). Kaymoor yielded a few more treasures in '93 as Thompson hummed the *Uninflatable Ewe* (12b), Cosby triumphed on his project *White Lightning* (13b), and Reed spanned the unrepeated *Fuel Injector* (13b). Kenny Parker tweaked a couple of ultra-thin arêtes at Fern Buttress, *Total Sex Package* (12a) and in the spring of '94, *Bosnian Vacation* (12d).

During an extended stay at the Gorge in the fall of '94, Thompson completed two long standing projects, *The Weatherman's Thumb* (13a) at Diamond Point and *The Ruchert Motion* (13a) at Beauty Mountain. Interest then shifted to Upper Endless, where the first sport routes went in around the Jacob's Ladder climb out. *Espresso Yourself* (12a) and *Stubble* (12b/c) by Thompson, *Fat Back* (12c) by Reed, and the entertaining *Churning in the Butter* (11b) by Samples began an upstream reassessment of this quiet section of Endless Wall. Late that year, Reed added *Slide Rule* (12a) and *Overkill* (13a), and equipped a number of ambitious projects in anticipation of the next season.

Long-time activist Bob Rentka.

photo: Doug Cosby

Strangely, in '95 the spotlight for new routes was shifted to crags along the river valleys north of the New, and the futuristic lines at Upper Endless would stay quiet a while longer. The Gorge meanwhile was enjoying its stature among the best cragging areas in the country, its reputation for excellent rock and routes only tempered by that of its weather. The '96 season would prove that all was not done though, as Reed, along with Brian McCray and Roxanna Brock, threw themselves against the colossal inverted walls of The Cirque at Upper Endless. Reed began with the unlikely 5.11's *Spurtual Reality* (11a/b) and *Powerlung* (11c), the latter highlighted by a depleting handrail finish across the cantilevered wall. Brock added *New Life* (11b), then upped the ante with *Finders Keepers* (12b/c) and *Holier Than Thou* (12c/d). McCray rang up an impressive tally, powering through such quality routes as *Live and Let Live* (12b), *Blacklist* (12b/c), *Xanth* (13b), *Ride the Lightning* (13b), and *Ragnarock* (13b). This inspired season may only be a taste of what the future holds; one look at the routes still in progress at The Cirque will leave you wondering...How far away is the New River's first 5.14.

THE ACCESS FUND – AT WORK AT THE NEW RIVER

The Access Fund is a national, non-profit organization dedicated to keeping climbing areas open and conserving the environment. As America's leading climber advocacy group, the Access Fund has been actively involved at the New River since it was founded in 1990. Because of their local commitment, a diverse slate of environmental and outreach projects have been effectively completed. Grass roots support has been instrumental in the realization of a number of these. With the help of nearly 150 volunteers the Access Fund has sponsored five environmental cleanups which were staged in partnership with the National Park Service. These cleanups have achieved remarkable results, having removed more than ten tons of garbage from in and around the cliff environment.

In 1994 the Access Fund provided a $1300 grant for the purchase of sorely needed building materials to replace the deteriorating access ladders along Endless Wall. On this project more than 40 volunteers helped to reconstruct the ladders, this time using high quality, enduring components. They've also provided a grant to publish two educational climber brochures which were developed in conjunction with the National Park Service. Additionally, a 1996 grant paid for educational trailhead signs.

Access Fund representatives have worked closely with the National Park Service to address impacts and provide solutions to management concerns. Currently, they are working with the National Park Service to develop a first-ever climbing management plan for the New River Gorge National River.

The Access Fund needs your support in order to continue it's efforts. Whether its acquiring threatened lands, funding trail projects or facilities like climber toilets, or negotiating on behalf of climbers, the Access Fund's continued commitment here, and across the nation, is crucially needed. For more information or to join the ranks of more than 8,000 current members, call the national office in Boulder, Colorado at 303.545.6772 or log on to their home page at *http://www.outdoorlink.com/accessfund* for more information.

LEAVE NO TRACE OUTDOOR SKILLS AND ETHICS

Leave No Trace is a national non-profit organization based in Boulder, Colorado that educates outdoor recreation user groups, federal agency personnel, and the public about minimum impact techniques. The following information is taken from their Rock Climbing booklet. Whether you're a backcountry trad-master or on the road to a 5.13 redpoint at the local crag, these principals and practices are for you. They are not rules, but rather guidelines based on climbers' abiding respect for and appreciation of wild and unique places and their inhabitants. To apply them effectively they must be tempered with common sense and adapted to the specific environment or situation. Adventure, beauty, and the freedom to pursue our craft remain essential to climbers. Continued access to the crags and the freedom to choose the rules of our game depends on making Leave No Trace a part of our daily climbing routine.

The original Honeymooner's Ladder – key to Endless Wall's popularity. The Rungmaster General can be seen putting the finishing touches on its construction.

photo: Carl Samples

American Climbers have historically been a group with a high standard of environmental care. However, the ethic that carried us through the early days of climbing is not enough anymore due to the combined effects of ever-growing numbers of climbers and ever-changing technologies. As an area's popularity increases, impacts to the land and to other visitors accelerate and become difficult to reverse. Litter, fire scars, and poorly planned trails are some of the unfortunate signs of carelessness that exist at some of our nations climbing areas.

We are appealing to all climbers to accept personal responsibility for the care of our fragile resources. Toward this goal, we offer the following principles, developed through the collaborative efforts of climbers, land managers, and climbing organizations including the Access Fund.

The Access Fund at the New: Senior Policy Analyst Sam Davidson (left), and National Access & Acquisitions Director Rick Thompson (center) with local activist Doug Reed at the Endless Wall.

photo: Armando Menocal

The General Principles of Leave No Trace are:

- Plan Ahead and Prepare
- Camp and Travel on Durable Surfaces
- Pack It In, Pack It Out
- Properly Dispose of What You Can't Pack Out
- Leave What You Find
- Minimize Use and Impact from Fires

And for climbers they all add up to the seventh principle:

- Minimize Climbing Impacts

These principals are applicable to the numerous crags and rock routes across North America. Success in decreasing the impacts created by climbers depends on understanding how these principles apply to different types of climbing in various environments.

Leave No Trace depends more on attitude and awareness than on rules and regulations. Minimum-impact techniques continually evolve and improve. Consider variables such as rock type, typical forms of protection, vegetation, wildlife, and the use the area receives - then determine the best way to leave no trace. Your climbing will be even more rewarding if you help to reduce changes to the land and foster relations with other recreationists, land managers and land owners.

Plan Ahead and Prepare

You've probably done a bit of research on routes, their difficulty, and the kinds of protection you might need on your next climbing day. But what about the aspects of planning that allow you to improve your Leave No Trace efforts? Make a decision to decrease your impact on the next visit to the crag.

Discarded tape and cigarette butts are unsightly so consider bringing along a small plastic bag in your pack for trash. If all you do is pick up a bit of litter, you will have improved your own Leave No Trace habits.

Camp and Travel on Durable Surfaces

Climbing areas may lie above steep slopes that can be easily eroded, or along riparian zones with fragile vegetation. With the huge increase in the number of climbers, random access creates serious erosion and trampling problems.

At easy-access crags or areas that see frequent traffic, the natural impulse is to make a bee-line through the brush to the base of the climb. Instead, take a moment longer to seek out and follow established paths and trails. A few footsteps off the trail may cause significant damage to the vegetation and attract further trampling and erosion, so remaining on existing paths is crucial. Try not to use trails that have been closed and respect rehabilitation efforts.

Choose campsites carefully. Camp in existing sites, if possible, to center your activities on already barren areas. Consider sites where either the vegetation is very resilient (e.g. grasses), or the ground is bare (e.g. rock, gravel, or sand). Avoid cooking and congregating on delicate flowers and woody ground cover that can be easily crushed. Try not to "improve" campsites by moving things around. If you move a few rocks to make a flat place to sleep, put'em back before you leave. Choose a slightly raised site that will drain water so you won't need to dig trenches in the soil.

Wherever you climb, try and unload your gear and take breaks on large, flat rocks or other durable ground to avoid damaging vegetation. During mud seasons and after rain, soft trails and roads are easily rutted and damaged, accelerating erosion during future runoff. Try and avoid these soft areas or use an alternate approach.

The choice is ours: We can help preserve the natural feel of our favorite crag or let incremental change lead to an ugly maze of erosion.

Pack It In, Pack It Out

Stick to the old adage: "Take only pictures and leave only footprints." Pack out what you bring in. All food waste, including orange peels and apple cores should be carried out, not buried or scattered. Food scraps left behind attract insects, rodents and other animals, which can become a nuisance or even a danger, especially in established or popular areas.

Please pick up trash when you find it. Consider taking a trash bag along with you every day. Recently, climbing rangers removed over 50 pounds of slings from the West Ridge of Forbidden Peak in the North Cascades. Keep a knife handy to remove the old, unsafe slings you find littering rappel and belay sites.

Properly Dispose of What You Can't Pack Out
When you are beyond access to outhouses, urinate on bare ground away from vegetation, climbing routes, and trails. Though not a health hazard, urine smells bad and can attract animals to the salts it contains.

Dispose of solid, human waste in a "cathole" at least 200 feet away from trails, the base of climbs, water sources or campsites. Avoid small depressions that may be drainages during the next wet spell. This helps prevent human waste from leaching into potential water sources. Be sure your disposal site is not a likely pathway or at the base of a boulder problem.

Dig into the top, dark organic layer of soil, make your deposit, stir in soil until the hole is completely filled, and disguise the spot thoroughly. Pack your toilet paper out in a ziplock. Human waste left in alcoves, overhangs, under rocks, and in other dark, cool environments will not breakdown readily.

Leave What You Find
Climbers are adventurers. When you climb, give others the same sense of discovery by leaving unique artifacts and features in place.

Trampling vegetation at the base of climbs or removing it from rock can be minimized if you're careful. Vertical walls represent unique biological communities. Some of the plant and lichen species may be quite rare so if at all possible, don't disturb them.

Reduce disturbance to animals. Try to keep all animals from getting human food. It's usually unhealthy for them and certainly teaches them to become pests in search of handouts. The presence of raptors, such as peregrine falcons, and many hawks and owls, are indicators of the health of any ecosystem. Avoid nesting sites on or near the crag in the spring and early summer. Watch the birds as they circle and land near their nests to identify places to avoid. If you encounter nests on a climb, don't touch them. Human contact may cause the adults to abandon the nest and its eggs or young. Adhere to seasonal closures; you can always find another climb.

Minimize Use and Impact of Fires
Fire rings and pits at the base of any crag are unacceptable. Fires are often considered inappropriate in populated areas and have caused access problems for climbers. Check with local land managers so you can comply with regulations. Warm clothes and hot food can keep you as warm as a toasty fire (on both sides at once!). Consider using a stove instead of a fire for cooking. They consume no wood, leave no scars, and rarely get out of control.

If you decide a fire is necessary, build it in a pre-existing fire ring and keep current fire danger in mind. Collect your wood from a wide area, away from camps, trails and crags, to disperse impact. Gather only small pieces - wrist diameter or less - that are already dead and on the ground. This makes it easier to burn your fire down to pure ash and eliminates half-burned logs. Before leaving, make sure the ash is cold. Dispose of excess ash by dispersing it widely, well away from camps, trails, cliffs and roads.

Minimize Climbing Impacts

Treat the rock with care! Although there still seems to be plenty of room for new routes and new climbing areas, the rock resource is limited.

Impacts to natural resources - Chipping and drilling holds destroys the rock. And besides, it's against NPS regulations. While cleaning loose and friable rock from faces is sometimes necessary for safety on new routes, avoid changing the rock to make a route easier or more comfortable.

Use removable protection and natural anchors wherever practical. Before placing bolts or other fixed anchors consider local ethics and regulations affecting their placement as well as the validity and quality of the route. Above all, if you place a bolt, make sure it is secure.

If you are considering establishing routes at new cliffs, weigh whether the local ecology can withstand the increased traffic a set of new routes will create. Climbing activities focus use in specific areas. Once the new area becomes known, changes such as barren ground, new trails and disturbance to wildlife follow quickly. Is the new route or area you have found really adding diversity to the local climbing scene, or is it more of the same? Before you document a new route or crag, or place fixed anchors, ask whether its quality and uniqueness justifies the impact that will inevitably follow once people learn about it.

Impacts to other people - Most non-climbers fail to understand the importance and the various and vital ingredients of safe and enjoyable climbing, and are sensitive and concerned about the presence of slings, bolts, or human caused changes they see at climbing areas. These changes are often perceived as ugly or disruptive to the general surroundings. It is up to us to be sensitive to other people's perspectives, and to take every opportunity to educate climbers and non-climbers about Leave No Trace techniques. Consider the following ideas when climbing; you may come up with others as well.

- To lessen the visibility of sport climbs, use discreet anchors at the tops of climbs. Colorful slings are easily seen from the ground and they bother hikers and other users.

- Use dull or painted bolt hangers to better disguise those that are easily seen by other recreationists on nearby trails. Many climbers are now carrying a small stencil to keep paint off the rock when they camouflage their hangers - a little retro-camouflaging never hurts and might do your own crag some good!

- Rather than rappel with ropes directly around tree trunks, leave a sling instead. Pulling ropes around trees damages them permanently. The sling can be removed later when it becomes unsafe. If you do leave a sling, choose a color that is difficult to see from a distance.

- If you use chalk, try and use it sparingly. A Leave No Trace attitude means that we should at least consider our use of chalk and how it affects the experiences of others. Maybe you will choose to use colored chalk or none at all.

- Maintain a low profile by removing equipment at the end of each day. Sometimes climbers leave ropes in place overnight to make better time the next day, but protocol varies with the area, so check local trends. Either way, the practice should not be abused; try not to let those ropes stay up for multiple days.

Protecting access through courtesy - Noise - from the volume of your boom box to the words you let fly out of your mouth when you fail on a red point attempt - can have a huge impact on other people and on wildlife. Consider who else is around and try and keep your decibel level within reason.

Another practice that can result in access problems is parking. Park only in designated areas or along roadways that are not posted. Carpool, when it is practical.

Contact the climbing group in your area and see how you can help. Be active in planning and management of climbing areas. Volunteer for clean up efforts, trail maintenance, and rehabilitation efforts, or organize them for your local area. Regional Coordinators from the Access Fund can help you organize clean ups, fundraisers for local projects, and deal with access issues.

Help maintain positive relationships between climbers, other recreationists, local residents, land managers and land owners by obeying the regulations that apply to all users of these lands. Make a decision to Leave No Trace during your next climbing trip.

For more information on the Leave No Trace ethic call 303.442.8222. Access Fund Regional Coordinator Gene Kistler can be reached at 304.574.2425.

GEOLOGY

The deeply entrenched New River has carved its way through numerous rock formations of the Late Mississippian and Middle Pennsylvanian ages along its meandering course through south-central West Virginia. The extensive cliffs that rim the northwestern end of the gorge are comprised of 325 million-year-old, quartzose conglomeratic rock known as Nuttall Sandstone. What a fitting honor that the rock we climb on is named after the family that has owned Beauty Mountain and Endless Wall for more than a century. Though sedimentary in nature, it contains a high percentage of quartz, which makes it highly resistant to weathering. Its diamond hard nature accounts for the beautiful clean sweeps of cliff line that yield little talus. Major vertical fractures occur often with many running the entire height of the escarpment. Sedimentary bedding is common with horizontals appearing almost everywhere. Some of them rival those of the Shawangunks in user friendliness. The prominent vertical fractures and horizontal beddings have also worked to create the abundance of overhangs that proliferate on the cliffs. Some project more than 50 feet!

Nuttall Sandstone reveals a palette of captivating colors, particularly where it's sheltered from the effects of weather. Vivid pink, orange, and yellow hues can be found on many facets. Although a fine grained texture predominates, you'll occasionally encounter anything from cracks lined with ripper crystals to baby bottom smooth bulges. Top climbers from around the world have called this the finest rock in America.

LOCAL CLIMATE

Located in the Allegheny Plateau on the western slope of the Appalachian Mountains, this region is subject to a variety of climatic extremes. The rule of thumb is that spring and fall are the best seasons for climbing, but good weather can be found year round. For the same token horrible conditions can also be experienced just about anytime. Local climbers seem to have adapted to these cruel extremes in a sort of evolutionary twist but, if this area is a destination during your travels you'll want to be selective about the timing of your trip. Fall is far and above the most reliable season with spring offering the next best time to visit.

After the storm; Endless Wall

photo: Carl Samples

On average more than 40 inches of precipitation fall here each year. If you're from the eastern U.S. that won't seem like an inordinate amount, but if you're from the arid west that will sound like a constant deluge. July has the highest monthly average, while October the lowest.

The months of May through September are generally warm, November through March are moderately cold, and April and October are months for fairly rapid transition. Summer highs average in the 80s, but when combined with the often stifling humidity, nearly unbearable climbing conditions result. Fog is a fairly common occurrence. During cool fall nights it often settles into and fills the gorge to the rim, providing a dramatic morning vista. It usually burns off before later morning. Dense fog can also be associated with many of the slow moving low pressure cells and can make even the most perfectly sheltered rain day routes too manky for climbing. Call the Weather Center at 304.253.4000 for an up-to-date forecast.

AMENITIES

New River Gorge offers a plentiful supply of places to sleep, eat and entertain yourself at.

Camping

For camping there is a selection of private campgrounds including:

Chestnut Creek Campground - located on Lansing Road. Full service facility with showers - 574.3136

Mountain State Campground - located on Ames Heights Road. Full service facility with showers - 574.0947

Rifrafters - located on Laurel Creek Road. Full service facilities with showers - 574.1065

Rocky Top Retreat - located adjacent to Kaymoor - running water and portable toilet facilities, but no showers. no phone #

National Park Service - Primative camping is permitted on NPS land. However, it is prohibited within:

- 100 feet of roads, trails & trailheads, parking areas, boat launches.

- 100 feet of the top rim of the cliffs (defined as the Nuttall Sandstone member).

- 100 feet of any historic district or site. This includes most of Kaymoor with the exception of *Rocky Top Retreat*.

Camping is not recommended at any of the highway pull offs, or on any private property unless you have obtained explicit permission from the land owner. This includes the area adjacent to the upper Burma Road above the Junkyard Wall.

Lodging
A selection of motels and bed & breakfasts are located in the immediate area:

Comfort Inn, Fayetteville - 574.3443

Garvey House, Winona - 574.3235

Morris Harvey House, Fayetteville - 574.1179

Opossum Creek Retreat, Lansing - 574.4836

Whitehorse Inn, Fayetteville - 574.1400

Eating Establishments
Over the past decade an increasing number of eating establishments have opened in the immediate area. Here is a sampling of the ones in Fayetteville popular among climbers. There is also a Mexican and an Oriental restaurant, as well as a selection of fast food joints five miles south in Oak Hill.

Fat Tire Deli, Keller Ave., Fayetteville - located on the upper side of the Little General convenience store parking lot.

Gino's Pizza, Court St., Fayetteville - just above Hard Rock Climbing Services.

Aussie's, Maple Ave., Fayetteville - two blocks north of Court St. on the left. Currently serving breakfast and lunch.

Mountain Mercantile, Court St., Fayetteville - across from the Little General convenience store.

Sedona Grill, Maple Ave., Fayetteville - half a block north of Court St. on the right.

Smokey's Grill - located at Class VI in Ames Heights.

Western Pancake House - on Rt. 19 a few miles south of Fayetteville.

Groceries
A 24 hour full service Kroger is conveniently located five miles south on route 19

Climbing Equipment
Blue Ridge Outdoors - located at the corner of Court St. and Wiseman Ave., Fayetteville - 574.2425

Hardrock Climbing Services - located one block beyond the Court House on Court St., Fayetteville - 574.0735

SAFETY, WARNINGS & EMERGENCY INFORMATION

After more than two decades of climbing here, there has yet to be a climbing fatality. Knock on wood! But there have been a number of very serious accidents, a couple which easily could have been fatal. Always exercise your best judgement before getting on a route as well as once you're on it. Even the safest-looking sport climb can turn to disaster if you don't tie your knot correctly, blow a clip close to the ground, or have a belayer that's not paying attention. Over the past few seasons there have been numerous "lowering accidents" as a result of inattentive belayers allowing the loose end of the rope to pass through the belay device when lowering the leader to the ground. All it would have taken to avoid those accidents was a simple knot tied in the loose end of the rope. Remember, the fundamental doctrine of climbing is the assumption of risk. It means that you assume the risk and consequences of injury if you voluntarily expose yourself to injury with the knowledge and appreciation of the dangers involved. Beyond that basic legal description it also means taking responsibility for your actions.

Be forewarned; at the New there is no organized mountain rescue group awaiting your call for help. Many of the crags are a substantial distance from road access and therefore, a rescue can take a good bit of time to organize and implement. Climbers should carry a first aid kit at all times, be knowledgeable on how to use it, and employ self rescue if circumstances permit.

Here are a few tips to help make your day at the crag a safe and enjoyable one:

- Be sure you've received proper training on safe climbing techniques before you head to the cliffs. And remember, there's a huge difference between climbing in the gym and the real world!

- Always check your knot and harness buckle - twice.

- When sport climbing get in the habit of tying a knot in the loose end of the rope.

- Always be suspect of fixed gear.

- Beware of loose holds which can break off or dislodge unexpectedly.

- Keep your eyes peeled for copperheads, the small poisonous snakes which inhabit this area. They're especially fond of sunning themselves on the cliff tops.

- Poison ivy abounds in the region. As the saying goes, "leaves of three, let it be."

In the event of an accident call 911.

Additional emergency numbers are:

Plateau Medical Center in Oak Hill - 465.0561

Raleigh General Hospital in Beckley - 469.6213

National Park Service in Glen Jean - 465.0508

Remember, the best piece of safety equipment each of us owns is located in the space between our ears. Use it well!

ROUTE RATINGS

Technical Difficulty – The ratings reflected in this guide are considered the consensus grades by climbers who frequent this area. Many of the area routes feature bouldery and/or reachy cruxes and therefore, can occasionally feel more difficult than one might expect when compared to grades found at areas where difficulty is primarily endurance related. Unrepeated routes reflect the grade reported by the first ascent party.

Quality - A system of stars is used to assess the aesthetic merits of each climb. Though highly subjective, these ratings reflect the general opinion of many local activists. The concept of quality ratings is however, somewhat controversial. Many argue that it causes overcrowding on area classics. My experience suggests the opposite for the following reason; without quality ratings most visiting climbers find themselves constantly asking other climbers the magical question: "What are the good routes to do?" And generally, the same routes are recommended time and time again, which results in overcrowding of those same few routes, while scores of high quality two and three star routes go overlooked. As you go about selecting your daily tick list be reminded that stacks of quality two and three star routes await. And rarely will you find a line up at the base of them.

No stars indicates a route that is generally below average.

☆   One star indicates a route of average quality. It will most likely have some sections of quality rock or offer a sequence of intriguing moves, but be lacking in continuity.

☆☆   Two stars indicates a distinctly memorable route that will have great rock, great moves and continuity.

☆☆☆   Three stars indicates a premium quality route that ranks in the top ten percent of area climbs.

☆☆☆☆   Four stars designates an area classic. Perfect rock and position will be found on these routes.

Hazard – The system used to assess extreme hazard on a route is consistent with the standards generally embraced in the U.S. An **R** after the technical grade indicates the possibility exists for a moderately long fall, say 20 feet or more, onto good protection, or a shorter fall onto dubious protection that could pull. There is an increased risk of injury on these routes over what one would experience on a route with no hazard rating. If an **X** appears after the technical grade it imparts a very serious lead. There exists the chance of a very long fall with no gear, a chance of zippering a string of dubious pieces out and/or the likelihood of an unprotected ground fall. A substantial risk of severe injury or death exists. Unless you feel like a crash test dummy you may want to avoid the **R** and **X** routes.

Sport Climbs – are indicated by the bolt hanger icon 🅑. For purposes of definition, only routes which have 100% fixed gear are designated with the sport climb icon. Routes which require as little as one natural gear placement are not considered sport climbs.

Rain Day Routes – are indicated by the umbrella icon ☂. The New is blessed to have a selection of routes which generally remain dry during rain because they're either continuously overhanging or sheltered by a roof at the top of the cliff. These routes can provide options on those rain days when you might otherwise end up watching the latest flick at the theater in Beckley. However, when fog is associated with the storm or, it's been raining for a number of consecutive days even these routes can get wet.

RECOMMENDED EQUIPMENT

The Rack - Due to the diversity of routes here, there isn't what one would call a standard rack for the New. For sport climbs you'll need 12 to 15 draws. For traditional routes it's best to pack along a versatile selection of gear from which you can choose a more streamlined rack once you get to the base of your route. Your master rack should include a varied selection of brass nuts and stoppers, and a healthy collection of camming units including Friends and Camalots. Make sure you've also got a bunch of small TCUs or the equivalent since they're crucial for protecting many of the shallow slots and horizontals. Tricams, Sliders and the like are also reliable additions. Many of the route descriptions include tips on the gear needed. As you can see from the general lack of routes with hazard ratings most of the climbs are reasonably well protected.

The Rope - A 50 meter rope works on most climbs, but occasionally you'll encounter a route that requires a 55 meter one. I've noted this whenever possible. On many of the trad routes "double nines" are a definite advantage, especially on the highly technical face climbs.

NPS REGULATIONS THAT AFFECT CLIMBING

When climbing on NPS property please follow these regulations:

- The use of motorized drills is prohibited throughout the park.
- Do not disturb any cultural or natural objects.
- Pets must be on a leash at all times.
- Do not damage any vegetation.

LOCAL ETHICS

Ethics has never been the crux of any route here, but it has maintained its relative importance within the realm of the idiosyncratic social rules that

A young Duncan Pregnall gives Marc LeMenestrel the beta on the hottest new shoe.
photo: Rick Thompson

dominate climbing. This is best exemplified by the harmonious intertwining of sport and traditional routes. Nearly all the sport climbs have been sensitively established so as to not infringe on the traditional lines. It is the mutual respect for these often opposing climbing styles that makes the New a refreshingly unique place.

Here are a couple established New River traditions to consider:

- Adding to, removing or altering fixed gear on any route without the consent of the first ascent party is taboo.

- Retro bolting traditional routes without the consent of the first ascent party is considered blatant sacrilege.

- Squeezed-in routes and grid bolting is frowned upon.

- All fixed anchors should be camouflaged to blend with the rock and rappel slings should be of a natural color.

USING THIS GUIDE

Chapters begin with a description and brief history of the crag, followed by a section which discusses access and etiquette considerations. An overview map of the cliff is then presented which allows you to see how the individual detail maps interface with the bigger picture. Routes are described as if you're walking along the base of the wall and are presented in sequence from one end of the cliff to the other, or in the case of a few crags like Endless Wall, from relative access points. References to left and right assume you are facing the cliff. Upstream and downstream references are made throughout this guide and therefore it's critical to know which way the river flows. All distances are estimates.

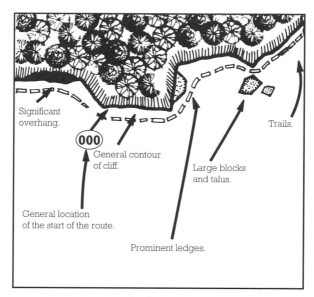

Significant overhang.

Trails.

000

General contour of cliff.

Large blocks and talus.

General location of the start of the route.

Prominent ledges.

Key to Map Symbols

NEW ROUTE INFORMATION & COMMENTS

Please send comments or new route information to:

Rick Thompson
C/O Chockstone Press
PO Box 3505,
Evergreen, CO 80437

Sunset on the majestic gorge.

photo: Rick Thompson

Rick Thompson on an early ascent of *Angel's Arête.*

photo: Peter Lewis

BRIDGE AREA CRAGS

A little more than two decades ago the New River escarpments were virgin to climbers. These outcrops are where it all began. It almost seems fitting that the first crags to be explored would be blessed with premium rock and an abundance of moderate classics. When combined with the near effortless access, one can easily understand why most visiting climbers make it a point to stop here. It's also the reason for the Bridge Buttress being the most poplar outcrop at the New. On weekends the place can feel like a stockyard, an appropriate analogy after you've witnessed the soil compaction at the base of the outcrop. Weekdays are the best time to climb here, and on occasion they're even crowded.

The Bridge Area Crags begin a short distance above from the bridge and stretch downstream for roughly a mile. All told more than 200 routes and variations are found on these flanks. The outcrops average 60 to 75 feet and for the most part are shrouded by dense forest, which accounts for them being the last cliffs in the gorge to dry after a storm.

To this day mystery surrounds the ascent of New River's first known climb, *Afternoon Delight* (5.5) which leads to the summit of the Pinnacle. This obscure 90 foot stack seems an unlikely candidate for such an historical event. In 1977, a rusting tin can was found on its summit. Inside lay a tattered scrap of paper on which the names of the first ascent team scribbled. Sadly, it was faded beyond legibility, thus preserving New River's most crucial and unanswered trivia question. The deteriorated condition of the can suggests the climb was done at least a decade prior to its discovery. Was it placed there by the Brit who was rumored to have climbed here in the '60s? We may never know.

In 1974 climbing made its debut at the Bridge Buttress. Initially a number of moderate routes were toproped. Rick Skidmore's 1975 ascent of *Zag* (5.8) was New River's first recorded lead. Bridge Buttress classics like Chockstone (5.9), *Jaws* (5.9), and *The Layback* (5.9) became the trade routes of those years. In addition, a number of the harder-looking lines were aided. In 1978 Greg Anderson led *The Tree Route* which was originally given a grade of 5.9. But over the years it's reputation as solid 10a confirms it as the New's first 5.10. By the early 80's most of the moderates had either been led or toproped. In 1981 Tom Howard added the Bridge Buttress's second 5.10 with *Underfling* (10b).

5.11 arrived in May of '83 with Doug Reed's ascent of *Englishman's Crack* (11b). June brought the second 5.11 when Rich Pleiss eliminated the aid on *Handsome and Wellhung* (11a). Soon the 11 grade became firmly rooted as a result of additions like Reed's *The Force* (11c), or Mike Artz classics such as *Marionette* (11c) and *Agent Orange* (11d). 1985 was another booming year. Cal Swoager contributions like *Blunder and Frightening* (10b), *Angel's Arête* (10a), and *Maranatha* (10c) are but a sampling of the numerous routes established by the core group of activists who were busy reaching out to the crags beyond the Bridge Buttress. Over the next few years things quieted down as Endless Wall and Bubba City became popular.

Spring of '88 brought the first 5.12s to the Bridge Area Crags when Eric Hörst led *Mega Magic* (12b/c) and *Team Machine* (12a), and Stuart Pregnall added *Frenzyed* (12a), all established on the same day. The season that followed was frenzied as routes like *The Stratagem* (12a), *Little Head Logic* (12a), *Pirouette* (12d), *Are You Experienced* (12c) and *Gag Reflex* (12d) helped firmly seat the 5.12 grade at this crag. John Bercaw's *Locked On Target* (13a) brought the first 5.13 to the crag. Additional routes have gone up since the late 80's and some of particularly high quality, but the intrinsic appeal of the Bridge Area Crags will always be the ultimate moderates that can be enjoyed here.

ACCESS & ETIQUETTE

The cliffs extending downstream from the Rostrum to the beginning of the North Bridge Wall are under ownership of the National Park Service. The North Bridge Wall, Pinnacle Wall and Ogre are currently owned by Alabama Properties. Access to most of the Bridge Area Crags is less than a 10 minute walk from the car. And for destinations like the Bridge Buttress it's less than 60 seconds.

But sadly, the convenient access has been a two edged sword, also serving as the fundamental cause of the climber impacts which threaten these cliffs. At The Bridge Buttress they're most noticeable. A decade ago a narrow path meandered along the base of the cliff. But with each passing year the zone of impact has crept. Today a near barren swath extends 20 feet to 30 feet out, and other impacts are apparent. The unstable trail at base of Angel's Arête is in danger of slipping down the bank. And there's the deteriorating ecosystem at the cliff top. What was once a healthy forest has been pummeled by hordes trampling around the top of the buttress. The thin soil layer near the cliff edge has become so severely compacted that trees have died, and many of the remaining specimens are in imminent danger. What were once pristine face climbs are now awash with the dirt and debris that erodes from those compacted soils. Then there's the litter, the greatest amount at any of the New River crags can be found here.

Here's what you can do to help preserve this area:

- Tread lightly at all times, particularly at the cliff top. Use top anchors (cold shuts) whenever available. This will help reduce additional soil compaction that occurs when setting up top anchors.
- Avoid using small diameter trees for anchoring.
- When hanging out at the cliff base make a conscious effort to keep your zone of impact as small as possible.
- Pick up all litter.
- Use permanent or portable toilet facilities whenever possible.
- If it's crowded, climb at other crags.
- Please, no rappelling from trees.
- Do not camp in this area.

A few tips on parking and getting to the cliffs - see Bridge Area Crags Overview maps for details:

- To access any of the crags from the Rostrum to the Central Bridge Wall use the pull offs in the area under the bridge
- To access the North Bridge Wall and the Ogre park at the switchback on Route 82. Be certain that you park well off the turn since rafting shuttle buses must be able to negotiate a three point turn here. Also, be conscientious how you park so other cars may also fit in this limited space.

Scott Garso doing the first ascent of *Boltus Prohibitus.*

photo: Rick Thompson

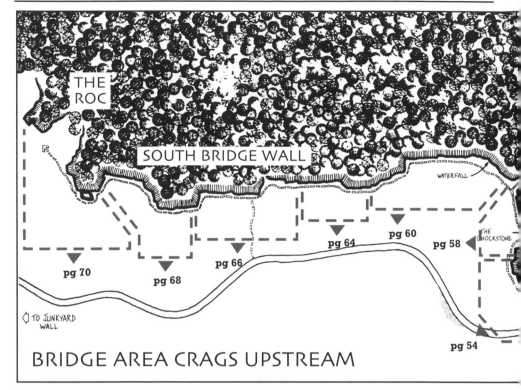

THE ROC

SOUTH BRIDGE WALL

WATERFALL

THE CHOCKSTONE

pg 60

pg 64

pg 58

pg 66

pg 70

pg 68

pg 54

TO JUNKYARD WALL

BRIDGE AREA CRAGS UPSTREAM

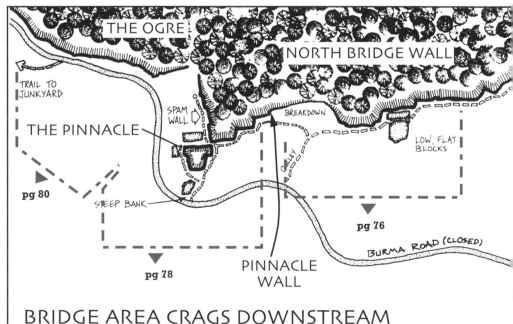

THE OGRE

NORTH BRIDGE WALL

TRAIL TO JUNKYARD

THE PINNACLE

SPAM WALL

BREAKDOWN

LOW, FLAT BLOCKS

pg 80

STEEP BANK

GULLEY

pg 76

pg 78

PINNACLE WALL

BURMA ROAD (CLOSED)

BRIDGE AREA CRAGS DOWNSTREAM

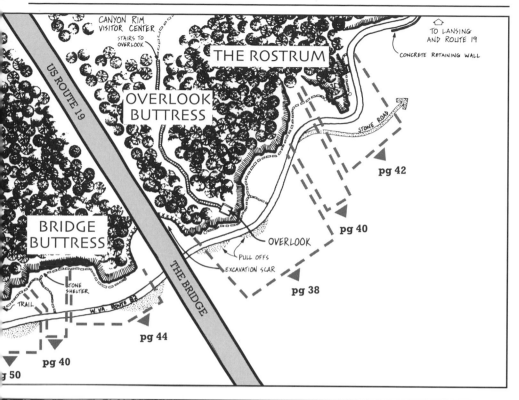

CANYON RIM
VISITOR CENTER
STAIRS TO
OVERLOOK

THE ROSTRUM

TO LANSING
AND ROUTE 19

CONCRETE RETAINING WALL

OVERLOOK
BUTTRESS

STONE ROAD

pg 42

US ROUTE 19

pg 40

BRIDGE
BUTTRESS

OVERLOOK

PULL OFFS

EXCAVATION SCAR

pg 38

STONE
SHELTER

THE BRIDGE

TRAIL

W. VA. ROUTE 82

pg 44

pg 40

g 50

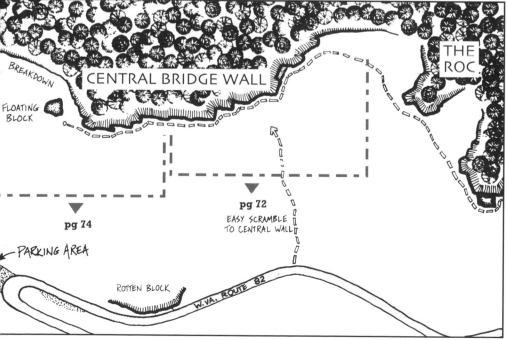

THE
ROC

BREAKDOWN

CENTRAL BRIDGE WALL

FLOATING
BLOCK

pg 74

pg 72

EASY SCRAMBLE
TO CENTRAL WALL

PARKING AREA

ROTTEN BLOCK

W. VA. ROUTE 82

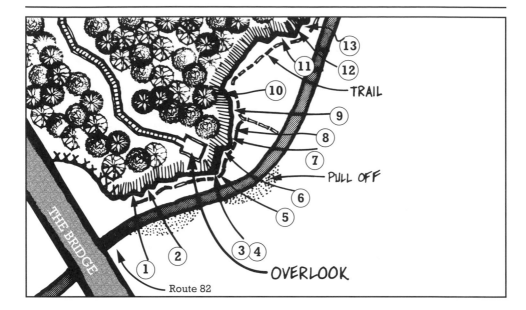

OVERLOOK BUTTRESS

The Overlook Buttress lies immediately east of the bridge and perched at its top is the Visitor Center Overlook Platform. In addition to its spectacular vantage point of the bridge, its also known amongst climbers as the local drop zone. When climbing here keep your eyes peeled for objects being hurled from above and climb smart: Wear a helmet!

1 Cheap Thrill 5.7
Locate a short, open dihedral capped by a triangular roof, just right of the rockfall scar. Climb the dihedral to the roof, bypass it on the left and venture up the face to the top. 40 feet. FA: Steve Erskine, solo, 1979.

2 Barefoot Alley 5.8
Begin 20 feet right of *Cheap Thrill*, at a prominent right-leaning dihedral. Follow the dihedral and face above to the top. 40 feet. FA: Rick Skidmore & Steve Erskine, 1979.

3 The Sandman 5.10a ☆
Sweet dreams! A former aid route named *Space Dumpling*, 5.9 A2. The aid version began with the thin crack to the left. The free line commences on the blunt arête, directly below the overlook platform. Climb up, then left past a short corner to a roof. Move left under the roof, then directly up the thin crack to easier terrain and a belay beside the platform. 70 feet. FA with aid: Rick Skidmore & Steve Erskine, 1979. FA: Rich Pleiss & Ron Augustino, November 1982.

4   House of Cards 5.10a

This deck is not stacked in your favor. In the words of the first ascent party, "super loose"! From the start of *The Sandman* climb directly up the prow and over two roofs which are pulled to the left side (bolt). Finish straight up. 70 feet. FA: Greg Collum & Rich Pleiss, June 1988.

5   The Overlooked 5.12 (?)

Just right of the arête is a line of five bolts. It's unknown if this route has ever been completed. 75 feet. FA: Unknown.

6   The Hall Effect 5.8+ ☆

Begin at the left-facing corner 20 feet right of *The Sandman*. P1: Climb the corner to the roof then move right and belay on the ledge. 35 feet. P2: Wander up the face, angling right past an orange and black scooped-out section to the top. 45 feet. FA P1: Steve Erskine & Rick Skidmore, 1979. FA P2: Rich Pleiss & Eugene Genay, May 1982.

7   The Incredible Overhanging Wall 5.10d

Toprope the center of the gently overhanging face to the ledge. 30 feet. TR FA: Steve Erskine & Hobart Parks, 1979.

8   Tree in Your Face 5.9

Climb the face between *The Incredible Overhanging Wall* and *Up to Disneyland*. 75 feet. FA: Fletch Taylor & Dan Friedman, February 1989.

9   Up to Disneyland 5.7 ☆☆

Touron time! Boulder up the short face near the right edge of the lower wall to the ledge then climb the face above aiming left for a short crack in a bulge. Finish directly to the top. 75 feet. FA: Hobart Parks & T.A. Horton, 1979.

10   Rocky Roads 5.8

Begin in the fractured corner system at the right side of the face (just left of the seepage) and follow the grungefest corner to a roof, which is pulled to the right. A short face leads to the top. 55 feet. FA: Rick Skidmore & Steve Erskine, 1979.

11   Out to Lunch 5.8

The obvious, lightning bolt crack to the right of the seepage. 40 feet. FA: Rick Skidmore & T.A. Horton, 1979.

12   Gunky Heaven 5.6 ☆

Reminiscent of the Gunks. Ascend the prominent, left-facing corner with two roofs. 60 feet. FA: Steve Erskine & Hobart Parks, 1979.

13   Under a Blood Red Sky 5.10d ☆

Begin 15 feet right of *Gunky Heaven* and move up the face past a bolt and pin to the arête. Clip another bolt and aim for the top. 55 feet. Gear: Camming units. FA: Jonathan Houck, John Baumert, Ian Wienholt & Bill Gaurin, September 1988.

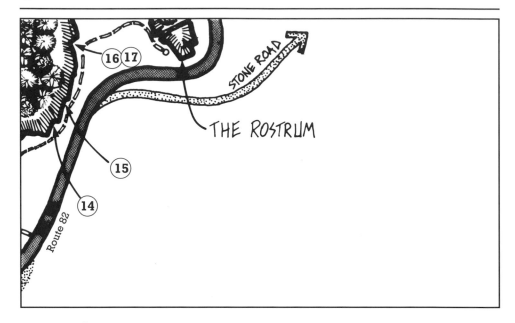

14 Ledge City 5.8

Right of *Gunky Heaven* is a dihedral with a rotten, roofy start. Follow the corner to a ledge and continue up a short corner to the top. 60 feet. FA: Rick Skidmore, Steve Erskine, T.A. Horton & Hobart Parks, 1979.

15 Be Bold and Be Strong 5.11b R

Steep and committing with marginal gear at the crux: a possible ankle breaker. Using the same crumbly roof start as *Ledge City*, reach right to a flake system which is followed past a pin (most likely original and rusty) to hairline cracks and the crux. Sketch up the cracks, past a small roof, finishing up and right. 60 feet. FA: Cal Swoager, Glenn Thomas & Mark Thomas, August 1985.

16 The Butler 5.9

Near the right side of the Overlook Buttress is a roof about 20 feet off the deck. Begin under the left side of it, at a tiny, right-facing corner. Follow the corner to the roof, then hand traverse right along the lip and pull onto the arête which is followed to the top. 35 feet. FA: Hobart Parks & Steve Erskine, 1979.

17 A Solitary Hang 5.6

Follow *The Butler* to the roof, then take the obvious, left-leaning crack to the top. 35 feet. FA: Rick Guierre & Eugene Genay, October 1983.

Eric Hörst crimping off the first ascent of *Mega Magic.*

photo: Rick Tompson

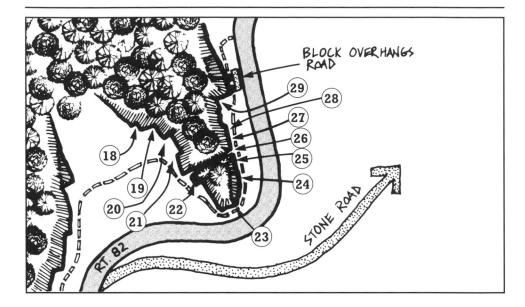

THE ROSTRUM

Some worthy routes can be enjoyed at this petite crag. The classic is *Mounting Madness*, one of the better 5.8 climbs in this part of the Gorge. Unlike most of the other cliffs in the Bridge Area, The Rostrum's south face tends to dry rapidly after rain.

18   Crack'n Clutch 5.7
Climb the first dihedral on the left side of The Rostrum's north face. 40 feet. FA: Eugene Genay & Rick Guierre, October 1983.

19   Beer Belly Roof 5.9+
Just right of *Crack'n Clutch* is a second dihedral. Stagger up it to a small roof then move out the three-inch crack finishing in the layback corner. 55 feet. FA: Steve Erskine & T.A. Horton, 1979.

20   Mortimer 5.11a ☆ ϐ﹒
A short distance downhill from *Beer Belly Roof*, follow the fixed gear up and right to an anchor. 40 feet. FA: Jonathan Houck, September 1990.

21   Kiss of the Spider Woman 5.10d ☆ ϐ﹒
Start right of *Mortimer*, on the right side of the alcove, and climb up and left past a pin to a small ledge. Continue up the face past two bolts to the anchor shared with *Mortimer*. 40 feet. FA: Jonathan Houck & Eric Hörst, September 1990.

22   The Mankey Monkey 5.9
Climb the first right-facing corner system left of the prow to its end, then step left and follow the offwidth to the top. 45 feet. FA: Nick Brash & Bruce Barton, August 1985.

23 Penalty for Early Withdrawal 5.11a ☆ 🎧

To reach the start of this route rappel off the prow to the ledge and set up a belay (camming units helpful). Follow three bolts up the clean face. 40 feet. FA: Jonathan Houck, May 1990.

24 Mounting Madness 5.8 R ☆☆

A fine climb with a maddening case of the runouts, which of course can lead to mounting fear. If you're comfortable leading at this grade, this one's highly recommended. Begin 15 feet left of *Rapid View*, under a large roof. Stem between a block and the right wall until it's possible to move onto the wall. Climb directly up past the left side of a small roof to a ledge then up a short flake. Angle left and up to gain a small, left-facing corner. Cruise the corner to the top. 60 feet. FA: Scott Garso, Rick Thompson, Eric Hoffman, Ron Kampas & Carl Samples, May 1986.

25 You Snooze, You Lose 5.10d R/X ☆

Don't fall asleep at the wheel on this serious pitch. Start immediately left of *Rapid View* and boulder up and left, then straight up to a roof which is pulled just right of Mounting Madness to the ledge. Make a bee line for the top, using imaginative protection. 60 feet. FA: Rick Thompson, Bob Rentka, Scott Garso, Carl Samples & Mark Van Cura, June 1986.

26 Rapid View 5.6 R ☆☆

A splendid introduction to offwidths. Finesse the obvious, offwidth crack. 60 feet. Gear: The biggest stuff you can get your hands on. FA: Nick Brash & Bruce Burgin, June 1979.

27 Boltus Prohibitus 5.10c ☆

Begin about six feet right of *Rapid View* and climb directly over a low roof to a ledge. Move straight up the face, past a bulge and finish up a short, left-facing corner. 55 feet. Gear: Sliders and small tri-cam are helpful. FA: Scott Garso, Carl Samples, Rick Thompson & Bob Rentka, June 1986.

28 Race Among the Ruins 5.10c ☆

Commence 12 feet right of *Boltus Prohibitus* and pull the low overhang past a pin. Continue directly up the face past another pin and bolt to the top. 50 feet. Gear: Small camming units and brass. FA: Jonathan Houck & Ian Wienholt, March 1989.

29 Palladium 5.9 ☆.

Defined as: Anything believed to afford effectual protection or safety. Approximately 50 feet right of *Rapid View* is an arête with an undercut, blank start. Begin 15 feet left of the arête, at a right-facing corner under a roof. Make a few moves up, then rail right, along horizontals, to reach the arête. Pull over a bulge and follow a left-facing flake for a short distance, making a delicate move back left to gain the open-book, which is followed to the top. 60 feet. FA: Rick Thompson, Carl Samples & Scott Garso, May 1986.

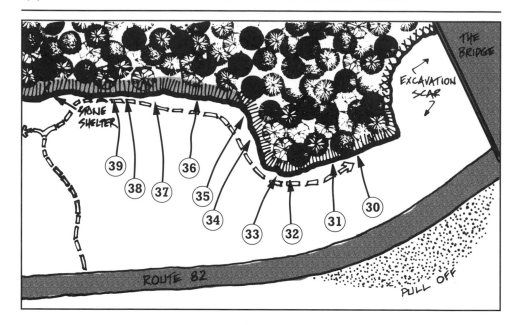

BRIDGE BUTTRESS

30   Gaye's Gaze 5.9+ ☆
Best approached on the trail from the *High Times* area due to the steep, loose slope below the route. Start about 30 feet left of the northwest corner of the bridge excavation scar and climb the prominent, right-leaning flake to a ledge. Rail left and pull the roof, finishing up a short dihedral. 40 feet. FA: Tom Howard & Bruce Burgin, November 1984.

31   Scarey 5.9 ☆
Start 15 feet left of *Gaye's Gaze*, just right of a shallow groove, and climb the face to a horizontal, then traverse left until directly below a roof. Move straight up past a second horizontal and an awkward mantel, then out the roof to gain a v-notch just above the lip. Finish up the face. 40 feet. FA: Nick Brash & Bruce Burgin, September 1983.

32   Golden Summer 5.11b 🔗
Left of *Scarey* are two sport routes. Climb the right-hand line of bolts. 35 feet. FA: John Black, 1991.

33   Wicca 5.13a 🔗
Climbs the left-hand line of bolts, just right of the clean arête. 40 feet. FA: John Black, 1991.

34   Macho Man 5.9+
Locate the parallel cracks in a steep, orange wall. Climb the right-hand, wider crack with the roofy start. 40 feet. FA: Steve Erskine & T.A. Horton, 1980.

35   Dog Fight 5.10b ☆

The left-hand, thinner crack is actually a face climb with a perfect protection crack. Lower from anchors at the top of the crack. 40 feet. FA: Ben Fowler, Tom Howard & Mike Brown, June 1985.

35a   Dog Fight Direct Finish — Bailing Wire 5.11b

From the anchors at the top of *Dog Fight* continue up a line of four bolts to the top. FA: John Black, 1991.

36   Horton's Tree 5.7+ ☆

This fun little route was one of the early Bridge Buttress moderates. A tiny tree used to grace the top of the crack, which naturally the route was named after. Sadly, a senseless climber cut down the sapling a few years back and installed chain anchors in its place. Follow the short, often wet crack just left of a small waterflow to it's end at the anchors. 25 feet. FA: T.A. Horton & Steve Erskine, 1980.

36a   H-Tree Direct Finish — Mean Old Mr. Gravity 5.12b

From the anchors on *Horton's Tree* continue up a line of bolts to the top. 60 feet. FA: John Black, October 1990.

37   Fat Factor 5.12c
aka Luv Jugs

The initial part of this route was formerly a trad, R-rated climb that moved left under the roofs and finished at the anchors on *High Times*.The climber who equipped the direct finish (*Luv Jugs*) ignored *Fat Factor*'s historical precedent and added two bolts to it. Begin right of *Let the Wind Blow* and climb past the two superfluous bolts to the ledge, then continue up the line of bolts through the roofs to the top. 60 feet. FA of initial section: Andrew Barry, Eric Anderson & Steve Lancaster, May 1985. FA of finish: John Black & Arthur Tsiamis, October 1990.

38   Let the Wind Blow 5.12a ☆

Historically significant, this former toprope was one of the first 5.12s at the New, testimony to Cal Swoager's powerful climbing. Begin just right of *High Times* and climb the crimpy face directly past three bolts to the *High Times* anchors. 35 feet. TR FA: Cal Swoager, August 1985. FA: Bob D'Antonio & Brian Mullin, April 1989.

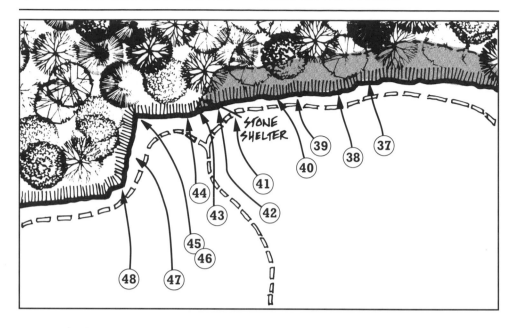

39 High Times 5.11a ☆☆ ℛ

A 1980 aid attempt on this route was aborted when a piton and a drill bit broke just below the roof band, forcing a retreat from the anchors which had been placed at the top of the hand crack. Subsequently, this portion of the route became exceedingly popular, the first of the New's rain day routes. In 1985 Andrew Barry added a spectacular finish through the roofs, though few climbers do this more challenging portion of the route. Start 30 feet right of the stone shelter and climb the arching finger-and-hand crack to anchors (5.10c). Continue straight up for a few moves, then follow the right-slanting weakness in the roofs to the top. 60 feet. Note: a recently added "fill-in" sport route starts right of the upper portion of this route and crosses over it. No details are known about it. FA of initial crack: Hobart Parks, 1980. FA of complete route: Andrew Barry & Eric Anderson, May 1985.

40 West Virginia Highway 5.12b ☆ 🅟 ℛ
aka Coal Miner's Daughter

Just left of *High Times* is a line of bolts that lead up the face and through the roofs to an anchor. 60 feet. TR FA of lower face: Doug Reed, November 1988. In 1991 John Black bolted it, extending the route through the upper roofs.

41 Labor Day 5.10c ☆☆ ℛ

Unbeknownst to the first ascent party, this route had been toproped in 1976 by Hobart Parks and called *Peter Pan*. On rain days some parties do the initial flake and lower from a threaded sling at the top of the flake, but it's never a safe practice to lower from a single sling. Start just right of the stone shelter and climb the right side of the giant, detached-looking flake to the roof. Toil left, out the pumpy horizontal, finishing at a pine tree belay. 55 feet. TR FA: Hobart Parks, 1976. FA: Doug Reed & Tom Howard, September 1984.

42   Whammy 5.13a

More a defacement than a rock climb, the holds on this route were heavily chipped by the first ascentionist. Under National Park Service regulations chipping and other forms of "hold creation" are considered defacement and therefore are illegal. Climb the short, bolted face left of *Labor Day*. 35 feet. FA: John Black, 1991.

43   Love Shack 5.12c

Unfortunately this tainted creation climbs directly over the historical route *Lotus Land*. In addition, the climbing takes place on the left side of the arête but the bolts are on the right, further adding to the "forced" feeling of the line. Considering the wealth of routes here, one can only ask himself why fill-in routes like this ever go in. Start just left of the stone shelter and follow the line of bolts up the arête. 55 feet. FA: John Black, 1991.

44   Lotus Land 5.10b ☆

An aid elimination of a 1980 route called *Gateway To Heaven*, 5.10 A0 (two moves of aid). Start ten feet left of the stone shelter and follow a right-leaning ramp to the arête. Climb up the face just left of the arête, then move left to a flake system that leads to the top. 55 feet. FA with aid: Hobart Parks & Steve Erskine, 1980. FA: Andrew Barry & John Burcham, June 1986.

45   The Mayfly 5.9– ☆

This was the second recorded route at the Bridge Buttress and was originally rated 5.7. Climb the large, right-facing dihedral left of the stone shelter. 40 feet. FA: Rick Skidmore, Hobart Parks & Phil Mooney, 1975.

45a   The Mayfly Variation Finish — The Gayfly 5.9 ☆

Climb *The Mayfly* until it is possible to traverse left across the face and follow a right-facing flake system to the top. Note: The placement of a piece high in the corner will protect the traverse. 45 feet. FA: Rick Skidmore & Hobart Parks, 1978.

46   The Midas Touch 5.11a

More like fool's gold. Begin five feet left of *The Mayfly* and bounce off the trunk of a tree to some face holds. Angle up and left to a good rest, then aim up and right to connect with the finish on *The Gayfly*. Note: Before starting, you may wish to place a piece in *The Mayfly* corner as high as your need for well-being dictates. 45 feet. FA: Andrew Barry & John Burcham, June 1986.

47   The Stratagem 5.12a ☆☆☆

Quite the gem indeed, one of the classic Bridge Buttress 5.12s. Unfortunately, erosion at the cliff top has caused the route to be a bit dirty. Begin 15 left of *The Mayfly* and boulder up and left to the first bolt, then follow the line of fixed gear to the cold shut station at the top. 60 feet. FA: Rick Thompson, Carl Samples & Stuart Pregnall, May 1988.

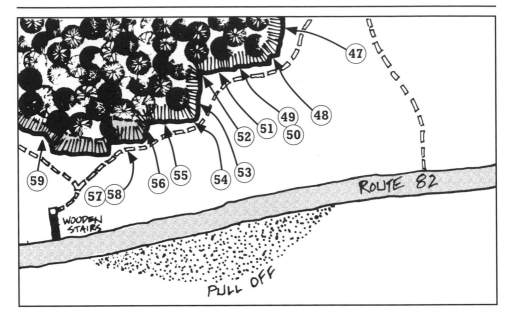

48 Pirouette 5.12d ☆☆

Formerly *Raindancer*, 5.8 A2, this was one of the New's last aid lines to be freed. Begin below the arête and climb an inside corner up and right past a short crack. Continue directly up the face to a pair of anchors at the top. 70 feet. FA with aid: Rick Skidmore & Steve Erskine, 1979. FA: Eric Hörst, Rick Thompson & Rob Turan, June 1988.

49 The Layback 5.9 ☆☆
aka Zig

One of the mandatory Bridge Buttress classics, but beware, looks are deceiving. Follow the sculpted, right-facing flake to the top. 50 feet. FA: Hobart Parks & Rick Skidmore, 1978.

50 Frenzyed 5.12a ☆

One of the "shoe routes." Seasoned veterans will remember the Frenzy by One Sport, a cutting-edge platform shoe. Climb the first ten feet of *The Layback*, then tip-toe up and left to a stance (right of *Blunder and Frightening*). Continue up and right past a bolt to a horizontal, then left to an old Leeper pin and master the perplexing bulge. 50 feet. FA: Stuart Pregnall, Eric Hörst & Rick Thompson, March 1988.

51 Blunder and Frightening 5.10b ☆

Like many of the early trad routes at the New, this one was named after a famous Gunks route, *Thunder and Frightening*. Beginning left of *The Layback*, face climb up to a thin crack, following it up and left until it peters out. Finish on the face above trending slightly left to the top. 45 feet. FA: Cal Swoager & Ed McCarthy, May 1985.

52   Penalty Situation 5.6
Climb the short-lived, wide crack in the corner. 35 feet. FA: Steve Erskine, solo, 1976.

53   Mega Magic 5.12b/c ☆ 🄟
The other "shoe route," this one was named after the magical qualities of La Sportiva's Mega. But most notably it was scene of the first power drill-placed bolts at the New River. Climb the line of bolts on the brilliant face right of *Angel's Arête*. 60 feet. FA: Eric Hörst, Stuart and Karen Pregnall & Rick Thompson, March 1988.

54   Angel's Arête 5.10a ☆☆☆☆
Heavenly! An immaculate arête with superb position on pristine rock, but don't expect continuous protectabilty. Please, tread lightly at the base of this route since the soil conditions are very unstable and the edge of the steep bank continues to creep closer to the cliff. Beginning on the right side, climb directly up the pink arête past a pin until it's possible to move left onto the face. Finish up and left. 60 feet. FA: Cal Swoager & Mike Artz, May 1985.

55   Pearly Gates 5.11b R ☆☆
Begin on the ledge, just right of *Zag*, and follow the thin face up and right to good holds. Step right and head straight to the top. 60 feet. FA: Eddie Begoon & Bill Moore, July 1988.

56   Zag 5.8 ☆☆☆
This highly visible and popular climb was the first known lead established at the Bridge Buttress and possibly at the New. Beginning from a ledge, climb the striking, wide crack that splits the face. 60 feet. FA: Hobart Parks & Rick Skidmore, 1975.

57   Handsome and Well Hung 5.11a ☆☆☆
aka Blood and Guts
Aptly descriptive, this route was first done as an aid line, with a traversing finish under the huge roof. A later ascent aided the fearsome looking roof crack at the top. The 1983 free ascent established it as the second 5.11 at the New. Start from the ledge left of *Zag* and strut your stuff up the superb, right-facing dihedral to the roof. Lower from the cold shuts or follow the historical traverse right along a line of old, rusty, not-so-trustworthy ¼" bolts. 80 feet. FA with aid: Steve Erskine, Rick Skidmore, & Hobart Parks, 1976. FA aid finish via roof crack: Sandy Giltinan & John Howe, 1977. FA: Rich Pleiss & Ron Augustino, June 1983.

58   Gag Reflex 5.12d ☆☆
This imaginative route takes a convulsive line out the exposed wall left of *Handsome and Well Hung*. From the same start as the previous route, traverse left across the face past a bolt to reach the arête and a second bolt. Continue left, on the unnerving traverse above the roof, to reach a right-facing corner which is followed to its end. Head up the face on "thank god" chickenheads to the top. FA: John Bercaw & Craig Miller, October 1988.

Phil Wilt on an early ascent of *Handsome and Wellhung.*

photo: Carl Samples

John Bercaw finishing off the second ascent of *Team Machine.*

photo: Rick Thompson

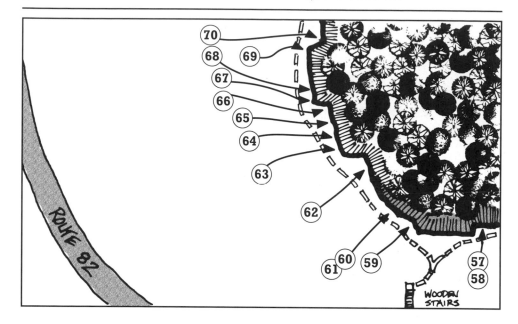

59 Englishman's Crack 5.11b ☆☆

Local legend rumors that a British climber visited here in the late 1960s. This one's in honor of that tale. Historically pivotal, this was the first 5.11 at the New. On the left side of the huge ceiling is a wide crack that splits a bulging roof. Climb through the roof to a stance at an aging bolt, then finish up the long, ramping flake (*Easily Flakey*). 70 feet. FA: Doug Reed, Tom Howard & Vernon Scarboro, May 1983.

60 Gymtonic 5.13a ☆ 🄟

Powerful, bouldery and exposed. A visit to the Gymtonic workout center in France may get you ready for this one. Begin left of *Englishman's Crack* and move up the face and pull the roof, stepping right to a stance above the roof on *Englishman's Crack*. Step onto the right wall and crank off a series of bouldery cruxes right, then directly up the exposed arête to a set of cold shuts. 75 feet. FA: Eric Hörst, June 1993.

61 Green Room 5.12b ☆ 🄟

Using the same start as *Gymtonic*, climb past the roof then continue directly up the slab until it's possible to step across *Easily Flakey* onto the steep, right wall. A short, cruxy face leads to the top and a pair of cold shuts. 75 feet. FA: Eric Hörst, June 1993.

62 Easily Flakey 5.7 R ☆☆

A highly fashionable route that is more often toproped than led. Start about 30 feet left of *Englishman's Crack*, at an inside corner, and climb up until you're standing in a good horizontal. Make a long, rightward traverse, staying above the roof band, to reach the bolt on *Englishman's Crack*, (or traverse up and right about ten feet higher) then follow the ramping dihedral to the top. 85 feet. Note: There are variations which continue up the initial corner or climb the slab. FA: Robie Gore, et al., 1977.

63   Team Machine 5.12a ☆☆☆☆ *ᶜ*

Solid Gold! Begin on the left side of the low-angle arête and climb up, then right along a slot and balance onto the slabby, right side of the arête. Move up on perfect rock following the line of bolts to cold shuts. 70 feet. FA: Eric Hörst & Rick Thompson, March 1988.

64   Stretch Armstrong 5.11c ☆ *ᶜ*

Just left of *Team Machine* is this squeezed-in route which climbs over part of *Raptured*. Follow the line of bolts to a cold shut station. 70 feet. FA: Rudy Ruana, Jonathan Houck & John Maguire, April 1990.

65   Raptured 5.11a ☆

Witness to Cal Swoager's visionary boldness. Beginning just right of *Jaws*, follow a small, right-facing corner up to a stance. Continue straight up the face to a prominent horizontal and traverse right 20 feet to another stance near the blunt arête (*Stretch Armstrong* crosses here). Wander up and left to the top. 70 feet. FA: Cal Swoager & Mike Artz, May 1985.

66   Jaws 5.9 ☆☆☆

Be forewarned, this handcrack is lined with crystalline teeth. Tape up and feed your hands to the flesh eating crack in the beautiful dihedral. Jam it to the top. 55 feet. FA: Rick Skidmore, et al, 1977.

67   Are You Experienced? 5.12c ☆☆☆

A masterpiece of intricacy. Just left of *Jaws* is a ravishing arête. Beginning in the bouldery open book, climb up and right, staying on the right side of the arête past a bolt. Move around to the other side of the arête and finish up the face. 65 feet. TR FA: Stuart & Karen Pregnall, May 1988. FA: John Bercaw & John McGowan, May 1988.

68   Tentative Decision 5.10d

A few paces left of *Are You Experienced?*, move up the face past a bolt, then rail left and up to a left-facing corner/flake which is pulled to the top. 70 feet. FA: Eddie Begoon & Bill Moore, July 1987.

69   Preferred Dynamics 5.11d

Climb the arête just right of *The Tree Route* past a bolt to the same finish as the previous route. 70 feet. FA: Kenny Parker & Blaze Davies, June 1988.

70   Tree Route 5.10a ☆☆☆

Unquestionably enchanting, just don't use the tree for aid. Start in the obvious left-facing corner with a large hemlock growing at its base. Climb the corner passing a small roof near the top. 70 feet. FA: Greg Anderson & Rick Skidmore, 1978.

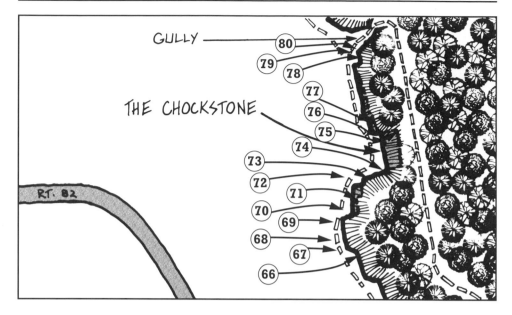

71   Marionette 5.11c ☆☆☆☆
This former aid climb is likely to string you out. Just left of *The Tree Route* is a thin crack in a small, left-facing corner that leads to a roof and a beautiful crack which is followed to the top. 70 feet. FA: Kris Kline & Mike Artz, August 1983.

72   A Touch of Tango 5.11b/c ☆☆☆
Put on your dancin' shoes for this dazzling arête. Climb the initial 15 feet of *Dresden Corner* then make an exposed traverse right to reach the hanging arête. Elegant moves up the arête and right-hand face lead to the top. 75 feet. FA: Kenny Parker & Blaze Davies, June 1988.

73   Dresden Corner 5.11d R ☆☆
Fifteen feet left of *Marionette*, at the left end of a low roof is a right-facing dihedral that begins 15 feet up. Move up a short arête to the start of the corner and follow the dihedral to the top passing a bolt at mid-height. 75 feet. Gear: Bring lots of brass. FA: Mike Adams, March 1986.

74   Chockstone 5.9 ☆☆
Popular and varied. On the right-hand wall of the Trashcompactor Roof is a left-leaning, thin crack that starts about 15 feet off the ground. Climb the face up and left to reach the start of the crack which leads to a right-facing corner. Up the corner to the top. 70 feet. FA: Rick Skidmore & Ian Swift, 1976.

75   Underfling 5.10b ☆☆
The left side of the Trashcompactor Roof sports a tasty undercling problem. Watch rope drag. Climb up the easy crack just left of the corner to the roof then undercling left and follow the short dihedral to the top. 75 feet. FA: Tom Howard, Jim Okel, Trip Collins, Nick Brash & Dan Perry, 1981.

76   Locked on Target 5.13a ☆☆
Reachy and continuous, make sure you're aiming for the right holds. Start ten left of *Underfling* and boulder up and left pulling the roof at a bolt. Fire up and right to the second bolt, then back left past the third. 55 feet. FA: John Bercaw, May 1988.

77   Let's Get Physical 5.12a ☆
This route's first ascent was done with a single bolt protecting the offwidth crux. Shortly afterward, the route was repeated on toprope and that party chopped the bolt, claiming it was unnecessary. Left of the previous route is an imposing, offwidth roof crack. Climb it. 65 feet. Gear: Really big stuff! FA: Alex Karr & Deb Orth, September 1988.

78   Butterbeans 5.10a ☆☆☆
The gourmet's offwidth. Near the left end of the Bridge Buttress is a stunning, four-inch offwidth. Follow it to the top. 45 feet. FA: Eddie Begoon & Mike Artz, August 1983.

79   Grapefruit Wine 5.11a
Right out of a Steely Dan tune! Begin approximately 20 feet left of *Butterbeans* and angle up and right past good gear to the obvious crux. Grope and launch for the top. 45 feet. Note: A #3 RP is essential to protect the crux. FA: Gene Kistler & Doug Houghton, 1989.

80   Monkey See, Monkey Do 5.5
Begin just left of the previous route and climb nearly straight up on good horizontals past a short open-book and the top. 40 feet. FA: Zeph Cunningham & Randy Boush, April 1988.

Eric Hörst on the exposed *Gymtonic.*   Photo: Rick Thompson

Rick Thompson on the first ascent of the *Stratagem*.

photo: Tom Clancy

Tom Howard on the landmark route *Englishman's Crack* in 1983.

photo: Bruce Burgin

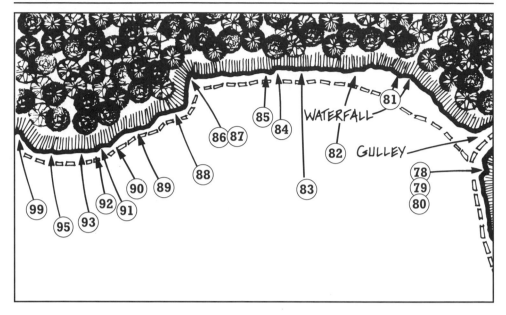

SOUTH BRIDGE WALL

81   Pipe Dreams 5.10c
This negative-starred extravaganza could send your dreams of fine climbing up
in smoke! Begin immediately left of the water line that runs up the cliff and climb
up to the obvious seam which is followed to the top. 45 feet. FA: Kenny Parker &
Blaze Davies, May 1987.

82   Desperados Under the Eaves 5.11a
Begin 25 feet left of *Pipe Dreams* and follow the line of six bolts to the top. 60
feet. FA: Brian Boyd & Nick Cocciolone, May 1993.

83   The Verge 5.12b ☆☆
Just right of *Two-Edged Sword* is a line of bolts that leads to a station. 60 feet. FA:
Doug Reed, 1994.

84   Two-Edged Sword 5.11a/b R ☆☆
Another of the former aid lines that went free with a slight variation, it was
originally called *Captain America* 5.9+ A2. Locate the obvious, black, right-
facing corner about 20 feet up. Climb straight up to it until just short of the roof
then move left across the black face to the arête. Duel your way straight up into
a small, left-facing corner that leads to cracks and the top. 60 feet. Note: Slightly
harder if you stay in the roofy corner. FA with aid: Rick Skidmore & Steve
Erskine, 1978. FA: Cal Swoager, Mike Artz & Andrew Barry, June 1985.

85   Sepultura 5.11d ☆ *(bolt symbol)*
Left of the previous route, climb the line of bolts to an anchor. 60 feet. FA: Doug Reed, 1994.

86   Trick or Treat 5.11a
Beginning just right of *Your Mother*, climb a chimneyish type affair to a small roof with a thin crack splitting it. Pull the roof and follow the crack (*Dynamite Crack* joins here) to the top. 45 feet. FA: Cal Swoager & Stuart Kuperstock, October 1983.

86a   Trick or Treat Variation Start — Dynamite Crack 5.10d
About eight feet right of *Your Mother* is a razor-thin flake that runs about halfway up the wall. Follow it to its end and make some hard moves left to gain the thin crack of *Trick or Treat*, just above the roof. Follow the crack to the top. 50 feet. TR FA: Hobart Parks & Steve Erskine, 1980. FA: Unknown.

87   Your Mother.... 5.9 ☆☆☆
A distinguished handcrack circa the days when everyone was possessed with *The Exorcist*. Climb the obvious handcrack in the right-facing corner. 50 feet. FA: Greg Anderson & Rick Skidmore, 1979.

88   Agent Orange 5.11d ☆☆☆☆
Please, no spraying here! At the time this route was put up a tiny tree grew above the crux which provided a good place to shake out. Since then the tree has died and the route is now considered to be a bit more sustained. Start in a small "pit," below an overhanging, orange flake and climb the face to the flake which is followed past a desperate bulge. Move left and follow the cracks to the top. 65 feet. FA: Mike Artz, Eddie Begoon & Kris Kline, August 1983.

89   Can't Find My Way Home 5.11a
Begin 15 feet left of *Agent Orange* and climb blocky rock to horizontals on the left wall. Continue up the face, staying left of the thin dihedral, past a hidden pin to the top. 65 feet. FA: Dave Moore & Bill Bradshaw, August 1988.

90   Not Bosched Up 5.11a
Start ten feet right of *Where Real Men Dare* and climb up to a ledge then crank directly up a short face past a crack to easier climbing leading to the top. 65 feet. FA: Rob Turan & Eric Hörst, April 1988.

91   Where Real Men Dare 5.8 ☆
A recommended climb of its grade. Begin in the obvious right-facing corner with a small roof at the bottom and follow it to the top. 55 feet. FA: Steve Erskine & Rick Skidmore, 1976.

Mike Artz on the bouldery start of *Marionette*. Belay by Andrew "Stoat" Barry.

photo: Carl Samples

Eddie Begoon cruxin' in fear on *Dresden Corner*.

photo: Rick Thompson

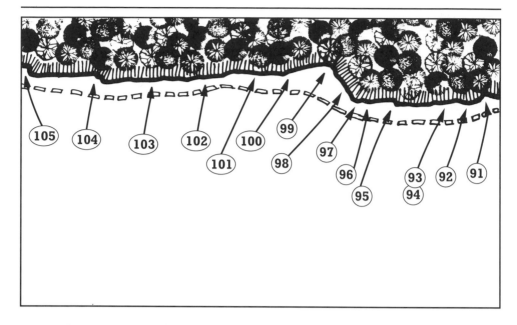

92   Are You Asparagus? 5.11a ☆

Start five feet left of *Where Real Men Dare* and climb a tiny, left-facing corner for ten feet then step left and move directly up, through overlaps, to a flake at the last overlap (about 15 feet left of arête). Pull onto the steep face (bolt), then angle up and right to a left-leaning flake and head straight for the top. 75 feet. FA: Carl Samples, Rick Thompson, Bob Rentka & Ed McCarthy, May 1988.

93   Ledge Lips 5.11b ☆☆

Reported in the first edition of *New River Rock* as a 5.10a toprope called *Improper Move*, the route turned out to be significantly more difficult. Commence directly behind a tall hemlock and power up a short, overhanging crack to a ledge. Move up the face, following a line behind the hemlock, past two bolts. Finish up and slightly right to the top. 75 feet. TR FA: Steve Erskine & T.A. Horton, 1980. FA: Rick Thompson, Carl Samples, Stuart Pregnall & Rich Cunningham, May 1988.

94   Little Head Logic 5.12a ☆☆

This masculine malfunction won't force you to think hard! Using the same start as *Ledge Lips*, climb the crack to the ledge then traverse left and climb a short, broken crack to its end. Continue up the face past three bolts to the top. 75 feet. FA: Rick Thompson, Bob D'Antonio & Carl Samples, April 1988.

95   Maranatha 5.10c ☆☆

A former aid climb called the *Flying Fool*, to commemorate the ground fall Rick Skidmore took on the initial attempt. Two points of aid were eliminated on the first free ascent. Start at a shoulder-high roof with a small, left-facing corner above it and climb up to a second, small roof which is pulled directly. Move right on broken rock passing a large hueco to reach the base of the prominent crack. Follow it with increasing difficulty to the top. 65 feet. FA with aid: Hobart Parks & Steve Erskine, 1977. FA: Cal Swoager, May 1985.

96   Bye Bye Bow Wow 5.10d ☆
Farewell Hangdog! Start 15 feet left of *Maranatha*, near the left edge of the face and climb a thin seam, just right of a left-arching corner to a good ledge. Step right and move up the face, angling slightly left to the top. 70 feet. FA: Andrew Barry, Carl Samples & Mark Van Cura, April 1988.

97   Min-arête 5.11a ☆☆
Begin immediately left of the previous route and boulder up the left-arching corner to a roof. Pull the roof and move up the right side of the sweet arête past two bolts to the top. 70 feet. FA: Carl Samples, Rick Thompson, Ron Kampas & Bob Cenk, May 1988.

98   The Freeman Route 5.11c
Not the ones from Montana. On the left wall of *Min-arête* is a line a bolts. 50 feet. FA: Mike Freeman, March 1988.

99   Beginners Only 5.7 ☆
This was the first route to grace the South Bridge Wall. Climb the obvious, left-facing dihedral. 50 feet. FA: Robie Gore, et al., 1975.

100   Mossy Groove 5.6
Climbs the left-facing, squarish flake that starts from a mossy ledge. 40 feet. FA: Unknown.

101   Sundowner 5.10b ☆
Affectionately known by locals as *Scumdowner*, a play on the perpetually dirty condition of this route. Climbs the conspicuous, straight-in fingercrack that begins as a tiny, left-facing corner. 40 feet. FA: Cal Swoager & Ed McCarthy, March 1983.

102   Kiss My Fingers 5.12c ☆
A real tips burner. Commence 20 feet left of *Sundowner*, at a short flake and climb the sustained face past a bolt, a pin and a bolt to the top. 40 feet. Note: No anchors. FA: Eddie Begoon & Mike Artz, July 1988.

103   In Tribute to Skid 5.7
Left of the previous route is a left-facing flake that forms a wide crack. Squirm to the top. 40 feet. FA: Steve Erskine & T.A. Horton, 1977.

104   Square Pegs 5.11
Originally rated 5.9+, a key hold has broken off since the first ascent. Left of *In Tribute to Skid* is a left-facing flake that develops a square slot near the top. 40 feet. FA: T.A. Horton & Steve Erskine, 1980.

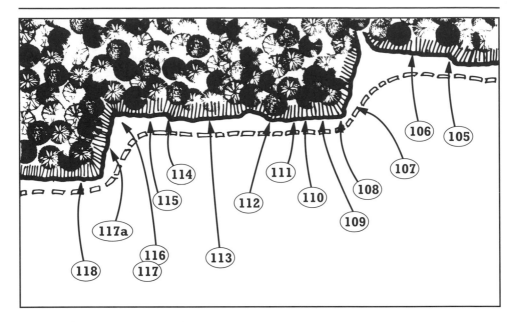

105 The Force 5.11c ☆☆

Features a frustratingly thin, devious and reachy crux. May the force be with you! Climb the black, left-facing dihedral past a roof to a crux encounter of the bulging kind. 40 feet. FA: Doug Reed & Tom Howard, October 1983.

106 Junk Food 5.10b X

More of a glorified boulder problem than a route. Start at a blank-looking face, about 25 feet left of *The Force*. Climb up the face, moving almost immediately right and continue on thin holds to a classic New River tree lunge finish. 20 feet. FA: Andrew Barry, John Eichenburger & John Burcham, May 1985.

107 Fast Asleep in a Dangerous World 5.12a ☆

Begin on the right side of the arête and climb low angle rock past a bolt to a horizontal. Move up and left, past a second bolt, then angle right to the top. 40 feet. FA: Eddie Begoon & Bob Rentka, August 1989.

108 The Last Tango 5.11b ☆☆ ☯

Climb the short arête past a bolt to the ledge, and continue directly up a white streak past four more bolts on a blunt arête to the top. 55 feet. Note: No anchors at top. FA: Stuart & Karen Pregnall, May 1988.

109 Blackberry Blossom 5.9

Begin just left of *The Last Tango* start and climb up and left to the edge. Continue straight up to a horizontal, then trend right, crossing over The Last Tango to reach a right-facing corner which is climbed to the top. 50 feet. FA: Mike Artz, Stanley Todd & Andrew Barry in April, 1986.

110   Unnamed 5.? ⓑ
Between *Blackberry Blossom* and *Catatonic Conflicts* is a line of bolts that leads to a cold shut station. Nothing is known about this route's origin or grade. 50 feet.

111   Catatonic Conflicts 5.10b
Start ten feet left of *Blackberry Blossom* and power up overhanging jugs to the ledge then continue up the steep face past a bolt to the top. 50 feet. FA: Randy Boush, September 1988.

112   The Third Dimension 5.9+
Locate the pair of waterworn cracks and follow the left-hand, thinner crack to its end. Wander up the easier face to the top. 45 feet. FA: Steve Erskine & Rick Skidmore, 1978.

113   Rob's Route 5.11b ⓑ
Just right of the *Gemini Cracks* is a sport climb protected by five bolts. 50 feet. FA: Rob Turan, June 1990.

114   Gemini Crack — Right 5.10a ☆☆☆
At the left end of the wall are a pair of charismatic fingercracks. Climb the right one. 50 feet. Note: It's possible to avoid the hard start by making a rising traverse in from the left. FA: Cal Swoager & Ed McCarthy, May 1983.

115   Gemini Crack — Left 5.10c ☆☆☆
The left-hand crack is a bit stiffer. 50 feet. FA: Cal Swoager, May 1983.

116   Lollipop 5.7+
Climb the wide crack in the right-facing corner. 35 feet. FA: Steve Erskine & Rick Skidmore, 1979.

117   Berlin Wall 5.10b ☆
Though a bit contrived, this route will certainly capture your attention. Follow *Lollipop* for a short distance until a small ledge on the left wall is reached. Hand-traverse left along it to gain a vertical flake near the center of the wall which is followed to a short face and the top. 45 feet. FA: Andrew Barry, Steve Lancaster & Eric Anderson, June 1985.

117a Berlin Wall Direct Start — Reunification 5.12b ☆☆
Start left of *Lollipop* and climb directly up the face, past two bolts, to join the regular route at the flake. Finish as normal. 35 feet. FA: Kevin Parker, March 1991.

118   My Wife is a Dog 5.10d ☆☆
Hangdog that is! A play on the 1988 Oscar-winning foreign film *My Life as a Dog*. Begin at the arête right of *Promised* and climb up and left then directly up to a bolt. Move up and right, then leftward to the top. 60 feet. FA: Stuart & Karen Pregnall, April 1988.

Scott Garso on *Underfling,* one of New River's first 5.10s.

photo: Rick Thompson

Pretending to find a hold, Kenny Parker on the second ascent of *Little Head Logic.*

photo: Steve Downes

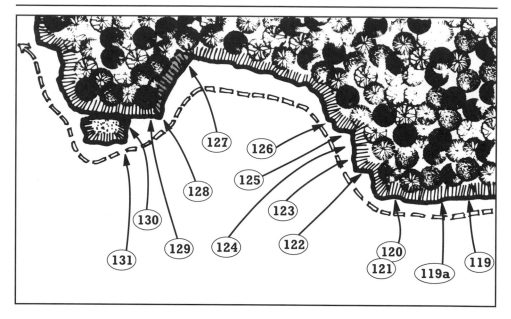

119   Promised 5.10b ☆☆☆
This fine New River face climb lives up to its promise of great climbing. Locate a distinctive, short crack in the center at mid-height. Start about ten feet right of the crack, just left of the previous route and climb up and left to a weakness below the crack. Head straight up the crack and the face above to the top. 60 feet. FA: Cal Swoager & John Govi, May 1984.

119a Promised Direct Start 5.10b ☆☆☆
It's possible to climb directly up to the crack. FA: Carl Samples & Ed McCarthy, May 1988.

120   Highlander 5.10a ☆☆
Begin a short distance left of *Promised* and climb the obviously awkward chimney to the ledge then directly up the face past a short crack to a stance. Continue up, trending slightly left to the top. 60 feet. FA: Sandy Fleming & John Vidumsky, October 1988.

121   Happy Head 5.8 ☆☆☆
This heady climb is sure to put a smile on your face. Follow the same start as *Highlander* to the ledge, then step left and climb the face and short crack to a stance. Move left to the arête and enjoy perfect rock and fine position on your way to the top. 60 feet. FA: John Vidumsky & Sandy Flemming, October 1988.

122   Chinese Style 5.8 R
Follow the raging offwidth in the corner to the top. 55 feet. FA: Hobart Parks & Steve Erskine, 1979.

123 Mind Shaft 5.12a/b ☆ 👤

Climb the line of bolts that leads to anchors to the right of *Eyes of the Mind*. 50 feet. FA: Roxanna Brock, 1994.

124 Eyes of the Mind 5.12b ☆☆

Begin immediately right of *Esse Crack* and pull the low roof to a bolt then continue straight up past a second bolt to a pin at the hueco eyes. Move right and finish up the dicey groove past a pin. 50 feet. FA: Dave Lanman, April 1988.

125 Esse Crack 5.10c ☆☆☆

Short, sweet, and a bit strenuous, this dihedral comes highly recommended. Climbs the open corner split by a curved, bulging crack. 40 feet. FA: Cal Swoager & Stuart Kuperstock, November 1983.

126 Sultans of Swing 5.12a

Protection difficult. Start ten feet left of *Esse Crack* and crank a short layback to some pockets. Continue up the face until it's possible to mantel onto the arête. Finish up and right. 40 feet. FA: Bill Patton & Matt Lamperti, October 1988.

127 Synaptic Lapse 5.10a ☆

Locate a right-facing corner with an alcove capped by a roof on the left wall. Climb the right-facing corner of the alcove to the roof, then move left around the roof and follow the short, opposite-facing corner to the top. 30 feet. FA: Tom Howard & Doug Reed, October 1983.

128 Welcome to Huecool 5.11d R ☆☆☆

This beautiful arête was first done using fixed wires as additional protection to the pin and bolt. Unfortunately, they frayed out over the years and the route is now a much more serious endeavor. Grope your way up the way-cool arête. 50 feet. FA: Mike Artz & Andrew Barry, April 1986.

129 Strongly Stationary 5.12a

One of the first 5.12s at the New. Commence ten feet left of *Welcome to Huecool* and climb straight up a smooth face past a hueco to the second horizontal. Move left five feet and follow easier moves to a bolt then finish directly to the top. 50 feet. FA: Andrew Barry & Mike Artz, April 1986.

The following two routes incorporate sections of a 1986 Andrew Barry route called *Go Go Ego* 5.10c. They were done without knowledge of the prior ascent and straighten out the former route's rather wandering line.

130 Salvation Salesman 5.11d ☆

Begin right of the arête, behind a large tree and climb past a bolt and a pin, finishing up a right-angling flake to the top. 60 feet. FA: Greg Collum & Rich Pleiss, May 1988.

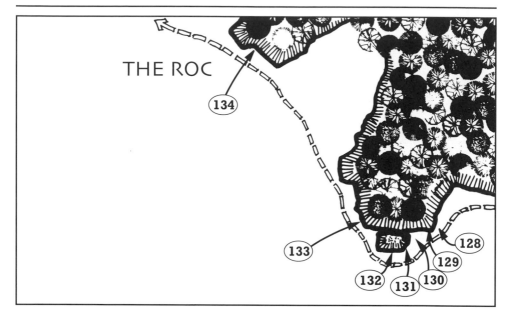

131 Jimmy's Swagger 5.10b ☆☆
Start on the right side of the arête and climb directly up the edge of the face past a bolt to the top. 60 feet. FA: Greg Collum & Rich Pleiss, May 1988.

132 Pancake Ledge 5.10b ☆
On the downhill side of the block is an obvious crack and flake system. Begin near the right edge of the face and follow the cracks up and left to a bulge in the center of the wall (beware of the loose block). Step right at the bulge and pull it at a short, vertical crack, finishing on the lower-angle face above. 60 feet. FA: Steve Erskine & T.A. Horton, 1979.

133 Big Mac Attack 5.11a
Climb an obvious, low-angle, right-facing corner for a short distance to reach broken cracks in the left wall. From the top of the cracks crank left to a stance on the arête and climb the left side past a bolt to the top. 60 feet. FA: Ed McCarthy, Mike Artz & Rob Turan, June 1988.

THE ROC
Just beyond *Big Mac Attack* is a breakdown in the cliff that marks the end of the South Bridge Wall. Continue following the trail for a short distance until a large block appears on your right. This tiny outcrop, known as The Roc, has but one route which can easily be identified by finding the small "pond" at the base of a right-facing corner system.

134 Ducks Unlimited 5.7 ☆
You'll probably see more mosquitoes here than ducks! Follow the right-facing dihedral to the top. 45 feet. FA: Steve Erskine & T.A. Horton, 1979.

Carl Samples sniffing out the first ascent of *Dr. Rosenbud's Nose.*

photo: Rick Thompson

CENTRAL BRIDGE WALL

Beyond The Roc is another break in the cliff and a gully. A low, grungy wall develops beyond the gully, marking the beginning of the Central Bridge Wall. Walk along the low wall until it increases in height to 40 or 50 feet. A large alcove capped by a roof locates the start of the first routes. It may be desirable to park above the switchback and hike directly uphill to reach this wall rather than parking at the Bridge Buttress pulloffs.

135 'Til the Cows Come Home 5.10b
Udderly awkward! Scramble up to a spacious platform and locate the obvious handcrack in the back of the alcove that begins as a low roof. Overcome the initial roof to gain a right-facing corner which is followed past a flared slot to the top. 40 feet. FA: Bruce Burgin & Carl Samples, May 1986.

136 Dairy Area 5.4 ☆
Or is it Derriere-rea? Variety and exposure with good protection. Watch rope drag. Begin on the left wall of the alcove, about 15 feet right of the arête and angle up and left on good horizontals to reach the outside corner, just below a roof band. Traverse left around the arête about ten feet on a good ledge, then angle right, following a right-leaning weakness up the steep face to the top. 50 feet. FA: Rick Thompson, Carl Samples & Bruce Burgin, May 1986.

137 Dairy Area Variation Finish — Quantum Meruit 5.4 ☆☆
This enjoyable link-up may well be the finest face climb of its grade at the New. Watch rope drag. Climb *Dairy Area* until you've reached the end of the leftward traverse along the good ledge. Strike out to the left and ascend the steep, delightful face straight to the top. This is the same finish as *Milk Run*. 55 feet. FA: Rick Thompson, Carl Samples & Bruce Burgin, May 1986.

138   The Big Cheese 5.10b ☆
Begin at the arête, just left of *Dairy Area*, and climb directly up to the ledge (crosses *Dairy Area* here), then reach right and pull the first overhang. Continue up the overhanging prow (right of *Dairy Area*) to the top. 45 feet. FA: John Vidumsky & Sandy Flemming, October 1989.

139   Hairy Canary 5.11c ☆☆
Start a short distance right of *Milk Run* and surmount the bulging wall directly then finish on *Milk Run*. 65 feet. FA: Mike Cote & Bill Moore, April 1987.

140   Milk Run 5.9+ ☆
Better climbing than it first appears. Start just right of the outside corner and angle leftward to an inside corner, then directly up to a four-foot roof with a crack. Pull the roof to a ledge and climb directly up the face, staying just right of a pie-shaped roof. 65 feet. FA: Bruce Burgin, Rick Thompson & Carl Samples, May 1986.

141   Rockin' Robyn 5.11d/12a ☆☆
Using the same start as *Midnight Moonlight*, climb directly up the overhanging face, past a piton to a ledge. Continue directly up the face past three bolts to the top. 70 feet. FA: Eric Hörst, April 1989.

142   Midnight Moonlight 5.7 ☆☆
Begin 20 feet left of the *Milk Run* arête and follow the left-leaning line of weakness to a short dihedral near the top. Up the dihedral to a small roof finishing left and up to the top. 65 feet. FA: Steve Erskine & T.A. Horton, 1979.

142a Midnight Moonlight Direct Finish —
Akron Motor Speedway 5.12a/b ☆ 🅱
From a ledge about a third of the way up *Midnight Moonlight*, step right and follow five bolts to the top. 65 feet. FA: Glenn Ritter & Mark Stevenson, August 1990.

143   Burning Bungee 5.11c ☆
Thirty feet left of the previous route, fire directly up the blunt, bulging arête past a bolt, then angle right and up to a ledge. From the right end of the ledge climb straight up the face to the top. 60 feet. FA: Rick Mix, Ken Needham & Eric Hörst, April 1989.

144   One Life at a Time, Please 5.10c/d R ☆☆
Get started approximately 35 feet right of the *Hopfenperle Special* and follow a right-angling ramp to a ledge. Climb crimpy flakes on the face just left of the thin seam (now equipped with a pin) up to a horizontal and step right, following the crack to the top. 60 feet. FA: Doug Chapman & Darlene Allison, July 1987. Note: In June 1988 a second party, unaware of the prior ascent, established a slightly more direct version to *One Life at a Time, Please*, naming it *Lichen Illusion* 5.11d. This version begins just right of the original start and climbs directly up a seam past a bolt to the ledge, finishing straight up the seam (pin) and crack to the top. Both pieces of fixed gear were placed by the second ascent party.

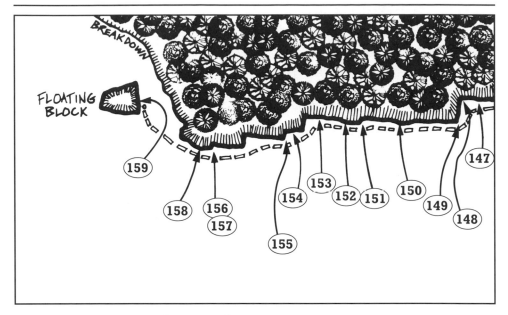

145   The Hopfenperle Special 5.7 ☆☆

Honoring the highly touted Swiss brew. Climbs the right-facing corner with a pair of hemlock trees growing at the base. 50 feet. FA: T.A. Horton & Steve Erskine, 1979.

146   Big Al's 5.9 ☆

Start about 25 feet left of the previous climb, on the left side of the arête at a short crack. Climb the crack to the arête and follow it to the top. 50 feet. FA: T.A. Horton & Steve Erskine, 1979.

147   First Strike 5.10a ☆☆☆

Supremo handcrack! Left of *Big Al's* is a sweeping orange wall split by a striking crack. Jam it! 50 feet. FA: Cal Swoager & Phil Wilt, March 1983.

148   Le Brief 5.10c

Begin about 15 feet left of *First Strike* and climb straight up the face past a bolt to a ledge. Rappel using same anchor as Slave to the Past. 25 feet. FA: Eric Hörst & Ken Needham, April 1989.

149   Slave to the Past 5.11c ☆

Engage at a distinctive, short, left-facing corner and climb it to the ledge. Step to the right end of the ledge and rappel with the utmost caution from the single pin. 30 feet. FA: Eric Hörst & Ken Needham, April 1989.

150   Bhopal West 5.10a R

An off-hands crack of a lethal nature. Bring your big gear. Jam the ever-widening handcrack in the brilliant orange wall to the top. 50 feet. FA: Dave Sippel & Eric Hoffman, June 1986.

151   Sphagnum Dopus 5.8–
Don't drop your schwaag in the moss. Twenty feet left of *Bhopal West* is a small, right-facing corner that ramps leftward. Follow it to the top. 35 feet. FA: Rick Thompson, Carl Samples & Bruce Burgin, May 1986.

152   Magnum Gropus 5.10d
Climbs the steep, broken crack left of the previous route. 35 feet. FA: Rick Thompson, Carl Samples & Bruce Burgin, May 1986.

153   Meth-iso-cyinate 5.10a
The toxin that killed the masses of Bhopal. About 40 feet left of *Magnum Gropus* is a bulging fingercrack. 30 feet. TR FA: Rick Skidmore & Steve Erskine, 1979. FA: Unknown.

154   Throw in the Rack 5.7+ ☆
Though a bit short, this is an aesthetic pitch. Climbs the clean, right-facing dihedral that begins from a narrow ledge. Either begin from the ledge or climb the short wall below it then follow the dihedral to the top. 25/40 feet. FA: Steve Erskine & T.A. Horton, 1979.

155   Romper Room 5.7
Climbs the arête left of the previous route. 45 feet. FA: Stuart & Karen Pregnall, summer 1989.

156   Dark Hollow 5.8 ☆
Climb the obvious, right-facing corner system in the center of narrow face. 50 feet. FA: T.A. Horton and Steve Erskine in 1978.

157   Joey's Face 5.10b ☆
Climb the first ten feet of *Dark Hollow* then move right and up through a bulge to a right-leaning flake. Finish left and up. 50 feet. FA: Markus Jucker & John Eichenburger, October 1989.

158   Needful Things 5.11c ☆☆
Just left of *Dark Hollow*, climb the line of four bolts. 50 feet. FA: Kevin Rock, 1994.

159   Impaled 5.10b
A short distance beyond *Dark Hollow* is a large boulder known as Floating Block. Begin on the upstream face, below an overhanging crack. Face climb up to a small, squarish platform and jam the crack to the top. 30 feet. FA: Steve Stanley, Bruce Burgin & Doug Perkins, June 1986.

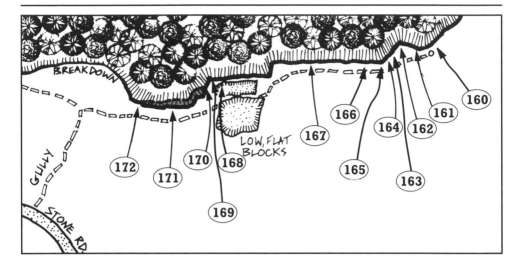

NORTH BRIDGE WALL

Beyond Floating Block is another breakdown in the outcrop culminating in a low, emungulated wall that stretches for about 200 feet. The cliff beyond this section is the North Bridge Wall. Routes are described as though you were approaching it from the Central Wall, but most climbers prefer to park at the switchback and walk out the stone road, as if approaching the Junkyard Wall. A short scramble from the road brings you to the Pinnacle.

160 Share the Faith 5.9
Climb the pinkish crack up to a small stance, then move left up a corner. Step right to a small ledge and up the face. 50 feet. FA: Jeff Horrocks & Phil Nelson, March 1989.

161   Dr. Rosenbud's Nose 5.10c ☆☆☆
Speaking of honkers, get a load of this one! Start ten feet right of *Midway* below a bolt and climb directly up the face to a stance under the roof on the left side of the arête. Pucker up and move up, then right on skimpy crimps to gain the beckoning arête which is followed to the top. 60 feet. FA: Carl Samples & Rick Thompson, May 1986.

162 Midway 5.8
An enjoyable start leads to an anticlimactic finish. Ascend the clean dihedral past a small roof at mid-height and finish up through a steep, dirt-filled corner. 50 feet. FA: Steve Erskine & T.A. Horton, 1977.

163   Hey Woody, Hinckley's Not the Center of the Universe Any More! 5.9+ ☆
For those not familiar, Hinckley Quarry is a popular crag in northern Ohio. Climb the face immediately left of *Midway* to a stance just left of a small roof. Move slightly right and climb the clean streak to the top. 60 feet. FA: Glenn Ritter & Tony Robinson, August 1990.

164   The Walrus 5.10a ☆☆
Begin on the right side of the arête and climb the pocketed face to a ledge at mid-height. Continue up the center of the face on steep horizontals to the top. 65 feet. FA: Eddie Begoon & Mike Artz, August 1987.

165   Ook Ook Kachook 5.11a ☆☆☆
Begin directly below the arête and climb up a few moves then traverse right eight feet and surmount the face staying left of a shallow right-facing corner. Trend up and left to a good stance below the arête. Follow the face on the left side of the arête to the top. 70 feet. FA: Mike Artz, Rick Thompson & Stanley Todd, June 1986.

166   The Egg Man 5.11b ☆
Ten feet left of the previous route is a pumpy start past a roof to a pin. Move left, then up to a good horizontal and continue up and left, finishing directly up the bulging face to the top. 70 feet. FA: Eddie Begoon & Stanley Todd, October 1987.

167   Orange Blossom Special 5.6 ☆
Left of *The Egg Man* is an attractive orange face dissected by a series of right-facing flakes. Begin in a keystone shaped recess and follow the flakes up and left to the top. 55 feet. FA: Hobart Parks & Rick Skidmore, 1977.

168   Gaye Belayed 5.7
Follow the obvious short crack to a ledge and rappel. 30 feet. FA: Bruce Burgin & Gaye Howard, July 1986.

169   The Gospel Trek 5.5
Start in the blocky corner that leads to a nice crack and follow it up to a roof. Crank out and over the roof to the top. 50 feet. FA: Phil Nelson & Jeff Horrocks, March 1989.

170   Chattasuga Choo-Choo 5.9
Begin just right of a rotten-looking overhanging corner and climb up the face to a horizontal. Move left into the alcove and pull over the roof to a ledge. Finish on the face just left of the arête. 50 feet. FA: Tom Howard & T.A. Horton, July 1986.

171   The Artful Dreamer 5.9
Dream on! At the right hand edge of this broken wall is a roof about 25 feet up. Begin under the left end of the roof and climb directly up to it. Exit left to a ledge and angle up and right to the base of a short white headwall. Follow cracks to the top. 55 feet. FA: Carl Samples, Rick Thompson, Bob Rentka, Scott Garso & Mark Van Cura, June 1986.

172   The Gloom Index 5.10a
The index that measures mediocrity. A gloomy start leads to a brief, dumpy finish. Locate a short crack near the left edge of the broken face and follow it to some green ledges. Move up and right to a short arête at the left edge of the headwall. Traverse right a couple of moves and follow cracks just right of the arête to the top. 50 feet. FA: Scott Garso, Mark Van Cura, Rick Thompson & Bob Rentka, June 1986.

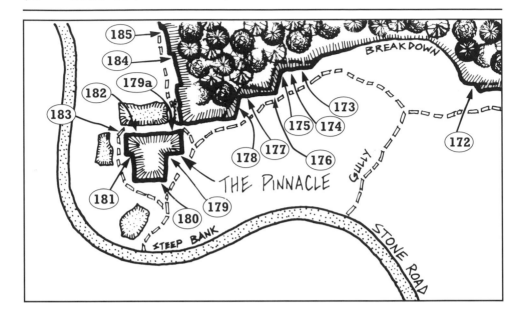

PINNACLE WALL

173 Meto Power 5.10c
Begin eight feet right of *Ode to Stoat* and boulder out a low roof to a stance below a second smaller roof. Follow the thin crack above the roof to a ledge and walk off right. 35 feet. FA: Stanley Todd & Rick Thompson, June 1986.

174 Ode to Stoat 5.10b ℝ
Andrew Barry is also affectionately known as Stoat. Begin 15 feet right of *Porcupine Crack*, at the left hand of a low roof band. Boulder up to a narrow roof and traverse left five feet to a good horizontal. Climb directly over the narrow roof past a bolt and finish straight to the top. 50 feet. Note: Can be a bit dirty. FA: Scott Garso, Rick Thompson & Carl Samples, June 1986.

175 Porcupine Crack 5.8 ☆ ℝ
You'll need some big gear for this route. After a few moves on broken rock, follow the clean, right-facing corner to the large roof and belay on the ledge to the right. 50 feet. FA: Hobart Parks & Steve Erskine, 1979.

176 Fat Cat 5.13a ☆☆ ℝ
You'll feel like a fat cat if you power up this purrfect little arête. Claw your way up the obvious, overhanging bolted arête to a rap station on the ledge below the large roof. 35 feet. FA: Scott Franklin, April 1989.

177   Mr. Peanut Head 5.9+ ☆

An intimidating line that, like its brother route, *Porcupine Crack*, requires some big gear. Follow the wide crack in the right-facing dihedral to the roof, then move right and pull into the right-facing corner which is followed to the top. 70 feet. FA: Hobart Parks & Steve Erskine, 1979.

178   Jams Across America 5.10b ☆

On the steep wall left of the *Mr. Peanut Head* corner is a short fingercrack. Climb it, then move up and left to a belay on a good ledge. Rap. 30 feet. FA: Unknown.

THE PINNACLE

The Pinnacle is a 90-foot detached tower with a serene summit. Its vantage point is one of the finest in the gorge for viewing the bridge. The moderate *Afternoon Delight* appears to be one of the first routes done in the gorge. In 1977, a tin can was found on its summit with some names scribbled on a piece of paper. But, the writing was illegible, thus preserving the mystery of its first ascent.

179   Afternoon Delight 5.5 ☆☆

The easiest route to the summit, this popular climb is recommended despite the inadequate protection at the start and the existence of a dreadful top 40 hit by the same name. Don't forget your picnic basket. Commence at an offwidth in a right-facing corner and brave your way up to a large ledge. Step across the ledge and climb the inside corner to the roof, exiting either left or right to more ledges. Climb straight to the top. 80 feet. Note: To avoid rope scars on the small summit trees it may be desirable to downclimb on the river side to a good ledge with a larger pine. A single rope will reach to the ground from here. FA: Will we ever know?

179a Afternoon Delight Direct Start — Pinnacle Flats 5.9

Climb the obvious, six-inch crack to the ledge and finish on *Afternoon Delight*. Note: Big gear. FA: Hobart Parks & Rick Skidmore, 1977.

180   The Vertex 5.10c/d R ☆☆

The highest point reached in the apparent motion of a celestial body. Begin just left of the outside corner at a short crack and climb it to a good horizontal. Move left, then up the thin face to a good stance, then climb up and rail right on a good horizontal. Surmount the left-hand margin of a bulge to reach the base of a short, left-leaning crack which leads to the ledge. Directly in front of you will be a short, white arête. Climb the face just right of the arête to another ledge and scramble up to the final short steep wall that leads to the summit. 90 feet. FA: Rick Thompson, Mike Artz & Stanley Todd, June 1986.

181   The Reverse Traverse 5.9

Locate the large offwidth in the north face of The Pinnacle. Follow it until you're about 15 feet below a good-sized roof then angle up and right to reach it. Pull it then track back to the left following a scooped out face to the ledge with the multi-branched pine. 70 feet. FA: Steve Stanley & Doug Perkins, June 1986.

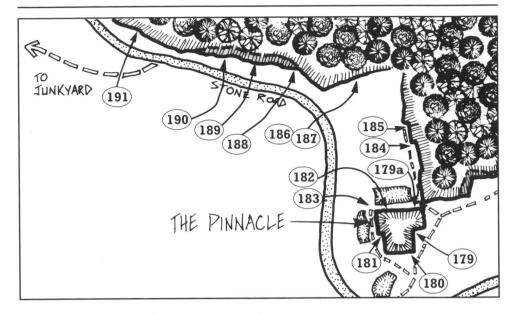

182   Destination Unknown 5.11d ☆☆

A complex and committing route done in the finest, ground-up tradition. Three years after the first ascent a visiting climber established a route which used a different start, but ultimately bolted over the upper two-thirds of the route. Because it infringed so significantly on this trad route all but the first three bolts were removed, thus preserving both the traditional route and the direct start. Initiate climbing ten feet left of the arête and climb the steep face for about 25 feet, then make a scary move right to reach the arête. Follow it to a roof which is pulled to a stance. Traverse left on good face holds, then up and back right to gain the start of an overhanging crack which is followed to the top. 85 feet. FA: Mike Artz & Andrew Barry, June 1986.

183   Destination Unknown Direct Start —
The Texas Bolt Massacre 5.11d ☆☆

Climbs the initial part of the blunt arête which is protected by three bolts. FA: Greg Brooks, 1989.

184   Spams Across America 5.6

For added excitement try it in the first ascent style — during a driving rain. Climb the right-hand, brown dihedral to broken rock and continue up and left to a stance. Finish up and left. 40 feet. FA: Carl Samples & Rick Thompson, May 1986.

185   The Spamling 5.7

Did you ever wonder what Spam is made of? Ascend the left-hand dihedral past a layback to reach broken rock. Scamper up and right to the top. 45 feet. FA: Scott Garso, Eric Hoffman & Ron Kampas, May 1986.

THE OGRE

The final outcrop included in the Bridge Area Crags chapter is a beastly looking crag most easily identified by the iron-ore colored seep at its base. Just beyond it is the trail that angles down and left to the Junkyard Wall.

186   Lucky Pierre at L.A.S.W.A. 5.9 R

Begin 30 feet left of the right-hand breakdown of the cliff, directly below a pin. Climb straight up past the pin to a small ledge, avoiding the blocky terrain on the right, finishing up the easier face. 45 feet. FA: Jonathan Houck & James Goodman, December 1987.

187   Lucky Pierre Direct Start — This One Is for Vicki 5.7

Begin just right of the regular start and climb blocky terrain to a small ledge. Hand traverse left above the pin, then mantel up and aim directly for the top. 45 feet. FA: Jonathan Houck & James Goodman, December 1987.

188   The Best Little Road Cut Out of Texas 5.12c ☆☆ 🎣

The right-hand line of six bolts. 50 feet. FA: Doug Reed, 1992.

189   Roadcutt Manor 5.12a 🎣

Follows the line of six bolts out the center of the roof. 50 feet. FA: Doug Reed, 1992.

190   Leechate 5.12a 🎣

Climbs the left-hand line of four bolts. 50 feet. FA: Doug Reed, 1992.

191   Food For Thought 5.8

Named for the junkyard that used to lie adjacent to this crag. Jam the obvious crack to its end and finish left. 35 feet. FA: T.A. Horton & Steve Erskine, 1979.

Eddie Begoon belayed by Mike Artz starting the first ascent of *The Bolting Blowfish,* New River's first sport climb.

photo: Rick Thompson

AMBASSADOR BUTTRESS

This modest crag first attracted climbers in 1983, though it went largely unexplored until four years later. Its initial surge in popularity paralleled that of Bubba City and the routes established here during the spring of '87 catalyzed an explosion of high standard face climbs that followed later that year at other crags. The most notable aspect of that influence lies in its bragging rights as the home of New River's first sport climb. At 12b, *The Bolting Blowfish* is a classic crimp-test that has never relinquished its reputation for technical challenge. And though you won't find this crag on the hit list of most visiting climbers, its versatile collection of quality 10s and 11s, complimented by a low-key setting, make it a deserving destination for the New River devotee.

The story behind the name of the crag unfolded one evening, when a group of us sat around the local pizza grotto, shooting the bull, when we were approached by a light-hearted fellow in a fading flannel suit. Immediately he struck up a conversation and it wasn't long before he casually advised us that he was the former Ambassador General of Zimbabwe. As we challenged his claim this cheerful man rambled on and on, insisting it was so. And just when we thought we'd called his bluff, he reached into his jacket pocket and proudly presented a handful of tattered, but official-looking letters that documented his claim. We were believers! It wasn't until he strolled off that it hit me, what would be more appropriate than to honor this local character by naming a crag after him? And so it became the Ambassador Buttress. We still see this gentleman on his daily strolls around the town, sharing his tale of diplomacy with all who will bend an ear.

ACCESS AND ETIQUETTE

The Ambassador Buttress was acquired by the National Park Service in 1989 as part of the Alabama Properties acquisition, a parcel which also contained Fern Buttress. In recent years, the annual Access Fund/National Park Service climber clean-ups have significantly mitigated the garbage ridden atmosphere it formerly had. However, it will most likely take the continued support of these yearly volunteer efforts to maintain the crag in a cleaner spirit.

All climbers should be aware of the prominent vantage point atop the Wall of Ill Repute. It's a popular place for viewing the bridge and occasionally is the scene of a party so be forewarned: Bottles are sporadically hurled from the top!

The most common access involves parking at the Fern Buttress pulloff. Follow the standard approach trail until just beyond the waterfall, where a trail cuts back to the right, passing under the waterfall. Follow the trail along the base of the cliff and you'll arrive shortly at *Nookie Monster*. It's also possible to park at either of the two small pulloffs just above the cliff. A brief descent to the top of the crag and a short rappel will get you to the routes.

Mike Artz on the first ascent of *New-veau Reach*.

photo: Rick Thompson

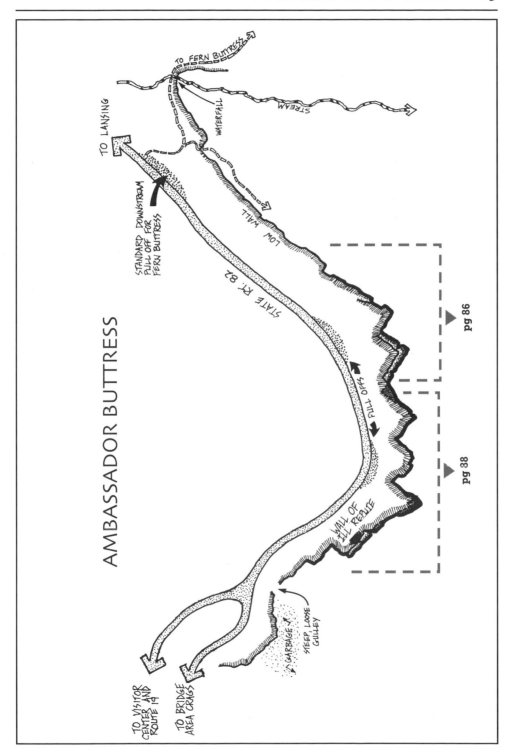

AMBASSADOR BUTTRESS

TO FERN BUTTRESS

TO LANSING

WATERFALL

STREAM

STANDARD DOWNSTREAM PULL OFF FOR FERN BUTTRESS

LOW WALL

STATE RT. 82

pg 86

PULL OFFS

pg 88

WALL OF ILL REPUTE

GARBAGE

STEEP LOOSE GULLEY

TO VISITOR CENTER AND ROUTE 19

TO BRIDGE AREA CRAGS

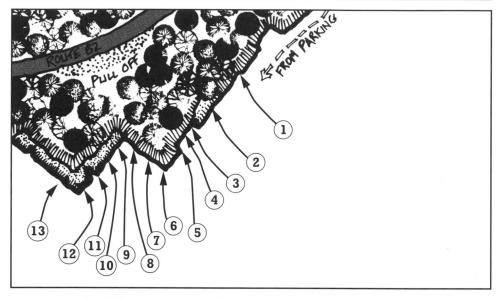

1 Nookie Monster 5.9+ ☆

Climb the obvious handcrack that leads to a flared slot. 40 feet. FA: Glenn Thomas, Mark Van Cura, Rick Thompson, Carl Samples & Scott Garso, March 1987.

2 Comfortably Numb 5.10d R

One of only a few routes at the New that were soloed on the first ascent. Just a week later it was led by another party with no knowledge of its prior ascent. That party gave it the R rating. Begin eight feet right of *Kidspeak* and climb directly past a cluster of pockets. Move up and right, then finish directly up. 40 feet. FA: Eddie Begoon, solo, June 1987.

3 Kidspeak 5.10a ☆☆

Climb the distinctly clean, left-facing dihedral to the ledge. Finish up and left or walk off right. 40 feet. FA: Eric Anderson, Doug Chapman & Paul Goesling, 1983.

4 Lunar Tunes 5.10a ☆☆

Commence five feet left of *Kidspeak* and follow the right-facing flake system to a roof, then traverse left, under the roof to reach the arête (joins *New-veau Reach* here). Finish straight to the top. 75 feet. FA: Tom Howard, Lee Carter, Rick Thompson & Carl Samples, April 1987.

5 The Underdiddled 5.10c R ☆

Crisscrosses *Lunar Tunes*. Begin just left of *Lunar Tunes* and frig your way up the small, right-facing corner, stemming past loose flakes (5.10a R) to reach the roof at half-height (crosses *Lunar Tunes* here). Step right and pull the roof at its widest point, past a bolt, finishing directly to the top. 75 feet. FA: Rick Thompson, Mike Artz & Rob Turan, August 1987.

6   New-veau Reach 5.11c ☆☆☆

Richly rewarding, this route yields a wealth of reachy moves. Begin on the left side of the gorgeous, blunt arête and climb directly up past a pin and a bolt (on the right side) on widely spaced horizontals, then move around to the right side. Continue directly up the arête to the top. 75 feet. Note: Bring plenty of TCUs. FA: Mike Artz & Rick Thompson, April 1987.

7   Clumsy Club Crack 5.10b ☆☆☆

More indicative of what your hands will feel like than reminiscent of Colorado's famed *Country Club Crack*. The initial 40 foot handcrack was the first climb done at the Ambassador. Tape up and begin eight feet left of *New-veau Reach* and jam the handcrack to its end at a ledge with two old pins. Finish directly up past two bolts and the crux. 75 feet. Note: The finish was added in traditional, ground up style and was originally R rated with serious, ankle breaking potential if you fell onto the ledge. The bolts were added later by the first ascent party. FA of handcrack to ledge: Eric Anderson, Doug Chapman & Paul Goesling, 1983. FA of the finish and complete ascent of route: Carl Samples & Rick Thompson, April 1987.

8   Unnamed 5.11d

Left of the previous route, follow the line of fixed gear to the top. 70 feet. FA: Unknown, 1990.

9   Unnamed 5.10d

Begin near the right side of the slab and climb directly up past two bolts to the ledge. Rappel. 35 feet. FA: Unknown, 1990.

10   Unnamed 5.10d

Sadly, this squeezed-in route infringes on the traditional line of ascent of *The Spineless Perpetrator*. Filler material. Climb the left-hand side of the face past two bolts to the ledge. Rappel. 35 feet. FA: Unknown, 1990.

11   The Spineless Perpetrator 5.10a ☆

Start five feet right of the chimney and climb directly past a letter box pocket to reach a left-facing flake which is followed to a ledge. Step right and follow a left-facing, white flake up the short wall to the top. 60 feet. FA: Carl Samples, Rick Thompson & Scott Garso, March 1987.

12   The Bolting Blowfish 5.12b ☆☆

This sweet, little crimp-test carries the honor of being New River's very first sport climb. Named after the look on Eddie's face as he hand drilled with Sachmo-looking cheeks. He was "all blowed-up" over this one. Start five feet left of the chimney, at the center of a narrow white face and crank directly past the bulging start and two pins, then continue directly up past two bolts to a roof. Step right or left and up to the top. 45 feet. Note: No anchors. FA: Eddie Begoon, Mike Artz & Rick Thompson, April 1987.

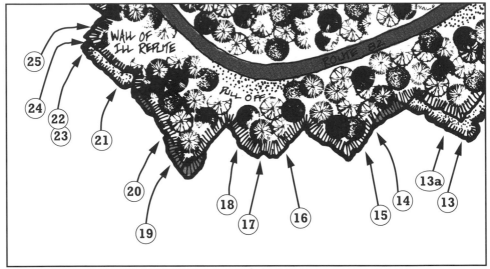

13   Dragon in Your Dreams 5.11b/c ☆☆☆

A serpentine route of tremendous popularity. Begin a short distance left of the arête and climb a wandering line up the mildly overhanging, pocketed face past two bolts to the top. 45 feet. FA: Kenny Parker & Danny Caldwell, April 1987.

13a   Dragon in Your Dreams Direct Start —
Enter the Dragon 5.12b ☆☆☆

Dream on! Begin 15 feet left of the previous route and climb up and right past three bolts to join *Dragon in Your Dreams* at the crux. Continue up to a cold shut station. 45 feet. FA: Kenny Parker, October 1990.

14   Auld Lang Syne 5.12b R ☆☆

The last route to be established in 1988, possibly in the country! It was completed in the fading daylight of New Year's Eve. Begin a short distance right of *Chasing Rainbows* and climb straight up the technical face past three pins to the roof, which yields at the obvious break. 60 feet. FA: Daniel Miller, Eddie Begoon & Kenny Parker, December 1988.

15   Chasing Rainbows 5.10a ☆☆☆

A spectrum of colorful climbing will be savored on this choice route. Start 12 feet right of the sweeping arête and climb up and left past an awkward mantel. Make a move right then back left again to reach a hollow flake on the arête. Power up and right on the white face to the top. 60 feet. FA: Eddie Begoon, Rick Thompson, Bill Moore & Bob Rentka, June 1987.

16   Reefer Derby 5.12c ☆☆☆

Smokin'! Climb directly up the face past a bolt to a horizontal, then fire up and right past a pin and cruise straight for the top. 60 feet. FA: Eddie Begoon & Mike Artz, January 1988.

17   Unnamed 5.11b
Start from the ledge and climb the slab up and right past two bolts to the top. 50 feet. TR FA: Rick Thompson, March 1987. FA: Unknown, 1990.

18   The Glitch 5.4
Major malfunction! What was I thinking? Climb the short wide crack in a low-angle, leaning slab and traverse right along a ledge to reach a large block. Step atop the block then move up and right on good horizontals to the top. 50 feet. FA: Rick Thompson, Carl Samples & Scott Garso, March 1987.

19   The Geneva Convention 5.11d R ☆
Convene on the left side of the arête, at a left-facing flake and move up and right to gain a seam which is followed past a pin to a ledge. Rail out the line of weakness in the roof and follow the face to the top. 60 feet. FA: Eric Hörst & Eddie Begoon, July 1987.

20   Liddlebiddanuthin' 5.10b R/X
I think you get the picture. Begin ten feet left of the previous route and climb an unprotectable grey flake to its end, then finish up and left to the top. 50 feet. FA: Eddie Begoon & Eric Hörst, June 1987.

21   Pleasure Principles 5.11a ☆☆☆
The pleasure game rules. Begin at a small, left-facing corner near the right side of the Wall of Ill Repute and climb up to a pin at a small roof. Pull directly over the bulge and continue up and slightly left past two bolts to the top. 55 feet. FA: Rick Thompson, Bob Rentka, Bill Moore & Eddie Begoon, June 1987.

22   Consenting Clips 5.10b ☆☆☆
Reminiscent of a classic Gunks face climb. Starting at the left edge of the Wall of Ill Repute, at a low roof, climb up and left to a good stance. Move up to the next horizontal, step right a few feet and head straight to the top. 60 feet. Note: Bring lots of TCUs. FA: Mike Artz, Eddie Begoon & Rick Thompson, April 1987.

23   The Happy Hooker 5.11a R
The skyhook protected crux on this pitch will put a smile of uncertainty on your face. Climb the first ten feet of the previous route then traverse left to the arête which is followed to the top. 60 feet. FA: Eric Hörst & Rob Turan, July 1987.

24   Wienie Roast 5.9 ☆
Follow the wide, right-facing flake to a roof. Traverse right under the roof and follow the second, wide, right-facing flake to the top. 35 feet. FA: Bill Moore & Eddie Begoon, June 1987.

25   Success Through Deception 5.12c ☆☆
Follow the obvious line past two bolts and a pin. 40 feet. FA: Eddie Begoon & Kenny Parker, spring 1989.

Glenn Thomas gearing up the start of *Rapscallion's Blues* on an early ascent.

photo: Rick Thompson

JUNKYARD WALL

A short trek downstream from the Bridge Area Crags will bring you to this fashionable destination. Don't let the name fool you, for here you'll find a profusion of traditional moderates on exquisite stone. And with access as easy as a walk in the park it's no wonder the Junkyard Wall runs a close second to the Bridge Buttress in popularity. Varying from 50 to 90 feet and stretching for nearly half a mile, this cliff is home to more than 60 routes. Dazzling finger and hand cracks, splendid dihedrals and roofs, brilliant faces; a little bit of everything can be found here. Not many years ago a massive garbage dump lay adjacent to the upstream end of the crag. Thankfully, that nasty eyesore was cleaned up by the West Virginia Department of Natural Resources and the NPS in the late 80's. Today, all that remains are some rusting cans, fragments of glass and the name of the crag to remind us of a day when environmental preservation ranked low in this region. Fortunately, a day gone by.

Although the initial routes were established here in 1978, it was the following year when the first of the significant lines like *New Yosemite* (5.9), *Jumpin' Jack Flash* (5.7+) and *V-Slot* (5.9), were climbed. During the following few years the crag remained dormant, but in the fall of '83 Phil Wilt established one of the Junkyard's most spectacular dihedrals, *Four Sheets to the Wind* (5.9+). Word of the quality sandstone began to spread and by the spring of '84 a surge of interest blossomed. Charismatic lines like *Enteruptus* (10a), *Rapscallion's Blues* (10c), *The Entertainer* (10a), and *Zealous* (10d) diversified the growing menu of premier climbs. 1985 brought a rush of new route exploration as many of the obvious opportunities were plucked. *New River Gunks* (5.7), *Chasing Spiders to the Right* (5.7 R), *Spoon Fed* (5.9+ R), *Realignment* (10d), and *Stuck in Another Dimension* (11a) are but a modest sampling of the cornucopia of routes established that season.

In November of '86 the crag's first 5.12 was completed with *Pilots of Bekaa* (12a/b), the first of a multitude of 5.12's to be established by Eric Hörst. The next three years brought a handful of sport climbs like *Reachers of Habit* (5.11b) and *Mystery Dance* (12b/c), routes that diversified the climbing opportunities here. And although these lines offer a quality clipping experience, the true curb appeal of the Junkyard Wall will always lie in the enduring qualities found in its collection of moderate trad classics.

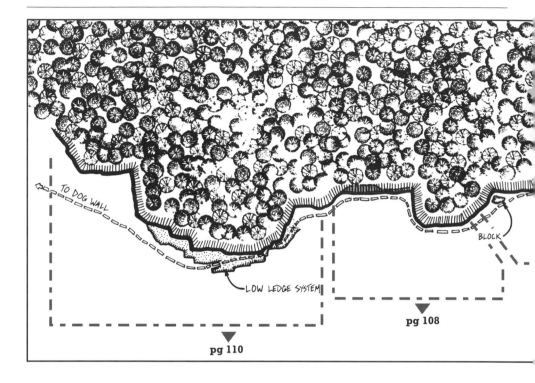

TO DOG WALL

LOW LEDGE SYSTEM

BLOCK

pg 108

▼
pg 110

ACCESS AND ETIQUETTE

The parcel on which this crag, as well as the Animal Escarpments and the majority of Bubba City sits is owned by Alabama Properties. Because these popular climbing sites are within the park boundaries, they are targeted for future acquisition by the NPS. Until that time, we are reminded that it is only by the good will of Alabama Properties that recreational use is permitted.

This crag suffers from the same recreational use impacts as the Bridge Buttress. A wide swath of compaction at the cliff base, erosion and dying trees at the cliff top, and human waste indiscriminately exposed near the base of routes are but a sampling of impacts we should consciously work to reduce.

Here's what you can do to help lighten the "footprint" of climbers at this crag:

- Tread lightly at all times, especially at the top of the cliff where additional soil compaction will cause further erosion and threaten the well being of trees.
- Avoid using small diameter trees for anchoring.
- Do not camp anywhere in this area. Use private campgrounds or camp on NPS property where such use is permitted.
- Pick up all litter.

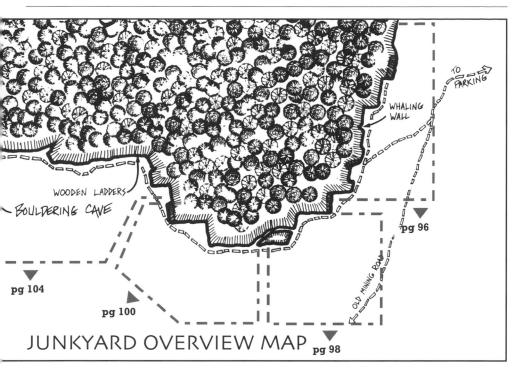

JUNKYARD OVERVIEW MAP

• When hanging out at the base of the cliff make a conscious effort to keep your zone of impact as small as possible.
• Follow Leave No Trace guidelines for the disposal of solid human waste as outlined in the Introduction Chapter.
• Do not rappel from trees.
• If crowded, climb at another crag.

To reach the Junkyard Wall, follow Route 82 beyond the Bridge Buttress until you reach the parking area at the first hairpin turn. This site is located on NPS land. See the Bridge Area Crags – Downstream Map for parking and access reference. Be certain that you park well off the switchback since shuttle buses use this road to access the river pull-out and must be able to negotiate a three-point turn here. Also be conscientious how you park so other cars may also fit in this limited area. To reach the crag follow the old dirt road (known as the Burma Road) which heads downstream from the parking area until you pass the Ogre, then follow the trail that forks downhill to the left. The cliff will appear a short distance ahead.

Over the past few years an alternate approach and parking area via the upper Burma Road has become popular. However, this access involves parking on private property and is not recommended. Camping in this area is also taboo.

Phil Wilt on the 1983 first ascent of *Four Sheets to the Wind.*

photo: Carl Samples

Cal Swoager soloing *New Yosemite* in 1985.

photo: Terry Swoager

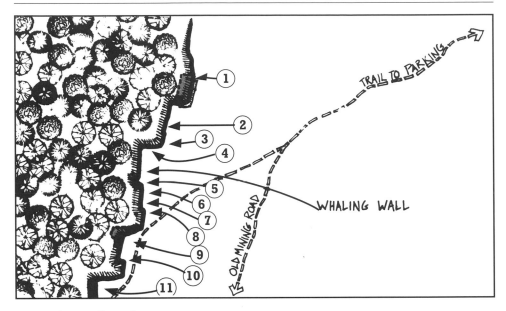

1   Long Reach 5.9+

Locate the low roof near the right side of the cliff and climb the handcrack on the right side of it. 40 feet. FA: Hobart Parks & Rick Skidmore, 1978.

2   Ann's Revenge 5.8+ ☆

Start about 20 feet left of the low roof and climb the small left-facing corner to its end at mid-height, then continue straight to the top via a squarish-looking crack. 60 feet. FA: Steve Erskine & Rick Skidmore, 1978.

3   Nine Lives 5.11c ☆☆

Climb the arête past four bolts to the top. 80 feet. Note: Bring small to medium camming units. FA: Bill Burgos, Kenny Parker, Marcus Jucker & Kevin Daney, November 1990.

4   Lapping the Sap 5.10a ☆

Better climbing than it may appear, but often wet. Begin in the major left-facing corner and chimney to gain the dihedral. Continue up to the roof and bypass it on the right wall. 85 feet. FA: Scott Garso & Rick Thompson, August 1985.

4a   Lapping the Sap Variation — The Hornet 5.9 ☆

This variation start avoids the initial chimney. Begin about 15 feet left of *Lapping the Sap* and angle up and right on flakes (5.9) to merge with the regular route just above the apex of the chimney. Finish as normal. FA: Steve Stanley & Bruce Burgin, April 1986.

The face to the left of *Lapping the Sap* is known as The Whaling Wall.

5   Crack Sap 5.9 ☆
Commence 30 feet left of *Lapping the Sap*, at a right-facing corner behind a tree. Strenuous jamming leads past the apex of the roof to easier climbing. At the top of the corner, move left to a ledge and belay. 50 feet. FA: Scott Garso & Rick Thompson, June 1985.

6   Danger in Paradise 5.10b ☆
Start six feet left of the tree at *Crack Sap* and climb the tiny corners past a pin, then follow a system of flakes and cracks that lead to the ledge above. Belay is the same as *Crack Sap*. 50 feet. FA: Rick Thompson, Scott Garso, Bob Rentka & Andrew Barry, June 1985.

7   Princess Diana 5.9+ R
A rather nondescript route considering it's named after the Princess of Wales...or is that Whales? Start 15 feet left of *Danger in Paradise* and climb directly up the face, passing the right-hand tip of the arching roof of *Whales in Drag*. Finish up and right to the ledge. 50 feet. FA: Andrew Barry & Glenn Thomas, June 1985.

8   Whales in Drag 5.10a
Whales crossdress? Climb the crumbly looking, right-facing corner that arches right to the roof, then traverse right under the roof to its end. Move up and traverse back to the left on easy ground then finish straight up the face to the ledge. 50 feet. Note: A #1.5 Friend is helpful for protecting the final moves. FA: Rick Thompson & Scott Garso, June 1985.

9   Rock Rash 5.11a
This beast resembles a whale-eating piranha. Begin under the low roof and climb the right wall of the alcove directly up to the wide crack. Undercling out the roof, passing the awkward lip to easy climbing and the ledge above. 50 feet. FA: Cal Swoager, May 1985.

10   Rapscallion's Blues 5.10c ☆☆☆☆
You won't be singing the blues on this upbeat pitch. Sustained climbing up the beautiful, right-facing dihedral leads to a short right-angling crack and the roof. Pull the awkward roof, then move left and finish up a short, v-slot crack. 60 feet. Note: It's possible to slither off right to a ledge after pulling the roof. FA: Doug Reed & Tom Howard, June 1984.

11   Four Sheets to the Wind 5.9+ ☆☆☆☆
Superior in every way, this Junkyard classic sports a series of Gunks-like roofs that are sure to fill your sails. Climb the wide crack in the left-facing dihedral to a lieback over the first roof, then continue directly through the roofs. Move left into an alcove and finish up the awkward slot to the top. 70 feet. Note: It's also possible to finish on the right wall. FA: Phil Wilt & Carl Samples, November 1983.

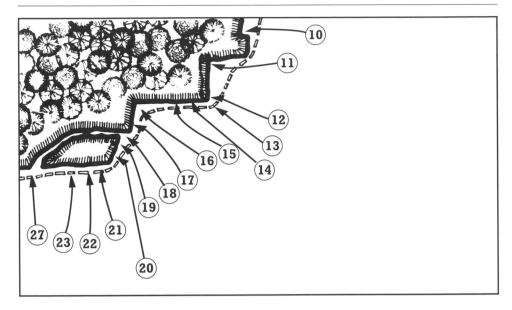

12   Enteruptus 5.10a ✰✰

Begin 20 feet left of *Four Sheets* at a crack just right of the arête. Climb for a short distance and move right onto a ramp, following a left-facing flake system to the roof. Pull it and crawl right to join *Four Sheets* at the alcove. Finish up the awkward slot. Note: It's possible to pull the roof directly at 5.11c. 70 feet. FA: Doug Reed & Tom Howard, June 1984.

12a   Enteruptus Variation Start — Scott's Turf Builder 5.10b ✰

Start between *Four Sheets* and *Enteruptus* and climb a short crack then move right to the base of a short, right-facing corner (just left of the actual corner of *Four Sheets*). Move up the corner until just below a roof and power left to link up with the upper flake of *Enteruptus*. FA: Scott Garso & Dave Sippel, May 1985.

13   Just Say No 5.11a R ✰✰

Begin just left of Enteruptus and follow the arête to the top. 75 feet. FA: Greg Collum & Rich Pleiss, July 1988.

14   Yew Nosemite 5.12b ✰

Begin immediately right of *New Yosemite* and climb a left-facing corner past a small roof then traverse eight feet right to a bucket. Thrash directly up past a pin and a ledge to the top. 60 feet. FA: Eric Hörst, October 1987.

15   New Yosemite 5.9 ✰✰✰
aka Climbing Under the Influence

This superlative handcrack is one of the best of its grade at the New. Jam it! 60 feet. FA: Steve Erskine & T.A. Horton, 1979.

16   Jumpin' Jack Flash 5.7+ ☆
It's a gas! Left of *New Yosemite* is a right-facing corner that begins with a tapering slot. Follow it to the top. 50 feet. FA: T.A. Horton & Hobart Parks, 1979.

17   Keep it Tight but Don't Give Me Aids 5.10a
A classic Andrew Barry pun. Begin left of *Jumpin' Jack Flash* and climb the left-leaning flake to the ledge at half-height. Go up, then left to another ledge to top out. 40 feet. Note: It's possible to finish further left at 5.7. FA: Andrew Barry & Frank Gibson, July 1985.

17a   Keep it Tight....Variation Finish 5.10a
Contrived. From the ledge at half-height, move up and right to finish past a small, orange corner. FA: Paul Heyliger, August 1985.

18   Andropov's Cold 5.11c ☆
Climb the 25 foot overhanging crack and finish by traversing off to the right or do the last part of *Keep it Tight*. 30 feet. FA: Shane Cobourn & Tom Howard, July 1984.

19   Frigidator 5.10b ☆
Great for cooling off on a hot day, but keep your distance during frigid weather! In the gaping chimney just left of *Andropov's Cold* is an obvious crack system on the right wall. Follow it until it's possible to exit out the gaping slot at the top. Note: The accepted style for doing this route precludes use of the wall behind you until the last move! 50 feet. FA: Tom Howard & Bruce Burgin, September 1985.

20   J.Y.D. 5.11c ☆
Start just left of the chimney and climb a short crack through a low bulge protected by a pin. Follow holds up and left, past a second pin to a gain a short finger crack that leads to a ledge. Finish up the easy arête. 65 feet. FA: Eric Hörst, Tom Eveler & Mark Guider, May 1987.

21   New River Gunks 5.7 ☆☆☆
New River meets the Gunks! This hybrid climb is the best intermediate route at the Junkyard. Start just left of the right-hand edge of the face and move up past a tiny right-facing corner to a good horizontal with excellent placements. Traverse right then directly up the short thin crack to a ledge. Move up the right-facing corner then angle up and right, pulling a wide crack over a small roof (or the face to the left) to the top. Note: It's also possible to continue up the final corner and pull some roofs at 5.7 or 5.8. This is the finish for *Team Jesus*. 65 feet. FA: Ed McCarthy & Cal Swoager, May 1985.

22   Reaching New Heights 5.11b/c
Begin just right of *Team Jesus* and climb the bouldery face to a good ledge. Use either of the finishes to *Team Jesus*. 65 feet. FA: Dave Petri, September 1986.

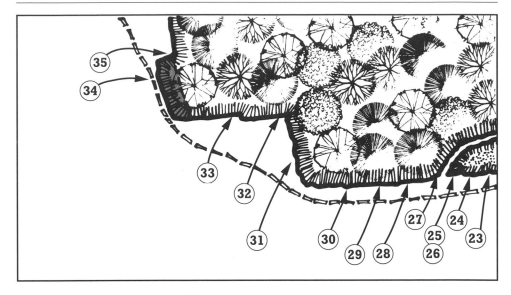

23   Team Jesus 5.10a/b ☆
Start 15 feet left of *New River Gunks* and climb the short crack to its end. A few dicey moves directly up the face lead to a good ledge, then traverse right and climb the easy, right-facing corner (same as *New River Gunks*) finishing directly over the roofs at the top. 65 feet. Note: It's also possible to climb a more direct finish up the face left of the final corner. FA: Cal Swoager & Bruce Cox, May 1985.

24   Bubba Meets Jesus 5.11a R
Begin ten feet left of *Team Jesus* and climb directly up past a pin then move up and slightly right to the top. 55 feet. FA: Dave Merrit, et al., June 1987.

25   The Distortionist 5.6
Near the left side of the slab is a short crack that leads to the low-angle arête. Follow the arête past a brief dihedral to the top. 50 feet. FA: Carl Samples & Bob Rentka, October 1986.

26   Cal n' Hobbes 5.11a
Follow *The Distortionist* to a platform over the chimney then step across and climb up to a roof, pulling it on the left side. Follow a short, offwidth dihedral then continue up the face, finishing just right of *The Contortionist*. 60 feet. FA: Fletch Taylor & Jim Porzelius, July 1989.

27   The Contortionist 5.9 ☆
Quite an awkward outing! Don't forget your big gear. On the left wall of the chimney is an offwidth crack that is followed to an easier corner and the top. 60 feet. FA: Rick Thompson & Scott Garso, June 1985.

28   Reachers of Habit 5.11a/b ☆☆ ℗
Begin just left of the chimney, directly in front of a tree. Climb up the face past a

pin aiming for a small right-facing corner and the second pin. Follow the corner past two bolts to a ledge. 50 feet. FA: Eric Hörst, Mark Guider & Tom Eveler, May 1987.

29   Mystery Dance 5.12b/c ☆☆ 🅟

Start 12 feet right of *The Entertainer* and climb a short face and fingercrack to a bolt. Traverse right a couple of moves and follow the line of bolts to the top. 65 feet. FA: Eric Hörst, October 1987.

30   The Entertainer 5.10a ☆☆☆

An entertaining variety of moves await you on the Junkyard's most popular 5.10. Follow the right-facing corner past a small roof to a good stance then climb directly up a short crack to a "Y," following the left-angling crack to a right-leaning flake. Follow the flake and face directly to the top. 70 feet. FA: Wes Love & Tom Howard, July 1984.

30a   The Entertainer Direct Finish — Realignment 5.10d ☆☆☆

This strenuous fingercrack finish makes a perfect encore. Follow the route as normal to the "Y" then follow the right-hand crack and face above to the top. 70 feet. FA: Cal Swoager & Ed McCarthy, June 1985.

31   Slip Trip 5.11c R ☆

Start 20 feet left of the arête and power directly up the poorly protected face (5.11c R) to a stance. Move up and left past a bolt in the bulges to the top. 70 feet. FA: Eric Hörst, Eddie Begoon & Bob Rentka, July 1987.

32   Mr. Ed 5.8

Follow the wide crack in the left-facing corner to the top. 65 feet. FA: Steve Erskine & T.A. Horton, 1978.

33   Rhododenema 5.10a ☆☆

A cruxy, exposed start leads to a tasty dihedral. In the center of the face is a left-facing, hanging dihedral. Begin 15 feet right of the dihedral and follow a leftward line of weakness past a pin to gain the start of it. Follow the corner until just below a small roof then move onto the left face and pull directly over the roof, finishing straight to the top. 75 feet. FA: Eric Anderson, Andrew Barry & Steve Lancaster, June 1985.

34   Stuck in Another Dimension 5.11a ☆☆☆

Intimidating, yes! Classic, absolutely! Climb the right-hand crack, finishing directly through the roof to the top. 75 feet. FA: Andrew Barry, Eric Anderson & Steve Lancaster, June 1985.

35   V-Slot 5.9 ☆
aka Ride A Rock Horse

Better climbing than it first appears. Climb the left-hand, varying-width crack until just below the roof, then escape left to the top. 55 feet. FA: Steve Erskine & Rick Skidmore, 1979.

Doug Reed on the bouldery *Andropov's Cold* in 1984.

photo: Rick Thompson

Bob Rentka on an early ascent of *Team Jesus.*

photo: Carl Samples

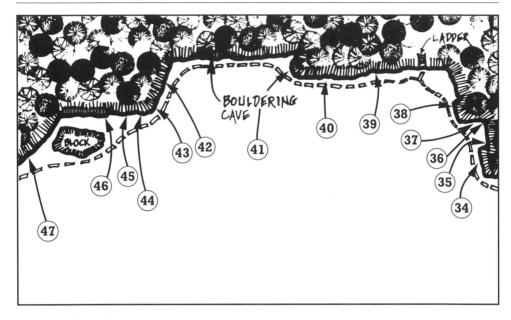

36   Who Knows? 5.7
The first known ascent party found a pin on this route. Who knows? Climb the prominent right-facing corner. 50 feet. FKA: Steve Erskine & T.A. Horton, 1979.

37   Anxiety Neurosis 5.11b R/X
Initiate climbing five feet left of *Who Knows?*, moving up and left past a short crack to a bogus bolt. Run it out, up and right to the top. 50 feet. FA: Eric Hörst & Tom Eveler, October 1987.

38   Churning in the Huecos 5.10c ☆
Start just left of a large tree and crank a gently overhanging start past a short crack, moving up and left to a pin. Continue directly up to three huecos and traverse right to a bolt, then move up and left past a ledge to the top. FA: Bill Gaurin, Steve Gaurin & Matt Watson, March 1988.

39   Walk in the Park 5.8+
Start at a bulge 45 feet left of the wooden ladders and climb past a pin through blocky rock to a pin at a ledge. Follow easy rock to the top. 55 feet. FA: Tom Eveler & Bill Gaurin, March 1988.

40   Anomalous Propagation 5.10a R
A route for meteorological misfits. The forecast for this route is mediocrity. Begin near the left edge of the grayish face and angle up and left past a pin then climb straight up the face (5.10a R) past a small roof, to a stance. Continue directly to the top. 65 feet. FA: Rick Thompson & Scott Garso, June 1985.

41   Beware of Eurodog 5.11d ☆
Start 15 feet left of *Anomalous Propagation* and climb a small corner to a low roof then exit to the right, making a difficult mantel protected by a pin. Step left and follow the face and arête to the top. 65 feet. FA: Eric & Kyle Hörst, March 1987.

The Junkyard Bouldering Cave
A short distance left of the previous route lies the popular Junkyard Bouldering Cave, well known for its roof problems. All of the bouldering takes place under a wide, low roof thus providing an ideal spot for getting horizontal without getting more than six feet off the deck. An infinite variety of problems and link-ups can be pieced together, even traverses exceeding 70 feet long are possible. Please, no fires or camping.

42   Redemption 5.11c
Sheer difficulty may be this route's only redeeming quality. Start at the roof crack near the center of the wall, pull the roof and follow a line of weakness up and right. Finish up the face just right of the wild-looking crack that leans to the right. 50 feet. FA: Cal Swoager & Ed McCarthy, May 1985.

43   Kansas Shitty 5.10c
Begin 15 feet right of *Zealous*, on the left side of the arête, and climb loose rock to a small roof. Move to the right side of the arête and up, passing a second small roof with a pin. Follow the crack to the top. 60 feet. FA: Tom Eveler & Eric Hörst, October 1987.

44   Zealous 5.10d ☆☆☆
Junkyard Top Ten! Pull the low roof crack and follow it to a horizontal. Move up and right and jam the eye catching fingercrack that splits the bulging wall, finishing directly to the top. 65 feet. FA: Cal Swoager & Bruce McClellan, September 1984.

45   Suck Face 5.11a
Begin about eight feet left of *Zealous* and climb a somewhat direct line up the face, paralleling *Zealous*. 65 feet. FA: Andrew Barry & Cal Swoager, September 1985.

46   Recreation 5.9 R
What a way to have fun. Bring plenty of skyhooks. Begin 20 feet left of *Zealous* and ramble up the face, again in a somewhat direct fashion, to the top. 60 feet. FA: Cal Swoager & Ed McCarthy, April 1985.

47   Modern Lovers 5.11c
Climb the right-leaning crack to its end then move back left following a broken crack until it dies out. Finish directly up the face above. 50 feet. FA: Andrew Barry, July 1985.

Nick Brash jammin' out a 1980 ascent of *V-Slot.*

photo: Bruce Burgin

Mike Artz immersed in the second ascent of *Zealous.*

photo: Carl Samples

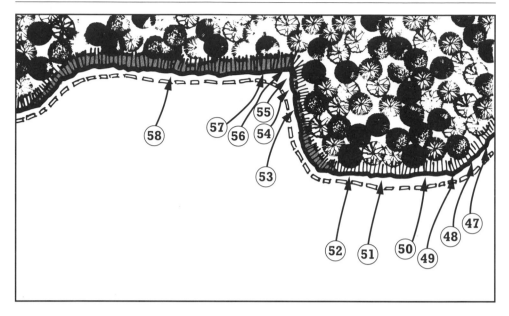

48   Five-Eight 5.11b ☆☆
Upon seeing this crack for the first time Cal Swoager declared: "Looks 5.8."!
And so it is, if only in name. Begin 25 feet left of *Modern Lovers* and follow the
thin crack that peters out about 30 feet up. Continue straight up the incipient
grooves and face past a bolt (barely visible from the ground) finishing straight
to the top. 60 feet. FA: Cal Swoager & Andrew Barry, July 1985.

49   Enemy Line 5.10c X
Not for the faint of heart. Start a couple of paces left of Five-Eight and climb the
runout face to gain a left-facing dihedral which is followed to a roof. Traverse
right under the roof to an awkward stance below a second smaller roof. Move
slightly left and over the roof, then back right (5.10c X) and battle your way up
the groove to the top. 60 feet. FA: Andrew Barry & Cal Swoager, July 1985.

50   Emotional Barbecue 5.10d ☆
This mentally grilling route is no picnic! Begin near the right end of the bulging
wall and follow the left-facing flakes to a jug-ledge. Continue up to a stance then
follow incipient cracks to a small right-facing corner and crack. Follow the crack
to another stance and traverse 20 feet right around the corner and up to the top.
70 feet. Note: The direct finish has been toproped at 5.11a by Andrew Barry. FA:
Mike Artz, Don Blume & Andrew Barry, September 1985.

51   Brown Dirt Cowboy 5.10c ☆
You'll have to be more than a gunslinger to succeed on this intricate line. Start
30 feet left of *Emotional Barbecue* and trend up and left via horizontals and
several small left-facing flakes. Continue straight onto a nubbly face then
directly up to a ledge via pockets. Ride the lichen to the top. 70 feet. FA: Mike
Artz, Don Blume & Mike Cote, September 1985.

52   Aimless Wanderers 5.10d
Start 15 feet left of the previous route and crank up and left on horizontals to a stance. Continue directly up the face to the top. 70 feet. FA: Jon Regelbrugge & Steve Bregman, October 1987.

53   Name It and Claim It 5.11a ☆
Start 15 feet right of *Childbirth* at a big bucket and climb up and right, through the roof (pin) toward the corner then up to a small ledge. Continue up the face past a second pin to the top. 75 feet. FA: Eric & Kyle Hörst, March 1987.

54   Lap Child 5.12a ☆☆
Start 10 feet right of *Childbirth* and climb the orange wall past four bolts to the top. 75 feet. Note: Bring a #1.5 and a #2 Friend for the top. FA: Dave Groth & Hassan Saab, May 1988.

55   Childbirth 5.11b ☆☆
This route delivers! Begin just right of *Squids in Bondage* and crank some hard moves over a small roof to gain a short left-facing corner. Labor up the crack and corner system to the top of the wall, then finish left out the roof crack. 75 feet. FA: Andrew Barry, July 1985.

56   Squids in Bondage 5.9- ☆
This climb isn't likely to tie you up for long. Climb the wide crack in the corner below the large roof and rappel from a station under the roof. 50 feet. FA: Rick Fairtrace & Cal Swoager, May 1985.

56a   Squids in Bondage — Childbirth Linkup 5.11b R
From the rappel slings traverse right (5.10b R) to join the final roof of *Childbirth*. FA: Andrew Barry, August 1985.

57   Faith Crack 5.10c ☆☆
Not to be missed by devoted crack climbers. Climb the fingercrack to the roof and rappel from the same slings as *Squids in Bondage*. 50 feet. FA: Cal Swoager & Rick Fairtrace, May 1985.

58   Pilots of Bekaa 5.12a/b ☆☆
The first of more than 100 5.12s established by Eric Hörst. Takeoff about 25 feet left of *Squids* and climb the short dihedral to a low roof, then traverse right and pull it to reach easier ground. Follow a corner to the second roof and pull it to the left, finishing directly up the steep face. 75 feet. FA: Eric Hörst, November 1986.

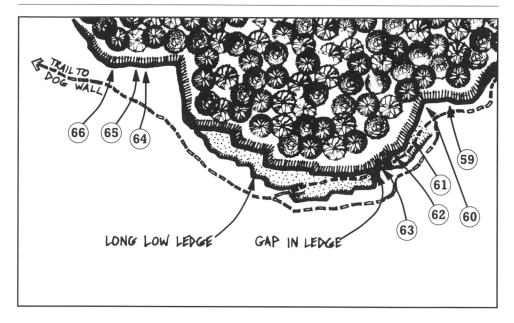

TRAIL TO DOG WALL

66 65 64

59

61

62 60

63

LONG LOW LEDGE   GAP IN LEDGE

59   Poison Ivy   5.10c R
Just beyond the flourishing poison ivy patch is a poorly protected, left-facing corner that leads to a crack. 40 feet. FA: Cal Swoager & Ed McCarthy, September 1985.

60   I Just Eight   5.8
Climb a small right-facing dihedral past a tiny overhang to the top. 35 feet. FA: Eric Hörst & Tammy Backenstose, June 1987.

61   Brother Sun   5.12 b/c ☆☆
Immediately right of *Never Alone* is a small, right-facing corner that is climbed to a low roof. Undercling the roof to the right, gaining a handcrack that leads to another corner capped by a roof. Exit the roof to the left along a thin rail (pin) and finish directly up the center of the face passing a second pin. 75 feet. FA: Eric Hörst, May 1987.

62   Never Alone   5.8
Begin about 12 feet right of *Chasing Spiders to the Right*, below a small right-facing corner. Climb the overhanging, juggy start to the corner and continue up to the large roof. Use the same finish as *Chasing Spiders to the Right*. 50 feet. FA: Cal Swoager, solo, August 1985.

63   Chasing Spiders to the Right   5.7 R ☆☆
An excellent route with some runouts. Begin just right of the void in the narrowing ledge and follow the right-facing dihedral to the large roof. Finish by traversing right below the roof. 50 feet. FA: Doug Chapman & Kevin Walsh, April 1985.

63a Chasing Spiders...Variation Finish — Chased by Spiders to the Left 5.9+ R ☆

Climb the route as normal to the roof and traverse off to the left. FA: Doug Chapman & Steve Lancaster, May 1985.

64 Deviated Septum 5.11a ☆

This swerving line is a bit contrived, however it sports some bouldery cruxes. Begin at the distinct right-arching crack and jam it to a stance below a large roof. Staying on the face below the roof, move up then right past a pin to reach the short, arching crack. Continue directly up the face (just right of the roof) to a stance below the final bulge, then pull it directly. 50 feet. FA: Rick Thompson & Scott Garso, September 1985.

64a Deviated Septum Variation — Direct Deviation 5.11a

For those wishing to avoid the first crux, start 15 feet right and uphill from *Deviated Septum* and climb the short, right-facing broken corner directly to the stance below the roof (5.9). FA: Scott Garso, September 1985.

65 Commuter Flight 5.11a ☆☆

A bit of fight time was logged on the first ascent of this improbable line. Begin by jamming the initial ten feet of *Deviated Septum* then breakout left, past a small, loose flake to a stance beside a tiny left-facing corner. Continue past the corner and conquer the bulging face to gain a sloping horizontal. Continue directly to the top (pin). 50 feet. Note: A #4 Friend will be helpful in protecting the crux. FA: John Harlin & Rick Thompson, September 1985.

66 Spoon Fed 5.9+ R ☆☆

A surprising variety of moves will reward you if you're willing to overlook the less-than-perfect protection. Start near the left edge of the face and climb directly up to some right-leaning flakes. Follow them up and right, past the crux to a right-facing flake which leads to a ledge. Make a few steps up and right, finishing up the short fingercrack. 50 feet. FA: Rick Thompson, Scott Garso & Eric Hoffman, September 1985.

First ascent of *Dingo* by Aussie Andrew Barry.

photo: Carl Samples

ANIMAL ESCARPMENTS

The Animal Escarpments are comprised of the Dog Wall and Cat Cliff, two modest, but rewarding crags that afford a ideal escape from more crowded sites like the Junkyard Wall of the Bridge Buttress. The Dog Wall's notoriety mainly stems from its medley of route names on the canine theme. *Poodle with a Mohawk* (5.1) and *Pit Bull Terror* (10b) are mere warm ups for the really twisted ones. There's little doubt they'll conjure up a few chuckles. If you're looking for sport climbs you'd best look elsewhere because the gallery here is limited to traditional routes, mostly in the 5.10 and 5.11 grades. There are however, a few meritorious moderates like *Nasty Poodle Chew* (5.6) and *Labrador Reliever* (5.8) that make these cliffs a worthy destination if you're searching for something with a little less bite.

The climbing history at these crags is limited to the '85 and '86 seasons, when they were hot with new route fever. This trend paralleled the growth years at the Junkyard Wall. But since then, these crags have slipped into obscurity. And for the many climbers seeking solitude this anonymity is a blessing in disguise.

ACCESS AND ETIQUETTE

Both outcrops are located on property currently under the private ownership of Alabama Properties, the same company which owns the Junkyard Wall and much of Bubba City. To reach the Dog Wall simply continue on the trail beyond the downstream end of the Junkyard Wall and follow it across the powerline cut and back into the woods. The Cat Cliff is found a short distance beyond the Dog Wall.

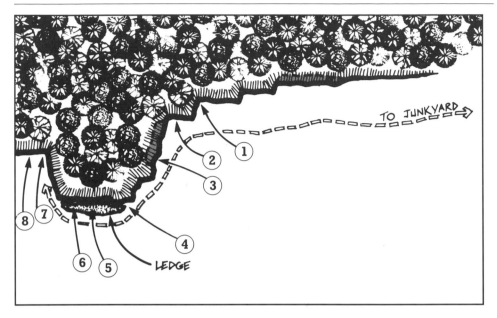

DOG WALL

Dog Wall has a rich concentration of traditional routes in the 5.10 and 5.11 grades. Here you can escape the crowds of the Junkyard and enjoy some excellent crack and face climbs.

1   Poodle with a Mohawk 5.1

One of the easiest routes in the gorge. Locate the first major right-facing dihedral and follow it to an easy leftward traverse under a roof. Finish up the short corner. 60 feet. FA: Andrew Barry, solo, May 1986.

2   Themetime 5.6 ☆

Recommended for its grade. Around the corner from *Poodle with a Mohawk* is another right-facing dihedral with a wide crack. Climb the crack until it's possible to move left into the corner. Continue up the corner to the top. 60 feet. FA: Mike Artz & Stanley Todd, May 1986.

3   Dreamtime 5.9+ ☆☆

The kind of roof cracks dreams are made of. Certainly looks harder than 5.9+! Splitting this tiered section are two separate crack systems. *Climb the left-hand crack through* three roofs to the top. 70 feet. FA: Andrew Barry & Eric Anderson, August 1985.

4   One-Eyed Viper 5.10b ☆

This kind of climbing can lead to tunnel vision. Begin at the right edge of the block that forms a ledge and climb the wide, right-facing corner until it's possible to traverse right to reach the start of a snaking crack system. Slither up it to the top. 65 feet. FA: Alex Karr & Phil Heller, November 1985.

5   Black Dog 5.8

Scramble up to the ledge near its left end and follow the obvious crack and flake system near the center of the face to the top. 60 feet. FA: Mike Artz & Andrew Barry, May 1986.

6   Born Under a Bad Smell 5.10c

Using the same start as *Black Dog*, scramble up to the ledge then jam the crack near the left end of the ledge until it dies out finishing directly up the face to the top. 60 feet. FA: Andrew Barry & Mike Artz, May 1986.

7   Nasty Poodle Chew 5.6 ☆☆

This well groomed moderate will expose you to some colorful & quality climbing. Ascends the major left-facing dihedral at the right-hand edge of the main face. 70 feet. FA: Steve Lancaster, Bill Shipman & Blaze Davies, June 1985.

8   Puppylove 5.10d ☆

A route only its master could love! Beware of the innocent look. Begin midway between *Nasty Poodle Chew* and *Pit Bull Terror* by bouldering up to the first good horizontal, then traversing left five feet. Move up and right to a solution pocket then run it out 20 feet to a tasty crack. Fire off the exciting finish. 80 feet. FA: Andrew Barry & Glenn Thomas, August 1985.

9   Pit Bull Terror 5.10b ☆☆☆

This frightfully fine climb demands a dogfight mentality. Indulge at the first crack left of *Nasty Poodle Chew* and follow it past a pin to a good ledge. Proceed up the face to a short crack and move left, following the crack under a roof that angles leftward. Conclude with a classic tree dyno to a good pine. 80 feet. Mike Artz & Ed McCarthy, July 1985.

10   Hangdog 5.11c ☆☆

Illusionistic moves that will keep you fighting to avoid being a hangdog. Just left of *Pit Bull Terror* is a crack that is jammed to a ledge. Continue up the face to a short, steep crack that ends at a big horizontal, then rail right and finish on *Pit Bull Terror*. 80 feet. FA: Cal Swoager & John Govi, July 1985.

11   Point the Bone 5.11a

Straight up! Left of *Hangdog* is a short, hanging, right-facing dihedral about 25 feet up. Climb the face leading directly up to the corner and follow it to a ledge. Finish on *Dog Day Afternoon*. 70 feet. FA: Andrew Barry & Mike Artz, May 1986.

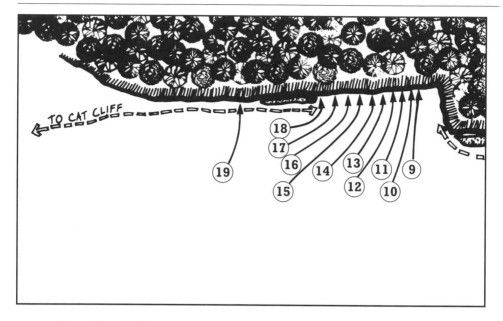

12   Dog Day Afternoon 5.11a

Not exactly a lazy dog's route. Climb the first line of weakness to the left of *Point the Bone* to the ledge, then crank a short crack and finish left and up to the top. 70 feet. FA: Carl Swoager & John Govi, July 1985.

13   Call of the Wild 5.11c

Begin immediately right of a ramp and climb up to a horizontal in a bulge protected by a pin. Move left ten feet and finish directly to the ledge and rappel. 35 feet. FA: Andrew Barry & Drew Bedford, September 1985.

14   A Dog Always Returns to Its Vomit 5.10c R

Repulsive indeed. Argh! Initiate climbing just right of *Dingo* and move up to a ledge below a bulge and a small roof. Strain up to a good horizontal and angle up and left around the roof. Finish directly to the ledge and rappel. 40 feet. FA: Cal Swoager & Andrew Barry, July 1985.

15   Dingo 5.10d ☆☆

This Australian bastard isn't domesticated in the least. Start directly below the stark fingercrack that splits the center of the wall and climb the face directly up to it. Paw your way to the ledge and rappel. 40 feet. FA: Andrew Barry & Cal Swoager, July 1985.

16   Bitch in Heat 5.11a R

This nasty mongrel sports a poorly protected crux. Begin just left of *Dingo* and pant your way up the thin seam to a horizontal break then finish directly to the top. 45 feet. FA: Andrew Barry & Drew Bedford, September 1985.

17   Doggy Style 5.11c R

Definitely bordering on obscene. No matter what style you do it in, it will be unprotected. Start at the first seam right of *Underdog* and climb directly up to a horizontal. Move left and up a flake finishing straight to the top. 50 feet. FA: Andrew Barry, September 1985.

18   Underdog 5.11a ☆

A mixed bag. About 40 feet left of *Dingo* is a conspicuously overhung, right-facing corner. Technical moves protected by a pin lead to the corner which is followed to its end. Finish directly up. 50 feet. TR FA: Carl Samples. FA: Andrew Barry, July 1985.

19   Mongrels 5.10a

Forty feet left of *Underdog* is a shallow sweeping face leading to a long roof. Climb the face until it is possible to traverse left to several small ledges directly beneath the roof. Pull the roof to more small ledges then continue directly up to the top. 60 feet. FA: Mike Artz & Andrew Barry, May 1986.

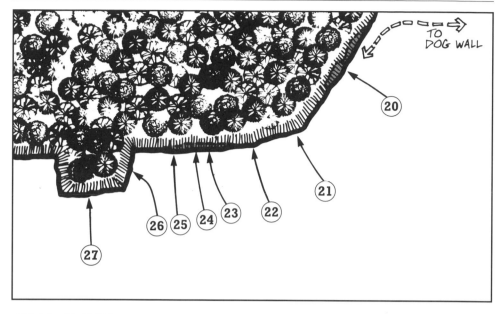

CAT CLIFF

A short walk beyond the Dog Wall lies this small crag. It features a savory little collection of trad routes that makes it well worth a visit. At the top of the charts is undoubtedly *Labrador Reliever*, which is one of the better 5.8s at the New.

20   More Bum, More Fun 5.10d ☆☆

More pumpy roof and crack climbing! Tackle the right-leaning, right-facing dihedral to a large roof and move right, turning the roof into the right-facing corner. Climb the corner to a second, larger roof, surmount it and continue to the top. 60 feet. FA: Greg Smith & Eric Anderson, June 1985.

21   Morning Glory 5.11a ☆

Left of the previous route and around the corner is a crack which is jammed to its end. Move left five feet and climb past a small roof-corner, finishing straight to the top. 60 feet. FA: Mike Artz, Andrew Barry & Greg Smith, June 1985.

22   Labrador Reliever 5.8 ☆☆☆

This climb shines as one of the New's best 5.8s. Well worth the travel. Start at a prominent left-leaning crack and follow it to a roof. Step left around the roof to gain the face above and pet the short crack to the top. 60 feet. FA: Don Blume & Mike Artz, September 1985.

23   Australian Whore 5.11a ☆

Begin 15 feet right of *Kentucky Whore* and pump your way out the groin-straining roof to gain a crack that starts just above the lip. Labor up the crack to a second roof which is pulled straight on. A brief face leads to the top. 65 feet. FA: Andrew Barry, Eric Anderson & Mike Artz, June 1985.

24   Kentucky Whore 5.11c ☆☆

This pumpy excursion will wear down you muscle-bound grunters. Begin near the center of the roof and crank the roof crack to a stance then continue up the fingercrack to a small ledge. Move up a short right-facing corner to an undercling which is followed to its end. Finish directly up the face via the path of least resistance. 65 feet. FA: Greg Smith, Mike Artz & Andrew Barry, June 1985.

25   Neuva Vida 5.11b ☆

Begin a short distance downstream from *Kentucky Whore* and jam the roof crack past the lip, continuing up the crack to the top. 60 feet. FA: Cal Swoager & John Govi, July 1985.

26   The Good Life 5.10c ☆

Follow the crack that splits this face to the top. 50 feet. FA: John Govi & Cal Swoager, July 1985.

27   Amarillo Dawn 5.11a ☆☆

Not exactly the scene from an old western, this fine line will reward you with the best bounty imaginable — superior crack climbing! Begin near the left side of the narrow face, at a right-facing corner and follow it to a ledge. Tackle the crack above, following it past an energy depleting roof to the top. 50 feet. FA: Mike Artz & Mike Cote, September 1985.

Eric Hörst on the first ascent of *Harmonic Jello.*

photo: Rick Thompson

BUBBA CITY

Bubba City is as much a phenomenon as it is a cragging destination. Appropriately, it reads "brother city," an apt exegesis of the friendships fostered among the tiny circle of climbers who shared its golden years. Bubba routes are characteristically technical face climbs, though there are some scattered dihedrals and cracks. Rock quality ranges from good to premium and some sections are arguably as impeccable as it gets. It was here that New River face climbing standards were consolidated and thus ushered the New into the national limelight for the first time.

It all began during a winter warm spell in February of '87 when Kenny Parker's curiosity lured him downstream from the Cat Cliff. Eureka! He stumbled upon this remarkable congregation of crags. A beckoning fingercrack at Bubba Buttress was the first to catch his fancy, a route he christened *Face It Bubba* (11a). It was the first of more than 200 routes to be established at Bubba City. It was equally important as the debut of the Bubba-isms, a theme entrenched in the seemingly endless number of routes with Bubba names.

In 1987 these crags yielded a cornucopia of new routes, more than 100 in all. But more notably Bubba City rapidly evolved into the testing grounds for pushing the area standards. By early summer a number of easier 5.12s were already established. Then, in August, Eric Hörst dialed the meter up a few notches with the completion of *Bubbacide* (12c). More classics like *Desperate but Not Serious* (12b), *Incredarête* (12c), and *The Innocence Mission* (12c R) soon followed. The waning days of October brought the most significant route of the season when Hörst established *Diamond Life* as New River's first 5.13! Other prolific trends also emerged that year including the establishment of the New's first 5.10 sport climb, *The Raptilian* (10d). Also of distinction was the trend for an increasing number of new routes to follow lines up blank-looking faces, and the accompanying increased use of fixed anchors. Nineteen eighty-seven was a pivotal year as Bubba City swiftly gained a national reputation as one of the finest crags in the east.

The '88 season was one of maturation for these crags, both in terms of trends and the saturation of routes. In April, Bob D'Antonio established *Boschtardized*, the New's first 5.11 sport climb. And top gun 5.12s the likes of *Bubba Black Sheep* (12b), *Mercenary Territory* (12a), *Likme'* (12a) and *Masterpiece Theater* (12d) became commonplace. A new crop of 5.13s were also added such as *A-Pocket-Leaps-Now* and *Dreams of White Hörsts*. By the end of '88 Bubba City had grown up. Nearly 200 routes had been established in a mere two seasons.

ACCESS AND ETIQUETTE

In 1978 the National Park Service established the original boundaries of the New River Gorge National River. At that time the western extent of the park bisected the North Bridge Wall, thus excluding a number of outcrops from long term protection under NPS management. Fortunately, a 1988 boundary adjustment extended the park perimeter to a point downriver, just beyond the Head Wall, forever ensuring their preservation and the publics' access to this significant climbing resource. Currently, all of Bubba City's crags remain under private ownership, but as future funding is appropriated, the NPS will acquire these properties.

Due to its sprawling nature, the crags of Bubba City are presented in two groupings, each with their own access trail(s). The upstream group includes Bimbo Buttress, Bubba Buttress, Central Bubba, Ames Wall and the Head Wall. This group is best reached from the rim-top trail which became popular in 1990. It can also be accessed via the traditional approach, which begins from the old Ames Mine Road and ascends the steep hillside directly up to the crags. The downstream group includes The Little Head Wall, Ameless Wall, Kingfish, Sandstonia and Rubble Rock. These crags are best accessed from a trailhead at the end of the Ames Mine Road. See the Bubba City Map for an overview.

To reach the parking area for the rim-top trail from Route 19, travel 1.5 miles northwest on Ames Heights Road (past Class VI Outfitters) and locate the pulloff on the left. Park as close to the road as possible to give your vehicle maximum visibility and as always, secure your valuables. Walk along the dirt road for a couple hundred yards, keeping your eyes peeled for a well-worn trail on the left. Follow it a short distance to a short downclimb (there may be a tiny ladder here) that will deposit you between Bubba Buttress and Central Bubba. The routes are described first in an upstream direction ending with Route 40 on Bimbo Buttress, which is just short of the Cat Cliff. Returning to the downclimb, they are then arranged in a downstream direction ending with route 166, which is the last route on The Head Wall.

The other two access trails begin from the old Ames Mine Road which is reached from Route 82, below the hairpin turn at the Junkyard pulloff. Be forewarned of the muffler-crunching crossings along this rugged road. A high clearance vehicle is a definite advantage. Follow the red-dog (a sort of reddish gravel) road past the abandoned Ames Mine entrance and park in a small area on the right. This five or six car spot provides parking for the upstream cliffs. The trail rises to the right about 100 feet beyond the cinder block building. A five- to ten-minute grunt up the trail will place you at *The Golden Escalator.* The arrangement of the route descriptions works equally well when using this approach trail.

To reach the downstream cliffs, continue to the end of the Ames Mine Road and park. The trail starts from the end of the road and yields a casual approach, reaching the cliff line just to the left of the upstream edge of Kingfish. The routes in this grouping are first listed in an upstream direction ending at Route 179, then returning to Kingfish, they're listed in a downstream direction.

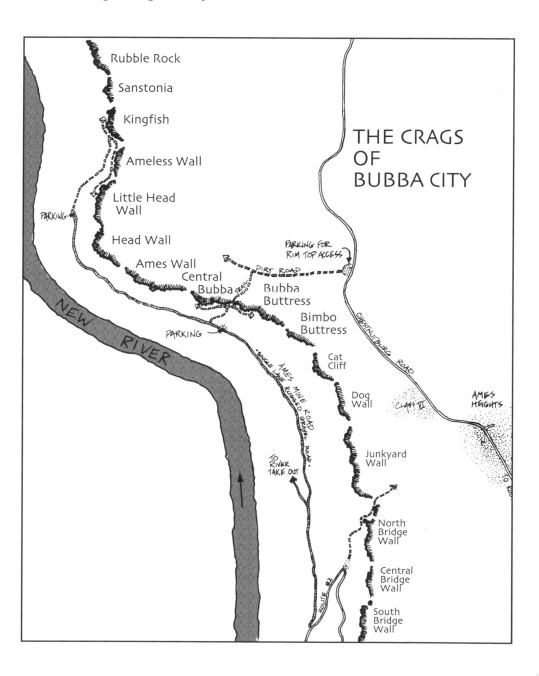

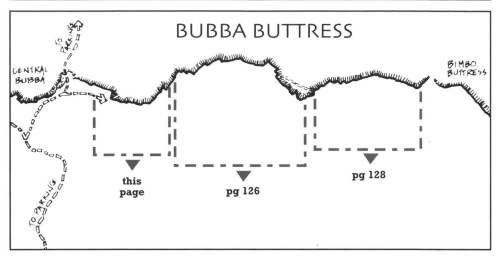

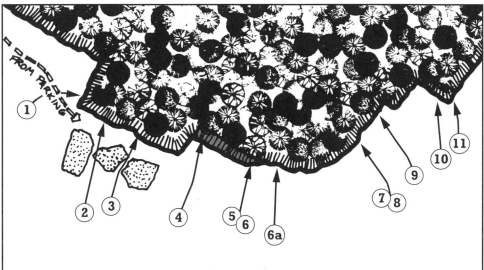

BUBBA BUTTRESS

1 Life-O-Suction 5.11a ☆
Follow the obvious arête past four bolts to the top. 65 feet. Note: Bring large TCUs. FA: Dave Moore, Randy Boush & Dwight Atkinson, March 1991.

2 Harmonic Jello 5.12b ☆☆☆ 🄿
Vibratory! Begin ten feet left of *Face It Bubba* and follow the line of bolts up the face and over a bulge. Continue up the moderate face to yet another bulge and an exciting finish and a cold-shut station. 75 feet. FA: Eric Hörst & Rick Thompson, April 1988.

3   Face It Bubba 5.11a ☆☆☆
This classic 5.11 was the first route at Bubba City. Begin at the left-leaning fingercrack and follow it past a small roof then angle up and right to a bolt. Aim directly up past a pin in a right-facing corner to the top. 75 feet. FA: Kenny Parker & Jon Regelbrugge, February 1987.

4   Basic Bubba Crack 5.9 ☆☆
Jam the crack in a right-facing dihedral past the roof and follow the wide crack to the top. 75 feet. FA: Kevin Parker & Garret Dudley, March 1987.

5   Bubbarête 5.10b ☆☆
Ten feet right of *Basic Bubba* is a fingercrack that's jammed to the right-hand end of the roof. Make a rising traverse to the right, past a flake to reach the beautiful white arête which is followed to the top. 80 feet. FA: Jon Regelbrugge & Kenny Parker, May 1987.

6   Veni, Vedi, Veci 5.12a ☆☆
In climber Pig Latin: We came, We saw, We equipped. Originally done by climbing the initial crack on *Bubbarête*, it's now most commonly climbed in combination with the *Flexible Strategies* start. If done this way the grade is 12b. Follow either start (*Bubbarête* or *Flexible Strategies*) to the *Bubbarête* traverse and continue directly up the line of fixed gear to a cold shut station. 75 feet. FA: Eric Hörst, Mike Artz, Rick Thompson & John Bercaw, April 1988.

6a   Veni, Vedi, Veci Direct Start —
Flexible Strategies 5.12b ☆☆☆ ⑫
Intended to be linked up with *Veni, Vedi, Veci*, this combination creates a stellar sport climb. Start just right of the crack and follow the line of bolts paralleling the crack to the traverse on *Bubbarête*. Finish on *Veni, Vedi, Veci*. 75 feet. FA: Eric Hörst, summer 1991.

7   Immaculate Combustion 5.10d ☆☆
A breath of fresh air, please! Start eight feet left of *Bubba Safari* and balance up and left past the first bolt, then continue up a left-rising line past a second bolt to a ledge. Climb directly up the steep white wall past a bolt, a pin, and a large hueco to the top. 80 feet. FA: Rick Thompson, Eric Hörst, Mike Artz & Bob Cenk, April 1988.

8   Fierce Face 5.11b ☆
Climb the start of *Immaculate Combustion* to the first bolt then continue straight up past a second bolt to a ledge. Finish directly to the top passing a bolt, a pin, and a bolt. 75 feet. FA: Karen & Stuart Pregnall, May 1988.

9   Bubba Safari 5.8
Follow the obvious short crack to the ledge then continue up the right-hand side of the face to the top. 65 feet. FA: Jon Eichenberger & Kenny Parker, June 1987.

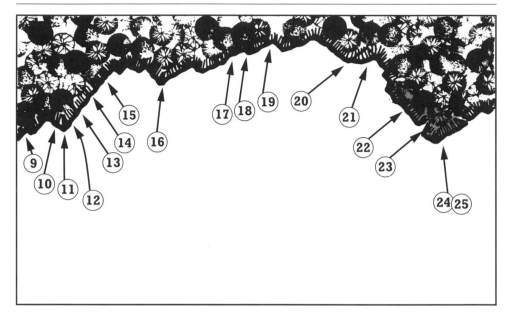

10   Dubious Young Lizards 5.11c ☆☆
Commence just left of the clean arête and follow a short lieback crack to moderate rock. Crank the left-angling short crack past a bolt to a pin, finishing up and left. 55 feet. FA: Jon Regelbrugge & Kenny Parker, June 1987.

11   Dumbolt County 5.10b ☆☆☆
Another of the early Bubba City beauties. Follow the right side the stunning the arête to the top. 55 feet. Note: There is a pin on the left side of the arête that must be clipped. 55 feet. FA: John Trautwein, Kenny Parker & Jon Eichenberger, May 1987.

12   Truth or Contra-Expenses 5.12a ☆ ⌐
Oliver North would love this route name. Begin at twin cracks, just right of *Dumbolt County* and follow five bolts to a cold shut station. 55 feet. Note: Shares cold shuts with *Reason over Might*. FA: Eric Hörst & Bob Rentka, November 1987.

13   Reason over Might 5.12a ☆ ⌐
Begin just right of the previous route and follow the line of bolts to the shared station. 55 feet. FA: Eric Hörst & Rick Thompson, September 1990.

14   The Man from Planet Zog 5.11a ☆
The Man from Planet Zog IS Stevie Dambois. Start 25 right of *Dumbolt County* and climb directly up the face past two pins to the top. 55 feet. FA: Eric Hörst & Bob Rentka, November 1987.

15   Jaded Vision 5.6
Follow the conspicuous right-facing corner system to the top. 35 feet. FA: Mark Van Cura & Carl Samples, August 1987.

16   El Routo de los Contrivadores 5.8

Start ten feet left of the large oak tree and climb a short, twin-sided flake then move up and right to a stance. Move up and left to another stance then follow the blunt prow past a small roof to the top. 40 feet. FA: Carl Samples, Mark Van Cura, Rick Thompson & Bob Rentka, August 1987.

17   Just Plain Dirty 5.4

Start 15 feet left of *Exit If You Can* and follow a crack past a ledge to the top. 60 feet. FA: Dwight Atkison & Zeph Cunningham, May 1988.

18   Exit If You Can 5.8+

Climb the short, orange, left-arching flake to a tree at the top. 35 feet. FA: Dave Moore & Dave Merrit, June 1987.

19   Fossilized Faggits 5.8

Spelled as the first ascentionists wished. Begin 20 feet right of *Exit If You Can* and follow a crack to a small overhang. Move right past a pin to the top. 50 feet. FA: Blaine Womock, Dwight Atkison & Zeph Cunningham, August 1988.

20   Cumberland Blues 5.11b ☆

Start at the orange arête and climb through bulges passing a pin to reach a right-leaning lieback flake. Follow the flake up to the roof which is pulled past a spot of loose rock to reach the top. 70 feet. FA: Kenny Parker & Jon Regelbrugge, June 1987.

21   Perpendiculus 5.10c/d ☆

Enter the world of right angles. Begin in the right-facing corner under the square, low roof and climb up, moving onto the right wall (pin) to reach the roof. Undercling right to the roof's end and follow the right-facing dihedral to the top. Belay up and right (loose rock). 50 feet. FA: Rick Thompson, Bob Rentka, Carl Samples & Mark Van Cura, August 1987.

22   A Pound of Prevention 5.8+

Start on the face below the left end of a ledge and climb directly up past a pin to reach it. Step right and follow an open-book to the top. 55 feet. FA: Mark Pell & Danny Caldwell, March 1987.

23   Thank God I'm Bubbafied! 5.8

Follow the chimney system to the top. 60 Feet. FA: Danny Caldwell, et al., October 1987.

24   Leave it to Bubba 5.9 ☆☆

Highly recommended for its grade. Begin at the left edge of the face and scramble up easy rock, then step left and follow a short crack to the roof. Hand traverse left around the corner and jam the beautiful crack to the top. 75 feet. FA: Danny Caldwell & Mark Pell, March 1987.

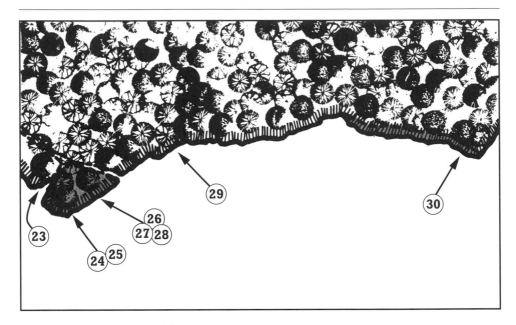

24a Leave it to Bubba Variation Finish - Fred Sandstone Flake 5.9+ ☆
Follow *Leave it to Bubba* to the roof and pull it, following a right-leaning flake to the top. 65 feet. FA: Danny Caldwell, Mark Pell & Jon Regelbrugge, March 1987.

25 Werewolf 5.10a ☆
First climbed under the midnight full moon. Start the same as *Leave it to Bubba* and climb directly up the center of the face to reach the roof. Pull the roof at a flake/crack and aim directly for the top. 65 feet. FA: Danny Caldwell & Mark Pell, March 1987.

26 Exhaust Pipe 5.8 R
Climb the center of the face for 25 feet then trend up and right to reach a right-leaning, orange corner. Climb the corner to a ledge then finish up and left to top. 65 feet. FA: Mark Pell & Jon Regelbrugge, March 1987.

27 Doo-Wah Woof 5.4 ☆
Use the same start as *Exhaust Pipe* and climb up then step right to a good ledge. Step to the right end of the ledge and follow the corner system to the top. 65 feet. FA: Jon Regelbrugge, solo, March 1987.

28 Creamy 5.8– R ☆
Climb *Doo-Wah Woof* to the right end of the ledge then follow enjoyable knobs up the right margin of the right-hand wall to the top. 65 Note: Bring a #0 slider or small Rock 'n Rollers and a TCU. FA: Rick Thompson, Bob Rentka & Eric Hörst, October 1987.

29   My Sister Makes Cluster Bombs 5.11b ☆☆

An amazing variety of moves are packed into this short, explosive route. Start a few paces right of the chimney, at a leaning block and crank directly up past a pin to a good horizontal. Jug right to a ledge and continue straight up to the roof, pulling it to gain a short left-facing flake. Power up the flake then step up and right past a short, steep face and the top. 60 feet. FA: Eric Hörst, Rick Thompson & Bob Rentka, October 1987.

30   Eating Bimbo Pie 5.7

Begin 40 feet left of the end of Bubba Buttress and follow a small open book then move up and right to a second open book. Continue up to a ledge. 50 feet. FA: Mark Van Cura & Carl Samples, August 1987.

Mike Artz on second ascent of *Taming the Shrewd.*

photo: Rick Thompson

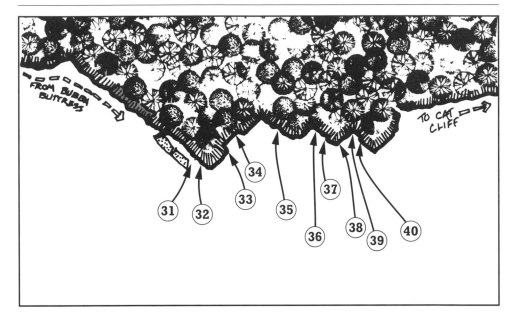

BIMBO BUTTRESS

This obscure crag is best known for its testpiece route, The Innocence Mission (12c R). In addition, a small selection of quality 10s and 11s can be found here along with a semblance of solitude.

31   Peanut Bubba and Jam 5.8 ☆
Just right of the large, leaning blocks is a finger-and-hand crack that leads to the top. 40 feet. FA: Dave Merrit & Dave Moore, May 1987.

32   The Ikon of Control 5.10c ☆
Not! Start six feet right of *Peanut Bubba and Jam* and climb directly up the center of the face past a bolt near the top, aiming for a small roof. 40 feet. FA: Rick Thompson & Bob Rentka, August 1987.

33   The Wong Woute 5.7
Start 20 feet right of the arête at a short, right-facing corner and follow the broken crack up and left to the top. 35 feet. FA: Unknown, 1987.

34   The Wang Way 5.6
Start at a left-facing corner, 15 feet right of *The Wong Woute* and follow cracks up and right to the top. 35 feet. FA: Unknown, 1987.

35   Crank to Power 5.11d ☆
Begin 15 feet left of the arête and climb directly up the overhanging, orange wall to a pin. Crank up and left to the top. 35 feet. FA: Eric Hörst, Rick Thompson, Carl Samples, Kyle Hörst & Bob Rentka, September 1987.

36   The Power Line 5.11c ☆

Follow the glaring, thin fingercrack to its end and step up and left past a pin to the top. 45 feet. FA: Eric Hörst, Rick Thompson, Bob Rentka & Mike Artz, August 1987.

37   Airwaves 5.10c ☆

Begin just right of *The Power Line*, at a left-facing dihedral which is climbed to its end at a tiny roof, then power up and right to the small roof on the arête. Staying on the left face, climb directly to the top. 45 feet. FA: Rick Thompson, Eric Hörst & Scott Garso, August 1987.

38   The Innocence Mission 5.12c R ☆☆

Considerably less innocuous than the name implies, a slip from the wrong place could land you party to a rescue. Currently unrepeated. Start at the right end of the low roof and move up, then traverse left and up to a stance (5.12a R) and clip the lone bolt. Move past the bolt angling slightly left to reach a good horizontal (5.12c R) and a crucial Friend placement. Continue up to the roof then finish up and right to the top. 50 feet. FA: Eric Hörst, Rick Thompson & Bob Rentka, October 1987.

39   It Comes In Spurts 5.7

Follow the crack system in the grungy corner to the top. 45 feet. FA: Scott Garso, August 1987.

40   Taming the Shrewd 5.10c ☆☆

Climb the small left-facing corner in the center of the face to its end. Continue directly up on widely spaced horizontals past a left-arching flake system to the top. Note: Bring TCUs. 50 feet. FA: Rick Thompson & Bob Rentka, August 1987.

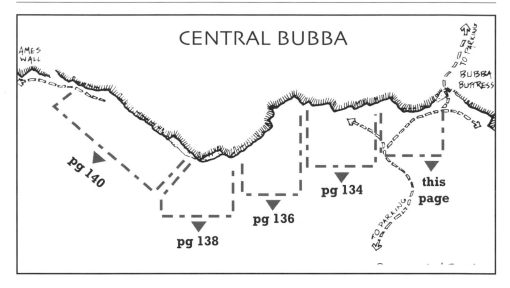

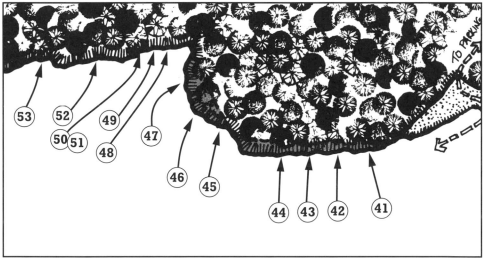

CENTRAL BUBBA

The most popular crag at Bubba City, Central Bubba offers a diverse and hearty collection of dead vertical sport routes.

41   Mr. Pudd's Wild Ride 5.12a ☆

Begin near the right edge of the face and climb a short, left-facing corner to a roof. Crank a short crack past a bolt then run it out up a thin face to a pin and easier climbing. Continue up to the ledge and belay. Walk off to the right. 45 feet. FA: Bob Rentka, Rick Thompson & Eric Hörst, October 1987.

42   Rattle and Hum 5.11b ☆ 🎧

Start ten feet left of *Mr. Pudd's Wild Ride* and rattle past a bolt and over the roof band following the line of bolts directly up a black steak to the top. 55 feet. FA: Eric Hörst & Rick Thompson, October 1988.

43   Mind's Eye 5.13a ☆☆ 🎧

Begin just left of *Rattle and Hum* and follow the line of bolts past powerful pocket moves. Continue up and right joining *Rattle and Hum* at the last bolt. 55 feet. FA: Eric Hörst, summer 1992.

44   It's Brutal Bubba 5.12c ☆☆

Though the initial section is a tad bit crumbly, the latter half features a pocketed crux on perfect rock. Start about 30 feet left of *Mr. Pudd's Wild Ride* at a left-facing tan and brown corner. Climb the corner to the roof band then traverse left and up to a bolt. Power through the overhanging, pocketed bulge and finish directly to the top. 65 feet. FA: Jeff Morris & Paul Pomeroy, March 1988.

45   The Cutting Edge 5.12a/b ☆☆☆ 🎧

Sharpen your skills for this exposed line. A must do thang! Begin ten feet right of *The Raging Tiger* and climb a short, flared dihedral to a good horizontal. Rail right and follow the line of bolts up the blunt arête to slings and a tree belay. 65 feet. FA: Eric Hörst, Rick Thompson & Stuart Pregnall, May 1988.

46   Jesus Wept 5.12d ☆☆☆ 🎧

The deceptive crux on this one can be a real tear jerker. Using the same start as *The Cutting Edge*, climb directly up the brilliantly colored face past five bolts finishing at cold shuts near the right edge of the large roof. 65 feet. FA: Eric Hörst, Rick Thompson, Mike Artz & Stuart Pregnall, May 1988.

47   The Raging Tiger 5.10d ☆☆☆☆

Feline fury. This outrageous line may well be the best 5.10 at Central Bubba. Commence eight feet right of the corner and climb past a small, left-facing flake to a good stance at a ledge. Follow a line of pockets up to a bolt, then continue up past a bulge to a cold shut station under the roof. 65 feet. FA: Kenny Parker & Steve Bregman, July 1987.

48   Bubba Bath 5.9

Five feet left of the corner, follow the lichen-covered, left-facing flake system to the top. 65 feet. Note: Wet during spring water flows. FA: Danny Caldwell & Mark Pell, March 1987.

49   The Golden Escalator 5.11a ☆☆

Step up and take this popular ride to the top. Begin five feet left of *Bubba Bath* and climb the narrow golden streak past three bolts to a cold shut station at the top. 65 feet. Note: wet during spring water flows. FA: Mike Cote & Bill Moore, July 1987.

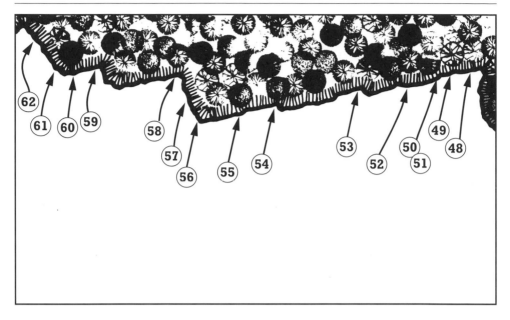

50   Brown Out 5.11d ☆ *(P)*

Using the same start as *Happy Campers*, climb directly up the face past four bolts to cold shuts. 65 feet. Note: Wet during spring water flows. FA: Eric Hörst, Rick Thompson & Scotty Greenway, September 1990.

51   Happy Campers 5.11a ☆

Start ten feet left of *The Golden Escalator* and climb increasingly difficult moves to reach the right end of a roof band. Arch up and left above the roof then finish directly up the clean streak (just left of *Brown Out*) passing a pin to the top. 65 feet. Note: Wet during spring water flows. FA: Bill Moore & Eddie Begoon, June 1987.

52   Hydroman 5.11c ☆☆ *(P)*

Hydration: a key component to athletic performance. Begin ten feet left of *Happy Campers* at an orange face under a roof and follow the line of six bolts to cold shuts. 65 feet. Note: First done as a mixed route, it was later retrobolted. FA: Rick Thompson & Eric Hörst, October 1988.

53   Bedtime for Bubba 5.9+

Follow the obvious broken left-facing corner system to the top. 65 feet. FA: Mark Pell & Danny Caldwell, March 1987.

54   Sheer Energy 5.11b ☆☆ *(P)*

Originally established as a frightful, R-rated trad line, it's now one of the more popular routes of its grade at the City. Begin in the next dihedral downstream from *Bedtime For Bubba* and climb the bolt protected right-arching corner up to a roof on the left wall. Pull it and move up and right along a ramp, then finish directly to a station at the top. 65 feet. FA: Eric & Kyle Hörst, May 1987.

55   Diamond Life 5.13a ☆☆ ℗
A brilliant stretch of power dependent techno face climbing. This renowned route glitters as New River's first 5.13. Begin a short distance left of *Sheer Energy* and follow the line of fixed gear to the top. 60 feet. FA: Eric Hörst & Rick Thompson, October 1987.

56   Bubbacide 5.12b/c ☆☆☆☆ ℗
Bubba's ultimate exterminator! One of the early trend setting 5.12s at Bubba, this line has an amazing amount of variety and is packed into 60 feet. Begin directly below the arête and climb the short dihedral past a bolt to the roof, which is pulled on the left side to gain a short crack. Move up and around to the right side of the arête and follow the bolts directly to the top. 60 feet. FA: Eric Hörst, August 1987.

56a   Bubbacide Direct Finish — Lean Productions 5.12c ☆☆ ℗
Follow *Bubbacide* until past the roof and finish directly up the left side of the arête. 60 feet. FA: Eric Hörst, spring 1991.

57   Into the Fire 5.12b ☆☆☆ ℗
During the fall of 1987 hundreds of forest fires raged across southern West Virginia. This route was put up during the peak of those infernos, as ashes fell from the sky like a snow squall. Start eight feet left of *Bubbacide* and follow the line of bolts directly up the center of the face to a sling station in the trees. 60 feet. FA: Eric Hörst & Rick Thompson, November 1987.

58   Pig Pen 5.10a
Please, no squealing as you wallow up this filthy left-facing dihedral. 60 feet. FA: Eddie Begoon, Rick Thompson, Mike Artz, Eric Hörst & Bob Rentka, August 1987.

59   Shear Strength 5.11b ☆☆☆
Stem-sational! The classic dihedral at Bubba City! Climb the flawless, left-facing orange dihedral past two pins to its top and rappel from a double bolt rap station. 55 feet. FA: Mike Artz & Eddie Begoon, May 1987.

60   Stop the Presses Rico Suavé! 5.12c ☆☆ ℗
Though a bit cramped this route climbs impeccable stretch of rock. Begin immediately left of *Shear Strength* and power up the slightly overhanging face past five bolts to cold shuts. 50 feet. FA: Eric Hörst & Mark Guider, spring 1991.

61   Bubba Lou 5.12c ☆☆
Start five feet right of *Desperate but Not Serious* at a short crack and follow it to a pin at a horizontal. Rail right to another pin at the arête then balance directly up past a bolt to a ledge. Step left and follow a pair of small, right-facing dihedrals and the face above to the top. 60 feet. Note: Bring lots of brass for the upper dihedrals. FA: John Bercaw & Craig Miller, April 1988.

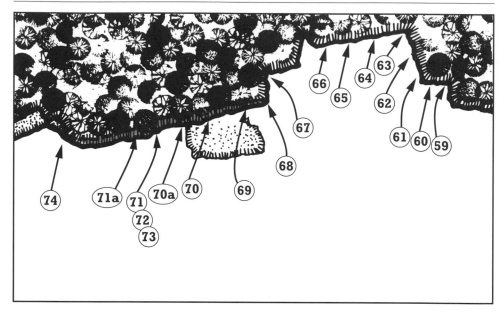

62 Desperate but Not Serious 5.12b ☆☆☆ 🐝

Like many of Bubba City's early 5.12s, this pitch was put up as a mixed route with just two pins protecting the start. The balance of the route took natural gear. The name is derived from the desperate, but not serious struggle one encountered while hanging out to make the tricky brass placements in the upper dihedrals. Start eight feet right of *Axis Bold As Bubba* and climb directly up the line of bolts to a cold shut station. 50 feet. FA: Eric Hörst & Rick Thompson, October 1987.

63 Axis Bold As Bubba 5.9+ ☆☆

This Central Bubba trade route climbs the clean, left-facing dihedral to a not-so-clean mantel finish. 50 feet. FA: Kevin Parker, Blaze Davies & Kenny Parker, March 1987.

64 Little Wing 5.10d ☆ 🐝

Start ten feet left of *Axis Bold As Bubba* and climb the face past two bolts, a pin and another bolt to a sling belay. 50 feet. FA: Eric & Lisa Hörst, June 1988.

65 The Raptilian 5.10d ☆☆ 🐝

New River's first 5.10 sport climb. Popular and enjoyable, but be prepared for a sporty fall factor. Start 20 feet left of *Axis Bold As Bubba*, at a small pedestal and follow the line of fixed gear directly to a sling station at a large pine. 50 feet. FA: Rick Thompson, Bob Rentka, Eddie Begoon, Eric Hörst & Mike Artz, October 1987.

66 Puddsucker 5.11a R

Begin five feet left of *The Raptilian* and climb straight up the faint orange streak past a mantel, then pull a small roof to the left and head up and right to the large pine, clipping the last bolt on *The Raptilian*. 50 feet. FA: Mike Artz, Eddie Begoon, Eric Hörst, Rick Thompson & Bob Rentka, October 1987.

67   Tosha Goes To The Gorge 5.4
Follow the easy right-facing corner system to the top. 45 feet. FA: Mike Artz, Amy Boyer & Rick Thompson, May 1987.

68   Whamawête 5.11d R ☆☆☆
A classic Begoonism, I swear this name came right out of the honemaster's mouth. Short for wham-a-wet-one! Climb the flawless arête passing a pin en route to the top. 60 feet. FA: Eddie Begoon, Mike Artz & Eric Hörst, October 1987.

69   Arapiles Please 5.12b/c ☆☆☆ ᕫ
You won't have to be Mr. Manners to savor this trade route. Begin 15 feet left of *Whamawete* and levitate directly up the line of fixed gear to a pair of cold shuts. 65 feet. FA: Eric Hörst & Rick Thompson, April 1988.

70   Hah! 5.11b ☆☆
The joke's on you. Left of *Arapiles Please* is a snaking seam that splits the face. Begin under the roof, to the left of and below the ledge, and climb up and right through the roofs to gain a stance at the start of the seam which leads to the top. 70 feet. FA: Jon Regelbrugge & John Trautwein, July 1987.

70a   Hah! — Direct Start 5.11b
Begin from the ledge below and right of the scam. Pull up and left (difficult pro) through the roof to reach a stance at the bottom of the scam. Finish on the normal route. FA: Jon Regelbrugge & John Trautwein, May 1987.

71   Bubba Meets She-Ra 5.10a
Start in the center of the wall and follow the small left-facing corner (bolt) up to the roof, then traverse left under it to reach the wide flake which is followed to the top. 70 feet. FA: John Trautwein & Stanley Todd, April 1987.

71a   Bubba Meets She-Ra Direct Start —
Psychotic Turnbuckles 5.10c
Commence ten feet left of the normal start and climb directly up through the roofs to join standard route. FA: Jon Regelbrugge & Kenny Parker, April 1987.

72   Look Who's Pulling 5.11b/c ☆☆ ᕫ
Using the same start as *Bubba Meets She-Ra*, climb the initial corner then move right and up, following the line of bolts out the tiered roof to a cold shut station just above the lip. 40 feet. FA: Eric Hörst, September 1992.

73   Bubba Meats Savannah 5.12a ☆ ᕫ
Once again use the same start as *Bubba Meets She-Ra* and follow the line of bolts that angle leftward out the tiered roof to a cold shut station. 40 feet. FA: Eric Hörst, September 1992.

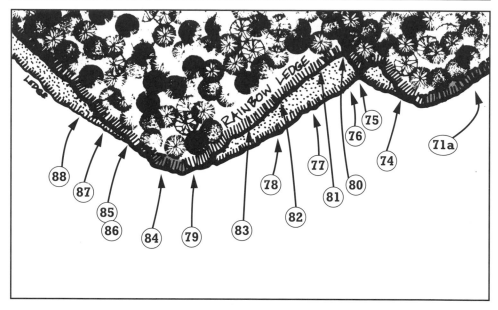

74   Bubbas on a Landscape 5.11d *b*
Begin immediately right of *Wasted Woute* and follow three bolts up the short bulging arête to a tree belay. 30 feet. Note: Stick clip the first bolt. FA: Eric Hörst & Mark Guider, spring 1990.

The following five pitches lead to Rainbow Ledge, home to a sizable lone pine. As a result of the popularity of these routes, the soil layer around the pine's roots has become increasingly compacted thereby threatening the tree's long term health. Please tread lightly when you're on the ledge and minimize your impact. Many parties rappel from the single anchor at the left end of the ledge.

75   Wasted Woute 5.7
Climb the wide crack in the left-facing corner to Rainbow Ledge and step right to another ledge. Climb a left-facing flake, then move left and follow a short crack to the top. 70 feet. FA: Jon Regelbrugge & Kenny Parker, April 1987.

76   Insistent Irony 5.10c/d ☆☆ *b*
The second 5.10 sport route established at the New. A bit bouldery for its grade, this route has recently become subject to dirt washing down it from Rainbow Ledge. Start five feet left of *Wasted Woute* and balance directly up the steep face past a bolt and two pins to the pine. 40 feet. Some subtle variations at the crux will vary the grade a bit. FA: Rick Thompson & Eric Hörst, October 1987.

77   D.S.B. (Deadly Sperm Build-up) 5.10b
Begin 12 feet left of *Wasted Woute* and follow the broken crack up to Rainbow Ledge. 40 feet. FA: Jon Regelbrugge & Jon Eichenberger, April 1987.

78   Dyno Pleas — First Pitch 5.11c R ☆
Start 15 left of *D.S.B.* and fire off a dyno and some scary moves up to a bolt. Angle up and left, then straight up to Rainbow Ledge. 40 feet. Note: Belay from the anchor at the left end of the ledge and back it up with camming units as required. FA: Eric Hörst & Rick Thompson, April 1988.

79   Mack the Knife 5.11d ☆☆
Initiate climbing ten feet left of *Dyno Pleas*, just left of the blunt arête, moving up and right through the roof past three bolts to Rainbow ledge. 40 feet. FA: Kenny Parker, March 1991.

The following four pitches lead from Rainbow Ledge to the top.

80   Bumbling Bubbas 5.10a
At the right-hand end of Rainbow Ledge is a left-facing, orange corner which leads to a short, dirty crack and the top. 40 feet. FA: Jon Reggelbrugge, Danny Caldwell & Jon Eichenberger, April 1987.

81   Absolute Reality 5.12d ☆☆☆ 🌢
No question this is the real thing. Begin eight feet left of *Bumbling Bubbas* and crank the desperate face up and left past a bolt and a pin. Power up and left over a bulge (bolt) then aim straight for the top past two more bolts to a cold shut station. 40 feet. FA: Eric Hörst & Rick Thompson, April 1988.

82   More Studly Than Puddly 5.12a ☆
Start eight feet left of *Absolute Reality* and climb directly past two bolts, then move left to a right-facing flake which leads to the top. 40 feet. FA: Rick Thompson, Stuart Pregnall & Eric Hörst, May 1988.

83   Dyno Pleas — Second Pitch 5.12b ☆☆ 🌢
Start six feet left of *More Studly Than Puddly*, near the left end of Rainbow Ledge, and climb directly up the gently overhanging, black streak protected by three bolts to cold shuts. 35 feet. FA: Eric Hörst & Rick Thompson, April 1988.

84   Bubba Has Balls 5.10a ☆
Start at the arête under the low roof and climb directly through the roof following a crack to the arête. Follow the white face on the left side of the arête to top. 70 feet. FA: John Trautwein & Stanley Todd, April 1987.

85   Eat at the Wye 5.10b ☆☆
Begin 15 feet left of *Bubba Has Balls* and climb a wide, broken crack to a face, then wander up and right on increasingly better rock past a right-arching seam to the top. 65 feet. FA: Kenny Parker & Blaze Davies, April 1987.

86   Trashed Again 5.10d ☆☆
Using the same start as *Eat at the Wye*, climb a slightly more direct line up the wall aiming for a black seam in the center of a bulge. Follow the seam to the top. 65 feet. FA: Kenny Parker & Ben Bulington, April 1987.

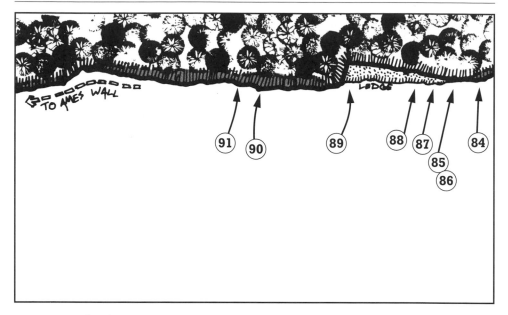

86a Trashed Again Variation Finish — Arch Bubba 5.9+ R
Climb *Trashed Again* to the bulge then traverse left and follow the left-arching corner and seam to the top. FA: Rick Fairtrace & Rick Fairtrace Jr., June 1987.

86b Trashed Again Variation Finish — Rock 'n Roll Hours 5.8
Climb *Trashed Again* to the bulge and traverse left, beyond the previous variation finish to a clean face. Finish directly up the face. Note: Best done with *Betty's Boop* start. FA: Bill Wilson & Blaze Davies, May 1987.

87 Betty's Boop 5.8
Historically listed as a separate route, it creates an independent line when combined with *Rock 'n Roll Hours.* Begin from the ledge and follow a broken crack to join *Rock 'n Roll Hours.* 60 feet. FA: Blaze Davies & Bill Wilson, May 1987.

88 White Bubbas On Dope 5.8
Begin 15 feet left of *Betty's Boop* from the ledge and climb up the lichen covered face to the top. 60 feet. FA: Wayne Sayre & Dennis Cole, May 1987.

89 Fat Chicks 5.10a R
Climb the prow just left of *White Bubbas* aiming for a small left-facing corner near the top. 60 feet. FA: Kenny Parker & John Trautwein, summer 1987.

90 Skinny Boys 5.10a ☆
Begin 15 right of *Bubba's Lament* and follow a blocky start up to a crack in an overhang then continue up to a ledge. Follow a clean streak to the top. 65 feet. FA: Norm Swan & Glenn Ritter, August 1988.

91   Bubba's Lament   5.9   ☆

Locate the crack system in the center of the face that begins as a left-facing corner and follow it through a series of roofs to the top. 65 feet. FA: Stanley Todd & John Trautwein, March 1987.

Eric Hörst at the crux of *Diamond Life* in 1987.

photo: Carl Samples

Mike Artz on an early attempt on *Bubbacide.*

photo: Rick Thompson

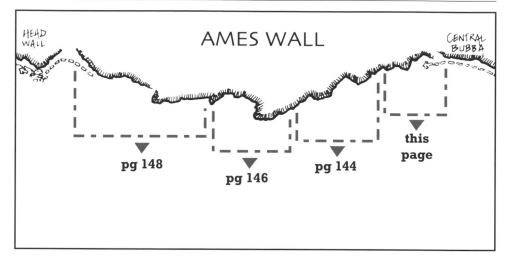

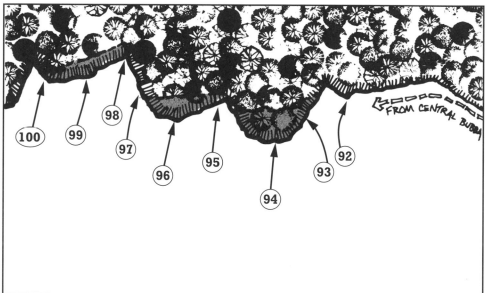

AMES WALL

A short walk from the Bubba City downclimb will get you to this excellent crag which features a plentiful supply of routes in the 5.10 to 5.13 grades.

92 Chicks in the Woods 5.11a ☆☆

Finer than it first appears, this one is definitely worthy. Follow a blunt arête up and right past a pin and a bolt, then step up to a ledge. Head straight for the top following the arête past a pin. 60 feet. FA: Stuart Pregnall, Rich Cunningham & Lisa Hörst, May 1988.

93 Galapagos 5.12a ☆☆ 🅟
Begin under the right side of the large low roof and follow the line of bolts to the top. 60 feet. FA: Kenny Parker & Eric Anderson, October 1989.

94 Darwin's Dangle 5.11d ☆☆
So this is where he hung out. P1: Begin just left of *Galapagos* and boulder up and right to the base of the roof. Power out the roof past two bolts to the lip and pull it up and left past a third bolt to a hanging belay. 45 feet. P2: Traverse up and right to a fingercrack, which is followed to a small ledge. A short face leads to the top (5.10b R). 35 feet. FA P1: Porter Jarrard & Kenny Parker, November 1988. FA P2: Steve Bregman & Kenny Parker, November 1988.

95 Tongulation 5.11d ☆☆☆
De-licked-able! Begin on the right margin of the brilliant orange and black striped wall and climb the left-facing corner to a stance. Crank past a bolt in the bulge and continue past two more bolts directly up a groove to reach a good horizontal at the roof. Move right and pull the roof past the fourth bolt, finishing up to a good pine at the top. 75 feet. FA: Bob D'Antonio, Rick Thompson, Rob Turan & Carl Samples, April 1988.

95a Tongulation Variation — Slip of the Tongue 5.11a ☆☆☆
This slight variation has become the more popular method of doing this route. Follow *Tongulation* to the third bolt, then step right, around to the far side of the arête, and directly up to the roof. Finish as normal. FA: Lynn Hill & Rick Thompson, April 1988.

96 Likmé 5.12a ☆☆☆☆ 🅟 🅡
This distant relative of the famous Eldorado route, *Lakmé*, is finger lickin' good! Start 30 feet left of *Tongulation*, near the left edge of the wall, and follow the weaving line of bolts to a station under the left edge of the roof. 55 feet. FA: Eric Hörst, Rick Thompson, Carl Samples & Bob Rentka, August 1988.

97 The American Sportsman 5.12c ☆ 🅟
Begin around the corner from *Likmé* and climb grey rock up and right past a low bolt to a stance and a hard-to-clip second bolt. Continue directly up the right margin of the face then angle up and slightly left past the third bolt finishing at a rap station. 55 feet. FA: Eric Hörst & Rick Thompson, May 1988.

98 La Bumba 5.9
Climb the left-facing, mossy corner to the roof then undercling right and follow the flake to the top. 60 feet. FA: Keith Smith & Bill Wilson, July 1987.

99 Space Truck'n Bubbas 5.11c ☆
Begin in the center of the wall, below a large roof band, and climb up and right to gain a small, right-facing corner which is followed to the roof. Pull the roof past a bolt and finish directly up. 65 feet. Note: This route was originally done to a rap station at the roof. FA to roof, 5.10c: John Trautwein & Kenny Parker, April 1987. FA of direct finish: Kenny Parker & John Trautwein, November 1989.

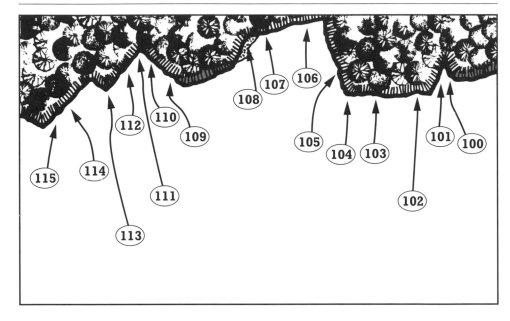

100 Lycrascopic 5.11a ☆
Begin a few feet right of *Lavender Chockstone*, below a grey arête, and climb past a critical .75 TCU placement, aiming for a bolt. Crank up the left side of the arête past a second bolt to the top. 60 feet. Note: Bring small TCUs or Friends for the top. FA: Rick Thompson, Andrew Barry & Eric Hörst, April 1988.

101 Lavender Chockstone 5.8+
Climb the v-shaped, short dihedral. 40 feet. Note: A bit dirty at the top. FA: Bruce Burgin, May 1987.

102 Boschtardized 5.11c ☆☆☆ ௺
A topflight continuously thin face climb. Start 15 feet left of *Lavender Chockstone*, on the right side of a clean face and crank past two bolts to a stance below a pin. Step right then straight up past two more bolts finishing up and left to the top. Note: No anchors. 65 feet. FA: Bob D'Antonio & Rick Thompson, April 1988.

103 Fingers in da Dyke 5.11b ☆☆ ௺
Plug it! Begin ten feet left of *Boschtardized* and follow the line of four bolts to the top. Note: The last bolt is a difficult clip. No anchors. 60 feet. FA: Gary Beil, Greg Flerx & Glen Ritter, September 1991.

104 Rock Waves 5.12b ☆☆
Lynn on-sight flashed the first ascent of this techno tweaker. Start on the left side of the arête at the *Arthur Murray Crack* and step around to the right side. Climb directly up the face past a small right-facing corner to a tiny roof, then step left to the arête. Move up to a pin, then up and right to the top. 60 feet. FA: Lynn Hill, Rick Thompson, Mike Artz & Andrew Barry, April 1988.

105 Arthur Murray Crack 5.10c/d ☆☆
The art of rock dance. Commence just left of the arête and tiptoe up the zig-zagging crack past a pin to the top. 45 feet. FA: Danny Caldwell & Mark Pell, April 1987.

106 Bubba Does Debbie 5.10a ☆
Jam the short fingercrack to the top. 30 feet. FA: Mark Pell & Danny Caldwell, April 1987.

107 Ba Boschka 5.11b ☆☆ 🄿
One of the New's early 5.11 sport climbs. Begin this popular route just right of *Tasty Flake*, at the extreme right end of a narrow ledge and boulder right then up past a bolt to a small roof. Continue directly up past three more bolts to the top. 45 feet. Note: No anchors. It's possible to avoid the crux start by mantling directly up, then traversing right along the roof band at 10d and scary! FA: Rick Thompson, Eric Hörst, Carl Samples, Jason Brooks & Bob Rentka, August 1988.

108 Tasty Flake 5.8+ ☆☆
This savory route is one of Bubba City's best moderates. Near the left edge of the amphitheater, follow the beautiful left-facing flake to the top. 45 feet. FA: Kevin Parker, Kenny Parker & Danny Caldwell, April 1987.

109 Bubba Black Sheep 5.12b ☆☆☆
Bubba said he was just helping the sheep over the fence. The first 5.12 to go up at Ames Wall. Start at a steep black face, just left of the arête, and climb directly past a pin, a bolt and a pin to the top. 50 feet. Note: Bring TCUs and Friends. FA: Eddie Begoon, January 1988.

110 Gone with the Bubba 5.7
Just right of the corner is an obvious crack which is followed to the top. 35 feet. FA: Wayne Sayre & Steve Bregman, April 1987.

111 Air Wailing 5.8+
Climb the corner without using the Gone with the Bubba crack. 35 feet. FA: Glenn Ritter, Bob Max & Barb Sheer, October 1988.

112 Bubbalicious 5.8+
Start ten feet left of *Air Wailing* and climb directly up the face to a ledge at mid-height. Follow small flakes to the top. 30 feet. Note: Bring small to medium TCUs. FA: Glenn Ritter, Barb Sheer & Bob Max, October 1988.

113 Stiff but Not Hard 5.10d ☆ 🄿
Begin on the right side of a short clean arête and follow the line of fixed gear to a tree belay at the top. 35 feet. FA: Eric Hörst, Rick Thompson & Carl Samples, July 1988.

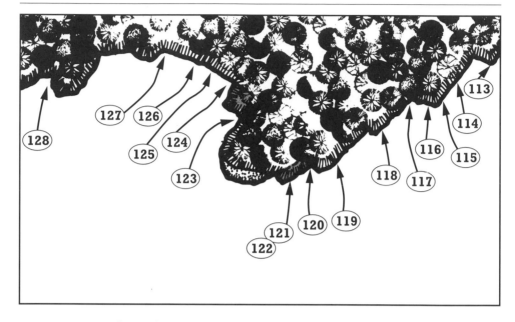

114   Parental Guidance Suggested 5.11a
Begin a short distance right of *The Attacktician* and climb the face past a bolt to the top. 50 feet. FA: Kelley Faust & Mike Kehoe, April 1989.

115   The Attacktician 5.11a ☆☆ 𝆑
A popular route of its grade. Start 15 feet right of the arête and climb the line of bolts up and left, finishing on the arête to a cold shut station. 55 feet. FA: Eric Hörst & Rick Thompson, October 1987.

116   Isotope Cemetery 5.10d/5.11a ☆
Begin by climbing the initial ten feet of *Prickley Bubba* until just above the low rotten roof, then step right and follow the face to the left of the arête to the top. 55 feet. FA: Eddie Begoon & Mike Artz, May 1987.

117   Prickley Bubba 5.6 ☆
Follow the wide crack in the open-book to the top. 50 feet. FA: Wayne Sayre & Steve Bregman, April 1987.

118   Radial Rimmed 5.10d ☆ 𝆑
Begin just right of the right-leaning offwidth and follow the line of six bolts up the face to a cold shut station. 50 feet. FA: Gary Beil & Greg Flerx, October 1991.

119   Michelin Man 5.12a ☆☆☆☆ 𝆑
One look at the route and you'll know what inspired the name. Start just left of the yawning offwidth and follow the line of bolts up the ballooning bulges, finishing directly up the pristine white face to a cold shut station. 75 feet. FA: Eric Hörst, Stuart Pregnall & Rich Cunningham, June 1988.

120 Camalot 5.10b ☆☆

One would guess New-vana could be found here. Begin on the left side of the arête, under the low, squarish roof and climb the face to reach the right end of the roof. Follow the right-leaning, left-facing dihedral until it peters out then hand traverse left and around the arête and climb the face to the top. 70 feet. FA: Danny Caldwell & Mark Pell, May 1987.

121 Scrubbing Bubbas 5.9

Start by climbing the corner which leads to the roof, then traverse leftward under it to reach the spacious ledge. Finish up the face to the top. 70 feet. FA: Mark Pell & Dan Caldwell, April 1987.

122 Suggestions 5.11b ☆

Follow *Scrubbing Bubbas* to the ledge and then move to the extreme right end of it. Step up and right then straight up past a bolt to the top. 70 feet. FA: Stuart Pregnall & Rich Cunningham, June 1988.

123 F.A.B. 5.10c ☆☆

Under the right side of the huge square roof known as the Bubba Compactor is a short overhanging face that is climbed to a small roof. Pull it to gain a gorgeous right-facing dihedral which is followed to the top. 70 feet. FA: Stanley Todd & John Trautwein, April 1987.

124 F.U.B. 5.10b/c ☆☆

Start by climbing the face under the left edge of the Bubba Compactor up to the roof. Using a crack on the left wall, climb up the burly-looking left corner of the Bubba Compactor to the top. 65 feet. FA: John Trautwein & Kenny Parker, May 1987.

125 Burning 5.12b ☆

Commence about ten feet left of *F.U.B.* by climbing directly up the face (Friend in letterbox) past a pin, then move up and right to a bolt. Continue past a second bolt to a small roof and the top. 50 feet. FA: Porter Jarrard & Eddie Begoon, October 1988.

126 Where's Bohemia? 5.12b/c ☆☆

Begin about 15 feet left of *Burning* and climb up past a low bolt and a pin to reach a good TCU placement. Continue up past two more bolts to the top. 50 feet. FA: Porter Jarrard, October 1988.

127 Bush Battle 5.5

At the left edge of the face is a vegetated crack that leads to the top. 35 feet. FA: Dave Merrit & Sandra Caldwell, May 1987.

128 Til' Tuesday 5.8

On the left side of the low blunt arête is a short, broken crack which is followed to the top. 50 feet. FA: Eric Hörst & Tammy Backenstose, June 1987.

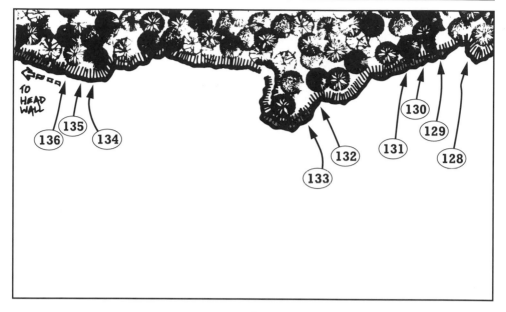

129 Pounded Puppies 5.12a ☆ ℗
Start in a short, right-facing corner on the right edge of the wall and climb up to a ledge (bolt) then continue up past a pin. Move left to a second bolt then dyno straight up aiming for a cold shut station. 40 feet. FA: Stuart Pregnall & Eric Hörst, June 1988.

130 A-Pocket-Leaps Now 5.13a ☆☆ ℗
The name says it all. Start just left of *Pounded Puppies* and power up the short, left-facing corner capped by a roof. Pull it and follow the line of bolts up the right side of the blunt arête to cold shuts shared with *Pounded Puppies*. 45 feet. Note: Stick clip first bolt. FA: Eric Hörst & Rick Thompson, July 1988.

131 Kama Futra 5.12c/d ☆☆ ℗
A bit more difficult than its Gunks counterpart. Begin ten feet left of *A-Pocket-Leaps Now* and climb a short, left-facing corner past a bolt to the roof then move left over the roof and follow the fixed gear to the top, using the same anchors as the two previous routes. 50 feet. FA: Eric Hörst, June 1988.

132 We're Having Some Fun Now 5.10b
Start on the face just left of the chimney and climb up and left to reach a right-leaning flake which is liebacked to the top. 50 feet. FA: Jon Regelbrugge, Mark Pell & Danny Caldwell, April 1987.

133 Keine Kraft 5.11d ☆☆
Rockwork orange. Begin a short distance left of the previous route and climb the face past a bolt, then move directly out tiered roofs past two more bolts to reach a lieback crack which is followed to the top. 50 feet. Note: Bring a light rack of Stoppers. FA: Scott Lazaar & Porter Jarrard, October 1988.

134   Farewell to Bubba 5.10a
Climb the short but clean, left-leaning crack to the top. 45 feet. FA: Kenny Parker & Jon Eichenberger, April 1987.

135   Pony Ride 5.3 ☆
Follow the wide crack in the center of the face to the top. 45 feet. FA: Sandra Caldwell & Dave Merrit, April 1987.

136   No Bubbas Allowed 5.9
Approximately 20 feet left of *Pony Ride* is a crack which is followed up to a ledge. Continue up the face above to the top. 55 feet. FA: John Trautwein & Doug Chapman, April 1987.

Bob D'Antonio poised on the first ascent of *Boshdardized.*

photo: Rick Thompson

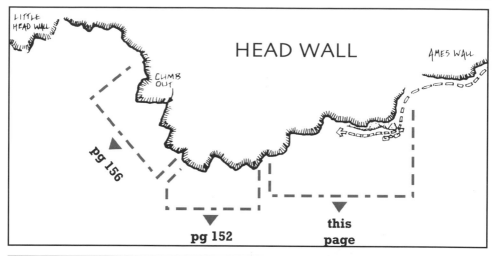

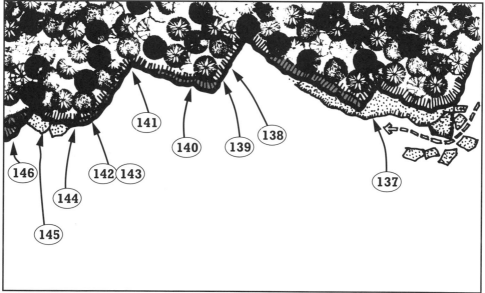

HEAD WALL

The super compact white and orange sandstone of the Head Wall is some of the finest rock to be found at Bubba City. Well worth the 15 minute walk from the Central Bubba access point, here you'll find an diverse selection of routes. From traditional gems like *Little Creatures* to power-packed sport routes like *Masterpiece Theater*.

137 Newvana 5.10d R ☆

It's unlikely you'll find it on this unnerving route. Start on the right side of the arête and boulder up past a stance, then follow the weakness up and right to a prominent horizontal at half-height. Hand traverse right and climb directly up the center of the face aiming for the middle of the roof. Step right to the top. 55 feet. Note: Bring plenty of RPs for the top. FA: Eddie Begoon, Rick Thompson & Bob Rentka, June 1987.

138   Bubba Down Under 5.12b/c ☆☆
More of that Arapiles-like rock. The original bolt placements are of questionable quality. Begin ten feet right of *Eurobubba* and do a bucket traverse left and then up to a stance. Continue up the face past two bolts aiming directly for the top. 75 feet. FA: Doug Hunter, Marc Gravatt & Dan Purcell, March 1988.

139   Eurobubba 5.10c R ☆
Begin on rotten flakes and climb past a low roof slot then step left and follow a short crack until you can hand traverse left eight feet. Crank directly up the polished face then move right to a poorly protected, left-facing flake that leads to the top. 70 feet. FA: Doug Reed & Rick Thompson, May 1987.

140   Crankenstein 5.11a ☆
Climb the beastly crack splitting the eight-foot roof and continue up the right-facing corner and face to the top. 65 feet. FA: Mike Artz & Eddie Begoon, June 1987.

141   Bubba Shitty 5.9
Follow the hand-and fist-crack in the corner to the top. 60 feet. FA: Ed McCarthy & Don Bloom, June 1987.

142   Skinhead Grin 5.11b ☆☆ 6ð
Follow *Reaches from Hell* to the second bolt, then move right on great holds through the bulge and continue directly to cold shuts at the top. 75 feet. FA: Eric Hörst & Mark Guider, summer 1991.

143   Reaches from Hell 5.11d ☆☆☆ 6ð
Be tall or be-damned! Begin 20 feet right of *Incredarête* and follow bolts up questionable rock past a small roof to gain the short, right-leaning crack. Move up and left on beautiful rock past a pin to a left-facing corner which is climbed until it's possible to make committing moves right to a short arête. Fire for the top. 75 feet. FA: Eric Hörst, Stuart Pregnall & Rick Thompson, October 1988.

144   Critical Path 5.12b ☆☆ 6ð
Begin a short distance right of *Incredarête* and follow the line of bolts up the right side of the arête to a cold shut station shared with *Incredarête*. 55 feet. FA: Eric Hörst & Mark Guider, June 1991.

145   Incredarête 5.12c ☆☆☆ 6ð
This ravishing arête is undoubtedly one of the most luring lines at the Head Wall. Originally done as a mixed route with a single bolt protecting the crux, it was later retrobolted. Begin on the left side of the smooth bulging arête and follow the line of fixed gear to the top. 50 feet. FA: Eric Hörst & Rick Thompson, September 1987.

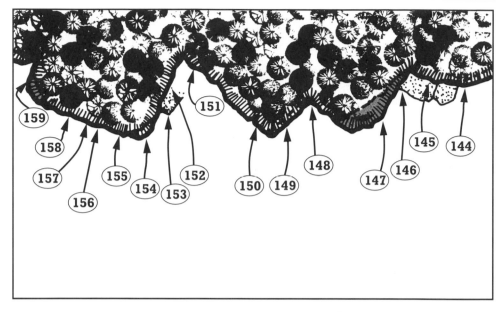

146   Masterpiece Theater 5.12d/13a ☆☆☆☆ 🅑

Magnum Opus! The best of its grade at Bubba City. Begin eight feet left of the offwidth corner, under a bulging orange roof, and follow the fixed gear to a rap station in trees. 65 feet. FA: Eric Hörst & Rick Thompson, September 1988.

147   The Great White Shark 5.12c ☆☆☆ 🅑

The Foops of Bubba City. If roofs are your bag, do it! Immediately left of the previous route is a looming roof split by a spectacular left-facing flake. Follow the line of four bolts to cold shuts just over the lip. 35 feet. FA: Eric Hörst, July 1990.

148   The Law of Diminishing Returns 5.9 ☆

The name hints at the values some associate with soloing. Follow the corner and hand crack to the top. 65 feet. FA: Doug Reed, solo, May 1987.

149   Perpetual Motion 5.11b ☆☆☆

If only this impeccable route could go on for an eternity. Beginning just left of the corner, climb up to a horizontal then hand traverse left (pin) until it's possible to climb up to a stance near half-height. Staying right of the arête, continue up the clean, bulging face past a second pin to the top. 65 feet. FA: Doug Reed, Mike Artz, Eric Hörst & Eddie Begoon, May 1987.

150   All Things Considered 5.11a ☆☆

Begin just right of the chimney and move up to a stance on a dinner plate shelf, then climb up and right over a bulge (bolt) to reach a jug on the left. Move up to a platform at half-height and finish directly up the arête. 60 feet. Note: Bring TCUs and Friends. FA: Stuart & Karen Pregnall, October 1988.

151   Nasty Body O'Dour 5.7
Follow the offensive offwidth in the corner to the top. 45 feet. FA: Mike Artz & Rick Thompson, May 1987.

152   China Crisis 5.11b ☆☆
A struggle of global proportions. Begin left of *Nasty Body O'Dour* and climb the painfully glaring, overhanging offwidth to the top (two pins in the right wall). 60 feet. FA: Eric & Kyle Hörst, June 1987.

153   Hubba Bubba 5.9+ ☆☆
This will give you something to chew on. P1: Begin from the ledge just left of *China Crisis* and climb a short wide crack to its end, then hand traverse left along the horizontal to reach a ledge at the arête and belay. 35 feet. P2: Climb directly up the left side of the arête on perfect white rock. 25 feet. FA: Eric Hörst, Rick Thompson & Stuart Pregnall, May 1987.

153a Hubba Bubba Direct Start - Skewered 5.12c/d ☆
Just left of the start of *Hubba Bubba* is a short, razor flake. Begin on the left edge of the ledge at a bolt and strain directly up the flake to meet the traverse of *Hubba Bubba* (#2.5 or #3 Friend). Finish on *Hubba Bubba* or for a more continuous sport climb link up with the upper half of *Dreams of White Hörsts*. FA: Eric Hörst & Rick Thompson, October 1988.

154   Dreams of White Hörsts 5.13a ☆☆☆ 🄿
Coined after the renowned British sea cliff climb. Begin below the beckoning white arête and ride directly up the right side past three bolts to a stance at mid-height. Continue up the enjoyable arête past a bolt and a pin to cold shuts at the top. 65 feet. FA: Eric Hörst & Rick Thompson, October 1988.

155   Burnin' Down the House 5.12a ☆
This traditional tester was Bubba City's first 5.12. Begin just left of the arête and climb the thin, overhanging corner/crack to a ledge with a pine tree. Rappel or finish on the second pitch of *Hubba Bubba*. 35 feet. FA: Eddie Begoon & Mike Artz, May 1987.

156   Take Me to the River 5.10a ☆
The second route to go up at Bubba City, it was done on the same day as *Face It Bubba*. Ten feet left of *Burnin' Down the House* is a crack in a small, left-facing corner which is followed up to the ledge. Continue directly up the face to the top. 70 feet. FA: Jon Regelbrugge & Kenny Parker, February 1987.

157   Regatta de Blank 5.12a ☆☆
Bubba City's second 5.12. Like the first, it was also put up on natural gear. Start between *Take Me To The River* and *Little Creatures* by pulling the low roof, then climbing up then slightly right to reach a horizontal. Shift left along the horizontal then climb directly up to reach a fingercrack that splits a small roof. Follow the crack and finish straight to the top. 75 feet. FA: Eric Hörst, Stuart Pregnall & Rick Thompson, May 1987.

Incredarête gets an early attempt. Doug Reed confronted by the crux.

photo: Ron Kampas

Dave Sippel on the third ascent of *Tworgasaminimum*

photo: Rick Thompson

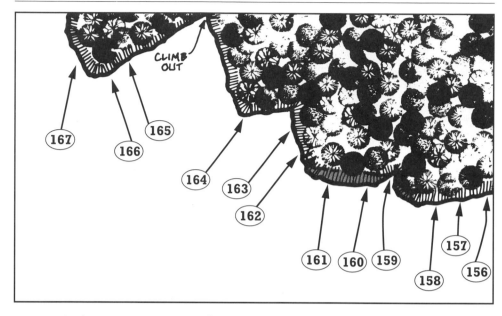

158 Little Creatures 5.10d ☆☆☆☆

A Bubba City classic. El Perfecto! Begin near the left side of the wall below a thin left-leaning crack, following broken rock up to gain the crack which is jammed to its end. Angle up and left, then back slightly right to a pair of short cracks that split a roof. Jam the cracks and follow the face to the top. 75 feet. FA: Mike Artz & Rick Thompson, May 1987.

159 Tworgasaminimum 5.10d ☆☆☆

Orgasmic position on a juicy arête. It's a two-fer! Start by climbing the first ten feet of the chimney then tiptoe along a good horizontal on the right wall to reach a bolt. Balance up and right, without chimneying off of the wall behind you, to gain a good ledge and climb directly up the blunt prow on horizontals. Balance up a short crack until it peters out and head up and right to the top. 75 feet. FA: Rick Thompson & Mike Artz, May 1987.

160 Tour de Bubba 5.11b ☆☆

Commence at the left edge of the chimney and climb up and left to a short, right-leaning flake which is followed to the first roof. Pull it and move to the left (critical TCUs) and surmount the second roof to gain a short fingercrack which leads to the top. 60 feet. FA: Mike Artz, Bob Rentka, Eddie Begoon & Rick Thompson, June 1987.

161 Head with No Hands 5.11b ☆☆

Think again. Begin at a small corner, 30 feet left of the chimney and follow it until it's possible to jog left to a second crack. Follow the crack up to the bulging roof which is conquered up and right to the top. 60 feet. FA: Doug Reed, May 1987.

162 Rites of Summer 5.12a ☆☆☆ ℗

A celebration of lock-offs awaits you on yet another Arapiles-like route. Begin at the left end of the low roof band and climb a moderate crack past a bolt then traverse right to the arête. Crank directly up (pin) then left to a "honker" flake (pin). Finish up and left past a bolt to slings at trees. 55 feet. FA: Eric Hörst, Rick Thompson & Carl Samples, August 1988.

163 Stories Without Words 5.12b ☆☆ ℗

Another Spyrogyra inspired line. Start just left of *Rites of Summer* and climb directly up past two bolts to a good stance. Move up and right past a third bolt then directly up to a fourth bolt. Traverse right along a thin horizontal and finish on the final moves of *Rites of Summer*. 50 feet. FA: Eric Hörst & Rick Thompson, October 1988.

164 Pump and Circumstance 5.12b ☆☆☆ ℗

This flamboyant arête delivers a series of pumpous cruxes. Begin at the base of the arête and climb directly up past a bolt protected start, then move up and right to a pin on the right side of the arête. Continue up the arête past three bolts to a cold shut station. 50 feet. FA: Eric Hörst, Rick Thompson & Carl Samples, August 1988.

165 Inventing Situations 5.11d ☆

Particularly deceptive. Climb the clean slab protected by a single ¼" bolt. 60 feet. FA: Doug Reed & Eric Hörst, May 1987.

166 Dementing Situations 5.10b ☆☆

From the same start as *Inventing Situations* immediately traverse left to the arête and move up past a tied-off pin (probably rusting by now) to a roof. Step left and follow the left-leaning corner for a short distance, then step back right and up to the top. 60 feet. Note: Bring TCUs. FA: Rick Thompson, Bob Rentka & Rick Fairtrace, June 1987.

167 Bubbatism by Fire 5.12a R ☆☆

Into the frying pan. Start 12 feet left of the arête at a crack and follow jugs up to the roof, then crank past the short, left-leaning corner to gain the face above. Aim straight past committing moves to the top. 60 feet. Note: Be sure you bring small to medium Friends to place after the runout. FA: Bob Rentka, Rick Thompson, Eric Hörst & Eddie Begoon, June 1987.

Eddie Begoon coming to grips with *Tour da Bubba* on the first ascent.

photo: Rick Thompson

John Bercaw finessing the delicate *Inventing Situations* on the second
ascent.

photo: Rick Thompson

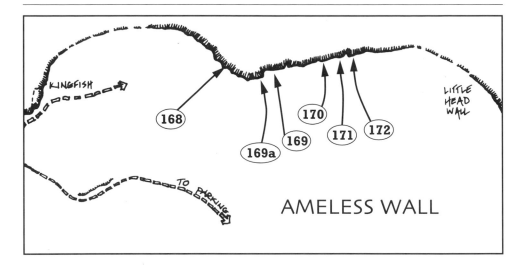

AMELESS WALL

168 Plastic Sturgeons 5.10b
Climb the face just right of the arête to a pin, then move to the arête and up to a thin horizontal. Continue up the arête a short distance then step right and follow the face to the top. 50 feet. FA: Doug Chapman & C.E. Blair, August 1987.

169 Face Lift 5.10a ☆
Begin by climbing a short, right-facing corner at the left end of the roofs to its end, then up to the end of a left-leaning corner. Move left and finish up the face passing a pin. 60 feet. FA: Doug Chapman, Darlene Allison & C.E. Blair, August 1987.

169a Face Lift — Direct Start 5.8 R/X
Climb straight up the face past the pin to the top. FA: Doug Chapman, August 1987.

170 Women Who Won't Wear Wool 5.10b
It ain't the itch. Climb the broken face and small ramps to gain a petite, right-curving corner. Continue straight up past an overlap to the top. 55 feet. FA: Doug Chapman &, Darlene Allison, May 1987.

171 Bloodtest 5.9
Climb the fingercrack which lies a short distance right of the previous route. 60 feet. FA: Doug Chapman & Darlene Allison, April 1987.

172 Men Who Love Sheep 5.10b ☆☆
Begin on the right side of the arête and follow it to the top, passing a pin en route. 60 feet. Note: It's possible to stem off the right wall to get the initial pro in. FA: Doug Chapman & Darlene Allison, July 1987.

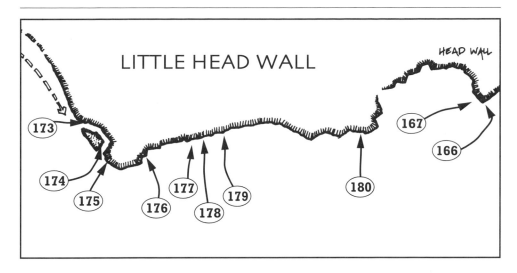

LITTLE HEAD WALL

173 Stalking the Wild Toad 5.7
Follow the dirty, left-facing ramp and corners to the top. 50 feet. FA: Gene Thompson & Doug Chapman, April 1987.

174 Helmeted Warrior of Love 5.7+
Suit up in the center of the pinnacle's face and climb up and left to reach the arête. Move a short distance up the arête then step right under a roof to a short crack which is jammed to the top. 50 feet. Note: A .5 TCU is helpful. FA: Doug Chapman & Darlene Allison, April 1987.

175 Comic Relief 5.7 ☆
Begin in a left-facing corner and follow the handcrack past some tiny roofs. Continue up, trending right at the end of a small left-facing corner. 60 feet. FA: Darlene Allison & Doug Chapman, April 1987.

176 Apostrophe 5.10a ☆
Start at the low roof and jam out the crack to gain the face, then follow broken cracks and face to the top. 65 feet. FA: Danny Caldwell & Kevin Parker, May 1987.

177 Cruise Slut 5.10a ☆☆
The start of this worthwhile route is 25 feet right of the large corner, at a small, right-facing dihedral. Climb a short distance, then traverse left to gain a seam which is followed to a clean, right-facing corner. Continue up to the second roof and traverse 25 feet right and up to the finish. 75 feet. FA: Doug Chapman & Darlene Allison, May 1987.

178   Crazy Ambulance Driver 5.10b R ☆
Commence on the left side of the arête and boulder the unprotected start to reach a pin. Continue up the face, then angle right to the arête which is followed to the top. 60 feet. FA: Doug Chapman & Darlene Allison, July 1987.

178a Crazy Ambulance Driver Variation —
Emergency Room Exit 5.10b R
Fire off the unprotected start of the previous route up to the pin, then angle up and left and climb the clean, right-facing dihedral. Move up and use the same finish as *Cruise Slut*. 70 feet. FA: Doug Chapman & Darlene Allison, July 1987.

179   The Hunger Artist 5.10b
Start on the low-angle face and cracks, slanting up and right to gain a pair of diverging cracks. Follow the left one to the top. 60 feet. FA: Doug Chapman & Darlene Allison, April 1987.

180   An Affair with the Heart 5.7 ☆
Immediately left of the arête, climb the attractive right-facing flake which curves leftward to the top. 50 feet. FA: Mike Artz & Amy Boyer, May 1987.

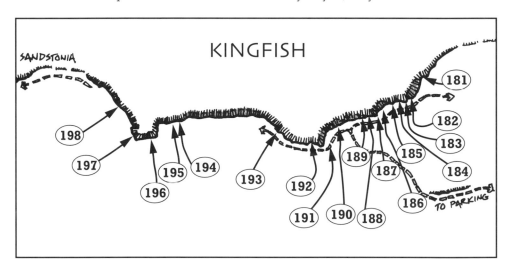

KINGFISH

181   If Frogs Had Wings 5.10a
Begin 40 feet right of *Iron Cross* and climb the left-facing corner, then traverse out the roof and pull into a short chimney that leads to the top. 25 feet. FA: Markus Jucker, Dave Moore & Pierre Lecavalier, June 1988.

182   Iron Cross 5.12a ☆☆
Begin at the left end of the large, low roof and climb a small right-facing corner to its end. Reach right and pull into a small right-facing dihedral which is followed to the top. 40 feet. FA: Eric Hörst, July 1987.

183 Silly Little Corner 5.6
Start ten feet left of *Iron Cross* and climb the right-facing, low-angle corner to the top. 40 feet. FA: Bill Burgess & Kevin Parker, April 1987.

184 The Trial 5.8 ☆
Climb the broken crack to the top. 40 feet. FA: Doug Chapman and Darlene Allison, April 1987.

185 Goodbye Mr. Lizard 5.5
Follow the large crack in the right-facing corner to the roof, then traverse left 15 feet and pull through a break in the roof to the top. 45 feet. FA: Doug Chapman & Darlene Allison, April 1987.

186 Fortitude 5.12c R
Start ten feet left of *Goodbye Mr. Lizard* and solve the desperate moves straight up to a mantel at the first horizontal, then finish directly to the top. 40 feet. FA: Eric Hörst, July 1987.

187 Solitude Standing 5.10b ☆
Begin on the right face of the prominent arête and climb directly to the top. 50 feet. FA: Eric Hörst & Tammy Backenstose, July 1987.

188 Not 'til Verdon 5.12b ☆☆
Begin at a small crack five feet left of the arête and climb directly up the overhanging face to a pin, then move right to the arête and a second pin. Finish up and slightly left. 50 feet. FA: Eric Hörst & Bob Rentka, July 1987.

189 King of Swing 5.11a ☆☆☆
One of the best routes at the downstream end of Bubba City. Climb the striking finger-and-hand crack that splits the center of the wall to a stance below the final roof band. Rappel. 55 feet. FA: Kenny Parker & Doug Chapman, March 1987.

189a King of Swing — Direct Finish 5.11b ☆
Jam the crack that splits the final roof band, aiming straight for the top. FA: Jon Regelbrugge & Kenny Parker, June 1987.

190 Bubba's Big Adventure 5.10a ☆
Locate the large, right-facing dihedral to the left of *King of Swing*. Start in a short, left-facing corner that lies just right of the main dihedral and follow it up and left to the dihedral. Continue to the corner's end and traverse left and up to the top. 50 feet. FA: Kevin Parker, Kenny Parker & Mark Pell, April 1987.

191 Bubba's Big Adventure — Direct Start 5.11b ☆
Set sail slightly left of the regular start and boulder directly up to the main dihedral. Finish as normal. FA: Kevin & Kenny Parker, April 1987.

192 Ratz Holm 5.7 ☆
Begin to the left of the arête in a small, right-facing corner and follow it up, then move left to gain a larger corner which is followed to the top. 60 feet. FA: Gene Thompson & Wayne Sayre, April 1987.

193   The Metamorphosis 5.9
Start atop a block, at a crumbly, left-facing corner, and follow it until it's possible to crank up and right to gain the start of a snaking crack. Climb the crack and face to the top. 70 feet. FA: Doug Chapman & Darlene Allison, April 1987.

194   Just Another Crack 5.9 ☆
Begin 15 feet right of the large, right-facing dihedral and follow the crack to a ledge. Rappel. 40 feet. FA: Wayne Sayre & Gene Thompson, April 1987.

195   Mid-Height Crisis 5.10a
Commence eight feet right of the corner, in the center of the face, and move directly up to a pin. Continue up, then angle left to a protruding block. Climb up to a good horizontal and traverse right to a ledge. Rappel. 50 feet. FA: Doug Chapman & Darlene Allison, May 1987.

196   Daily Waste 5.10b ☆
Pull a low overhang and angle up and left to gain a distinct crack which is followed to the top. 60 feet. FA: Jon Regelbrugge & John Trautwein, April 1987.

197   Face Value 5.11a R ☆
Begin just left of the nose and crank up and right on flakes and edges into a shallow, seamed scoop. Climb directly to the top. 60 feet. FA: Kris Kline & Eddie Begoon, May 1987.

198   C.T. Crack 5.8
Follow the overhanging handcrack to the ledge and rappel from a large tree. 35 feet. FA: Dennis Cole & Gene Thompson, April 1987.

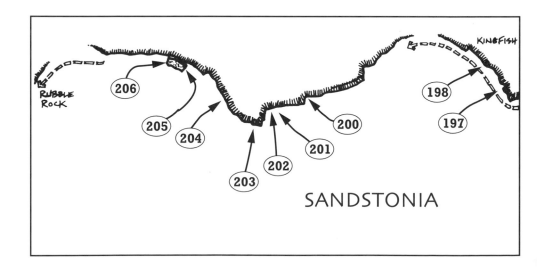

SANDSTONIA

199   Double Twouble   5.10c   ☆☆
Start at the prominent right-facing corner and follow it to a ledge, then step left and jam the fingercrack to the top. 80 feet. FA: Kenny Parker, Mark Pell & Kevin Parker, April 1987.

200   Risky Business   5.11a   ☆
Follow *Double Twouble* to the ledge and step right to a tasty looking crack which is followed to the top. 80 feet. Note: The first ascentionist placed pro at the lip of the roof from aid. It may be R-rated without it. FA: Kris Kline, May 1987.

201   Beef Boy Field Day   5.9
Start at a wide chimney in a large, right-facing dihedral and climb the crack on the right wall to its end, then traverse right to a ledge with trees. Jam the crack in the center of the face to its end, angling up and left to the top. 85 feet. FA: Jon & David Eichenburger, April 1987.

202   Mixed Emotions   5.8+
Using the same start as the previous route, follow the crack to its end and angle up and left to gain a right-facing dihedral that leads to the top. 80 feet. FA: John Trautwein & Blaze Davies, April 1987.

203   To Bubba or Not to Be   5.11a   ☆☆
Begin just left of the arête, at a small left-facing dihedral which is followed to a ledge. Step left and pull the roof via a gorgeous crack which is followed to the top. 80 feet. FA: Kenny Parker & Jon Regelbrugge, April 1987.

204   Cool Crack   5.10a
Jam the overhanging handcrack that leads to a ledge. 40 feet. FA: Kenny Parker & John Trautwein, May 1987.

205   Slip Sliding Away   5.4
Ascend the center of the low angled, upstream face of the same detached block the previous route is located on. 25 feet. FA: Kenny Parker & Bill Wilson, May 1987.

206   Lord of the Jungle   5.12a   ☆
Climb the short, overhanging finger-and-hand crack in the downstream face of the detached block. 35 feet. FA: Kenny Parker, Kevin Parker & Jon Regelbrugge, June 1987.

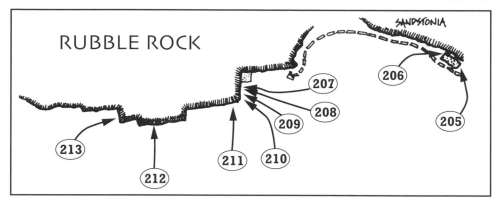

RUBBLE ROCK

207   Mercenary Territory 5.12a ☆☆☆
Start ten feet right of *Waka Jawaka* and boulder past a good letterbox to the first
bolt, then trend right to the second bolt. Move up to a small ledge on the left
(pin), then traverse left, joining *Waka Jawaka* at the ledge. Rappel. 60 feet. FA:
Kenny Parker, Kevin Parker & Kelly Faust, October 1988.

208   Waka Jawaka 5.11a ☆☆
Commence in the center of the face and climb the crack and flake system to a
ledge. Rappel. 50 feet. FA: John Trautwein & Kenny Parker, June 1987.

209   Thing Foot 5.10b ☆
Begin 20 feet right of the arête, at a small seam and climb up and left to reach
the arête. Step left to the other side and follow the easy face to the top. 65 feet.
FA: Danny Caldwell & Kevin Parker, June 1987.

210   Metabolic Optimizer 5.11d/12a ☆☆
Start immediately left of the previous route and climb the tiny, right-leaning
corner and face, crossing over *Thing Foot*. Aim for a right-angling, overhanging
crack which is pumped to the ledge. Rappel. 60 feet. FA: Steve Bregman, Kenny
Parker & Kevin Parker, April 1988.

211   Gift from the Mayor 5.10b ☆
Commence about eight feet left of the arête and solve the boulder problem start
to reach the easier face above. Finish directly to the top. 60 feet. FA: Tom Kees,
Kenny Parker & Kevin Parker, October, 1987.

212   The Hideosity 5.10a ☆
Start at the short, left-facing corner and follow it up to a roof which is pulled on
the right to reach a pair of cracks. Jam either one to the top. 60 feet. FA: John
Trautwein & Kenny Parker, June 1987.

213   Frilled Dog Winkle 5.11a ☆☆
A species of conch. Climb the eye-catching fingercrack and flake in the center
of the face. 60 feet. FA: Doug Reed & Vernon Scarborough, May 1987.

Eric Hörst doing the first ascent of *Likmé.*

photo: Carl Samples

Mike Artz on the dihedral finish of *Can I Do It 'Till I Need Glasses* in 1986.

photo: Rick Thompson

ENDLESS WALL

Sprawling for nearly four miles and boasting more than 600 routes, Endless Wall is the crown jewel of New River rock. Long sweeps of impeccable stone, a near perfect balance of traditional and sport climbing routes, and its spectacular position high above the New River make Endless Wall a remarkable crag. And when topped off with the amazing selection of high of caliber climbs, you have what many believe is one of the finest crags found anywhere. Most of the cliff averages 80 to 100 feet, but in a few sections it rises to nearly 150. Here, the longest routes in the area are found. The height of the crag also means much of the rock is exposed above the tree tops and drys quickly after storms. Another bonus is its southern orientation. Because of its sunny exposure, perfect climbing days can be enjoyed during the cool, crisp days of spring and fall. But beware of the sweltering summer months, it can feel like a blast furnace.

During the early 80's climber visits to Endless were sporadic at best. The first route to grace its miles of cliff line was established in the summer of '81 when the Fern Buttress classic *Anal Clenching Adventures* was climbed with a spot of aid at 5.9 A1. Later that year the first 5.10's were put up when Tom Howard climbed *New Fangled Dangle* (originally rated 10b) and Nick Brash led the plumline crack *Springboard* (10b). But the most notable climb of the '81 season was Howard's ascent of *The Undeserved* (10c), a line which today is recognized as one of the crags' finest. Endless Wall remained virtually dormant during the '82 and '83 seasons. Even '84 brought surprisingly little climber interest. The handful of local activists had their hands full at popular spots like Beauty Mountain and the Bridge Area Crags. The only significant routes established that year were *Bisect* (10c), *Mud and Guts* (10b)and *Triple Treat* (10a), all put up by the team of Howard and Reed, and Rich Pleiss's *Fantasy* (5.8).

Endless Wall's first real wave of interest arrived in October of '85. Bruce Burgin had scoped the access to the cliff and found a short approach from Lansing Road. On a hemlock which was ideally positioned at the rim he established a rappel, one that has since become the standard access point along Upper Central Endless. Word of this convenient approach and nearly unlimited rock spread quickly to core activists like Mike Artz, Andrew Barry and Rick Thompson. During the weeks that followed Endless experienced the most significant new route explosion in the history of the New. Eye catching cracks and flakes went down quickly. *Celibate Mallard* (10c), *The Grafenberg Crack* (5.9-), *Wire Train* (10c), *Can I Do It 'Til I Need Glasses?* (10b), *Remission* (10b), and *Leave it to Jesus* (11d) are but a few of the early gems. Within the month more than 50 routes had been done, most of them along Central Endless.

During November the momentum continue to swell. At Fern Point treasures like *Smooth Operator* (5.9+), *Mellifluus* (11a), *Autumn Fire* (10a) and *Linear Encounters* (11a) were found. And Fern Buttress became a spot for plucky opportunities as well. *Ritz Cracker* (5.9), *Berserker* (11c) and *Cresenta* (10a) are but a sampling of the early Fern findings. By the end of '85, Endless had already earned the reputation for having some of the finest rock and routes at the New. But, things were just beginning to unfold.

The hum of exploration escalated during the spring of '86. *The Prowesse* (5.9 R), *Riding the Crest of a Wave* (5.9), *Emerald Dance* (5.9) and *Surge Complex* (11a) were early additions. By fall, the collection of unclimbed cracks and dihedrals began to dwindle and activists increasingly turned their attention to the astonishing array of blank-looking faces and arêtes that remained. It quickly became apparent the quality of the faces was on par with the cracks. Mega lines like *Rock Lobster* (10c), *The Diddler* (10a), *Technarête* (10a), and *Do the Funky Evan* (10d) opened the door. By year's end more than 200 routes, nearly half the climbs at the New could be found on the Endless Wall. During the following season most local activists turned their attention to newly evolving crags like Bubba City and the Ambassador Buttress. Things quieted down at Endless Wall.

Spring of '88 brought a mild return in interest. In March, Eric Hörst established *Welcome to Conditioning* (12d/13a) the cliff's hardest route yet. Then, in May, Reed polished off *Dissonance*, a solid 13a testpiece. Standards were on the rise and by late summer activists were again frequenting the Endless. In August it was Reed's *Sacrilege* (12b), that became the crag's introductory sport climb. *Hold the Dog* (11d), *Freaky Stylee* (12a) and *Aesthetica* (11c) followed closely. The sport climbing trend quickly solidified as some of the finest faces at the New were climbed. The high quality rock at Fern Point and Central Endless were the first to feel this trend, and it wasn't long before they yielded an impressive array of routes. Sport climbs soon graced the Wall of Points, Diamond Point and Fern Buttress as well. By 1992 the supply of unclimbed rock began to dwindled and the push for new routes began to fade. More than 500 hundred routes had been established in the span of just seven years.

And although the golden days of new route exploration have long passed at Endless Wall, the lure of this wondrous cliff will never fade. For its true colors lie in the rainbow of classic climbs that abound here. It's no wonder Endless Wall is the cornerstone of New River rock.

ACCESS & ETIQUETTE

In the fall of 1988 the National Park Service acquired a 265 acre parcel from Alabama Properties which included the Fern Buttress portion of Endless Wall. The balance, which includes the three miles of outcrop that lie upstream from Fern Creek, currently remain under private ownership by the John Nuttall Estate. On this same tract are also Beauty Mountain and Keeneys Buttress. The

NPS has been negotiating to acquire this parcel for nearly a decade. But until it has completed the acquisition, climbers and all others who enjoy use of this property are reminded that their ability to recreate here is a direct result of support for recreational use by the Nuttall Estate Trustees.

Due to the sheer length of this cliff there are numerous access points that will get you to the climbs efficiently. Underscore efficiently. So before heading out there, take a few minutes to read this section carefully. Becoming familiar with the system used to orient you to the routes will be time well spent.

The most important map to become familiar with is the Endless Wall Overview Map on pages 174 and 175. It illustrates:

- An overview of the cliff
- Parking areas
- Access trails
- Buttress or section names – ie.– Dr. Ruth's Big Buttress, Fern Point, Central Endless, etc.
- The extent of area covered by each of the four Section Maps, each indicated by the brackets. These maps are found on the four pages that follow the Overview Map.

The section maps provide an enlarged view of cliff segments, each approximately one mile in length. In addition to showing trails and indicators for the detail maps, they also include "route ordering direction arrows". The concept of these arrows is crucial to understanding the sequence on which the routes are described. The routes are not arranged in sequence from one end of the cliff to the other as they are in other chapters, but instead are organized based on how one would optimally get to the routes via the established trails and access points. For example, the Honeymooners Ladders provide access to routes that are both upstream and downstream from them and therefore, the descriptions have been arranged with that in mind.

When climbing here please remember to:

- Secure your valuables and car before heading to the crag.
- Always change your clothes out of view.
- Follow Leave No Trace principals for minimal impact climbing as detailed in the Introduction Chapter.
- Pick up all litter.
- Camping is not permitted on Nuttall Estate Property.

Following are some general parking and access guidelines to assist you in getting to your destination. The Overview Map will be useful for reference.

Upper Endless Parking – provides access to routes from the upstream end of the cliff to the upstream end of the Cirque, approximately a half mile of cliff. Parking is currently limited to about a half dozen cars and the access trail is on Nuttall

Estate property. The same parking and access trail also serves Beauty Mountain, which often creates a parking shortage. The parking site is identified on the Endless Wall Overview Map. Park only on the small triangle of grass directly in front of the Nuttall Estate Cemetery sign. There are three or four spots here. Pull straight in and please, no parallel parking and leave room for other cars. If these spots are filled, an alternative is to park along the side of the road to the cemetery which angles off to the right (see map). Pull well off to the side and do not park at, or walk through the cemetery. Do not park in front of any houses or along the narrow gravel road. If these parking sites are taken, please climb elsewhere.

A short stroll along the trail will lead you past two residences and some old cars. Please be courteous to these neighbors and respect their barking dogs, which will hopefully be chained. Remember, good relations with these folks are critical to future access. Just beyond the houses the trail will begin a gentle descent and as it bears to the left the Intestinal Wall will appear on your left. The short wall which develops on the right side of the trail is the start of Upper Endless.

Central Endless Pull Off – provides access to routes from the Cirque to midway along the Wall of Points, a total of nearly two miles of cliff, via the Central Endless trail. With the exception of a few head-in spaces, parking here is currently limited to a roadside parallel parking which can handle a maximum of about 30 vehicles, provided they're parked close together. A word of warning: this pull off is located on the crest of Lansing Road. When confronted with head-on traffic, cars are often forced off the narrow paving and onto the gravel berm. At times they come dangerously close to climbers and their cars. Make sure you park your vehicle off the road as far as possible and be cautious when getting in or out of your car. State law requires your vehicle to be parked a minimum of four feet off the paving. Violators are subject to ticketing and towing.

Fern Creek Parking Lot – provides access to routes from midway along the Wall of Points to midway along Fern Buttress, nearly one mile of cliff line, via the Fern Creek Trail. This gravel parking lot, which is located on NPS property, has a capacity of about 30 to 35 cars. Limited overflow parking is accommodated at the pull offs near the bridge on Lansing Road. However, as mentioned above, make certain your car is at least four feet off the paving and be very careful getting in or out of your vehicle since cars tend to throttle along at warp speeds through this section. An NPS Climber Information Kiosk is located adjacent to the lot, please check it for the latest info. Two bits of crucial beta when parking here: first, no overnight camping is permitted; second, this lot has been the scene of more car break-ins than any other at the New. Most of these break-ins occur after dusk, so secure your valuables before heading to the crag and don't leave your car parked here overnight.

Fern Buttress Pull Off – provides access to routes from the downstream end of the cliff to midway along Fern Buttress, about three quarters of a mile of cliff, via the Fern Buttress Trail. This pull off can handle less than a dozen cars so please park in such a way that other people can fit their cars as well.

Safety, a major consideration – of all the crags at the New, Endless Wall presents the most challenging scenario for mobilizing a timely rescue. The distance from the road combined with the rim top access (which means victims have to be hauled up the cliff in a stokes liter) creates an at-best difficult situation for EMTs to respond quickly in. Please, CLIMB SMART and CLIMB SAFE at all times. You may want to think twice before jumping on those R or X rated routes. You may also want to get in the habit of tying a knot in the loose end of the rope when sport climbing. A recent rash of "lowering" accidents (ie. – belayers allowing the loose end of the rope to pass through the belay device when lowering the leader and thereby dropping them to the ground) has resulted in numerous broken ankles and worse. Beware of loose holds, a number of accidents have resulted from a hold unexpectedly snapping off. In addition, it's a good idea to carry first aid kit and flashlight.

Fern Point Slab. Rick Thompson on *Mellifluus*.

photo: Carl Samples.

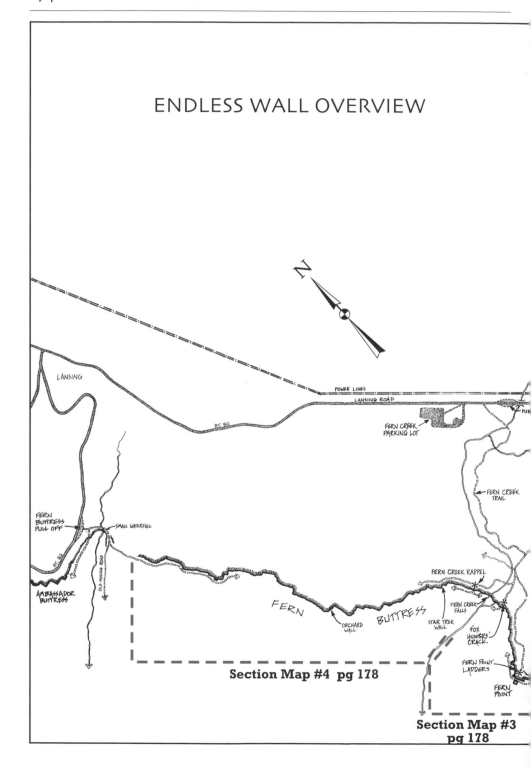

ENDLESS WALL OVERVIEW

N

LANSING

POWER LINES

LANSING ROAD

RT. 82

FERN CREEK
PARKING LOT

FERN CREEK
TRAIL

FERN
BUTTRESS
PULL OFF

SMALL WATERFALL

RT. 82

OLD MINING ROAD

AMBASSADOR
BUTTRESS

FERN

BUTTRESS

ORCHARD
WALL

FERN CREEK RAPPEL

FERN CREEK
FALLS

STAR TREK
WALL

FOX
HUNTERS'
CRACK

FERN POINT
LADDERS

FERN
POINT

Section Map #4 pg 178

**Section Map #3
pg 178**

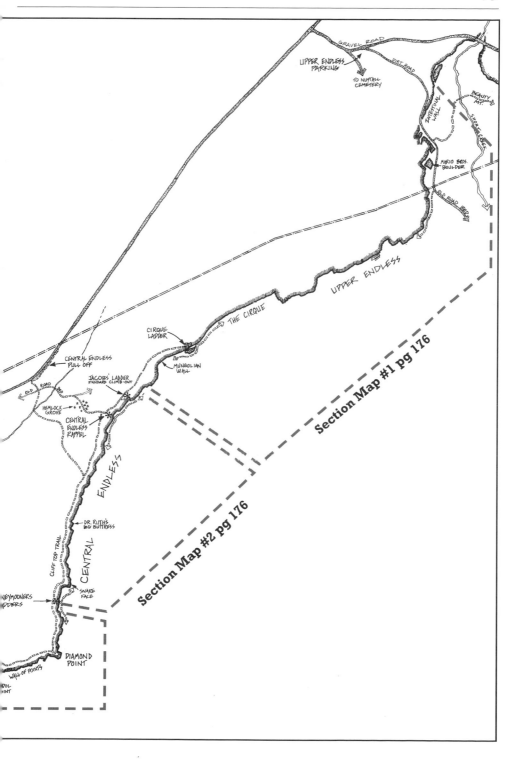

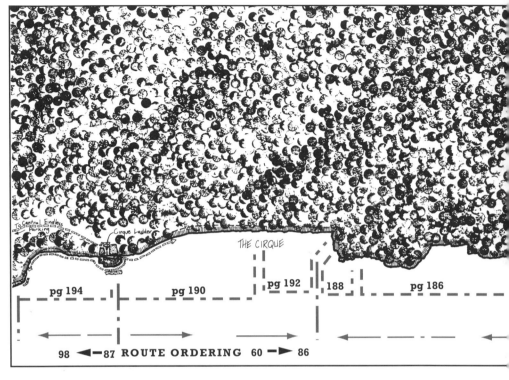

To Central Endless Parking

Cirque Ladder

THE CIRQUE

pg 194 pg 190 pg 192 188 pg 186

98 ◄─87 **ROUTE ORDERING** 60 ─► 86

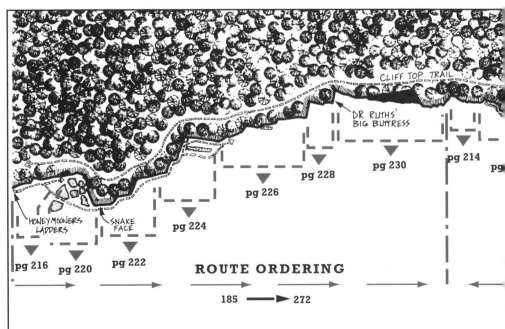

CLIFF TOP TRAIL

DR. RUTHS' BIG BUTTRESS

pg 214

pg 230

pg 228

pg 226

pg 224

HONEYMOONERS LADDERS

SNAKE FACE

pg 216 pg 220 pg 222

ROUTE ORDERING

185 ──► 272

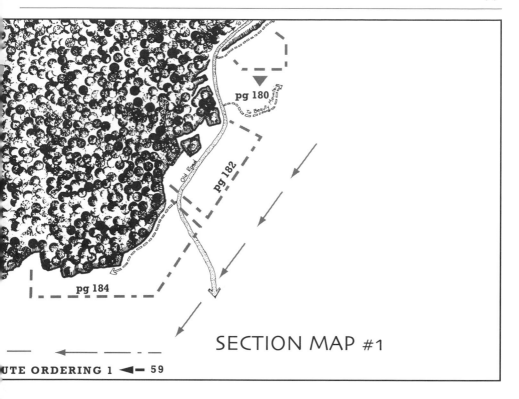

pg 180

To Beauty Mount

Old Road

pg 182

pg 184

SECTION MAP #1

UTE ORDERING 1 ◄— 59

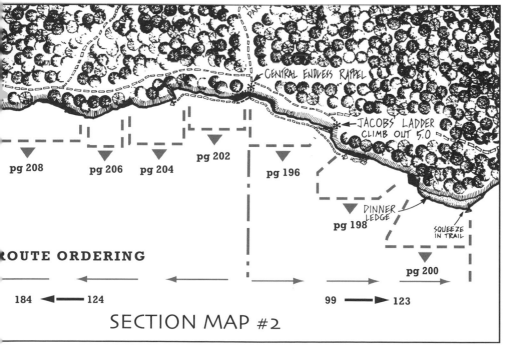

PAR

CENTRAL ENDLESS RAPPEL

JACOBS LADDER
CLIMB OUT 5.0

pg 208   pg 206   pg 204   pg 202   pg 196

DINNER
LEDGE

pg 198

SQUEEZE
IN TRAIL

ROUTE ORDERING

184 ◄— 124   99 —► 123

pg 200

SECTION MAP #2

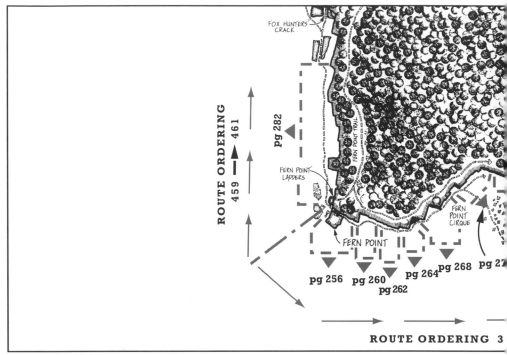

FOX HUNTERS CRACK

ROUTE ORDERING

459 ➤ 461

pg 282

FERN POINT LADDERS

FERN POINT TRAIL

FERN POINT

FERN POINT CIRQUE

pg 256   **pg 260**   **pg 264** **pg 268**   **pg 27**

pg 262

ROUTE ORDERING 3

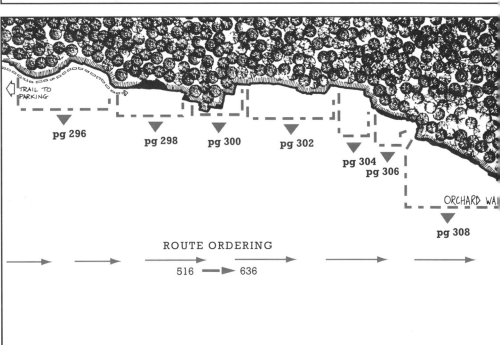

TRAIL TO PARKING

pg 296   **pg 298**   **pg 300**   **pg 302**

pg 304

pg 306

ORCHARD WA

pg 308

ROUTE ORDERING

516 ➤ 636

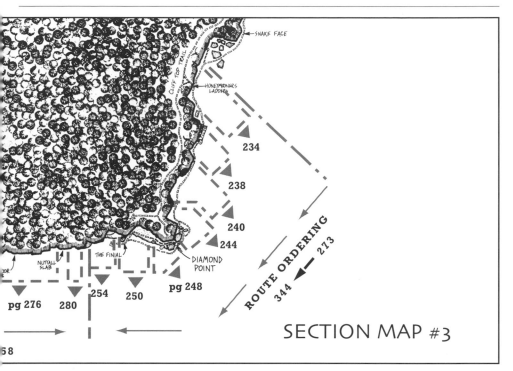

SNAKE FACE

CLIFF TOP TRAIL

HONEYMOONERS
LADDERS

234

238

240

244

ROUTE ORDERING

344 ◄— 273

THE FINIAL

NUTTALL
SLAB

DIAMOND
POINT

pg 248

254

250

pg 276

280

SECTION MAP #3

58

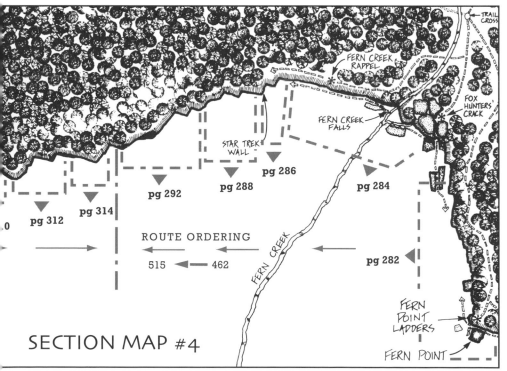

TRAIL
CROSS

FERN CREEK
RAPPEL

FOX
HUNTERS'
CRACK

FERN CREEK
FALLS

STAR TREK
WALL

pg 286

pg 292

pg 288

pg 284

pg 314

pg 312

ROUTE ORDERING

FERN CREEK

515 ◄— 462

pg 282

0

FERN
POINT
LADDERS

FERN POINT

SECTION MAP #4

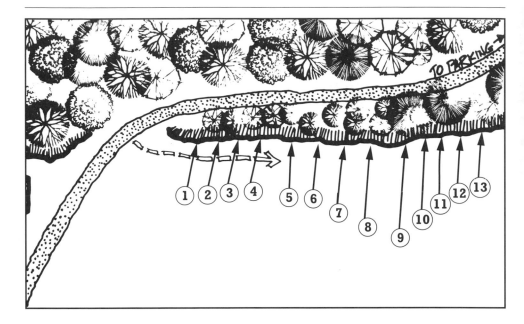

UPPER ENDLESS

THE INTESTINAL WALL

Welcome to the starless zone. Aptly named, The Intestinal Wall is a local anomaly, home to the shortest, dumpiest routes to be found along the New River's endless miles of cliff line. The following descriptions list the fixed gear as originally equipped. However, over the past few years many of the hangers have been stolen, rendering the routes unclimbable. They are described here mainly for historical reference and are ordered from left to right.

1   Batman 5.9
Near the left edge of the wall is a line protected by three bolts with a single cold shut. 30 feet. FA: Steve Zich & Deb Orth, 1989.

2   Robin 5.8
Holy choss, Batman! Just right of the previous route is a face protected by two bolts with a single anchor. 30 feet. FA: Steve Zich & Deb Orth, 1989.

3   Aquaman 5.9+
The next line is just left of a large poplar and has three bolts and a double bolt anchor. 30 feet. FA: Steve Zich & Charlie Rafferty, 1989.

4   Unnamed 5.9
Just right of the poplar tree is a route protected by three bolts with a single cold-shut anchor. 30 feet. FA: Unknown.

5   Unnamed 5.10 ᵇ
A few feet to the right is a route with two bolts and a single cold shut. 30 feet. FA: Unknown.

6   Mo 5.10 ᵇ
The next one is equipped with a bolt, a pin, a bolt, and a single cold shut. 30 feet. FA: Rob Turan, 1989.

7   Turan-ocaurus Wrecks 5.10 ᵇ
Five feet right of the previous route and just right of the dead stump is a line with three bolts. 30 feet. FA: Rob Turan, 1989.

8   Dispose of Properly 5.11b ᵇ
Looks like someone missed the message. The next route has three angle iron hangers and an anchor. 30 feet. FA: Kevin Lawlor, 1989.

9   Tools For Mutant Women 5.10c ᵇ
One of the early routes on this crag. Five feet right of the previous route is a line with two angle iron hangers and an anchor. 30 feet. FA: Sandi Carrick, 1989.

10   Project—Abandoned
Three bolts to a single bolt anchor. 25 feet.

11   Dueling Banjos 5.12a ᵇ
A three-bolt line that angles up and right to an anchor. 25 feet. FA: Metalhead & Drack, 1989.

12   Wonderwoman 5.11d ᵇ
Just left of the gnarly crack is a three-bolt line with a single-bolt anchor. 25 feet. FA: Steve Zich & Sandy Cox, 1989

13   Plastic Man 5.11a ᵇ
Right of the crack is a two-bolt route with an anchor. 20 feet. FA: Steve Zich & Alex Karr, 1989.

UPPER ENDLESS

14   In the Palm of His Hand 5.7+ ☆
Just plain fun. Begin on the right side of the blunt arête, just right of the large tree, and follow jugs directly to the top. 35 feet. FA: Van E. Eitel II, Alan Fuhr & Dan Russel, September 1990.

15   European Vacation 5.12b ☆ ⬡
Short and steep. Begin at the right edge of the overhanging face and follow the bolts to an anchor just over the lip. 35 feet. FA: Doug Cosby, October 1988.

16   Super Mario 5.13a ☆☆ ⬡
No kid stuff here. Begin just left of *Euro Vac* and thrust up the overhanging pocketed face to anchors at the top. 40 feet. FA: Scott Franklin, 1989.

17   The Rock 5.7 ☆
Begin just right of the arête and follow the left-facing flake to the top. 40 feet. FA: Kevin Rock, 1990.

18   Upper Crust 5.5 ☆
Climb the left side of the arête. 40 feet. FA: Kevin Rock, 1990.

19   Guides Route Right 5.5 ☆☆
With so few routes of this grade available, this one is sure to be popular. Start just right of the blunt arête and follow the featured face to the top. 40 feet. FA: Kevin Rock, 1990.

20   Guides Route Left 5.5 ☆☆

A fine companion to the previous line. Commence on the left side of the blunt arête and climb the left-facing flake and face. 40 feet. FA: Kevin Rock, 1990.

21   Guides Route Far Left 5.4 ☆

Just left of the previous route, climb the right-facing corner. 40 feet, FA: Kevin Rock, 1990.

22   The Pinkney Route 5.10d ☆ 🅟

Follow four bolts to an anchor. 40 feet. FA: John Pinkney, October 1989.

23   Sixteenth Rung 5.10c ☆ 🅟

The central line of four bolts with an anchor. 40 feet. FA: Steve Zich & Sandy Cox, September 1989.

24   Rival 5.10c/d 🅟

Begin just right of the chimney and boulder up 15 feet to the first bolt, then follow two more to an anchor. 40 feet. Note: Can be a bit dirty. FA: Steve Zich & Deb Orth, October 1989.

25   Project—In Progress

The bolt line just right of *Tubin' Dudes.* 35 feet.

26   Tubin' Dudes 5.13b ☆ 🅟

Another of Harrison Dekker's test-piece routes. Follow the line of fixed gear up the center of the clean white face. 40 feet. FA: Harrison Dekker, 1990.

27   Unnamed 5.11b ☆ 🅟

Begin from the ledge, just left of the arête and stick clip the first bolt, then follow three more to a chain anchor. 50 feet. FA: Unknown, 1991.

28   The Bunny Hop of Death 5.11b R ☆

Begin from the ledge, six feet right of the arête and boulder the unprotected start over the low roof, then follow the left-facing flakes to the top. 60 feet. FA: Carl Samples & Bob Rentka, October 1989.

29   Unnamed 5.10c 🅟

Begin at a blunt arête, just left of the chimney and follow four bolts up to a two-bolt anchor. 50 feet. FA: Doug Cosby, 1989.

30   Jack the Tripper 5.12a ☆

As of press time the hangers were missing. Begin at a blunt arête and climb past two bolts moving up and right and finishing via a left-facing flake. 50 feet. FA: Eddie Begoon & Bob Rentka, August 1989.

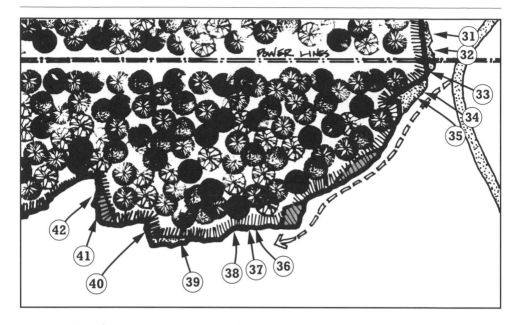

31   I Don't Want Her 5.11a ☆
Beginning on the right side of the face climb directly up past a small, left-facing corner to the top. 65 feet. FA: Eddie Begoon & Mike Artz, June 1989.

32   She's Too Fat For Me 5.10d ☆
Begin from the ledge left of the previous route and move up the face passing a left-facing dihedral enroute to the top. 65 feet. FA: Mike Artz & Eddie Begoon, June 1989.

33   White Powderête 11a ☆☆
Quite a nice line! Begin directly below the beckoning arête and boulder up to the ledge. Make a scarey clip of the lone bolt and continue directly up the arête and top out. 80 feet. FA: Mike Artz & Eddie Begoon, June 1989.

34   Project—Abandoned
Begin from the ledge, eight feet right of the chimney and follow the line of bolts up the brilliant orange face to an anchor under the roof. 45 feet.

35   Ramrod 5.12c ☆☆ 🄿
Send it home! Start from the same ledge as the previous route, 12 feet left of the chimney and follow five bolts to a cold-shut station below the roof. 45 feet. FA: Doug Reed & Bob Rentka, May 1990.

36   Unnamed 5.9 ☆
Climb the obvious right handcrack to the ledge and rappel from the fixed nut. 35 feet. FA: Paul Sullivan & Mike Roth, July 1989.

37 Unnamed 5.8 ☆
Climb the left-facing flake in the center of the face to the ledge and rappel. 35 feet. FA: Mike Roth & Paul Sullivan, July 1989.

38 Long John Jam 5.9+
The first route to be established on Upper Endless Wall. Follow the left-hand, thin crack up to the ledge at the roof and rappel. 30 feet. FA: Phil Wilt & Carl Samples, May 1982.

39 Tip Terror 5.12c ☆☆
What will your fingers feel like? Start just left of the blunt arête and climb the squeaky clean face past two perfect letter box slots and two bolts directly to the ledge. 35 feet. FA: Eddie Begoon & Mike Artz, July 1989.

40 Sweet Potatoe 5.9 ☆☆
How do you spell potato? Start ten feet right of the inside corner and climb directly up the face to a ledge, then step right to a crack in a small, left-facing dihedral. Jam the crack to a stance and follow the beautiful, right-facing dihedral to a chimney, which leads to the top. 65 feet. FA: Paul Sullivan, Mike Roth, & Kurt Klemperer, July 1989.

41 The Zee Crack 5.10a ☆ ☞
The second route established at the Upper Endless Wall. Begin under the huge roof, 10 feet left of the arête and climb the dogleg crack to the ledge. Walk off left. 35 feet. FA: Scott Garso, Jack Nard, Rick Thompson & Bob Value, June 1982.

42 Unnamed 5.10 ☞
Fifteen feet left of *The Zee Crack* is a toprope problem with a single cold shut at the ledge. 35 feet. FA: Unknown.

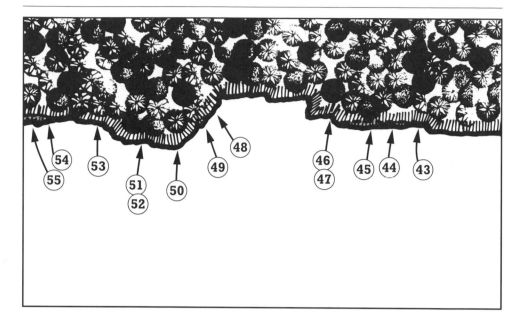

Immediately downstream from the previous routes lies the infamous Poison Ivy Grotto. If you're allergic to the dreaded stuff you had best exercise extreme caution when walking this section of trail.

43   Sheena is a Punk Rocker 5.11a ☆
Start 15 feet left of the corner and climb the slabby face past two bolts, then continue up the clean streak, aiming directly for the top. 60 feet. FA: Eddie Begoon & Mike Artz, June 1989.

44   Project—In Progress
Thirty feet left of the chimney is a right-facing flake with three bolts above it.

45   Barbecued Babies 5.12b ☆☆
aka Zeno's Route
Commence at the right-facing corner in a low roof and pull it to gain the overhanging, left-facing dihedral protected by two bolts. Continue to the top. 85 feet. FA: Bill Lutkus & Jim Damon, 1989.

46   Spurtin' Fer Certain 5.12a ☆☆☆
A real stimulator! Begin in the obvious open book, atop the short pedestal, and move up the left-facing flake to a small roof, then traverse right along the horizontal. Crank up the face past two bolts to the top. 90 feet. FA: Eddie Begoon & Mike Artz, June 1989.

47   Lactic Weekend 5.11c ☆☆
Pump it up! Using the same start as the previous route climb up to the roof and traverse left and up to a bolt, then climb up and right past an overlap. Finish directly past an orange scoop capped by a roof. 90 feet. FA: Mike Artz & Eddie Begoon, June 1989.

48   Garden Weasel 5.7
Begin four feet left of the small, left-facing corner and follow the dirty, right-facing flake to the ledge. Rappel from the two-bolt station at the top of *Basket Case*. 45 feet. FA: Keith Filter, May 1989.

49   Basket Case 5.11b ☆
Start at the right edge of the orange face and follow the thin, right-facing flakes to the ledge. Rappel from a station under the roof. 45 feet FA: Kenny Parker, Kevin Parker, Kelly Faust, Steve Downes, & Doug Houghton, June 1989.

50   Fiesta Grande 5.12c ☆☆ ⟨₽⟩
Begin by stick clipping the first bolt and step off the rock pile to grasp the first holds, then follow the line of bolts up the radiant orange face to a cold-shut station. 80 feet. Note: The fixed etrier, which originally was used to get started, has been replaced with the stack of rocks. FA: Porter Jarrard, June 1990.

51   Skiggle Von Wiggle 5.10b ☆☆
Start below an orange wall dominated by a right-facing, left-leaning flake system that begins at mid-height. Boulder up and right atop a block then skank past a left-facing flake and rail right to the start of an overhanging flake which leads to the top. 80 feet. FA: Paul Sullivan & Mike Roth, July 1989.

52   Unnamed 5.10a
Using the same start as the previous route, climb up and left to the top. 80 feet. FA: Mike Artz, Eddie Begoon & Mike Cote, August 1989.

53   Bat Cave 5.8
Start in the large, left-facing corner and climb the handcrack on the left wall to a stance at the cave. Chimney to gain the orange dihedral which is followed to the roof. Traverse right and up. 75 feet. FA: Paul Sullivan & Wayne Sayre, April 1989.

54   State of the Artz 5.11b/c ☆
Begin just left of the wide, broken crack and boulder up the blunt arête past a bolt, continuing up to the ledge. Climb directly up the right edge of the face passing two more bolts on the way to the top. 70 feet. FA: Mike Artz & Eddie Begoon, June 1989.

55   Even Cowgirls Get the Blues 5.11b ☆
Begin just left of the previous route and climb past three bolts to the ledge. 35 feet. Note: Bring TCUs. FA: Eddie Begoon & Mike Artz, June 1989.

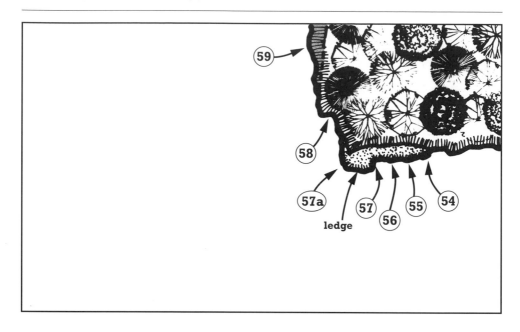

56 Fish Out of Water 5.12b ☆☆
Scale the smooth right-facing corner past two bolts and a pin to the ledge. 35 feet. FA: Eddie Begoon and Mike Artz, June 1989.

57 Wedgie 5.10b ☆☆
A classic blade arête. Start on the right side of the arête and climb the broken, right-facing corner to the ledge. Ride the knife edge to the top. 70 feet. FA: Blaze Davies & Bill Wilson, 1988.

57a Wedgie Direct Start—Out of Hand 5.11a ☆
Begin on the left side of the arête and jam the finger crack to the ledge. 30 feet. FA: Blaze Davies & Bill Wilson, 1988.

58 High and Lively 5.10b ☆☆
Start in the right-facing corner and chimney and climb into the wide crack. Move up and left to the ledge (possible belay) then continue up and left, following the crack and corner system to a small pine at the top. 90 feet. FA: Paul Sullivan & Mike Roth, July 1989.

59 Project—Mission Impossible 👀
A short distance left of *High and Lively* is a brief but desperate line of five bolts. Route 59 marks the last route listed in a downstream direction from the access point at the Intestinal Wall.

Doug Reed starting the wild
ride on the *The Mechanical Bull.*

photo: Carl Samples

Mike Artz on the first ascent of *Celibate
Mallard.*

photo: Rick Thompson

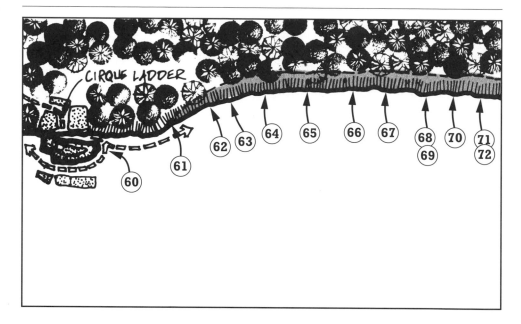

THE CIRQUE

The next key access point is the Cirque Ladder, which is best reached via the rim top trail from the Central Endless Pull Off. See the overview map for details. WARNING: USE THIS LADDER AT YOU OWN RISK OF INJURY OR DEATH! The route ordering now begins in an upstream direction from the Cirque Ladder and ends at the upstream terminus of the Cirque, just short of route 59.

60   Belly Up 5.12c ☆
At the bottom of the Cirque Ladder gully is a clean arête that is climbed a short distance to a right-angling crack which leads past two bolts to a ledge. Rappel. 60 feet. FA: Eddie Begoon & Mike Artz, August 1989.

61   Hourglass 5.12a/b ☆☆ 🄿
Begin at the downstream margin of the Cirque, just left of the chiseled initials dated 7.25.25. Begin at the right-curving, right-facing flake and follow bolts to an anchor. 85 feet. FA: Doug Reed & Phil Olnick, September 1989.

62   Spurtual Reality 5.11b ☆ 🄿 ↺
Pull the bouldery low roof and follow the right-facing corner for a short distance, then fire up and left through the series of roofs to cold shuts. 50 feet. FA: Doug Reed, April 1996.

63   Power Lung 5.11c ☆☆☆ 🅑 ℛ
This unique climb features a novel power traverse. Begin a short distance right of *Spurtual Reality* and crank directly to the fourth bolt, then rail right along the well-defined horizontal past three more bolts to cold shuts. 65 feet. FA: Doug Reed, April 1996.

64   Project - In Progress - Pooh's Corner 🅑 ℛ
The line of bolts in a severely overhanging right-facing dihedral.

65   Project - In Progress 🅑 ℛ
Located 20 feet right of the Paulownia tree (the one with the huge leaves that's growing beside the wall) is a line of bolts that angle up and right to the top.

66   Where's Bulimia? 5.9 ℛ
Wretch up the left-facing flake and corner to the ledge, and move right to anchors at the top of the first pitch of *Superstition*. 50 feet. FA: Doug Reed & Rick Thompson, March 1989.

67   Superstition 5.12d ☆☆☆ 🅑 ℛ
Two stout pitches will make a believer out of you. This was the first route to breach the imposing center section of the Cirque. P1: Begin right of *Where's Bulimia?*, at a low roof, and make bouldery moves to gain a tiny left-facing corner. Follow the line of bolts directly up to the ledge and belay. 45 feet. P2: Step right 25 feet and continue up the line of bolts to a station on a ledge near the top. 50 feet. FA P1: Doug Reed, Russ Clune & Rick Thompson, March 1989. FA P2: Doug Reed, September 1989.

68   Sloth 5.12c ☆☆ 🅑 ℛ
Originally bolted from the ground up by Begoon and Artz in 1989, it remained uncompleted until recently. Begin 50 feet right of *Superstition*, at a short left-facing flake, and climb to the second bolt, then traverse left and finish up and left to cold shuts. 60 feet. FA: Brian McCray, spring 1996.

69   Project - In Progress 🅑 ℛ
Using the same start as Sloth, after the second bolt continue up and right to cold shuts.

70   Xanth 5.13b ☆☆☆ 🅑 ℛ
Begin 20 feet right of *Sloth* at a thin start and follow the line of eight bolts through a roof at the top to a left-facing dihedral and cold shuts. 60 feet. FA: Brian McCray, spring 1996.

71   Project - In Progress 🅑 ℛ
Begins right of *Xanth* and follows the long line of bolts to cold shuts. 100 feet.

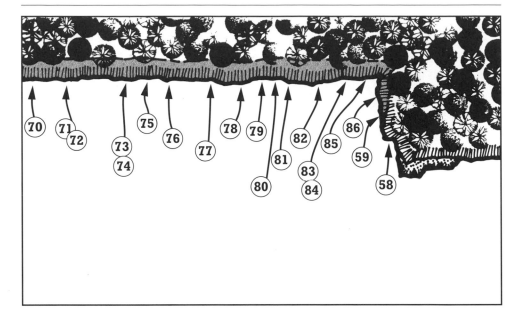

72 Project - In Progress - Dolores Clairborne 🄿 ℛ
Using the same start as the previous project move right after the second bolt and follow seven more bolts to cold shuts. Note: sometimes used as a warm up route when climbed to the bail-biner at the sixth bolt. 70 feet.

73 Finders Keepers 5.12b/c ☆☆☆ 🄿 ℛ
Begin at the left end of a low roof and power directly up, following the left-hand line of bolts along a series of right-facing flakes to open cold shuts. Nine bolts in all. 75 feet. FA: Roxanna Brock, spring 1996.

74 Project - In Progress - Losers Weepers 🄿 ℛ
Using the same start as *Finders Keepers* move right after the second bolt and follow six more bolts to a pair of open cold shuts.

75 Project - In Progress 🄿 ℛ
Climb the thin face to an undercling and a right-facing corner in the roof, then continue up the face to a large hole and a pair of cold shuts. More difficult climbing past two more bolts leads to a second pair of cold shuts.

76 Ride the Lightning 5.13b ☆☆☆ 🄿 ℛ
Begin six feet right of the previous project on thin face moves and strike up to a wide undercling flake, then continue up the face to a roof. Go left to gain a left-facing flared dihedral and fire up and right past the eleventh bolt to cold shuts. 90 feet. FA: Brian McCray, spring 1996.

77   Ragnarock 5.13b ☆☆☆☆ 🅟 ℛ
Begin 30 feet right of Ride the Lightning and follow bolts past left-facing flakes until it's possible to traverse left under the roof to finish on Ride the Lightening. 90 feet. FA: Brian McCray, spring 1996.

78   Project - In Progress - Sporticus aka The Woody 🅟 ℛ
The line of bolts just to the right of the sassafras tree that lead to a right-facing dihedral.

79   Project - In Progress 🅟 ℛ
Twelve feet right of *Sporticus* is a line of seven bolts.

80   Project - In Progress 🅟 ℛ
Start at left-facing flakes in front of a charred tree trunk and climb past 13 bolts.

81   Project - In Progress - Brian's House of Cards 🅟 ℛ
Fifteen feet right of the charred trunk is another 13 bolt project. Requires 2 ropes to get to the ground.

82   Project - In Progress 🅟 ℛ
Six bolts to cold shuts.

83   New Life 5.11b ☆☆☆ 🅟 ℛ
Begin from the left side of the hanging grape garden and climb up and left on right-facing flakes to a right-facing corner. Move up and over a roof, then continue up to the last bolt. Schwank left, then back right to get to the shuts. 90 feet. Note: subject to spray from the waterfall on windy days. FA: Roxanna Brock, spring 1996.

84   Live and Let Live 5.12b ☆☆ 🅟 ℛ
Using the same start as *New Life* move right after the first bolt and follow the line of nine bolts to a pair of cold shuts. 70 feet. Note: subject to waterfall spray. FA: Brian McCray, spring 1996.

85   Holier Than Thou 5.12c/d ☆☆ 🅟 ℛ
Start at a left-arching flake and climb to a roof, then move up reach a left-facing arched dihedral. Pull past the second roof to gain a slab that leads to cold shuts. Nine bolts in all. 70 feet. Note: subject to waterfall spray. FA: Roxanna Brock, spring 1996.

86   Blacklist 5.12b/c ☆☆☆ 🅟 ℛ
This route is located ten feet right of the huge chimney that separates the two walls. Start in a left-facing corner and follow the line of nine bolts to cold shuts. 80 feet. Note: subject to waterfall spray. FA: Brian McCray, spring 1996.

Blacklist is the last route ordered in an upstream direction from the Cirque Ladder access point.

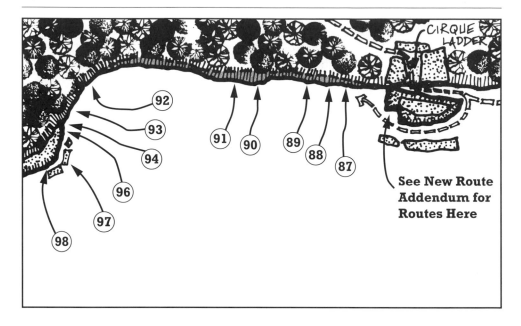

THE MUNGOLIAN WALL

The following routes are ordered in a downstream direction from the Cirque ladder to a point ending midway along Dinner Ledge. Beware of the bumper crop of poison ivy that flourishes along this section of cliff. The first landmark you'll encounter is the Stalactite, a massive splinter of rock that became embedded vertically in the ground when it fell from the roofs above just a few years ago.

87   Project--In Progress

The line of bolts located directly behind the Stalactite.

88   Slide Rule 5.12b ☆☆

Follow the line of seven bolts to a cold shut anchor. 75 feet. FA: Doug Reed, November 1994.

89   Pigtail 5.12b/c ☆

A short distance left of the previous route is a line of six bolts and a cold-shut station. 70 feet. FA: Doug Reed, November 1994.

90   Overkill 5.13a ☆☆

Follow the line of bolts until just below the roof and make a radical traverse left and pull the roof, finishing directly up to a station. 75 feet. FA: Doug Reed, November 1994.

91   Overkill Variation Finish—Future Proof 5.12b ☆☆☆

Follow the route as normal to the roof, then finish up and right over the roof to gain a right-angling corner which leads to the top. FA: Doug Reed, 1995.

92   Espresso Yourself 5.12a ☆☆☆ 🅟

Caffeination rules! Start near the right margin of the brilliant orange wall and climb the technical face up and left past three bolts to a roof band. Pull it directly and follow the overhanging left-facing dihedral to a cold-shut station. 80 feet. FA: Rick Thompson, November 1994.

93   Sunshine Daydream 5.10a ☆☆

Start approximately 30 feet left of *Espresso Yourself* and climb the orange, right-arching flake to a roof, which is pulled to a small ledge on the left. Step left to another right-arching flake, which is followed to a roof, then step right and pull the roof, finishing directly up. 90 feet. Note: Double ropes recommended. Can be bit dirty. FA: Paul Sullivan & Mike Roth, May 1989.

94   Blind Sight 5.10b ☆

Locate the clean left-facing corner and follow it directly up to a pine on Dinner Ledge. 40 feet. FA: Eddie Begoon & Mike Artz, April 1986.

95   Blood Donors 5.10d ☆

Typically done as the second pitch to *Blind Sight*. From the belay tree on *Blind Sight*, step left to a thin left-facing corner, which is followed until it's possible to move right to the arête. Climb straight up through two roofs, moving right to belay at a pine tree. 40 feet. FA: Mike Artz & Eddie Begoon, April 1986.

96   Blue Angel   5.10c/d ☆
aka Sport Climbing 101 🅟

This one was first done as a ground-up route and was named for the whipper Mike Roth logged while attempting it. A single bolt was subsequently placed by the first ascent party to protect the finish. A year or so later the line immediately to the left was bolted. The original bolt is just to the right of this line. Begin just left of *Blind Sight* and follow four bolts to Dinner Ledge. 35 feet. FA: Mike Roth and Paul Sullivan, May 1989.

97   High Octane 5.10c ☆☆

Begins five feet right of the "squeeze" in the trail and climb a right-facing flake up and left to Dinner Ledge. Step over to the flawless arête and climb the right side, passing two bolts. 70 feet. FA: Dean Metzler, Paul Sullivan & Mike Roth, May 1989.

98   Weenie Roast 5.8

Begin on the left side of the arête and climb the left-facing flake to it's top, then hand traverse right to stance on a blunt arête. Move up the left side of arête to Dinner Ledge. 30 feet. FA: Paul Sullivan & Mike Roth, May 1989.

Weenie Roast is the last route listed in a downstream direction from the Cirque Ladder access point.

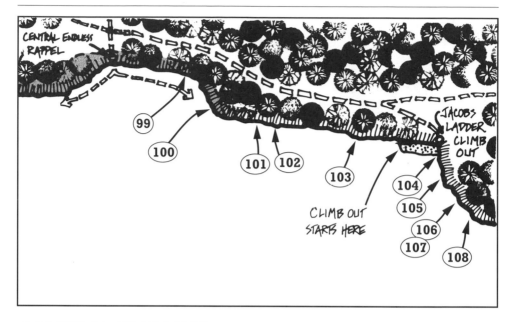

CENTRAL ENDLESS

The next major access point downstream from the Cirque Ladder is the Central Endless Rappel, which is most easily reached from the Central Endless parking area. See the overview map for details. Using this rappel as the next reference point, the following route descriptions are ordered in an upstream direction.

99 The Good Book 5.9 ☆

An attractive dihedral that unfortunately tends to be wet. The second pitch is called The Rainbow. P1: Jam the crack in the left-facing dihedral past some small roofs and belay on a ledge below the final roof band. 70 feet. P2: Make a long, easy traverse left, finishing on loose rock up to the Central Endless rappel tree. 70 feet. FA: Cal Swoager & Stuart Kuperstock, October 1985.

100 Project—In Progress 🔩

The line of bolts up the way steep prow.

The following three routes are located in a prolific sea of poison ivy. Beware!

101 Motivation 5.10d ☆ 🔩

Begin a short distance right of the arête and slab up and right past a pin and a bolt to a bulge, then continue directly up passing alternating bolts and pins to the top. 65 feet. FA: Tom Helvie, May 1991.

102 Cheez Boys 5.12a 🔩

Slabbin' on rock-cotta cheese. Begin 30 feet right of *Motivation* and follow the line of five bolts through a bulge. 55 feet. FA: Tom Helvie, October 1991.

103   Endangered Species 5.10c/d

Too bad it's not the ivy. Begin about 100 feet left of *Jacob's Ladder* and start with a stick clip, then climb directly past the second bolt aiming for a stance below the roof. Pull it directly past a pin and a bolt to the top. 70 feet. FA: Tom Helvie & Chris Kirkpatrick, April 1991.

Jacob's Ladder 5.0—Traditional Climb Out

Not a ladder! Most of us have become spoiled by the ladders that now grace Endless Wall's major access points. *Jacob's Ladder* climb out was the primary egress used when the crag was originally being explored by climbers in the mid-eighties. And though it earns a fifth class rating, it's typically climbed unroped. Be forewarned: There are some very exposed moves near the top, particularly the leftward traverse under the roof. Add the awkwardness of a pack on your back and you've got a potentially lethal situation. YOU ALONE ARE RESPONSIBLE FOR YOUR SAFETY! If you're not comfortable with the unroped exposure either rope up or hike upstream to the Cirque Ladder. Begin at the base of a left-facing corner and ledge system and follow it until it's possible to tiptoe leftward along a ledge under the final roof. Scramble up and right to the top. 60 feet.

104   Save the Human Race 5.5 ☆

Just right of the *Jacob's Ladder* climb out is a right-facing corner equipped with a handcrack. Climb the crack to a ledge with a tree and traverse left and finish on *Jacob's Ladder*. FA: Andrew Barry, solo, wearing tennis shoes and a pack, October 1985.

105   Just Forget It 5.12b ☆☆ ⌂

Just do it, just send it...*Just Forget It!* An improbable and action packed route on flawless stone. Begin just right of the blunt arête below an overhanging white face and follow four bolts up and left to the corner of the roof, then back right to a cold-shut station. 35 feet. FA: Rick Thompson, March 1995.

106   Senility 5.11a ☆

Just forget it? Begin in the open corner to the left of the huge hueco and climb the corner to its end, following the overhanging crack directly to the ledge. Meander up the ledgy face to the top. 70 feet. FA: Mike Artz, Andrew Barry, & Jon Regelbrugge, November 1985.

106a Senility Variation Finish—Captain Chaos 5.10a ☆

Climb the first 30 feet of *Senility*, then hand traverse left and follow the flake system up to a stance under a roof. Step left around the roof and scramble to the top. 70 feet. FA: Paul Sullivan & Dave Moore, June 1989.

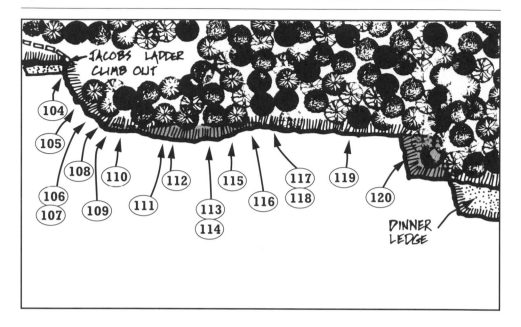

107 Route 66 5.11b R ☆
Get your kicks on Route 66. Bring sky hooks for protecting the finishing face. Climb the first few moves of *Senility,* then step right and up the face just above the hueco to gain an inside corner. Move up the corner (get good pro here) then angle up and right on good holds. Finish slightly left then directly to the top. 60 feet. FA: Andrew Barry, Mike Artz, & Jon Regelbrugge, November 1985.

108 Stubble 5.12b/c ☆☆ ℗
The initial moves of this route pass along the right edge of the magnificent hueco, which is composed of delicate sculpted formations. Help preserve this splendid natural creation by using extra care to avoid disturbing or touching it. Start just right of the hueco and crank up and left to a stance on the right side of it. Reach right, then up and left over the roof and follow the overhanging face on the left side of the arête to a cold-shut station. 50 feet FA: Rick Thompson, November 1994.

109 Almost Heaven 5.10b/c ☆
Wild, wonderful, Wet Virginia! Start just left of the twin maples and jug up and right to a stance at the left margin of the slab. Wander up the slab past a short crack to an orange roof and pull it, finishing up and left to the top. 70 feet. FA: Bill Bradshaw & Paul Sullivan, July 1989.

110 Churning in the Butter 5.11b ☆☆☆ ℗
This rich and creamy route is loaded with variety. Follow the line of nine bolts to a wild finish and a cold-shut station. 90 feet. Note: You'll need a 50-meter rope. FA: Carl Samples, November 1994.

111   The Alpha and the Omega 5.11c
P1: Begin just left of the collection of sport climbs, at a right-angling roof crack and follow pumpy moves out it to reach a flake above the lip. Climb up the flake past a bolt, then move left to a bolt belay in the huge hueco. 30 feet. P2: Traverse left a short distance, then climb directly up the face, aiming for a crack in a small roof. Continue out the roof crack to the top. 50 feet. FA: Cal Swoager & Stuart Kuperstock, October 1985.

112   Baby Rage 5.12a/b
Begin immediately right of the previous route and jump start, then follow the short line of bolts to a cold-shut station. 30 feet. FA: Doug Reed, November 1994.

113   Project--In Progress--The Mechanical Bull
Brace yourself for a wild ride! Begin about 30 feet right of *Baby Rage*, just right of a detached flake at the lip which resembles an ear. Stick clip and climb out and left, then back right to reach the ear. Move up the flake then follow the line of bolts up and left through the bulge, finishing directly up to a cold-shut station below the upper roof band.

114   Fat Back 5.12c ☆
Begin with the same start as *The Mechanical Bull*, climbing up to the ear, then follow the right-hand line of bolts to a station below the roof. Note: Some crumbly rock. 70 feet. FA: Doug Reed, November 1994.

115   Project—In Progress
A short distance upstream from *Fat Back* is a line with three bolts.

116   Shotgun 5.12b ☆
Just right of the end of the low roof is a left-leaning crack, which is followed to a station below the roof. 50 feet. FA: Doug Reed, 1991.

117   Fearful Symmetry 5.12b ☆☆☆
One of the early Endless Wall testpiece cracks and still one of the toughest. Begin at a low hueco with a double-sided flake above it and follow the left-hand flake to the roof. Crank over the roof and fibrillate up the lone, snaking crack and face above to the top. 85 feet. FA: Eric Hörst, May 1987.

118   Project—In Progress—The Gram Delusion
The bolt line which follows the right-hand flake out of the hueco.

119   Solitaire 5.10d ☆
Midway along the next wall is a low, right-facing roof-corner with a crack splitting the face above. Follow it, moving up and left to a stance below the roof. Climb the crack and jugs out the roof to the top. 90 feet. FA: Andrew Barry, Mike Artz & Jon Regelbrugge, November 1985.

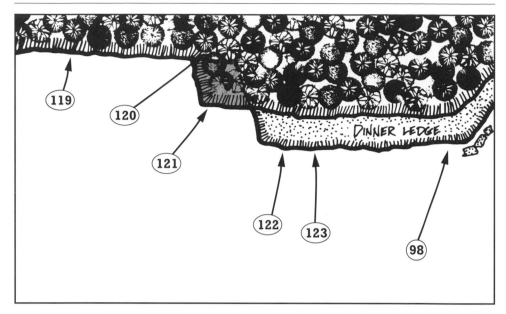

120   Petrified Pink Puke 5.10c ☆
P1: Begin at the flake system on the left wall of the roof-capped, left-facing dihedral by heaving up to the roof then traversing left a short distance. Pull past a roof to enter a left-facing dihedral and belay. 60 feet. P2: Continue up the corner until it is possible to make a long, rising traverse to the right, following the path of least resistance to the top. 50 feet. FA: Eddie Begoon & Mike Artz, April 1986.

121   Big Gulp 5.9+
Swallow hard and climb the layback crack on the dihedral's right wall to the roof, then hand traverse right to Dinner Ledge. 50 feet. FA: John Burcham & Andrew Barry, March 1986.

The next two routes start from Dinner Ledge. Either of them works well as a second pitch to *Big Gulp*. Please minimize your impact on Dinner Ledge. This pristine terrace shows virtually no signs of human impact and every effort possible should be made to preserve it in that state.

122   Caffeine Free 5.9 ☆☆
Start 15 feet to the right of *Big Gulp's* finish and jam the striking crack and face to the top. 40 feet. FA: Andrew Barry & Mike Artz, April 1986.

123   Nutrasweet 5.10a ☆
Begin a few paces right of *Caffeine Free* and ascend the crack system until it is possible to move left to finish on *Caffeine Free*. 45 feet. FA: Mike Artz & Andrew Barry, April 1986.

Nutrasweet is the last route listed in an upstream direction from the Central Endless Rappel. Just beyond this point you will come to route 98, *Weenie Roast*.

Mike Artz on *The Undeserved.* photo: Carl Samples

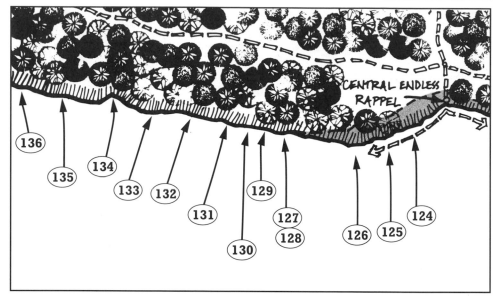

We will now return to the Central Endless Rappel and begin descriptions in a downstream direction.

124   Project—In Progress
The line of bolts which lies immediately left of the rappel.

125   Unnamed 5.13a ☆ 📖
Follow the line of six bolts out the exceedingly steep wall to a cold-shut station. 60 feet. FA: Doug Reed, 1993.

126   Suspended Sentence 5.12c ☆☆ 📖
Hangem' High! Start in an overhanging right-facing corner and follow it up to a stance below a roof. Crank out another overhanging corner and traverse out left to the arête and a rap station. 50 feet. Note: Bring a nut to back up the single bolt rap station. FA: Jeff Morris, Jason Stern, Jim Damon & Paul Pomeroy, October 1989.

127   Android 5.10d ☆
Don't expect robotics to help you here. Climb the short left-facing corner its end, then move right and up to a small, left-facing flake. Ascend the face above the flake to a roof, which is pulled directly up to a small pine. 75 feet. Note: A sky hook will be helpful for protecting the face above the flake. FA: Andrew Barry & Mike Artz, October 1985.

128   The Centurion 5.11c ☆
Using the same start as *Android* climb the initial corner, then move left and follow the line of bolts to a cold-shut station. 75 feet. Note: Carry some gear to protect the initial corner or use a very long stick to clip the first bolt. FA: Doug Cosby & Gary Beil, August 1990.

129   River Heart 5.11d ☆☆ ⑨

Follow the line of eight bolts to a pair of cold shuts. 70 feet. FA: Doug Reed, summer 1994.

130   Pearl River 5.12b ☆☆ ⑨

Begin by jumping up to a jug and pull the low roof, then follow the line of seven bolts to a cold-shut station. 70 feet. FA: Doug Reed & Eric Hörst, May 1990.

131   Gin and Bulls 5.12c/d ☆ ⑨

Begin 15 feet left of the *Pearl River* and follow the line of bolts to a cold-shut station. 80 feet. FA: Doug Reed & Russ Clune, September 1990.

132   Golden Years 5.11d/12a ☆☆☆

This climb was established on Minunni's thirtieth birthday, an apt welcome to golden years. Begin approximately 20 feet right of *Imperial Strut* by lunging up to a shelf. Hand traverse right to a pin, then move up and right through bulging eyebrows to a second pin. Thrutch up and left, then straight up to a bolt and continue up and right past a small left-facing flake. Angle left to a ledge system under the headwall and move directly up, exiting left below the top. 80 feet. Note: The fixed gear on this one is starting to show signs of aging. FA: Darrow Kirkpatrick & Frank Minunni, March 1987.

133   Project—In Progress

The line of bolts just right of *Imperial Strut.*

134   Imperial Strut 5.10a Ao ☆☆

Steep and strenuous liebacking. Begin at the right-facing dihedral with a mature beech tree at its base and march up the corner using the unavoidable aid offered by the tree for a short section near the bottom. Continue up the corner and flake system above to the top. 75 feet. FA: Rick Thompson & Scott Garso, October 1985.

135   Lying Egyptian 5.10c ☆

Commence about 20 feet left of *Imperial Strut* and climb past a bolt and huecos, then move up and left through a bulge and past a second bolt to the top. 75 feet. Note: Bring a light rack including TCUs and Friends. FA: Kelly Faust, Kenny Parker, & Gene Kistler, April 1989.

136   Kline The Billy Goat 5.11b ☆☆

Start 35 feet left of *Imperial Strut* and climb directly to a pin at 20 feet. Continue past three bolts until you're under a small roof, then step right and up to a ledge. Clip the fourth bolt and boogie to the top. 75 feet. Note: Tote a few TCUs along. FA: Eddie Begoon, Mike Artz, & Kelly Faust, April 1989.

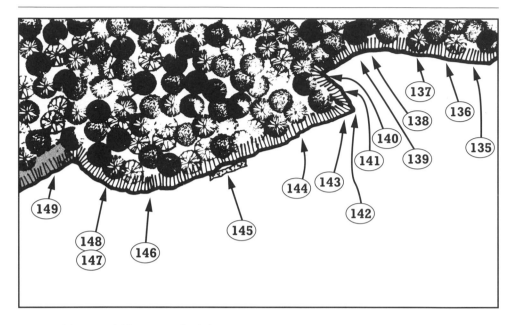

137   Man-o-War 5.12b ☆☆
Don't get stung on this seductive line. Start about 20 feet left of *Kline the Billy Goat* and climb past three bolts, then follow the left-facing flake to a ledge. Head up and slightly left to the top. 75 feet. Note: A handful of TCUs and a #1 1/2 Friend will be helpful. FA: Eddie Begoon & Mike Artz, April 1989.

138   Oyster Cracker 5.10a ☆☆☆
An elegant pitch featuring a classic flake system. Climb the conspicuous, right-leaning, orange flake system to a ledge above two small roofs, then finish up and right. 75 feet. FA: Mike Artz, Andrew Barry, & Bruce Burgin, October 1985.

139   Bubbas at Arapiles 5.12a/b ☆☆ 🎧
This popular line was one the earliest sport climbs established on Endless Wall. Begin just left of *Oyster Cracker* and climb up to an obvious hueco. Move up and left past a bolt, then straight up past a pin and two more bolts to the top. 50 feet. FA: Kenny Parker & Steve Bregman, October 1988.

140   Purity Made 5.7 ☆
Climb the crack in the right-facing corner to the top. 45 feet. FA: Tom Howard, Dan Perry, & Jim Okel, October 1981.

141   Dab Hand 5.10b
A creation of self serving rules. Climb the face left of *Purity Made* without using the corner or the nearby trees. The route finishes on the left side of the short dihedral near the top. 40 feet. FA: Andrew Barry & John Burcham, June 1986.

142 Double Negative 5.9 X

A slip from this poorly protected line is likely to leave you in the negatory zone. Begin on the lichen covered face just right of the low-angled clean streak and crunch and climb directly up the to the top. 60 feet. FA: Andrew Barry & Steve Lancaster, October 1985.

143 Alcan Highway 5.6 R

Begin by climbing the tree next the base of the wall as far as you desire, then step onto the rock and climb the clean streak to the top. Shares a couple of moves with *Double Negative* at the finish. 60 feet. FA: John Burcham & Andrew Barry, June 1986.

144 Wad Cutter 5.12a/b ☆☆

Begin 20 feet left of *Alcan Highway*, about eight feet left of a fallen tree and climb directly past a pin and a bolt to a tied-off pin. Continue to a second bolt, then angle up and right to the top. 80 feet. Gear: Bring a selection of TCUs. FA: Kenny Parker & Mike Cote, April 1988.

145 Brain Death 5.10c ☆

Begin atop a long, flat boulder and angle up the face to a crack in a small left facing bulge, which is pulled to gain a ledge. Angle up and left over a second bulge, then finish up and right to the top. 80 feet. FA: Jeff Laushey & Bruce Burgess, October 1985.

145a Fun With Jello 5.11a ☆

Follow *Brain Death* as normal up to the ledge, then finish up and right past a pin to the top. FA: Jeff Laushey & Bruce Burgess, October 1985.

146 Give a Boy a Gun 5.11c ☆

Begin about ten feet right of start to *Never Cry Tuna* and crank a small right facing feature, then follow a line of holds up and right to a good horizontal. Climb straight up past a pin, then shoot up and right on widely spaced protection to the top. 90 feet. Note: Bring a heap of TCUs. FA: Eddie Begoon & Kevin Parker, April 1988.

147 Never Cry Tuna 5.11c ☆☆☆

Begin 25 feet right of the *Tuna Fish Roof* dihedral at a right-facing corner and climb directly up to a bolt on the blunt arête. Continue up, then left, joining *Hot Tuna* at the last bolt. Finish on *Hot Tuna*. 80 feet. Note: Lots of TCUs, Friends to #2, and a small selection of stoppers will do ya nicely. FA: Eddie Begoon & Kevin Parker, July 1989.

148 Hot Tuna 5.12b ☆☆☆

Using the same start as the previous route climb the corner, then move up and left past two bolts to a horizontal. Move right to the arête and continue past a third bolt to a rap station. 80 feet. Note: Bring TCUs, small Friends, and medium to large wires. FA: Kenny Parker & Steve Downes, May 1989.

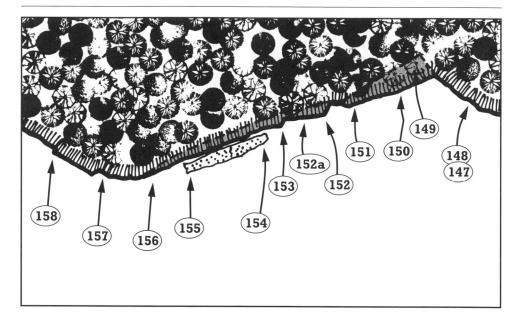

149 Tuna Fish Roof 5.11d
This classic-looking route is unfortunately a one move wonder. P1: Begin at the dihedral below the perfectly flat bottomed roof and follow it to a no-hands rest at the roof. Move right to the roofs end and set up a hanging belay just above the lip. 60 feet. P2: Follow the easy corner to the top. 30 feet. FA: Andrew Barry & Mike Artz, October 1985.

150 Somethin' Fierce 5.11b
On the wall just left of *Tuna Fish Roof* is a line of bolts that lead to a cold-shut station below the roof. 45 feet. FA: Glenn Ritter, August 1991.

151 Celibate Mallard 5.10c ☆☆☆☆
No quack climbing here, just exquisite flakes, corners and roofs. Begin in the right hand, right-facing flake system and follow it past an awkward start and a good layback to a small roof. Pull the roof and follow the right-arching corner to the top. 90 feet. FA: Mike Artz & Andrew Barry, October 1985.

152 Roy's Lament 5.9 ☆☆
A varied and stimulating climb of great popularity. Begin at the left-hand, right-facing flake system and follow it to a ledge. Climb a varying width crack in a corner up to a roof and traverse off right to a belay in the trees. 90 feet. FA: Dan Perry, Jim Okel, & Tom Howard, October 1981.

152a Roy's Lament Direct Start 5.9
Fifteen feet left of the regular start is a crack (5.8) that is followed up to the ledge. Finish on the normal route. FA: Andrew Barry, Kenny Hummel, & Mike Artz, October 1985.

152b Roy's Lament Direct Finish 5.10b ☆
A touch of the Gunks! Consensus has recently upgraded this from its original 5.9+ grade. Follow *Roy's Lament* as normal until you reach the roof at the top of the corner and pull it directly. Move right to a belay. FA: Scott Garso, Rick Thompson & Bruce Burgin, October 1985.

153 No Mas 5.12b ☆
Start 15 feet left of the *Roy's Lament Direct Start* and climb directly up the gray streak, passing two bolts near the steak's right margin. 80 feet. FA: Mike Artz & Eddie Begoon, April 1988.

154 Tatoo 5.12a ☆☆ ⓟ
Begin from the right end of the shelf and follow the line of bolts to a cold-shut station below the roof. 70 feet. FA: Doug Reed, September 1994.

155 Young Whippersnapper's Route 5.11b X
A pair of wings and a harp could be yours if you blow it before the first clip. Commence ten feet right of *The Undeserved* at the left end of the shelf and climb straight up the thin face passing a pin until you're ten feet below a small overlap. Traverse right past a fixed tricam to a flake then move up and traverse right to the end of the overlap. Finish up, then right to a small belay tree. 100 feet. FA: Phil Heller & Andrew Barry, April 1986.

156 The Undeserved 5.10c ☆☆☆☆
One of the first routes established at The Endless Wall, this paramount climb is also heralded as one of the finest of its grade. Lieback the initial flake past a knobby bulge and follow the continually narrowing crack past a rattly, but seemingly secure block until you reach a good horizontal. Hand traverse left to gain a left-facing dihedral and follow it to a tree belay at a good ledge. 90 feet. FA: Tom Howard, Jim Okel, & Dan Perry, October 1981.

156a The Undeserved Variation—Mig Squadron 5.11a ☆☆☆☆
A variation that avoids most of the crack on the normal route in lieu of an outstanding dihedral. Layback the crack as normal until it's possible to make a tricky leftward traverse to reach the start of the hanging, left-facing dihedral. Follow it to the top, finishing as normal. FA: Rich Pleiss & Tim Mein, August 1984.

157 Back With My Kind 5.11c/d ☆☆☆
In 1987 Andrew Barry moved west to California, leaving his beloved New River behind. He established this route on a return visit, hence the name. Begin just left of *The Undeserved* at a short, left-facing dihedral. Climb the dihedral for a short distance and move left to good holds just below the dihedral's end. Move up and right past a bolt and continue up an open book past two more bolts. Power up and right to a fourth bolt then left to the base of a short, overhanging dihedral that leads to the top. 80 feet. Note: Carry a light rack plus a #3 and 3½ Friend. FA: Andrew Barry & Mike Artz, April 1988.

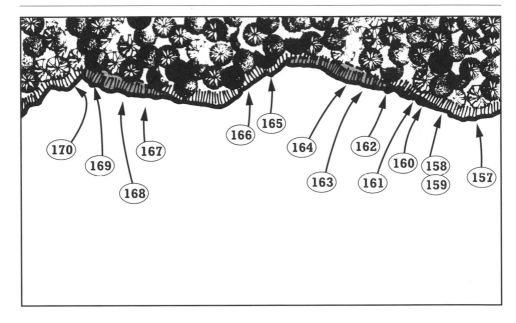

158 The Erogenous Zone 5.10c ☆
Climb the short left-facing corner to its top, then move up and left to gain a crack that splits a small overhang. Jam the crack to a flake which is followed to its end, then angle left and up to a tiny ledge finishing directly up to a small pine. 90 feet. FA: Mike Artz & Andrew Barry, October 1985.

159 Caption 5.12b/c ☆☆
Using the same start as *The Erogenous Zone*, climb the short, left-facing corner then move left to a bolt. Follow the line of six more bolts to a tree at the top. 90 feet. Note: Bring small stoppers for corner and a #1 Friend for top. FA: Porter Jarrard & Doug Reed, May 1989.

160 Sparks 5.12c ☆☆ 🄿
Begin just right of *New Fangled Dangle* and pull the low overhang and follow the line of bolts to the top. 75 feet. FA: Doug Reed, May 1989.

161 New Fangled Dangle 5.11a ☆☆
Historically important as Endless Wall's first 5.10, it has since been upgraded due to the elimination of a chockstone that graced the opening moves on the first ascent. Climb the left-facing V-slot dihedral that splits the wall to the top. 80 feet. FA: Tom Howard & Bill Newman, October 1981.

162 Rebel Spade 5.12b ☆☆ 🄿
On the left side of the *New Fangled Dangle* dihedral is a low roof that is pulled to gain a line of bolts that are followed up the blunt arête to the top. 80 feet. FA: Doug Reed, September 1990.

163   Project—In Progress
Line of bolts right of the *Old Duffer's Route.*

164   Old Duffer's Route 5.12b
One of the first 5.12s at the New. Start 40 feet left of *New Fanged Dangle,* at a
point where the low roof is at its widest. Pump your way out the long, low roof
crack to some slings a short distance above the lip. 40 feet. FA: Alex Karr &
Mike Kehoe, April 1986.

165   Flirting With VMC 5.9
P1: Begin in an off-width right-facing flake that lies 15 feet left of the end of the
long, low roof. Climb the flake to a right-facing dihedral, which is followed to its
end, then move right to a belay ledge. 60 feet. P2: Follow a right-facing flake
and chimney to the top. 30 feet. FA: Stanley Todd, Mike Artz, & Eddie Begoon,
June 1986.

166   Flirting With Apollo Reed 5.12a ☆ ⓟ
Begin a short distance left of *Flirting With VMC* and follow the line of six bolts to
a pair of cold shuts. 65 feet. FA: Doug Reed, 1992.

167   Four Star 5.11b ☆
Roof climbing of a celestial nature. Start in a small left-facing corner that lies
about 20 feet right of *The Tide* and climb the corner and crack above to a pair of
cold shuts (used for *Back With My Chyme*) at the base of a huge roof. Belay here
to reduce rope drag. Move up to the giant roof and power out the 25-foot crack
to the top. 100 feet. FA: Maurice Reed & Doug Reed, October 1985.

168   Back With My Chyme 5.12a ⓟ ⓡ
Wretch and hurl! Begin left of the start to *Four Star* and climb directly up the face
to the cold shuts. 60 feet. FA TR: Rick Thompson, Doug Reed, Carl Samples and
Bob Rentka, August 1990. FA: Aaron Fullerton & Matt the Ectomorph, October
1995.

169   The Tide 5.8 ☆
P1: Start in the large right-facing dihedral and follow it until it ends at a large
roof band, then traverse left along a horizontal to a triangular ledge and belay at
a pair of bolts. 70 feet. P2: Step left around the arête and follow unprotected
moves to the top. 30 feet. FA: Mac McNeese & Andrew Barry, October 1985.

170   The Beach 5.10b
Commence 15 feet left of *The Tide* and boulder up to a crack, which is followed
to its end and a good ledge above. Continue directly up the eroded face
passing an Aussie bolt (no hanger, bring a wired stopper for clipping) and join
The Tide at the halfway point of the leftward traverse. Finish on *The Tide.* FA:
Andrew Barry & Mac McNeese, October 1985.

Cal Swoager on the burley direct finish of *Fantasy* – Scott Garso dozing off on belay duty.

photo: Carl Samples

Ed McCarthey on the second ascent of *Night Galley*, one of the
first routes established on Endless Wall.

photo: Carl Samples

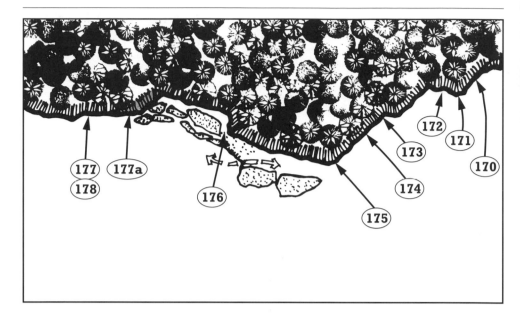

171 Jet Cap 5.12a ☆☆ 🎣

Begin at the enticing arête right of *Liddlebiddariddum* and follow line of six bolts to rap station on the ledge. 80 feet. FA: Doug Reed & Bob Rentka, October 1989.

172 Liddlebiddariddum 5.10d ☆☆

Do you have the rhythm? It just requires a little. Locate a short, left-arching corner that lies below a striking finger crack and climb it for a short distance, then breakout up and right through the bulges to gain the crack. Follow the crack to its end and finish up and right. 80 feet. FA: Mike Artz & Eddie Begoon, July 1986.

173 Gut Feeling 5.7 ☆

Approximately 20 feet left of *Liddlebiddariddum* is a right-facing flake which is climbed until it merges with a right-facing corner. Ascend the corner to its top and traverse right to the top of *Liddlebiddariddum*. 90 feet. FA: Mike Artz & Andrew Barry, June 1986.

174 Statistical Reminder 5.9+ R ☆

Start 20 feet right of *Two Step Arête* below the right side of a scallop in the face and climb past the right side of the dish, then wander up the face using the same finish as *The One Step*. 90 feet. FA: Eddie Begoon & Stanley Todd, June 1986.

175 Two Step Arête 5.8+ ☆☆

A low-angle arête that requires some route finding skills. Start at the base of the arête and climb up to a good ledge then continue straight up a narrow face to a ledge with some large, loose blocks. Step around to the left side of the arête and follow the path of least resistance until it's possible to move up and right to a small ledge on the arête at the base of a tiny inside corner. Climb the corner to a horizontal break and move directly up the right face of the arête to easier climbing and the top. 90 feet. FA: Tom Howard, October 1985.

175a Two Step Arête Variation Finish—Steppin' Out 5.7+
Follow the regular route until you reach the horizontal just below the top. Hand traverse right past the finish of *The One Step* to gain a good ledge and a short, left-facing corner. Move up the corner and shift right to a tree belay. Watch rope drag. 100 feet. FA: Charlie Rafferty & Carl Samples, April 1986.

175b Two Step Arête Variation—The One Step 5.8+ R ☆
Add a star and delete the R-rating if done in combination with the normal finish on *Two Step Arête*. Step onto the ledge at the base of the route and move around to the right side of the arête. Climb directly up the right side of the arête past a small roof until you merge with the regular route at the tiny inside corner and follow it to the horizontal. Hand traverse right 12 feet (get good pro here) and climb up the unprotected face (big air potential!) to the top. 90 feet. FA: Rick Thompson & Eric Hoffman, June 1986.

176 The Orgasmatron 5.10d ☆☆
Guaranteed to get you juiced! Left of *Two Step Arête* is a group of long, ledgy blocks along the base of the wall. At the upstream end of these is a large block that's slipped away from the base of the wall. Start behind it in the back of the wide chimney and follow a short left-facing corner up to a left-leaning crack. Pump your way up the crack to a ledge and rappel. 80 feet. FA: Andrew Barry & Mike Artz, October 1985.

177 Vidassana 5.11d ☆ ⑫
A Buddhist expression for "single pointed concentration." Start at the downstream end of the ledgy blocks below a brilliant, orange face and climb up to the first bolt then move up and right under an overlap and follow the right angling line of bolts past a large hueco to an anchor on a ledge. 50 feet. FA: Doug Cosby, June 1989.

177a Vidassana Direct Start—Wu Wei 5.12c ☆☆ ⑫
A Chinese Taoist expression for "doing without doing." Start under the roof to the right of *Vidassana* and follow the line of bolts out the roof joining *Vidassana* above the roof. 40 feet. FA: Doug Cosby & Rod Hansen, October 1989.

178 Progresso 5.11d ☆
Using the same start as *Vidassana* climb past the first bolt to the left, then straight up trending right to the second bolt. Aim for brilliant orange rock and the third bolt then up to a ledge just below the top. Rappel 95 feet. Note: Rack up with lots of TCUs, small Friends, and medium wires. Double ropes are also helpful. FA: Porter Jarrard, Eddie Begoon, & Peter Noebels, September 1989.

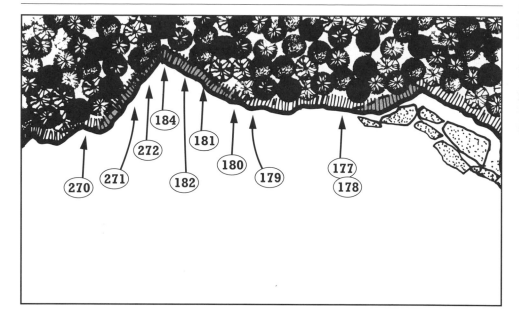

179   Super Face 5.11c ☆☆
Begin near the right edge of the face below a small right-facing dihedral and follow it to a good horizontal, then climb the face past three bolts to a ledge. Continue straight up and finish on the last part of the second pitch of *Fantasy*. 100 feet. FA: Glenn Ritter, Mark Stevenson & John Plum, June 1989.

180   Dreams of White Toilet Paper 5.11a R ☆☆
Start 20 feet right of *Fantasy* and boulder up to a short, right-facing corner. At the top of the corner aim straight up for a bolt, then continue up the enjoyable face joining the second pitch of *Fantasy* where it traverses right. Finish on *Fantasy*. 95 feet. FA: Eddie Begoon & Mike Artz, April 1989.

181   Fantasy 5.8 ☆☆☆☆
The New's premier crack of its grade. Most parties rap from the top of the first pitch. P1: About 25 feet right of the large right-facing corner (*Pink Pooka Party*) is a fantastic left-angling crack which is followed to belay anchors on the large ledge below the roof. 80 feet. P2: Traverse right, then up the path of least resistance to the top. 50 feet. FA: Tim Mein & Rich Pleiss, September 1984.

181a   Fantasy Direct Finish 5.10b ☆
This dynamic finish is recommended but tends to be a bit dusty. Variation P2: From the ledge climb up and left through a left-facing dihedral to the top. 45 feet. FA: Mike Artz & Mike Cote, October 1985.

182   Fantasy Face 5.12a ☆ 🄯
Start 15 feet left of *Fantasy* at a small roof and follow the line of bolts up the face to a pair of anchors on the ledge. 80 feet. FA TR: Glenn Ritter & Mark Stevenson, June 1989. FA: Paul Harmon, 1993.

183   Mr. Fantasy 5.11c ☆ 🖉

From the anchors at the top of *Fantasy Face* follow the line of bolts up and left through the tiered roof to a pair of anchors. 45 feet. FA: Rick Mix, 1993.

184   Pink Pooka Party 5.9+

Ramble up the large, right-facing corner to the roofs and traverse left. Rappel from the station on *Doce Doe* or finish on that route. 100 feet. FA: Jim Overbey, Jeff Burton & Monty Reagan, November 1985.

Pink Pooka Party is the last route listed in a downstream direction from the Central Endless Rappel access point.

Rick Thompson on the first ascent of *Lobster in Clevage Probe*.

photo: Tom Howard

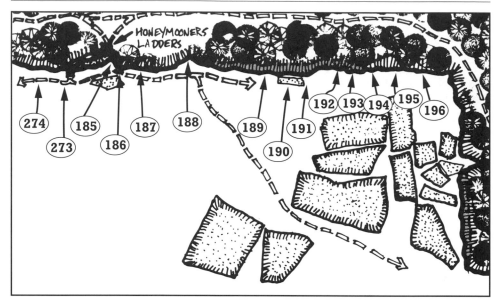

The next routes are listed in an upstream direction from the Honeymooners Ladder access point (see map).

THE HONEYMOONERS LADDERS

These ladders provide optimal access for routes located from midway along the Central Endless to the Nuttall Slab, which is located about halfway down the Wall of Points. Originally a 5.4 climb called The Honeymooners (FA: Andrew Barry and Suellen de Waard, July 1986), the first ladders were erected in the spring of 1989 using indigenous materials. As a result of a generous grant from The Access Fund and labor provided by numerous volunteer activists the original ladders were replaced with new ones in the summer of 1994. WARNING: USE THESE LADDERS AT YOUR OWN RISK OF INJURY OR DEATH! Use of them involves considerable exposure, particularly at the bottom of the chimney that connects the two ladders. In wet conditions the risk is increased. YOU ALONE ARE RESPONSIBLE FOR YOUR OWN SAFETY. Please be courteous to other climbers using them and wait until their ascent or descent is complete prior to beginning you own.

185   The Jackie Gleason Flake 5.9+ ☆

Just right of the lower ladder is a wide crack in a left-facing corner. Follow it to the top. 75 feet. FA: Buddy Brazington, et al. 1989.

186   Muckraker 5.11a ☆☆☆ 🄿

Artfully intricate, this climb is deservingly popular and considerably cleaner than the name implies. Start on the left side of the arête and follow the line of bolts up the blunt prow to a station at the top. 80 feet. FA: Doug Cosby & Phil Olnick, October 1989.

187   Perserverence 5.10a/b
Start about ten feet right of *Muckraker* and climb the face past two bolts to stance, then ramble directly to the top. 75 feet. FA: George Powell, Bill McCray, Dawn Parr, & John Burcham, May 1990.

188   Wire Train 5.10c ☆☆☆
This exceptional flake system will keep you chugging all the way. Begin in the obvious right-facing corner and follow the right-leaning flake to its end. Angle up and right to gain a left-facing flake and follow it to the top. 80 feet. FA: Doug Reed & Maurice Reed, October 1985.

189   Stink Bug 5.12c
Begin near the right side of the low roof and pull it, following the line of bolts to cold shuts. 70 feet. FA: Doug Reed, fall 1993.

190   Free Flow 5.11c/d ☆☆
Begin from boulder in the center of the low roof and pull onto the slightly overhanging wall, then follow the line of seven bolts to a cold-shut station. 75 feet. FA: Doug Reed, May 1990.

191   Channel Zero 5.11c ☆☆
Dial up just right of the previous route and pull the roof, then surf the up the face past six bolts to a cold-shut station. 75 feet. FA: Doug Reed, spring 1993.

192   Motor King 5.11d ☆
Begin near the right edge of the roof and pull a low roof to gain a short, right-facing dihedral capped by a roof, then traverse left and continue up the face to the top. 75 feet. FA: Doug Reed, spring 1993.

193   I Feel Like a Wog 5.12b
Bercaw's characterization of how he felt after groveling up this lichen covered face on the first ascent. And though climber traffic has since cleaned up the route a bit, the question remains: What's a wog? Start around the corner from *Double Flat* and crank past a bolt to a narrow roof which is pulled past a second bolt to gain a groove. Continue past a pin, then trend left over a second roof and follow the face directly to the top. 70 feet. Note: Bring TCUs and small Friends. Shares the finish with *Double Flat*. FA: John Bercaw & Craig Miller, December 1988.

194   Double Flat 5.9 ☆
Start on the face left of the roof-capped dihedral (*Walking on the Moon*) from a ledge short and climb the bolt-protected face to a station. 60 feet. FA: Doug Reed, spring 1993.

195   Walking on the Moon 5.11a
Begin in the roof-capped dihedral and climb to the roof, then move out the right wall to the roof's end. Step right and follow the easy cracks to the top. 70 feet. FA: Monty Reagan, Bruce Burgess, & Jeff Laushey, October 1985.

Jon Wilson on the *Legacy*.

photo: Tom Isaacson

Doug Reed on the *Racist* in 1989.

photo: Peter Noebels

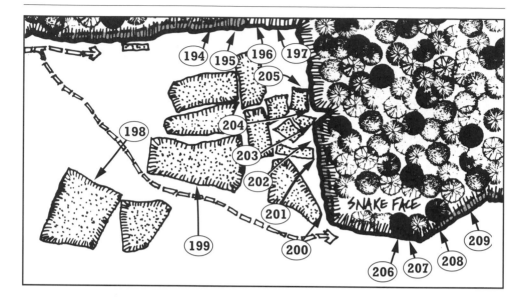

196   Walking on the Moon Direct Start—Moonraker 5.7+ ☆
Start around the corner from the *Walking on the Moon* roof and move up and left
to the start of the obvious cracks which are followed to the top. 70 feet. FA: Mark
Van Cura & Carl Samples, November 1988.

197   Off Like a Prom Dress 5.10d ☆
Begin just right of the previous route and climb directly up the face past two
bolts to the top. 70 feet. Note: Carry a rack of small to medium camming units
and wires. FA: Frank Orthel, Neil Ofsthun, & Mike Stewart, November 1990.

Returning to *Perserverence* the trail descends toward the river, then angles
upstream between two large boulders. The next route is on the triangular face
of the right-hand boulder.

198   Bouldergiest 5.12b
Climb the line of bolts to a cold-shut station. 40 feet. FA: Doug Reed, April 1992.

199   I Advanced Masked 5.12b ☆
Begin below the obvious flake and climb the overhanging face up and left past
four bolts to rap slings. 40 feet. FA: Eric Hörst, August 1989.

Beyond *I Advanced Masked*, the trail rises to meet the main wall at the Snake
Face. The distinctive arête that defines the left edge of the wall is:

200   Favorite Challenge 5.11d ☆☆
If mixed routes are your bag, this could turn out to be one of your favorite
arêtes. Climb the arête and face on the right side past a pin and a bolt to the top.
85 feet. FA: Doug Reed, Eddie Begoon, and Mike Artz, October 1987.

201 The Racist 5.13b ☆☆☆☆ (bolt)
This tried-and-true area test piece will definitely discriminate against you if you're shorter than 6-feet tall. Start in the center of the overhanging pristine white face and step off the boulder below the first bolt following a complex sequence of pumping moves past eight more bolts to a station. 85 feet. FA: Doug Reed, May 1989.

202 Dial 911 5.13a ☆☆☆ (bolt)
More popular than MCI's Dime-A-Minute Deal. Climb the technical face just left of *The Racist* to cold shuts. 70 feet. FA: Doug Reed, summer 1991.

203 Mississippi Burning 5.12b ☆
Climb the bolted arête on the left side of the gaping chimney to a cold-shut station on the face below the final roof band. 70 feet. FA TR: Doug Reed & Rick Thompson, May 1989. FA: Doug Cosby & Jim Woodruff, June 1990.

204 Sugar Bubbas 5.11a ☆☆☆ (bolt)
This sweet little treat was one of the early Endless Wall sport routes. And sporty it is! Start on the left face of the wide chimney and climb up and left on the blunt arête past two bolts, a pin and two more bolts to a wild, top-out mantel. Lower from the *Harvest* anchors.65 feet. FA: Mike Artz, Eddie Begoon & Don Wood, October 1988.

205 Harvest 5.12a ☆ (bolt)
Start just left of *Sugar Bubbas* and follow the line of bolts to a cold-shut station on the ledge below the top. 65 feet. FA: Doug Reed, September 1992.

206 Snake Patrol 5.10c ☆
This contrived route snakes its way over a good portion of the face. Watch for rope drag. Start ten feet left of the arête and slither straight up until holds fizzle out, then traverse right to the arête. Make a few shared moves with *Razor Sharp*) up the arête, then traverse left to the start of a short, right-facing corner near the center of the face. Follow it to the base of a seam, then make a rising leftward traverse to the arête on the far side of the face which leads to the top. 110 feet. Note: Double ropes recommended. FA: Eddie Begoon & Mike Artz, July 1986.

207 Razor Sharp 5.11b ☆☆
Begin on the blunt arête and follow it to a small inside corner. Move slightly right, then back left to gain a ledge below a razor sharp flake that is followed to its end. Traverse along the top of it and finish directly up. 90 feet. FA: Andrew Barry & Doug Chapman, October 1985.

208 Discombobulated 5.11a ☆☆ (bolt)
Begin behind the mature oak and follow the line of eight bolts to cold shuts. 85 feet. FA: Doug Reed, April 1991.

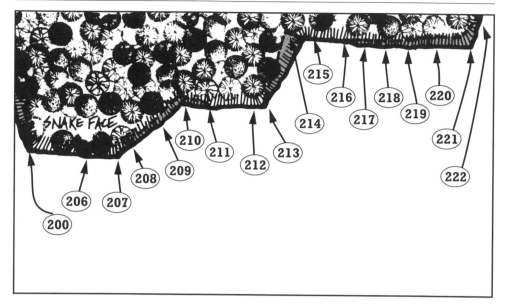

209   The Legacy 5.11b or 11d ☆☆☆☆ 🐝

Supremely popular. Start behind the oak and climb the face to the beginning of a right arching corner which leads to an overhang. There are two different finishes which can be used from here. The original involves stepping back left above the overhang on exposed terrain and continuing up and left to cold shuts (11d). The second and more popular finish moves up and right from the overhang to cold shuts (11b). 90 feet. WARNING: Both finishes require a 55 meter to get to the ground. FA: Doug Reed & Bob Rentka, July 1990.

210   Stolen Kisses 5.9+ ☆

Locate a large right-facing flake on the right-hand wall of the fractured inside corner and lieback it, then continue up the corner to the top. 100 feet. FA: Nick Brash, Wes Love & Bruce Burgin, October 1985.

211   Adam Ant 5.11a

Start 15 feet right of *Stolen Kisses* and boulder up on small flakes to gain a shallow ramp (same ramp as on *Rock Lobster*) and follow it up and left and mantel on a ledge. Continue up, then left to join *Stolen Kisses* at the finish. 85 feet. FA: Fletch Taylor & John Gill, February 1989.

212   Rock Lobster 5.10c ☆☆

An arduous route that will expose you to some superb rock. Begin at a right-facing flake near the arête (this is immediately left of *Bullet the New Sky*) and follow it to a small roof, then move left and follow a short ramp to its end. Climb straight up to a stance and traverse right along a thin horizontal until it's possible to move up to a bolt, then climb directly up to a large crack that is followed to the top. 100 feet. Note: Double ropes recommended. FA: Eddie Begoon & Mike Artz, August 1986.

213   Bullet the New Sky 5.12b ☆☆☆☆ 🄿
Big brother of Penitente Canyon's famed *Bullet the Blue Sky*, which was ironically also established by D'Antonio. If riding arêtes is your thing, you're in for a real treat. Begin five feet right of *Rock Lobster* and follow the line of bolts up the arête to a pair of cold shuts. 85 feet. Note: Keep your eyes open for a hunter's bullet that's imbedded in a horizontal just below the top. It was at least a partial impetus for the name. FA: Eric Hörst, Rick Thompson, Doug Reed, & Bob D'Antonio, May 1989.

214   S.T.A.N.C. 5.10b ☆☆☆
One of Nick Brash's finest off-widths, this domineering line is a classic of its genre. Follow the obvious, right-leaning off-width corner past a roof and continue to the top. 100 feet. FA: Nick Brash, Mac McNeese, & Wes Love, October 1985.

215   Bloodshot 5.13a ☆☆ 🄿
Begin a few paces right of the corner and follow the line of eight bolts to a pair of cold shuts. 85 feet. FA: Doug Reed, November 1994.

216   The Pocket Route 5.13a ☆☆☆ 🄿
The next line to the right is protected by nine bolts. 85 feet FA: Doug Reed, summer 1992.

217   Silent But Deadly 5.13a ☆☆ 🄿
Begin a few feet right of the previous route and crank the line of nine bolts to a cold-shut station. 85 feet. FA: Doug Reed, spring 1992.

218   Vulcan Block 5.12c ☆☆☆ 🄿
Commence from the stack of rocks and follow clips along a thin right-arching flake and past a roof to cold shuts. Nine bolts in all. 90 feet. Note: Someone recently removed the starter blocks. FA: Doug Reed, fall 1991.

219   Shovel Jerk 5.13b ☆ 🄿
A short distance to the right is a line of eight bolts, which lead to cold shuts. 85 feet. FA: Doug Reed, 1993.

220   Dissonance 5.13a ☆☆☆ 🄿
This noteworthy route was the first of many 5.13's Doug Reed has established at the New. If you're shorter than 6-feet tall, the crux on this one could leave you with a feeling of utter discord. Start about 15 feet left of the arête and power past the roof start following a line of eight bolts and a pin to the top. 80 feet. FA: Doug Reed, May 1988.

221   New World Order 5.12a ☆☆☆
**   aka Masoko Tango** 🄿
Start on the left side of the arête and climb the line of seven clips directly to a pair of cold shuts. 85 feet. FA: Eric Hörst, July 1989.

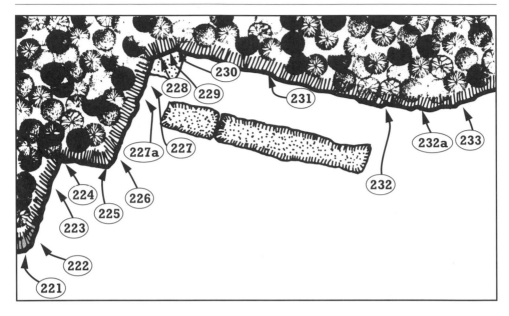

222   Unnamed 5.11c ☆ ⌒

On the right side of the arête is a five-bolt route that ends at a single cold shut. 50 feet. FA: Doug Reed, 1992.

223   New Speedway Boogie 5.10d

Begin about 15 feet left of *Gang Bang* and follow a short, left-facing flake to a crack in a tiny right-facing corner, then continue up the crack until it ends and wander up the face to the top. 85 feet. FA: Jon Regelbrugge & Andrew Barry, November 1985.

224   Gang Bang 5.9 ☆

The first ascent party was short on big gear so Brash, in his typical style, ran it out to the top. Follow the off-width corner-crack past a claustrophobic squeeze to the top. 75 feet. Note: Bring large gear. FA: Nick Brash, Wes Love, Tom Howard, Bruce Burgin, & Rick Thompson, October 1985.

225   Do the Funky Evan 5.10d R ☆☆☆

An Australian rock ritual. Begin directly below the gorgeous arête and climb up to a stance atop a right-facing flake, then continue directly up the left side of the arête past a bolt, a pin, a bolt and a runout to the top. 85 feet. FA: Andrew Barry, Mike Artz, & Eddie Begoon, July 1986.

226   Martini Face 5.12c ☆☆☆ ⌒

Not exactly straight up or on the rocks, this high potency route packs a punch. Begin just right of *Do the Funky Evan* and crank past a low roof to a bolt, then continue up the weaving path past six more bolts finishing up and right to the top. 80 feet. Note: No top anchors. FA: Doug Reed, March 1989.

227 Translate Slowly 5.10c R ☆
The unprotected start will most likely translate into a limited number of ascents. Start just left of the block in the corner and follow dicey face moves up and left to a ledge, then jamb the strenuous crack up and right to the top. 75 feet. FA: Maurice Reed & Doug Reed, October 1985.

227a Translate Slowly Direct Start 5.11a R
Begin about 10 feet left of the normal start and climb directly up the unprotected face to the ledge. FA: Phil Heller & Andrew Barry, April 1986.

228 What a Jamb 5.9+ ☆
Recommended for the handcrack aficionado. Jam your way up the left side of the huge flake to a stance below a roof, then move up and left through the roof to the top. 65 feet. FA: Nick Brash & Bruce Burgin, September 1985.

229 Lobster in Cleavage Probe 5.10a ☆☆
Aesthetic stems and laybacks will greet you on this sustained pitch. The center of the twin-sided flake is split by a thin left-facing flake. Claw your way up the thin flake until it peters out and continue up the center of the face past a bulge, then step up and right to a tree (joins *Pink Eye* here) and either rappel or slog up the grunge to the top. 65 feet. FA: Rick Thompson & Tom Howard, October 1985.

230 Pink Eye 5.8
Step off the right edge of the block and follow the right side of the twin-sided flake to the top. 65 feet. Note: It may by desirable to rappel from the tree about 20 feet below the top to avoid the grungy finish. FA: Jeff Laushey & Bruce Burgess, October 1985.

231 Night Gallery 5.10b ☆☆
The first ascent party finished this route as the shrouds of darkness were closing in. Recently upgraded. Follow the conspicuous crack system to the top. 75 feet. FA: Jim Okel, Dan Perry, & Tom Howard, October 1981.

232 Sneak Preview 5.10b ☆
Start 20 feet right of *Night Gallery*, just right of a small left-facing corner and climb up to a ledge, then step right to a thin crack behind a tree. Climb the crack to a left-facing flake, then wander up the face to the top. 80 feet. FA: Doug Chapman, October 1985.

232a Sneak Preview Variation Start - Ray-Hauls Redemption Round 5.9 R
Begin about 20 feet right of the normal start and climb directly up the unprotected face to the ledge. Finish as normal. Note: The 5.9 grade only applies to the start. The upper face involves 5.10 climbing. FA: Fletch Taylor & John Gill, December 1988.

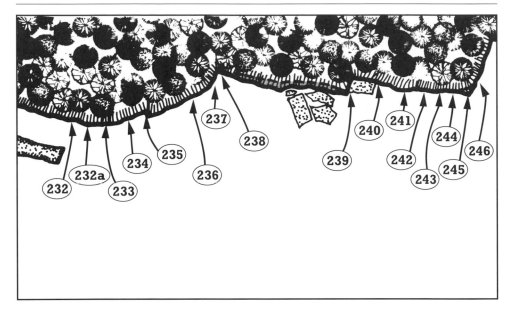

233 Drug Virgin 5.11d 🄿

Start just left of *Cosmic Thing*, on the left side of the tree and climb past three bolts to a ledge. Note: No cold shuts; rap from anchors around the tree. 40 feet. FA: Bob D'Antonio & Brian Mullin, May 1989.

234 Cosmic Thing 5.13b ☆ ℞

Begin immediately right of the tree and followed sustained climbing along the line of four bolts to a ledge. Rap from anchors around the tree. 40 feet. Note: bring a .5 Friend to protect the finishing moves. FA: Eric Hörst, October 1989.

235 Scream Seam 5.11a ☆ ℞

A screaming good little climb. Directly behind a tree is a flawless left-facing corner that is followed to a ledge. Step left and rap from anchors around the tree. 35 feet. FA: Doug Chapman & Jon Regelbrugge, October 1985.

236 Two Fish Limit 5.12a/b ☆ 🄿 ℞

Start 20 feet right of *Scream Seam* and follow the line of bolts to a station below the roof. 60 feet. FA: Eric Hörst & Rick Thompson, October 1989.

237 Monster in My Pants 5.10a

Fifteen feet left of *The Separator* is a short arête. Start on the left side and move past a low bolt to a good ledge, then continue up cracks in the left wall to the top. 75 feet. FA: Ed McCarthy & Carl Samples, June 1988.

238 The Separator 5.10a

Named for the shoulder separation Samples suffered on the first attempt to lead this route. Doing it as two pitches will reduce rope drag. Begin in the right-facing dihedral behind a mature beech tree and struggle past the tapering chimney to a roof. Move left and up to a ledge, then follow the crack in the center of the face to the top. 80 feet. FA: Ed McCarthy & Bob Rentka, July 1986.

239   In Real Life 5.12a ☆

Scramble up the corner described in *Amigo Bandito* to gain a ledge on the left and step over to an attractive arête. Climb the right side of the arête past three bolts until it's possible to step left to good holds and a ledge. 40 feet. Note: Bring a #0 TCU and #1 Friend. FA: Eddie Begoon & Mike Artz, May 1989.

240   Amigo Bandito 5.10a

Climb a short right-facing corner to its end, then step onto the right wall and follow a mankey finger crack to the top. 75 feet. FA: Jeff Laushey & Bruce Burgess, October 1985.

241   Leave Me Bee 5.11c ☆

Start about 15 feet right of *Amigo Bandito* at a thin seam that is followed to its end, then continue up a wandering line of holds to the top. 80 feet. Note: Carry a light rack of HBs and nuts to medium size, three sets of # 0 and #1 TCUs and Friends to #2 1/2. FA: Mike Artz, Eddie Begoon, & Doug Reed, April 1989.

242   The Wasted Armenian 5.11c R ☆

Begin 15 feet left of *Sufficiently Wasted* by bouldering up and left, then back right to a bolt. Finger traverse along a narrow orange overhang, then past a second bolt and continue to top finishing just left of the *Sufficiently Wasted* crack. 95 feet. FA: Ward Smith, Chris Smith, & Dave Vartanian, November 1989.

243   Sufficiently Wasted 5.11a ☆☆

Hanging around too long on the initial crack will ensure this condition. Get started by climbing the crack in the orange face until it's possible to make a thin move left and mantel onto a ledge below the roof. Move left and follow a varying width crack to the top. 95 feet. FA: Jon Regelbrugge & Kenny Hummel, October 1985.

244   The Wasted Weeblewobble 5.10b ☆

Start five feet left of *Black Noise* at a thin crack, which is followed to a ledge, then step right and up staying just left of *Black Noise* to pass a small roof on the right. Continue up a crack and face to the top. 95 feet. FA: Jon Regelbrugge, Doug Chapman, & Andrew Barry, October 1985.

245   Black Noise 5.9+ ☆☆

Begin just left of the arête and boulder past the low roof on good horizontals, then climb directly up the face to a good ledge staying about eight feet left of the arête. Continue past a small overlap and a bulge, then follow a groove in the lower angle face to the top. 95 feet. FA: Andrew Barry, Jon Regelbrugge, & Doug Chapman, October 1985.

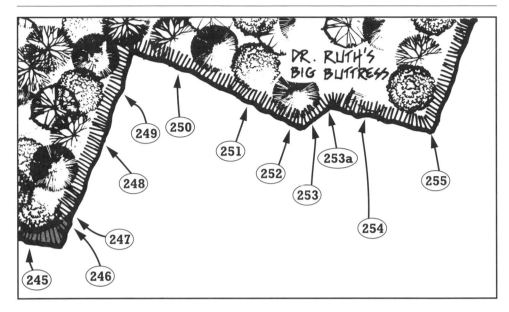

246 Technarête 5.10a ☆☆☆
Superior exposure, position and rock create a climb of impeccable character. Start just left of the tree below some left-facing overlaps and climb up and left under the overlaps, then layback to a small stance. Continue up and left on good horizontals and move around to the left side of the arête to reach a small ledge. Climb past a right-facing flake and step right above a roof to follow the right-facing flake to its end, then up the low angle arête to the top. 100 feet. FA: Rick Thompson & Mark Van Cura, July 1986.

247 Arms Control 5.11b ☆☆☆
Follow Technarête for first few moves, then climb straight up the face on the right side of the arête to a roof. Move right and continue up the overhanging face to the top. 90 feet. Note: Bring TCUs and keep your eyes peeled for a hidden HB placement. FA: Mike Johnson & Mike McCombs, May 1987.

248 Recondite 5.11b ☆☆☆☆
Steep and intricate, this classic line will test your imagination. Begin just right of the tree that grows midway along this face and climb up and slightly left on horizontals, then move right aiming for the start of a small left-facing corner. Climb the corner and short handcrack above and finish directly up the face to the top. 90 feet. FA: Andrew Barry, Jon Regelbrugge, & Doug Chapman, October 1985.

249 Power Source 5.12b ☆
Begin 20 feet uphill from Recondite near the right side of the face and climb up to a good horizontal then directly up to a pin. Continue up and right to the second pin, then up to a bolt. Finish up and right past a hidden pin to the top. 75 feet. Note: Small Friends and TCUs. FA: Eddie Begoon, October 1988.

250   Pride of Cucamunga   5.10d R

Tends to be filthy. Begin about 20 feet left of *The Diddler* and climb the obvious flared crack and knobby face directly to a large tree. 75 feet. FA: Dave Moore & Bill Bradshaw, June 1988.

251   Idiotsyncracies   5.11b ☆☆

Perfect protection with three fine cruxes. Start ten feet left of *The Diddler* and climb directly past a bolt to a ledge then continue past a pin and three bolts to the top. 80 feet. Note: Bring a light rack including small to medium camming units. FA: Rick Thompson, Bob D'Antonio, Eric Hörst & Brian Mullins, May 1989.

252   The Diddler   5.10a ☆☆☆

A big buttress classic that'll keep you entertained. Start on the left side of the arête and climb straight up to a ledge, then continue up the left side of the blunt arête past a hidden pin to a good horizontal. Move around to the right side of the arête and finish directly to the top. 85 feet. FA: Dave Sippel & Rick Thompson, July 1986.

253   The Grafenberg Crack 5.9- ☆☆☆

This sensual line will hit the spot. Start five feet left of the prominent dihedral and jam the handcrack to its end at a ledge, then finesse up and right to gain a layback flake. Follow the flake to its end, then step left and up the easy face to the top. 85 feet. FA: Tom Howard & Rick Thompson, October 1985.

253a The Grafenberg Crack Direct Start—Dr. Ruth's Variation
5.8 ☆☆☆

An excellent start that lowers the overall difficulty of the route. Begin just right of the normal start and climb the right-facing dihedral to its end and move onto the right face past a couple horizontals, then back left to link up with the normal route at the start of the flake. FA: Mark Van Cura & Rick Thompson, July 1986.

254   Between Coming and Going 5.10c ☆

Begin by climbing the thin crack between *The Grafenberg Crack* and *Insertum Outcome* to its end, then continue directly up the center of the face past a bulge. Climb past a small right-facing corner to a tiny roof, then step left and finish on *The Grafenberg Crack.* 80 feet. FA: Lynn Hill & Rick Thompson, April 1988.

255   Insertum Outcome 5.10b ☆☆

This thought-provoking route sports an unique finish. Begin on the right side of the arête and follow thin cracks to a small roof. Pull the roof on the left side and continue up cracks and laybacks to a good stance below a narrow, blank face that bisects the arête. Devious moves lead directly to a ledge, then finish on the easy arête to the top. 85 feet. Note: Be sure to carry a couple small TCUs. FA: Rick Thompson, Mark Van Cura, & Bob Rentka, July 1986.

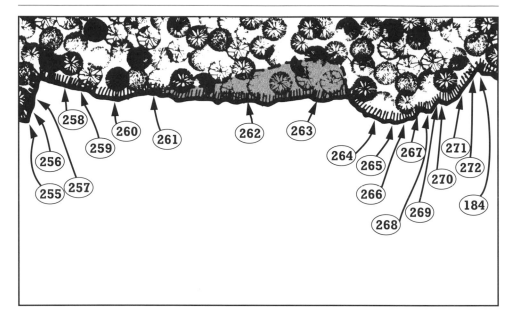

256   Giant Steps 5.11d ☆
Start a short distance right of the previous route and follow the line of bolts up the slabby face to the top. 70 feet. FA: Danny Caldwell, September 1990.

257   Crystal Vision 5.10a R ☆
Elegant face climbing with a touch of poor pro. Begin climbing 15 feet left of the inside corner at a clean streak and ascend a direct line to the top. 70 feet. FA: Eddie Begoon, Mike Artz, & Stanley Todd, July 1986.

258   Bad Head of Lettuce 5.10a
Start beneath a small roof and climb up to a shallow, right-facing corner and a bolt. Continue up the corner moving left at its end (bolt) and up the face past the third bolt to the top. 65 feet. FA: Frank Orthel & Mike Stewart, August 1990.

259   Closer to the Heart 5.9+
Begin directly below a prominent right-arching corner and climb straight up to its start, then face climb just right of the corner moving up and right to an arête that is followed to the top. 70 feet. FA: Mike Artz, Eddie Begoon, & Stanley Todd, July 1986.

260   The Growing Hole 5.12a ☆☆ 🔗
Climb the line of bolts up the blunt arête to a cold-shut station. 70 feet. FA: Doug Reed & Greg Phillips, April 1990.

261   Celluloid Vipers 5.9+
At the left end of the huge roof is a short right-facing dihedral that is climbed past a roof, then follow an off-width crack to the top. 75 feet. FA: Mike Cote & Mike Artz, October 1985.

262 Titan's Dice 5.13b ☆☆ 🎣

Start about 30 feet right of the previous route and crank the awkward and powerful moves out the left-angling roof crack to cold shuts. 65 feet. FA: Doug Reed, 1991.

263 Permission Granted 5.10a ☆

A roof of gargantuan proportion that turns out to be much easier than it first appears. P1: In the back corner below the 40-foot roof is a dihedral that leads to the roof. Face climb and undercling right using the roof crack for protection until you reach its end and set up a hanging belay in the handcrack above the lip. 60 feet. P2: Continue up the crack to a small roof and step left to a ledge. Move left 30 feet to an established rappel (pins). 40 feet. FA: Mike Artz & Mike Cote, October 1985.

263a Permission Granted Direct Finish 5.10b ☆

P2: Instead of traversing left to the anchors, continue up the headwall over a small roof to the top. 65 feet. FA: Mike Eviston & Chris Schmich, October 1991.

264 Virgin Thing 5.12a ☆ 🎣

Begin just left of the arête and follow the line of bolts past a distinct roof crack near the top to a station. 85 feet. FA: Kevin Rock & Brian McCray, 1992.

265 The Stick 5.11d ☆ 🎣

Start at a low roof on the right side of the arête and follow the line of clips up the arête and headwall to a pair of cold shuts. 95 feet. WARNING: A 55-meter rope is required! FA: Doug Reed & Rick Thompson, March 1989.

266 Blackhappy 5.12b ☆☆☆☆ 🎣

An undisputed Endless Wall winner. Begin just left of *Black and Tan* and follow the line of bolts to a cold-shut station. 85 feet. FA: Doug Reed, 1993.

267 Black and Tan 5.10a ☆☆☆☆

Hyperclassic!. Just left of *Doce Doe* is an immaculate, right-facing orange and black corner. Follow elegant laybacks and stems up the corner until just below the roof and angle up and right across the face. Climb past a small roof to the top. 85 feet. FA: Rich Pleiss & Ron Augustino, September 1985.

268 Aesthetica 5.11c ☆☆☆☆ 🎣

Impeccable rock, impeccable moves, an all star event. Start 12 feet right of *Black and Tan* and follow the line of bolts to a cold-shut station. 85 feet. FA: Doug Reed & Rick Thompson, October 1988.

269 Erotica 5.12a ☆☆ 🎣

Start by climbing the first part of *Doce Doe* then move onto the left wall and follow the line of bolts over an stimulating roof to a cold-shut station at the top. 85 feet. FA: Doug Reed, 1991.

270   Doce Doe 5.9 ☆

Follow the right-ramping dihedral with a wide crack in it to its end and step right to a right-facing corner in an overhang. There are a pair of anchors here. Pull through the first overhang then past a second to the top. 100 feet. Note: If done to the anchors the route is 5.7. FA: Tom Howard, Bill Newman & Bruce Burgin, October 1981.

271   Veil of Addiction 5.10d ☆

The first half of this route was done by Doug Chapman in 1987 as a variation start to *Men Under Water*. Unaware of the previous ascent, Begoon established this more direct line nearly three years later. Begin a short distance right of the arête and climb straight up past a bolt and a seam to a hueco. Continue up past a second bolt to the station on *Doce Doe*. 75 feet. FA: Eddie Begoon, Howard Clark, Amy Riopel, & Doug Houghton, March 1990.

272   Men Under Water 5.10a ☆

Begin ten feet left of *Pink Pooka Party* (the last route that was previously described in a down stream direction) and climb the low angle face to the left side of a flake which is followed to its end. Step left about ten feet and follow pockets directly past a bolt to a ledge. Finish on *Doce Doe* or rap from the station. 80 feet. FA: Doug Chapman & Darlene Allison, October 1987.

Men Under Water is the last route described in an upstream direction from the Honeymooner's Ladders access point. Returning to the Honeymooner's Ladders the routes are now described in a downstream direction.

Mark Van Cura on the 5.7 classic *Crescent Moon.*

photo: Carl Samples

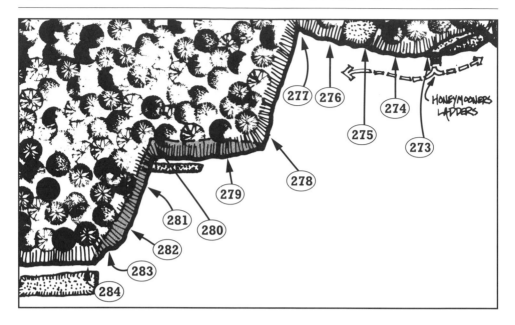

273 Sooner or Ladder 5.11b

This route begins from the tree at the top of the lower Honeymooners Ladder and therefore can cause quite a traffic snarl on busy days. Follow the line of five bolts to a cold-shut station. 45 feet. FA: Jack Beatty & Doug Cosby, 1990.

274 The Bonemaster Gear Fling 5.11b/c ☆☆

Or was it a Honemaster Gear Sling? Start a few paces left of the ladder and follow the line of bolts past a perplexing crux on the blunt arête to cold shuts. 80 feet. FA: Carl Samples & Bob Rentka, March 1989.

275 Double Feature 5.11d ☆☆☆

This endlessly featured climb will make for an entertaining experience. Begin ten feet right of *Crescent Moon* and either stick clip or boulder up to the first bolt, then follow six more bolts to cold shuts. 80 feet. FA: Rick Thompson, Ron Kampas, Doug Reed, & Bob D'Antonio, May 1989.

276 Crescent Moon 5.7 ☆☆☆☆

The New's classic offwidth of its grade. Bring a selection of large gear. Locate the beautiful, left-arching off-width that lies just to the right of the *Lunar Debris* dihedral and follow it to the top. 70 feet. FA: Mike Artz, Stanley Todd, & Eddie Begoon, July 1986.

277 Lunar Debris 5.9 ☆☆

An off-width of inter-stellar proportions! Jam, layback, and improvise your way up the off-width corner to the top. 70 feet. FA: Eddie Begoon, Stanley Todd, & Mike Artz, July 1986.

278   The Rabbit Almost Died   5.12a ☆☆

Hop on the arête and climb past a bolt, then continue up until its possible to move right to a second bolt. Climb directly to the third bolt and make hard moves left to reach good holds and a stance above. Finish straight up the crack or climb the face just left of it to the top. 90 feet. FA: Doug Reed, Eddie Begoon, & Mike Artz, April 1989.

279   Rainy Day Route   5.12b ☆☆ 🄿 ⌒

Follow the shallow corner to the roof and skirt to the left. Pull the roof and solve the tricky finishing moves to reach the anchor. 65 feet. FA: Doug Reed, 1992.

279a Rainy Day Route Variation Finish-Big Boss Man   5.12d 🄿 ⌒

Follow the regular route to the roof and pull it directly. Lowering from the last two bolts. 60 feet. Note: No anchors. FA: Doug Reed, 1992.

280   Crimes of Fashion   5.10c ☆☆

Don't let this route's menacing appearance intimidate you. Begin in the brilliant orange right-facing corner and follow the wide crack to a massive roof. Traverse left to the roof's end and climb the corner above until it's possible to exit left to the top. 100 feet. Note: Double ropes will help you avoid rope drag. FA: Mike Artz & Andrew Barry, October 1985.

281   Quinsana Plus   5.13a ☆☆☆☆ 🄿

This magical looking route may be the New River's most popular 5.13. Start immediately left of the block and follow the line of bolts up the tiger-striped, overhanging face to cold shuts below the final roof. 80 feet. FA: Doug Reed, April 1990.

282   Noelle   5.12c R ☆☆☆

Although spectacular, this intimidating line rarely gets done due to the dicey gear. Start a short distance left of *Quinsana Plus*, in a left-facing corner, and follow it to a bolt at a roof. Pull into an overhanging left-facing corner which leads to the face above, then diagonal up and right to gain a mantel under roof. Traverse to the left edge of the roof and climb face above topping out under a small pine. 90 feet. Note: Bring a selection of small to medium camming units and stoppers. FA: Jim Damon & Mick Avery, November 1988.

283   Satanic Verses   5.13b/c ☆☆☆ 🄿

Fiendishly fine! Start a few feet left of *Noelle* and climb directly up the face, then out the diabolically overhung stretch of rock to join *Get Thee Behind Me Satan*, which is climbed to its normal finish at cold shuts. 85 feet. FA: Doug Reed, spring 1993.

Jim Taylor engaged at the crux of *Jesus and Tequila.*

photo: Carl Samples

Porter Jarrard on *Libertine.*

photo: Carl Samples

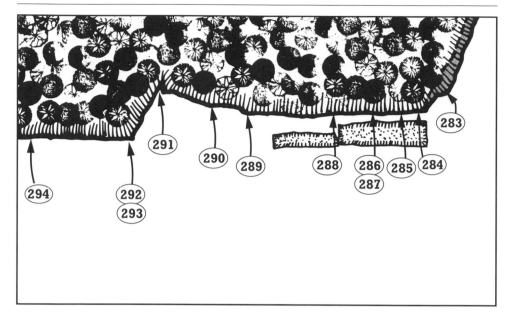

284 Jesus and Tequila 5.12b ☆☆☆☆ 📖

You couldn't pray for a finer climb. Most parties start by stick clipping the first bolt and stepping off the block. Follow the line of bolts past a sobering crux to a cold-shut station. 85 feet. Note: Originally done with some fixed wires protecting the initial arête, it finished at a rap station below the final roof. It was retrobolted after Woodward added the finish. FA: To the original station by John Scott & Dave Groth, May 1988. FA: Complete route by Jonny Woodward, April 1989.

284a Jesus and Tequila Variation Finish—Get Thee Behind Me Satan 5.13a/b ☆☆ 📖

Don't look back. Climb *Jesus and Tequila* to the fourth bolt and continue to the right on very exposed ground to reach the far side of the arête. Finish directly up the face on the right side of arête to cold shuts. 95 feet. Note: Two ropes recommended. FA: Porter Jarrard, May 1990.

285 Sacrilege 5.12b ☆☆☆☆ 📖

This was the first sport route on the Endless Wall, and a brilliant one at that! The tenuous crux has seen the demise of many a redpoint. Start from the block just left of *Jesus and Tequila* with a stick clip and follow the line of fixed gear to cold shuts at the top. 85 feet. FA: Doug Reed & Porter Jarrard, August 1988.

286 Libertine 5.13a ☆☆☆ 📖

Another on the morally unrestrained theme. Begin a few paces left of the previous route with a stick clip and follow the right-hand line of bolts to a cold-shut station. 80 feet. FA: Porter Jarrard, April 1990.

287   Oblivion 5.12d ☆☆ ⓟ
Climb *Libertine* until it's possible to diverge leftward, following a line of bolts to the cold-shut station which is shared with *Libertine*. 80 feet. FA: Porter Jarrard, April 1990.

288   Harlequin 5.12b ☆☆☆ ⓟ
Websters defines it as a conventional buffoon of the commedia. Climbers will most likely define it as seriously big fun. Start ten feet right of *Staticline*, in front of a tree, and follow the line of fixed gear up and right to a cold-shut station. 85 feet. FA: Doug Reed, July 1989.

289   Staticline 5.11d ☆
Begin a few feet right of *Open Mouths*, at the blunt arête, and boulder up to a bolt, then aim directly past two more bolts and a pin. Finish on the last section of *Open Mouths*. 85 feet. Note: Carry medium wires and a .5 TCU for the top. It's possible to climb the first ten feet of *Open Mouths* and traverse right to the first bolt, thus avoiding the crux. FA: John Scott & Dave Groth, May 1988.

290   Open Mouths 5.11a ☆
Begin about 20 feet right of the distinct off-width dihedral (*Southern Hospitality*) at a shallow corner and follow a thin right-facing flake to its end. Move up past a bulge to a stance on the left, then climb the blank-looking face to reach an overlap. Follow the overlap to its end then directly to the top. 85 feet. Note: Small camming units will help protect the face below the overlap. FA: Andrew Barry, Doug Chapman & Tom Howard, October 1985.

291   Southern Hospitality 5.10a ☆
A cordial West Virginia welcome to off-widths. Climb the off-width right-facing dihedral to the top. 90 feet. FA: Dick Ramsey, April 1990.

292   Struck by Lichening 5.11d ☆☆
This deceptive line boasts an adequate dose of adventure. Shares the start with *Brass Monkey*. Begin on the left side of the arête with a stick clip and crank up and left to a right-facing corner. Make a right-rising traverse after the first bolt, then up the right margin of the face (hidden TCU slots) to an orange bulge. Continue past two bolts and the crux finishing up the easy crack to the top. 90 feet. FA: Rick Thompson & Carl Samples, April 1990.

293   Brass Monkey 5.10b R ☆☆☆
Unfortunately the popularity of this high quality route is overshadowed by the serious runout below the ledge. From the same start as *Struck by Lichening* continue directly past the bolt to the corner's end. Rail left a short distance and head directly for the ledge. Step left and follow the splendid right-arching corner to the top. 85 feet. Note: Bring a mixed rack with plenty of TCUs. FA: Eddie Begoon & Howard Clark, February 1989.

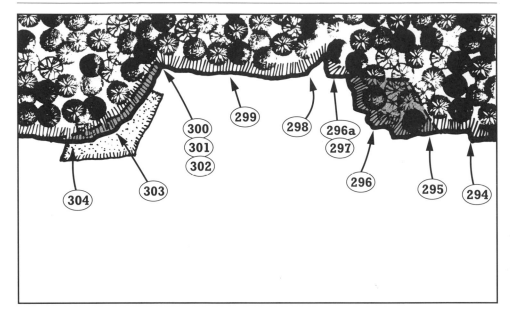

294 The Height of Flashin' 5.11b/c ☆☆☆
A multi-cruxed, action packed route on high grade sandstone. Start at the left edge of the face below an arête undercut by a low roof. Stick clip first bolt and improvise awkward moves over the roof to gain the arête. Climb up, then right to a good stance, then move directly up the dicey slab to the ledge. Follow a line of bolts to the top. 95 feet. Note: Carry a light rack of camming units. FA: Stuart Pregnall & Ron Kampas, April 1990.

295 Can't Find My Guernsey Cow 5.12b ☆☆
Tailored for the all you bovine aficionados. Begin right of *Nestle Krunch Roof* at a short crack. Get a good Friend as high as you can in the crack, then traverse right past a bolt and up to reach the arête. Climb the arête (bolts), then move up and right past three more bolts to a ledge. Step left and up to a pin and aim directly for the top. 95 feet. Note: Bring Friends, TCUs, and small stoppers. FA: Eddie Begoon & Mike Artz, April 1989.

296 Nestle Krunch Roof 5.10c ☆☆☆
Schweeeeter than candy! Two short, select pitches add up to an Endless Wall extravaganza. P1: Start in a left-facing corner under the huge roof and climb up to a small roof. Traverse left to the honker ear and pull the cumbersome flare moving up to the ceiling. Make a tricky leftward traverse to reach the end of the roof, then pull into the left-facing corner (the *Direct Start* joins here.) and set up a hanging belay. 55 feet. P2: Follow the pleasant corner to the top. 50 feet. Note: Double ropes are helpful in avoiding rope drag on the first pitch. FA: Mike Cote, Mike Artz, & Rick Thompson, October 1985.

296a Nestle Krunch Roof Direct Start 5.10a ☆☆
Begin on the right side of the chimney and climb directly up the face past two

bolts to reach the left-facing dihedral, which is the start of the second pitch. Follow the dihedral to the top. FA: Doug Reed & Bob Rentka, May 1990.

297 Voyeur's Hand 5.12c ☆ 𝄞

Do the *Nestle Krunch Roof Direct Start* and make a couple moves up the dihedral, then traverse right along horizontals to reach the center of the hanging face. Finish directly to anchors at the top. 85 feet. FA: Doug Reed & Bob Rentka, May 1990.

298 The Glass Onion 5.10b ☆☆ 𝄞

This popular outing has some unique holds. Scramble a few feet up the chimney and move to a ledge on the left wall. Follow the line of five bolts to a cold-shut station. 75 feet. FA: Angie McGinnus, fall 1994.

299 Dust Bowl 5.10a R

Begin about 30 feet right of *The Frictional Heat Experiment* and climb up to a hanging finger crack which is followed to its end. Step left and continue straight up to a small pine (you are now run out and about to get a lot more so). Move slightly right, then head for the top through the fields of lichen on lower angled rock and rounded holds. Sounds like fun. 95 feet. FA: Eddie Begoon & Howard Clark, February 1989.

300 The Frictional Heat Experiment 5.10a

One of those slow grinds. Begin under the roof and boulder up a short face to reach the wide roof crack. Grunt and undercling to the right, then follow the off-width right-facing dihedral to the top. 100 feet. Note: Originally done as a trad route, the two bolts that protect the start were added when *Hell Bound for Glory* was put up. FA: Rick Thompson & Scott Garso, April 1986.

301 Hell Bound for Glory 5.12a ☆☆☆ 𝄞

More like hell bound for exposure. Follow the *Frictional Heat Experiment* past the roof, then step onto the left-hand wall and follow the line of bolts leftward to a very exposed position. Power directly up the line of bolts to a cold-shut station at the top. 85 feet. FA: Doug Cosby & Jim Woodruff, May 1990.

302 Clean Sweep 5.12c ☆ 𝄞

Follow *Hell Bound for Glory* to the third bolt and continue leftward, then directly up, following a line of six more bolts to a cold-shut station. 85 feet. FA: Doug Cosby, September 1990.

303 Maximum Leader 5.12c ☆☆ 𝄞

Begin atop the large block, under the low roof. Stick clip the first bolt and crank directly up the line of nine more bolts to cold shuts. 85 feet. FA: Doug Cosby, May 1990.

304 Project—In Progress

Line of bolts on the right edge of the face.

Doug Reed reaching for a crimp on the first ascent of *Voyeurs Hand.*

photo: Carl Samples

Mike Artz on an early ascent of *Leave it to Jesus.*

photo: Carl Samples

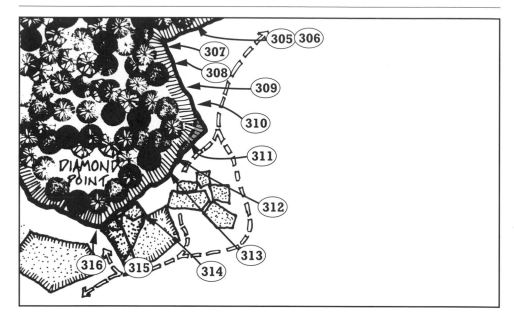

305   Hog Wollor 5.10d ☆☆
Begin right of the corner and climb the face aiming for a crack that splits the roof and face above. At the end of the crack step left to a flake and follow it to the top. 90 feet. FA: Eddie Begoon & Mike Artz, August 1988.

306   Luck of the Draw 5.11c/d ☆☆ 🄲
With a really, really long stick you can clip the first bolt and make this a sport climb. Otherwise you'll need gear or some big cojones for the start. Climb the initial moves of *Hog Wollor*, then follow the line of five bolts to a station. 80 feet. FA: Doug Cosby & J.P. Ginchereau, July 1990.

307   Strange Duck 5.11c ☆
Begin about 15 feet left of the dihedral and climb up to a good horizontal at the base of the right-facing corner. Continue up until it's possible to traverse right to reach a pin. Power straight up passing a hard-to-see pin and a bolt enroute to the top. 90 feet. FA: Eddie Begoon & Mike Artz, August 1988.

308   The Dark Side 5.11c ☆☆ 🄲
Start about 15 feet left of *Strange Duck* and follow the line of bolts to an anchor. 80 feet. FA: Doug Cosby, July 1990.

309   Leave It to Jesus 5.11d ☆☆☆☆
Glory Hallelujah! Considered by many to be the finest finger crack in the gorge. Jam and layback the dream-like splitter crack to its end at a narrow roof band, then hand traverse left to reach a ledge on the arête. Move around to the left side of the arête and follow the moderate but runout face to the top. 110 feet. Note: Most parties lower from the station on the ledge (station for *The Gift of Grace*). Double ropes are recommended if you're going to top out via the original line of ascent. FA: Cal Swoager & Stuart Kuperstock, October 1985.

309a Leave It to Jesus Direct Finish 5.11d ☆☆☆☆
For the true directissima tack on this finish. From the end of the finger crack move left a short distance, then pull the roof and follow the right-facing corner to the top. 95 feet. Note: The finish in-of-itself is 11b. FA: Jonny Woodward & Rich Gottleib, November 1988.

310   The Gift of Grace 5.12b ☆☆☆☆ 🄿
A divine arête, but be prepared for some sporty climbing. Begin just left of *Leave It to Jesus* by stick clipping the first bolt. Power along the edge of the roof then pull past the bolt to a stance above the lip. Continue up line of bolts on right side of arête to a station at the ledge. 75 feet. FA: Eric Hörst, Bob Rentka, Carl Samples, & Phil Olnick, November 1989.

311   Stupendid Animation 5.11b/c ☆☆☆
A mixed bag, both in terms of gear and variety of moves. Start about 15 feet right of *Ovine Seduction*, where the left margin of the low roof meets the ground and stick clip the first bolt. Climb directly past the bolt, then angle up and right past a second bolt and the crux until it's possible to move up to a good horizontal. Angle up and right past the third bolt, then directly up the face past more Friend placements and two more bolts to the top. 100 feet. Note: Bring a selection of small to medium Friends and TCUs. FA: Rick Thompson, Eric Hörst, & Carl Samples, November 1989.

312   How Hard Is That Thang? 5.12b/c ☆☆☆ 🄿
A question I've heard so many times. Begin ten feet right of *Ovine Seduction* and follow five bolts through a technical bulge to a ledge (crosses *Ovine Seduction* here). Step up, then left following five more bolts up the dazzling blunt arête to a cold-shut station. 85 feet. FA: Rick Thompson & Eric Hörst, September 1990.

313   Ovine Seduction 5.11a ☆☆
Pump time! P1: Start at the broken, gently overhanging crack and jam it until you're forced to rail right to a good ledge and a belay. P2: Follow the right-leaning crack to its end and angle left to the top. 100 feet. FA: Mike Artz & Andrew Barry, October 1985.

314   Supersymmetry 5.7 ☆☆
Scramble to the spacious ledge (*Strike a Scowl* also starts here) and set up a belay. Step over to the wafer thin flake that forms the right edge of the face and follow it until it ends. Finish up the face past a small roof to the top. 75 feet. Note: Bring large gear. FA: Andrew Barry & Mike Artz, October 1985.

Scott Garso on *Raging Waters* in 1986.

photo: Rick Thompson

Rick Thompson on *The Weatherman's Thumb.*

photo: Carl Samples

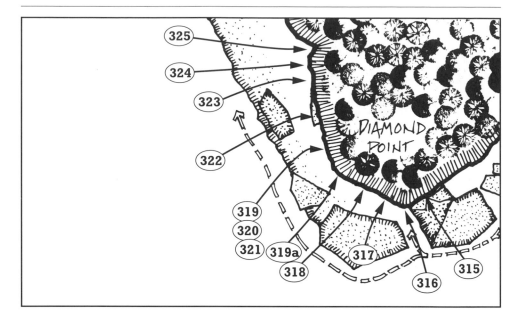

315 Strike a Scowl 5.10b ☆☆☆

You might say this route is too popular. Occasionally the scene of waiting lines. Originally established as a hair-raising 10d R trad route, it was mistakenly bolted by a party not aware of the previous ascent. Begoon agreed to "let it be." Start from the same ledge as the previous route and step atop a leaning block. Follow the line of bolts directly up the center of the face past a small roof to cold shuts. 75 feet. Note: The trad line started in the hairline crack just to the right of the bolted start. FA: Eddie Begoon & Kris Kline, May 1987.

316 Crack a Smile 5.10a ☆☆

Grin and bear it! Start just left of the block and jam the handcrack past a bulge. Enter the flared left-facing off-width corner and follow it to a ledge. Finish up the face of the leaning block. 90 feet. FA: Eddie Begoon & Glenn Thomas, September 1986.

317 Raging Waters 5.11a ☆☆☆☆

White water rules say don't get caught in the torrent! Begin just left of the previous route at a short, open corner and power past the bouldery crux to a stance. Continue up a short corner, then follow the spectacular left-facing flake until it forms a ledge. Finish directly up the face to the top. 90 feet. FA: Rick Thompson & Tom Howard, October 1985.

318 Fine Motor Control 5.12a ☆☆

A complimentary face route to the collection of Diamond Point cracks. Begin six feet left of Raging Waters and throttle up the initial bouldery face past two bolts to a stance. Continue up the line of bolts on good horizontals to a pair of cold shuts. 85 feet. FA: Eric Hörst & Bob Rentka, June 1989.

319   Can I Do It 'Til I Need Glasses? 5.10b ☆☆☆☆
This reputed gem is a Diamond Point favorite. Stay focused and keep your mind on the crack. P1: Using the same start as *Remission* climb up a few moves, then traverse right to the start of a gently overhanging finger crack. Follow strenuous moves up the crack for 25 feet or so until it's possible to hand traverse right to the base of a right-facing hanging dihedral. Set up a hanging belay. 50 feet. P2: Follow the beautiful corner to the top. 45 feet. Note: A direct start (5.11a) is possible by climbing the short flake/crack that lies directly below the main crack. FA: Rick Thompson & Mike Artz, October 1985.

319a Can I Do It....Variation - Straight Up and Stiff 5.10d ☆☆☆☆
A visionary direct finish that comes strenuously recommended. Climb the route as normal and continue straight up the crack past the hand traverse until the crack ends at a roof. Finish directly up the face. 90 feet. Note: It's also possible to move right at the roof and finish on the final part of the normal route. FA: Andrew Barry & Jon Regelbrugge, November 1985.

320   Durometer 64 5.10b ☆
Start by climbing the first 15 feet of *Remission*, then forge up the face above aiming directly for the top. 85 feet. Note: Rack up with lots of small Friends and TCUs. FA: Steve Bregman, John Eichenberger, Kenny Parker, & Jon Regelbrugge, June 1988.

321   Remission 5.10b ☆☆☆☆
Increasingly demanding moves lead to a crescendo on the final jams. Start at the right-hand end of a block and follow the beautiful leftward snaking crack to the top. 85 feet. FA: Mike Artz, Mike Cote, & Rick Thompson, October 1985.

322   Zygomatic 5.11c ☆
Established simultaneously with *Raging Waters*. Left of *Remission* is a shocking pink left-facing corner, capped by a roof. Begin by bouldering directly up to the start of corner, which is climbed until just below the roof. Move onto the right face and up a few moves, then back left above the roof following the crack and face to the top. 85 feet. FA: Maurice Reed & Doug Reed, October 1985.

323   The Weatherman's Thumb 5.13a ☆☆☆ 🄿
Dedicated to Eric Hörst, the weatherman. Don't TV meteorologists use their thumbs to click that remote control device that changes the forecast? Begin a few paces left of the corner on *Zygomatic* and follow the line of bolts to a pair of cold shuts. 85 feet. FA: Rick Thompson, Carl Samples, & Doug Reed, November 1994.

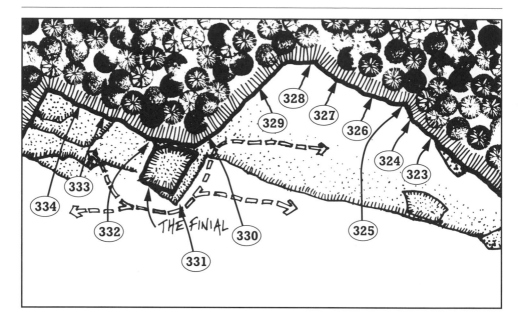

324 Homer Erectus 5.11b/c or 12a ☆☆☆ 🄿

Ancestral to Homer Simpson, this is one may be more popular than the TV show. Some major air has been logged going for the shuts. Begin a few feet right of *Carcus Tunnel Syndrome* and climb to a right-facing corner. Continue up the line of bolts until you reach the top of a right-facing overhanging flake (the 12a original version powers directly up here). Rail rightward along a good horizontal until it's possible to move up, then back left. Finish up and left to the cold shuts. 85 feet. FA: Rick Thompson & Michelle King, May 1992.

325 Carcus Tunnel Syndrome 5.8

Climb the ever-widening chimney system to the top. 85 feet. FA: Doug Reed, solo, May 1992.

326 This Sport Needs an Enema 5.12b/c ☆☆ 🄿

Some say that the current problems in climbing will take more than an enema to clean up. Begin about 15 feet left of *Carcus Tunnel Syndrome* and climb the face past two bolts, then directly up to a stance below a left-facing, overhanging flake. Follow bolts up the flake and short crack to a station below the roof that caps the top. 80 feet. FA: Eric Hörst & Rick Thompson, October 1989.

327 Bodyphobic 5.11c

Begin about 20 feet right of *The Diving Swan* at a short groove in the left side of a slabby face. Climb past a bolt, then right and up a steep white face to a ledge. Continue up a left-facing, curving flake to a bolt, then pull the roof and follow the face to the top. 85 feet. FA: Greg Collum, Rich Pleiss, Jim Nonemaker, & Ron Augustino, June 1988.

328   The Diving Swan 5.11a ☆☆
Named for the stylish dive performed by Mike Cote on the first ascent. Begin at the distinct orange and green right-facing flake and follow it to a roof. Move right and continue up a right-facing corner until an obvious traverse to the right is reached. A few moves right lead to a crack that splits a roof. Bazaar jams lead to the top. 75 feet. Note: The top tends to be a bit dirty. FA: Mike Cote & Mike Artz, October 1985.

329   The Ex-Puddition 5.11c ☆☆
From a small ledge just left of a grungy left-facing flake follow the sustained face past six bolts to a pair of cold shuts. 65 feet. Note: Some prefer to stick clip the first bolt. FA: Rick Thompson, Carl Samples, & Bob Rentka, April 1990.

330   The Nutcrafter Suite 5.10c ☆
A rock symphony celebrating the essence of traditional climbing: the craft of placing gear. Start just left of *The Ex-Puddition*, immediately right of the Finial chimney and move up and left to a left-facing flake. Climb the flake, then go left to a crack that leads to an easy dihedral and the top. 65 feet. FA: Carl Samples, Rick Thompson & Bob Rentka, April 1990.

331   Thought Crime 5.7 ☆
Begin from a ledge on the downhill side of the Finial and climb the right side of the arête until it's possible to traverse right below a small roof band to reach a crack in the center of the face. Follow the crack to the right shoulder of the pillar, then finish up and left to the top. Belay and rappel from cold shuts on the summit. 50 feet. FA: Rick Thompson & Glenn Thomas, April 1986.

331a Thought Crime Variation Finish—Stroke Victim 5.8 ☆
Instead of traversing right along the roof band, continue directly up the arête to the top of the pillar. FA: Mark Van Cura & Dave Sippel, June 1986.

332   Flying Sideways 5.9
Begin in the chimney on the left side of The Finial and climb awkwardly up until it's possible to follow a weakness that leads leftward and up. Continue up broken cracks to the top. 80 feet. Note: The first ascent was none in two pitches (to reduce rope drag) with a belay at the top of the initial chimney. FA: Howard Clark & Amy Riopel, March 1989.

333   Shudder Bugger 5.12b/c ☆☆ ◔
And when you smile for the camera.... Start 25 feet left of the Finial and scramble up to a ledge under the line of bolts. Stick clip, then crank directly up the seemingly endless array of slopers to cold shuts at the top. 65 feet. FA: Carl Samples, Rick Thompson, & Bob Rentka, September 1990.

Eric Hörst on *This Sport Needs an Enema.*

photo: Carl Samples

Kevin Rock on the fabulous finish of *Euro Nation*.

photo: Carl Samples

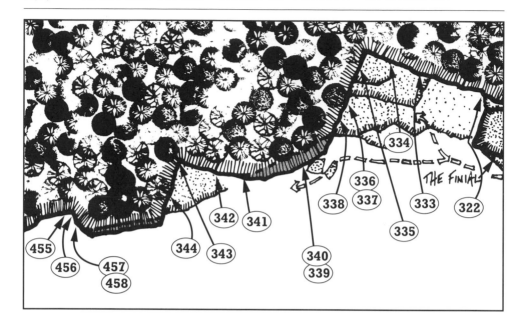

334 Thilly Puddy 5.10d ☆
Scramble to the same start as *Shudder Bugger*, then move leftward up the ramping corner until directly below a hanging handcrack. Climb the face to gain the short crack which is jammed to its end, then finish directly up. 50 feet. FA: Carl Samples, Bob Rentka & Jason Brookes, September 1988.

335 April Fools 5.11c
Scramble up the mossy slabs above the ledge to a platform of sorts and climb directly up the face past two welded cold shuts to the top. 50 feet. Note: Bring a light selection of camming units up to a #2½ Friend. FA: Eddie Begoon, April 1990.

336 The Ed Sullivan Show 5.11c ☆ 🖝
Start from the corner of the ledge and step onto the wall following the line of bolts up and slightly right to a pair of anchors at the top. 75 feet. Note: Prone to being scruffy. FA: Paul Sullivan, summer 1993.

337 The Stratowienie 5.11a R ☆
Honoring the namesake feature one must honk on when doing this committing line. Begin from the same start as the previous route and climb past the first bolt (placed on the first ascent of *The Ed Sullivan Show*), then move up and left to reach the right margin of the bulge. Move up the right side of it, then left to a pine on a ledge. Finish directly up pulling a narrow roof at the top. 75 feet. FA: Carl Samples, Bob Rentka, & Jason Brookes, September 1988.

338 Euro Nation 5.10a/b ☆☆☆ 🖝
First done at 5.11d as a mixed route without what has become the traditional

start: a stem off the tree. Was it Janet Jackson or the retro equipping that inspired the name? Begin near the left end of the ledge, at the base of a tree and stem past the initial boulder problem until it's possible to step onto the wall. Follow the line of bolts to the top. 75 feet. Warning: Be sure to back clip when lowering so you can swing back onto the ledge. FA: Carl Samples & Rick Thompson, March 1990.

339   Flash Point 5.11d/12a ☆☆☆☆ &

This hyperclassic should elevate your excitement to the brink of ignition. Begin in center of the orange overhanging wall and scramble to a ledge on the left, then reach right pulling an awkward roof. Step right and up a rising flake to its top, then up impeccable white rock to an airy leftward sequence. Power directly over a bulge, then move around to the right side of the arête. Climb directly up the face and either top out or lower from the last two bolts. 100 feet. WARNING: 60 meter rope required. FA: Rick Thompson, Carl Samples, Stuart Pregnall, & Ron Kampas, April 1990.

340   Project—In Progress—Jazz Rock Confusion

Shares the start of *Flashpoint* and climbs directly up the overhanging seam.

341   Lisa's Lunge Time 5.12b/c ☆☆ &

Start left of the arête and boulder up and right to reach the first bolt on the arête proper, then continue up the line of bolts to a ledge. Step left and climb directly to anchors at the top. 80 feet. FA: Eric & Lisa Hörst, August 1989.

342   Stop and I'll Shoot 5.11b ☆☆ &

The popular sport of target shooting. Begin from nearly the same start as *Lisa's Lunge Time* and climb up and left past a dicey slab, then right over a bulge to a stance. Move up the right-facing corner and pull the roof to anchors below the top. 70 feet. FA: Carl Samples, Rick Thompson & Mark Van Cura, April 1990.

343   Ambiance 5.8

Climb the glowing off-width. 85 feet. FA: Andrew Barry & John Regelbrugge, November 1985.

344   The Americans, Baby 5.10c R/X ☆

A tale set in Australia, about the promulgation of "the American way" as carried out by a Coca-Cola salesman. A few years back Andrew Barry was asked for his consent to retrobolt this route. When articulating to his opposition to the idea, he stated that if such a thing were to occur, the route would more appropriately be named "The Frogs, Baby." Start at the left-hand end of the ledge and venture up and left on increasingly frightening ground to reach the start of a long flake system that parallels the arête. Follow flakes to the top. 85 feet. FA: Andrew Barry & John Regelbrugge, November 1985.

This is the last route listed in a downstream direction from the Honeymooners Ladders.

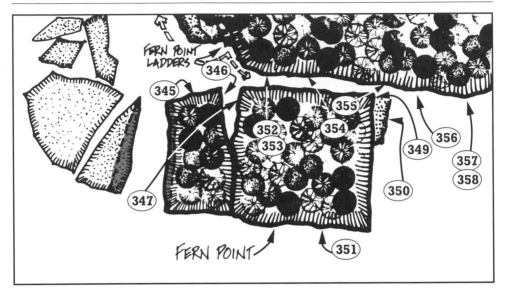

The next major access point is the Fern Point Ladders. See Endless Wall overview map for details on how to reach the Fern Point Ladders. Descriptions will now begin from the bottom of those ladders in an upstream direction.

345 Standing Up in the Big Tent 5.12c ☆ 𝄞
Sort of like a Barnum and Bailey side show. Begin on the right side of the tree and follow the line of three bolts and a pin to the top. 35 feet. FA: Eric Hörst & Rick Thompson, May 1989.

346 Unnamed 5.9
Start on the left side of the arête and follow the short face past a pin to the top of the block. 30 feet. FA: Kelly Faust, et al., 1990.

347 Whip It 5.12b ☆☆ 𝄞
A fall at the second bolt will provide insight to the route name. Get started on the right side of the arête and move up and left past a bolt, then around to the left side of the arête and the second bolt. Continue directly up the left side of the arête past a ledge to the top. 70 feet. FA: Eric Hörst & Rick Thompson, May 1989.

348 Salvador Raleigh's Blow Up Dolly 5.12b/c ☆ 𝄞
Rock artist or just another bag of air? Commence 15 feet left of *Whip It* and follow the line of six bolts to cold shuts. 70 feet. FA: Eric Hörst & Rick Thompson, October 1990.

349 The Ribbon 5.11d ☆☆☆
The hyper-classic arête at Fern Point. Follow the beautiful ribbon edge arête past a bolt and two pins to the top. 70 feet. Note: Carry small to medium stoppers and TCUs. FA: Phil Heller & Joseph Schwartz, April 1988.

350 Fidget 5.11c

Start 15 feet left of *The Ribbon* at the left end of the ledge and climb directly up a short distance, then follow an angling line up and right to the top finishing five feet left of the arête. 70 feet. Note: Bring a set of Rock'n Rollers or the equivilent. Protection is difficult to place, but bomber when you get it in. FA: Phil Heller & Joseph Schwartz, April 1988.

351 Express Yourself 5.12d ☆☆ (b)

In this case an expression of difficulty. Climb the thin crack past two bolts its end, then continue up the face past three more bolts to a station. 60 feet. FA: Eric Hörst, June 1989.

352 George, George, George of the Gorge, Watch Out For That Tree 5.9 (b)

Begin in a shallow green scoop (this is also the start of *Positron* and is protected by a bolt) and move up to a horizontal, then traverse left to a ledge. Climb directly past a bolt and move left around a small blocky roof to the top. 60 feet. FA: John Burcham & Kelly Faust, August 1989. Note: recently retrobolted by Burcham.

353 Positron 5.12a ☆ (b)

Using the same start the previous route follow the line of bolts directly to cold shuts. 55 feet. FA: Eric Hörst & Mark Guider, May 1991.

354 Civilizing Mission 5.12b ☆☆ (b)

This mission, should you choose to accept it, will be techno packed every move of the way. Stick clip or boulder to the first bolt to reach a three-foot roof and pull it, then follow the line line of bolts to cold shuts. 60 feet. FA: Eric Hörst & Rick Thompson, May 1989.

355 New Age Equippers 5.11c ☆☆☆ (b)

Continuously diverse, pumpy, and entertaining. Get ready to red-line your fun meter. Begin directly accross from *The Ribbon* and follow a line of six bolts to cold shuts. 65 feet. FA: Rick Thompson, Ron Kampas, Bob Rentka, & Eric Hörst, May 1989.

356 Dangerous Liasions 5.12b ☆☆☆ (b)

Invariabley sustained with a sequential crux and a knock out finish. Begin a short distance downhill from *New Age Equippers* and follow the line of eight bolts to cold shuts. 75 feet. FA: Rick Thompson & Eric Hörst, April 1989.

357 The Exqueetion 5.12a ☆☆ (b)

More on the incessantly thin theme. Start about ten feet right of *Dangerous Liasions* and climb the line of nine bolts that lead directly to cold shuts. 80 feet. FA: Carl Samples & Rick Thompson, October 1990.

Doug Cosby *Standing Up In the Big Tent.*
photo: Doug Cosby collection

Bob Value on the first ascent of *Mellifluus* in 1985.
photo: Rick Thompson

Scott Garso on *The Prowesse*.
photo: Rick Thompson

Mark Guider leading the first ascent
of *Stim-o-Stam.*
photo: Eric Hörst

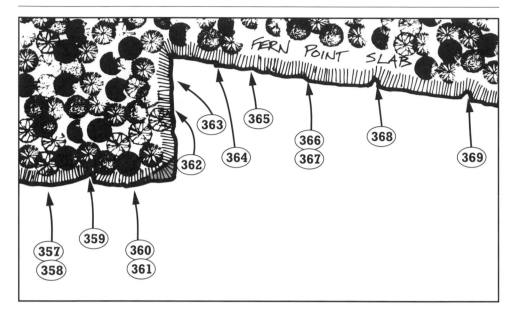

358   Texas Wine 5.11c R ☆
Using the same start as *The Exqueetion* climb past the second bolt, then follow the rightward diverging line of three widely bolts to a unruly finish. 80 feet. Note: Carry a light mixed rack. FA: Porter Jarrard & Kenny Parker, October 1988.

359   Linear Encounters 5.11a ☆☆☆☆
A crack encounter of the Endless kind. Start in a left-facing corner and awkwardly jam to an opposite facing corner which leads to a roof. Follow the sensational crack directly above the roof to its end and continue along the left-angling seam to the top. 85 feet. Note: Small TCUs will be crucial for protecting the final section. FA: Mike Artz & Andrew Barry, November 1985.

360   Eurobics 5.12d/13a ☆☆☆ 🄟
The grade on this sequencer is distinctly height dependant. Begin 15 feet right of *Linear Encounters* (shares the start with *Le Futuriste*) and boulder over the low roof to gain the first bolt, then move left and follow the line of bolts past the slab and through a right-facing corner to a pair of cold shuts. 80 feet. FA: Rick Thompson, Eric Hörst, & Bob Rentka, September 1989.

361   Le Futuriste 5.12b ☆☆☆ 🄟
Extraordinary position and flawless rock make this one a Fern Point requisite. Using the same sart as *Eurobics* move up to the first bolt, then follow the bolts up and right to gain a stance at the base of the white arête which is finessed to a pair of cold shuts. 80 feet. FA: Doug Reed & Rick Thompson, November 1988.

362 Be-Attitudes 5.12c ☆☆ 🎣

Begin at the center of the wall and follow the line of seven bolts to a cold shut station. 75 feet. FA: Eric Hörst, June 1990.

363 The Whetterbox 5.11d ☆☆

A highly prized line with a cute surprise. Start at the base of the chimney by stepping onto the left wall and move up to a bolt, then make a blind move to the left around a blunt nose. Crank up a short left-rising flake to the *Whetterbox* (get a good TCU here) and fire directly up the improbable wall past two pins to a bolt. Aim up and right past a sobering, but solid runout to the top. 75 feet. FA: Mike Artz, Doug Reed, Rick Thompson, and Bob Rentka, December 1988.

364 Terminus 5.10a ☆ 🎣

This overly popular outing used to finish at a group of mature pines on the ledge. However, a 1991 epic ice storm encrusted the trees so heavily they toppled to the ground. Begin near the left end of the Fern Point Slab, at base of short, left-facing corner and boulder up to first bolt then move right onto the face. Climb directly up the slab past three more bolts to the ledge. 40 feet. Note: Currently climbers traverse right and lower from the cold shuts at the top of *The Vertical Wench*. FA: Rick Thompson, Ron Kampas, & Bob Rentka, August 1989.

365 The Vertical Wench 5.12d

Once the bouldery crux has been mastered it's easy street. Follow the hairline seam past three bolts and some TCU placements to a pair of cold shuts. 50 feet. FA: Rick Thompson & Eric Hörst, April 1989.

366 Is It Safe? 5.11d/12a ☆☆ 🎣

Unquestionably so, but be prepared for a sporty slabbin'. Using the same start as *De-Funked*, climb up to the top of the right-facing flake, then continue directly up the clean streak to a ledge. Step right and fire straight up the headwall past three more bolts to cold shuts. 85 feet. FA: Rick Thompson, Bob Rentka, Carl Samples, Ron Kampas, & Mark Van Cura, August 1989.

367 De-Funked 5.12b ☆☆ 🎣

Or is it defunct? Try the crux and find out. Climb to the top of the right-facing flake, then make a delicate rightward traverse to reach a right-facing crescent. Follow the groove past two more bolts to the right side of the ledge, then power straight up the steep headwall past two more bolts and an uplifting finish to cold shuts. 85 feet. FA: Rick Thompson, Porter Jarrard, & Mike Artz, November 1988.

368 The Reception 5.8+

Begin in the left-hand chimney and follow the wideness up to a large, seemingly detached block. Climb this on its right side, then hand traverse left to the nose and make the final moves straight up. 85 feet. FA: Jim Van Buren & Paul Ledoux, April 1988.

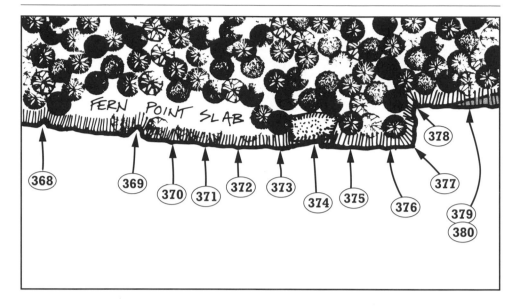

369 Seventh Sign 5.7
Climb the right-hand chimney until its possible to lieback a right-facing flake.
Step back left and up to the top. 85 feet. Note: With some traffic this scruffy route
should improve. FA: Ellen Nichols, Chris Holmes, & Mike Hientz, April 1988.

370 Slabbers of Habit 5.11b/c ☆☆
A slabathon in the finest Begoon tradition. Start about ten feet right of *Seventh
Sign* and boulder directly up to a bolt, then continue past a ledge and aim for a
second bolt. Angle right, then up a steepening headwall past a pin and a bolt to
the top. 90 feet. Note: Carry TCUs and small Friends. FA: Eddie Begoon & Bob
Rentka, October 1988.

371 Dead Painters Society 5.12a ☆☆☆☆ 👀
May those who paint route names at the base of climbs retire to this honorary
society forever. Considered the classic 5.12 slab route at the New. Commence
just right of *Slabbers of Habit* and follow the line of eight bolts directly to cold
shuts. 85 feet. FA: Rick Thompson, Bob Rentka, Carl Samples, Eric Hörst, &
Doug Reed, June 1989.

372 Son of Frankenstein 5.11d ☆
This monster begins with an incipient crack that's climbed to its end at a ledge.
Trend slightly right, then back left to hollow-sounding flakes under a bulge
which is pulled directly. Head up the clean streak past a pin to the top. 85 feet.
FA: Stanley Todd & Eddie Begoon, March 1987.

373 The Magnificent Puddcasso 5.12a ☆☆ 👀
Or is that Picasso? Not a classic piece of art but certainly an expressive slab
climb. Start ten feet left of *Mellifluus* and follow the line of nine bolts to cold shuts
at the top. 90 feet. FA: Rick Thompson, Eric Hörst & Bob Rentka, June 1989.

374   Mellifluus 5.11a ☆☆☆☆
Late Latin meaning: flowing with honey. And oh how sweet it is! The classic
5.11a crack on the Endless Wall and the second route established at Fern Point.
Follow the hand, finger and tips crack past a low angled crux, then continue up
the crack until it merges with an orange right-facing flake. Climb the flake until
just below the roof and traverse off left to a tree belay. 90 feet. FA: Rick
Thompson & Bob Value, October 1985.

375   Roll it Over in Your Mind 5.11d ☆☆
This one will have ya chewin' the fat. Start ten feet right of *Mellifluus* by climbing
directly past a bulge and onto a steep face until its possible to move right and
up past a pin to reach a bolt. Continue straight up the brilliant orange wall past
another bolt and several lunges to a second pin, then angle right to the top. 90
feet. Note: Bring plenty of TCUs. FA: Mike Artz & Eddie Begoon, May 1987.

376   Slick Olives 5.10d R
Pull a low roof 15 feet right of the previous route and move up and right aiming
for the top of a large flake. Continue directly past a bolt to a stance below a
headwall, then climb to a small pine and exit right to the arête and the top. 90
feet. FA: Mike Artz & Eddie Begoon, May 1987.

377   Driven to the Edge 5.11c R ☆
Established ground-up. Start on the right of the arête and clamber up to the first
bolt on the left face of the arête, then continue directly past the second bolt and
move back to the right side of the arête. Follow unnervingly crunchy rock to top.
80 feet. FA: Jay Smith & Mike Best, July 1989.

378   Nasty Groove 5.9
Awkwardly jam the right-facing corner to a ledge with a good pine and either
rappel or continue up easy climbing to the top. 65 feet to the ledge. FA: Bob
Burgher & Phil Heller, November 1985.

379   The Acid Atomizer 5.12a ☆
Using the same start as *Live Wire* and The *Fly'n Hawaiian*, climb up and left,
following the line of bolts to slings in the pine trees. 65 feet. Note: Shares some
moves with *Live Wire*. FA: Eric Hörst & Mark Guider, November 1990.

380   Live Wire 5.10d ☆☆
Continuous thin face climbing on shockingly perfect white stone. Using the
same start as *The Fly'n Hawaiian* climb the initial five feet, then crank a bee line
up the electrifying face to a belay on the pine tree ledge. 65 feet. Note: Bring a
selection of nuts, 2 # 0 TCUs and Friends to #2. FA: Eddie Begoon, Mike Artz, &
Jim MacAuther, November 1987.

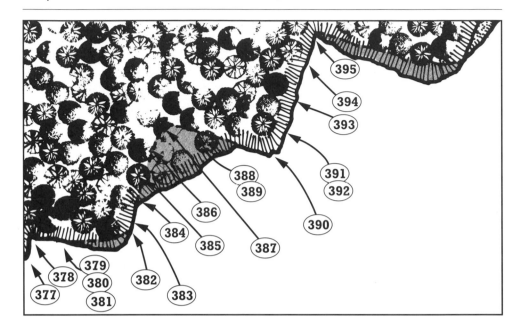

381   The Fly'n Hawaiian 5.9+ ☆☆
A prime-quality face climb that honors Garso's Hawaiian heritage and his
propensity for logging major whippers. Begin ten feet right of *Nasty Groove* and
boulder up and right on a big flake, then hand traverse right along a horizontal,
staying just above the lip of the roof to reach an aging pin. Climb directly up to
gain the rounded white arête, then continue up the left side of the arête (staying
left of *The Prowesse*) and either move left to the pine tree belay or finish on *The
Prowesse*. 65 feet to the pine tree belay or 110 feet to the top. Note: Carry a
selection of small to medium TCUs. FA: Scott Garso & Rick Thompson, August
1986.

382   The Prowesse 5.9 R ☆☆☆☆
Considered by many to be New River's finest 5.9. Features ethereal position
and perfect rock! The name is of Middle English origin meaning: valiant or
daring deed. Inexperienced leaders be forewarned this route is intricate and
the gear is sparse at times. If 5.9 is your leading limit you might think twice
before jumping on this one. P1: Start on the right side of the blunt white arête, on
the face to the right of the low roof and boulder up and left to a good horizontal
and get some bomber gear. Traverse left around the arête and climb up the
blunt prow for 15 feet, then move left past a rounded outside corner and climb
directly up the white highway that bisects the prow to a hanging belay at a point
level with the ledge on your left. 70 feet. P2: Continue up the highway and pass
a small overhang on the left to a stance below the final arête. Get good pro
here, then follow a line of flakes and knobs on the left side of the arête (5.7 R) to
the top. 50 feet. Note: Can be done in one long pitch, but expect hellacious rope
drag. FA: Rick Thompson & Glenn Thomas, April 1986.

382a The Prowesse Direct Finish—The Repossessed 5.8+ R ☆☆
Your well-being will most certainly be repossessed if you blow it above the crux on this finish. Climb Pitch #2 until you reach the stance below the sharp arête. It is prudent you get good protection here. Step around to the right side and make a couple of moves up the arête then angle up and right to the top. 60 feet. FA: Rick Thompson & Glenn Thomas, June 1986.

383 Stim-o-Stam 5.11c ☆☆ ⓟ
Using the same start as *The Prowesse* climb directly up the line of bolts to cold shuts on the right side of the arête. 70 feet. Note: At the final two bolts it may seem a bit forced to stay on the right side of the arête. Most parties move left here. FA: Mark Guider, Eric Hörst, Jodie Rozen & Ray Kallio, October 1990.

384 Freakly Stylee 5.12a ☆☆☆☆ ⓟ
If 12a is your grade, this one is compulsory. A killer route! Commence just right of the start of *The Prowesse* and climb up (you can use a #2 1/2 Friend to protect these moves) to the first of five bolts that are followed to a cold-shut station. 70 feet. Note: In light drizzle this can work as a rain day route; however, the bottom section may get a little wet. FA: Porter Jarrard & Doug Reed, October 1988.

385 Techman 5.12c ☆☆ ⓟ ℞
Engage just right of the previous start and follow six bolts up and slightly left to join *Freaky Stylee* at the last bolt. 70 feet. FA: Doug Reed, 1991.

386 Stealth' n Magic 5.12c/d ☆☆☆ ⓟ ℞
Those Keebler elves did it again, this time with sticky rubber. Start five feet left of *Biohazard* and follow the line of seven bolts to a pair of cold shuts. 70 feet. FA: Rick Thompson, Eric Hörst, Carl Samples & Bob Rentka, November 1989.

387 Biohazard 5.10a ☆☆ ℞
A long and enjoyable pitch with a delicate and thought-provoking crux. Expect some rope drag. Start at twin cracks in the dihedral and romp up moderate ground to the massive roof (there are slings around a flake here which some parties use to lower from on rain days). Follow elegant moves up and right across the face until it's possible to finish up a short corner to the top.110 feet. FA: Rick Thompson, Dave Sippel, Mark Van Cura, & Glenn Thomas, November 1985.

388 Fascist Architecture 5.12c/d ☆☆☆ ⓟ ℞
A politically correct sport climb of superior design. Begin ten feet right of *Biohazard* and move up the right-facing flake until it's possible to move left and up a striking finger crack to its end, then overcome the fascist bulge to reach a rap station. 65 feet. FA: Eric Hörst & Bob Rentka, June 1989.

389 Inexorably Delicious 5.10d R ☆
Particularly scrumptious if you have an appetite for run outs. Using the same start as *Fascist Architecture* move up the flake until it's possible to do an unprotected hand traverse to the right, then wander up the long face finishing on the last 20 feet of *Biohazard*. 90 feet. FA: Phil Heller & Bob Burgher, November 1985.

389a Inexorably Delicious Variation Start - Exquisite Lace 5.10b ☆
Start on the arête and climb a short dihedral to its end at a small ledge, then step up and left and follow *Inexorably Delicious* to the top. 90 feet. FA: Eddie Begoon & Freddy Young, March 1987.

390 Party Till Yer Blind 5.10b ☆☆☆☆
One of the finest 5.10 arêtes at the New. Using the same start *Exquisite Lace* climb the short inside corner to the ledge, then move directly up the left side of the arête past a bolt at mid-height to the top. 90 feet. Note: Bring TCUs and Friends to #2, and keep your eyes peeled for gear placements on the right side of the arête . FA: Kenny Parker, Blaze Davies & Tracey Ramm, May 1989.

391 Party in My Mind 5.10b ☆☆☆☆
This impressively steep face climb will reveal some of the nicest incuts imaginable. Begin with the same start as *Party All the Time* and after 15 feet diverge left and up the bulging orange wall staying about 10 feet right of the arête until you reach a ledge. Finish on the headwall just right of the arête. 90 feet. FA: Carl Samples & Bob Rentka, November 1988.

392 Party All the Time, Party All the Time 5.10b ☆
Originally this route featured an R-rated start; however, an unknown party subsequently added a bolt to the start. Commence 15 feet right of the arête at a short left-facing flake and climb up and right, then follow a line of flakes up and back left to a ledge about 20 feet below the top. Move right and follow a short inside corner to the top. 90 feet. FA: Andrew Barry & Mike Artz, November 1985.

393 Fatlburger 5.11d ☆ 🎧
Follow the line of bolts past a dazzling series of mono doigts to a pair of cold shuts. 50 feet. FA: Eric Hörst & Rick Thompson, October 1990.

394 Meat Is Murder 5.12b ☆ 🎧
The question may be: Will veggie power get you up this one? Begin about 15 feet left of the *Smooth Operator* dihedral and follow the line of six bolts to cold shuts. 50 feet. FA: Eric Hörst & Mark Guider, October 1990.

Ken Cline experiencing *Party In My Mind.*

photo: Carl Samples

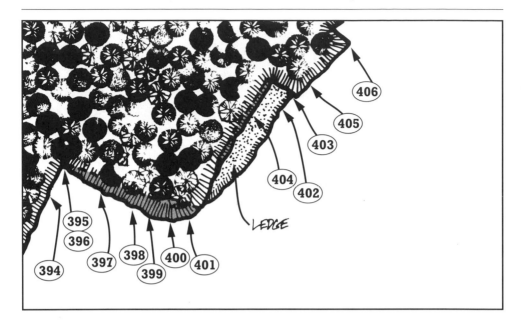

395 Smooth Operator 5.9+ ☆☆☆☆

Exceptional hand and fist jams will lead you to ecstasy on this outrageous pitch. The first route to be established at Fern Point. On the left wall of the offwidth corner is a handcrack that is followed to an alcove. Move left and up liebacks, finishing up a left-facing flared slot. 90 feet. FA: Rick Fairtrace & Scott Jones, October 1985.

396 Timberline 5.10b ☆

The first ascent of this route was protected in classic retro-tech fashion: Two pieces of log slinged and cammed into the initial off-width. Begin immediately right of *Smooth Operator* and struggle up the offwidth, then move to a ledge on the right and finish up the dihedrals. 90 feet. Note: In addition to the normal mixed rack bring some Big Bro's. FA: Andy Zimmerman & Laura Novak, October 1989.

397 Modern Primative 5.12b/c ☆☆ 🅟 ℛ

Requires a subtle blend of brute force and technical mastery. Begin near the left edge of the face and climb the line of four bolts to a station below the roof. 50 feet. FA: Doug Reed & Rick Thompson, October 1988.

398 Plyometrics 5.12c/d ☆☆ ℛ

The art of leaping. Begin 15 feet right of *Modern Primative* and climb up and right past two bolts, then follow a series of huecos up and left past two more bolts and a letterbox (good small TCU). Move left, then up to finish on *Modern Primative*. 50 feet. FA: Doug Reed & Rick Thompson, October 1988.

399 Harbinger Scarab 5.12c ☆☆
Looking like something out of Buoux, this route is certainly one of Endless Wall's more intimidating lines. Get going by climbing the left edge of a twin-sided flake up to the first bolt, then step onto the prow and up to the huge roof. Power out the flake and follow the line of bolts up the bulging headwall to the top. 100 feet. Note: Bring some small camming units to protect the start; the rest of the route is a clip-up. Using two ropes will help avoid rope drag. There are no anchors at the top. FA: Doug Reed, November 1989.

400 Back in the Saddle 5.10c ☆ ℛ
Start in an obtuse right-facing dihedral and ride it to slings under the roof. 45 feet. FA: Mike Artz & Bill Moore, February 1986.

401 The Sweetest Taboo 5.13b ☆☆☆ 🖑 ℛ
aka Swedish Taboo
A stellar testpiece. Start immediately right of *Back in the Saddle* and follow the line of six bolts up the charismatic blunt orange arête to cold shuts below the roof. 50 feet. FA: Eric Hörst, May 1990.

402 'Bout Time 5.13b ☆ 🖑
Immediately left of the *Diversity in Microcosm* dihedral is a line of four bolts that leads to cold shuts. 40 feet. John Logan, 1993.

403 Diversity in Microcosm 5.9 R ☆
An ocean of climbing diversity. The R rating is eliminated if done using the variation finish. Start in a clean right-leaning dihedral and follow it into a flared alcove, then move left under the roof to gain a picnic-sized ledge. Make a couple moves on the left side on the arête, then climb around to a good ledge on the right side and directly up the poorly protected arête (5.6 R) to the top. 80 feet. FA: Tom Howard & Dan Perry, November 1985.

403a Diversity in Microcosm Variation Finish 5.9 ☆
From the ledge at mid-height follow the obvious left-facing dihedral to the top. FA: Steve Lancaster & Doug Chapman, November 1985.

404 Crimes of Flashin' 5.12a ☆☆ 🖑
Surealistic position on immecable rock. An ideal choice during cooler weather due to its southern exposure. Begin in the center of the vibrant orange wall that rises above the ledge and follow the line of bolts to a pair of cold shuts. 50 feet. Note: Most parties gain access to the ledge by rapping in. FA: Rick Thompson, Eric Hörst, Carl Samples, & Bob Rentka, October 1989.

405 Pocket Pussy 5.12b ☆☆☆ 🖑
Characterized by a pumping series of pocket dynos. Stick clip the first bolt and begin by climbing the first ten feet of *Diversity in Microcosm*, then traverse right around the arête on a small ledge and follow the line of four bolts to cold shuts on the ledge. 45 feet. FA: Rick Thompson, Eric Hörst, Carl Samples & Bob Rentka, October 1989.

Doug Reed bearing down on the
first ascent of *Modern Primitive.*

photo: Rick Thompson

Immersed in his *Sweetest Taboo*,
Eric Hörst.

photo: Rick Thompson

Rick Thompson on the first ascent of *Crimes of Flashin'.*

photo: Carl Samples

Lisa Hörst on *Exoduster*

photo: Eric Hörst

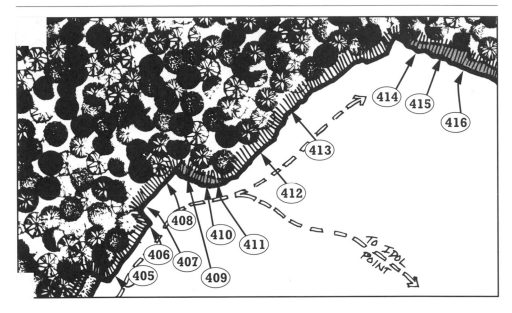

406 The Plug 5.12d or a/b ☆☆ ⓟ

This companion route to *Pocket Pussy* features more on the pocket plugging theme, except these are of a smaller variety. Originally done via the 12d direct start on the left side of the arête, a slightly easier one can be found by beginning on the right side. Stick clip the first bolt and use either start to gain the pocketed face which is followed past two more bolts to gain the ledge. Lower from the same cold shuts as *Pocket Pussy*. 45 feet. FA: Rick Thompson, Eric Hörst, & Carl Samples, November 1989.

407 Autumn Fire 5.10b ☆☆☆

This undisputed classic should not be missed. Another of the early Fern Point routes. Jam the small right-facing corner to the ledge, then lieback the great flake to the top. 70 feet. FA: Glenn Thomas & Rick Thompson, November 1985.

408 Exoduster 5.10b/c ☆ ⓟ ⓡ

Too popular. Begin a few feet right of the previous route and follow four bolts to a pair of cold shuts below the roof. 45 feet. FA: Lisa & Eric Hörst, August 1990.

408a Exoduster Direct Finish—Eat My Dust 5.11b ☆ ⓟ

From the cold shuts move left and around the roof, then follow three more bolts to a second pair of cold shuts. 35 feet. FA: Gary Beil & Greg Flerx, September 1991.

409 Pre-Marital Bliss 5.9 ☆☆

A fashionable bachelor's farewell. The weekend after the first ascent Sippel got married and he hasn't been seen on the rocks since! O.K., it's a joke! Follow moderate cracks in the left-facing dihedral past a roof at mid-height and continue up the corner to a small triangular roof (eight feet below the big roof), then traverse left across the face to a belay or lower from the *Eat My Dust* cold shuts. 80 feet. Note: Originally finished on the *Autumn Fire* belay ledge. FA: Dave Sippel & Mark Van Cura, November 1985.

410 Through the Never 5.12b

Begin in the center of the orange face and follow the line of bolts to a pair of cold shuts. 80 feet. FA: Dan Osman & Jay Smith, September 1991.

411 Mental Wings 5.12c ☆☆☆

Ethereal position on an elegant arête, it's almost like soaring. Start on the left side of the undercut arête and follow the right-arcing line of bolts to the arête , then crank directly to the ledge. Continue up the perfect arête to cold shuts at the top. 85 feet. FA: Eric Hörst & Harrison Dekker, October 1989.

412 Smore Energy 5.11b ☆☆☆

Now who would believe climbers derive their energy from marshmallow candies? Commence a few paces right of the arête and thug your way up the right-hand line of bolts and a pin at the finish to cold shuts below the top. 85 feet. FA: Eric & Lisa Hörst, October 1989.

412a Smore Energy-Mental Wings Link Up-Chouinard-Steck Variation 5.11d ☆

Follow *Smore Energy* to the third bolt, then follow bolts angling leftward to connect with the finish of *Mental Wings*. 85 feet. FA: Eric Hörst & Mark Guider, May 1991.

413 Manute Bol 5.10d

Begin immediately right of *Smore Energy* and follow the overhanging crack up to a ledge, then climb a right-facing corner until it's possible to move up and left to the top. 90 feet. FA: Pete Absolon, April 1986.

414 Hooked on Bionics 5.11c

Shock your way past three bolts to a pair of cold shuts. 30 feet. FA: Eric Hörst & Mark Guider, May 1991.

415 Idols of the Tribe 5.13a ☆☆

Get started to the left of the dihedral start of *Life's a Bitch* and follow the line of nine bolts up and over a roof to a pair of cold shuts near the top. 85 feet. FA: Porter Jarrard, October 1990.

416 Life's a Bitch and Then You Climb 5.10b ☆

P1: Begin from a ledge and climb the left-facing dihedral moving right at the roof to gain a ledge and belay. 40 feet. P2: Follow the broad right-facing dihedral to the top. (This is the same finish as *Fist Fodder*) 35 feet. FA: Rick Fairtrace & Scott Jones, March 1986.

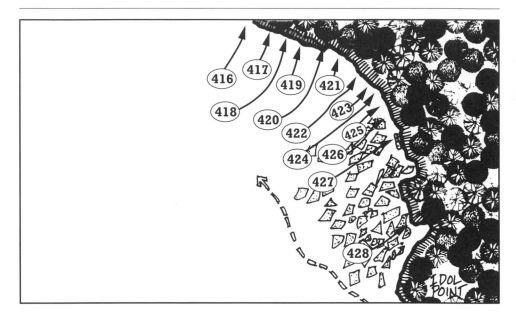

417 Fist Fodder 5.9 ☆
Food for the fist crack connoisseur. To the right of *Life's a Bitch* are a series of cracks that split a short wall above a low roof band. P1: Begin under the most left-hand crack at a short left-facing corner and move up and left to gain the crack that is jammed to the large ledge. Belay. 40 feet. P2: Step left and follow the right-facing corner to the top. 40 feet. FA: Tom Howard & Dan Perry, November 1985.

418 Aquarian Conspiracy 5.10c ☆
Start just right of *Fist Fodder* and climb up and right past a jug-ledge to reach a horizontal along the base of the roof. Traverse right to the crack and follow it to the ledge, then step across the ledge and climb the face past a right-facing flake to the top. 80 feet. FA: Mike Artz & Rick Fairtrace, March 1986.

419 Guns of Sassoun 5.11d ☆
David Sassoun was a legendary Armenian who fought back the invading Turks. Commence a short distance right of *Aquarian Conspiracy* and climb up and left through the overhang with a bolt to reach a bottomless fingercrack that is jammed to the ledge. Step right and finish up the easier face. 80 feet. FA: Dave Vartanian & Ward Smith, May 1990.

420 Jane 5.9+
Start behind the large hemlock tree and climb the right-facing corner to the ledge, then step left and continue up the right-facing corner to the top. 80 feet. FA: John Burcham, et al., November 1985.

421   Grin Reaper 5.10b R/X

It's doubtful the bogus protection will bring a smile to your face. Start 15 feet right of *Jane* on a clean white face and climb directly to a roof (5.8 R/X) and pass it to the left, continuing up to a ledge. Finish straight up. (5.10b R). 75 feet. Note: Skyhooks could be helpful. FA: Rick Fairtrace & Scott Jones, October 1986.

422   Tarzan 5.10a

Begin left of a large poplar tree at a short orange-and-white left-facing corner. Climb the corner, then move left and follow a short crack to its end. Continue up and right to a good ledge and belay. Rappel from the tree. 50 feet. FA: John Burcham, Andrew Barry, & Mike Artz, November 1985.

423   Golden Olympics 5.10a ☆

Commence just right of *Video Waves* at a thin left-leaning crack that is followed to a brief right-facing corner. Continue up the face past an orange bulge to the top. 70 feet. FA: Eddie Begoon & Tracy Ramm, February 1990.

424   Video Waves 5.9

Start ten feet right of the gross-looking chimney at a short, thin flake and follow it to a rhodi-choked ledge, then climb the left face of the clean dihedral past a squarish, white face (looks like a TV tube) and finish up and left. 70 feet. FA: Rick Fairtrace & Bob Rentka, September 1986.

425   Soft Torture 5.11d ☆☆

A short distance right of the previous route is a thin left-leaning crack that brings you to a line of five bolts and the top. 75 feet. Note: Bring wires for the crack and small TCUs for the top. FA: Eddie Begoon, February 1990.

426   Radford Rockers 5.11d ☆

Get rockin' a short distance right of *Soft Torture* and crank the line protected by four bolts to the top. 65 feet. Note: Carry a light mixed rack. FA: John Maguire, et al., October 1990.

427   Dead Animal Crackers 5.9

Lieback a flake and jam the obvious short hand crack to the top. 40 feet. FA: Ed McCarthy & Carl Samples, April 1986.

428   Reed's Ladder 5.4

This route is not a ladder and is typically used as a climb out. Scramble to a high point on the talus and follow the path of least resistance up the broken arête. 50 feet. FA: Doug Reed, solo, 1990.

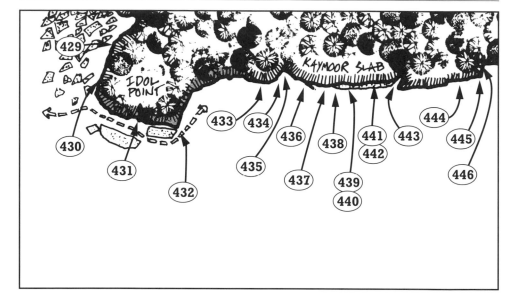

429   French Tickler   5.12b/c ☆☆ ℗

Begin approximately 30 feet uphill from *The Saint* and follow the line of eight bolts to a pair of cold shuts. 80 feet. FA: Rick Thompson, Carl Samples, & Eric Hörst, July 1990.

430   The Saint   5.12d ☆☆ ℗

At left side of Idol Point is an overhanging arête with a line of six bolts that lead to cold shuts at a half-height ledge. 65 feet. FA: Doug Reed, July 1990.

431   The Spectre   5.11c ☆☆

Oh, the haunting possiblities! Some have felt rather ghostly when, mistakenly thinking the line of bolts indicated a sport route, failed to bring a mixed rack. Begin in a rotten-looking corner in the center of the face and follow the widely spaced bolt-protected crack past an unruly flake and a techno-jam finish to a pair of cold shuts. 90 feet. FA: Doug Reed & Bob Rentka, June 1990.

432   Idol Point Arête   5.12a ☆ ℗

Start in the wide crack on the right side of the arête and follow the line of bolts to cold shuts. 80 feet. FA: Doug Reed, 1990.

433   Riding the Crest of a Wave   5.9 ☆☆☆☆

Not only is this one of New River's most classic moderates, but it's also the longest route in the gorge. P1: Begin ten feet left of the outside corner and face climb to a ledge, then move through a short left-facing corner to the face above it and continue up and right to a good ledge with a small pine. 45 feet. P2: From the right end of the ledge climb a short arête to a crack below the long right-facing flake. Ascend the flake until it's possible to step right to another flake which is followed to a small ledge. Continue up the clean right-facing corner to a roof and step left to a stance above it. Finish by angling right above the roof, then directly up a short white face to the top. 100 feet. FA: Rick Thompson & Scott Garso, April 1986.

434 Meniscus Burning 5.11c *b*
Begin ten feet left of the corner and follow three bolts to cold shuts. 35 feet. FA: Eric Hörst & Mark Guider, November 1990.

435 Command Performance 5.10b ☆☆
Possibly the longest single pitch in the gorge, this one will dispense a cornicopia of jams. Begin in the varying-width right-facing corner and follow it until a roof is reached near the top. Climb through the cleft and skirt right on the ledge to belay. 130 feet. Note: Bring a monster rack including double #3, 3 1/2, and 4 Friends as well as some large Tricams or Big Bros. FA: Sandy Flemming & John Vidumsky, November 1990.

436 What Will People Think? 5.12c/d ☆☆☆ *b*
This multi-cruxed thought provoker will dish out plenty of action. Begin atop the blade of rock and step onto the wall and follow the line of bolts to a pair of cold shuts. 80 feet. FA: Rick Thompson & Carl Samples, October 1990.

437 Slab-o-Meat 5.11d ☆☆ *b*
Commence just right of the blade and follow the line of bolts up the long slab to a tree belay at a ledge. Rappel or walk left and scramble to top. 110 feet. Note: There are no anchors. FA: Rick Thompson, Ron Kampas, Stuart Pregnall et al., April 1990.

438 Fool Effect 5.9+ ☆☆ *b*
Originally done as a ground-up R-rated route, the name references the fool effect often associated with poorly protected routes. But alas the name took on new meaning after the route was retrobolted. Since then it's become the scene of constant crowds and debacles. Begin left of the ledge and follow the line of 13 bolts to the top. 125 feet. Note: Two ropes are needed to rappel from the top. FA: Tom & Sharon Clancy, Bob Cenk, & Mark Van Cura, June 1990.

439 Paralleling 5.10d R ☆
That's rappelling spelled sideways, sort of. Begin at the left end of the ledge (same start as *A Date With Disappointment*) and angle up and left of the bolts, then follow a parallel line with *A Date With Disappointment*. Continue directly past a orange left-facing flake to a prow and wander through the final overhangs to the top. 115 feet. Note: Bring a healthy selection of small to medium camming units. FA: Andrew Barry & Mike Artz, June 1986.

440 A Date With Disappointment 5.12b ☆☆ *b*
An apt depiction of the crux holds. Begin near the left end of the ledge and follow the line of eight bolts through an orange bulge to a cold shut station. 85 feet. Warning: The belayer must pay careful attention not to lower the leader off the ledge; a 165-meter rope just gets there. FA: Rick Thompson, October 1992.

441 New Wave 5.11a R ☆

Intricately committing. Bring a couple of skyhooks and be prepared for some body surfing! Using the same start as *The Upheaval* climb directly past the first bolt, then float up and left (hooks and 10c R) to an undercling. Continue up and left aiming for a bolt, then finesse the face to the right of the bolt to reach several horizontals. Continue to an incipient crack and follow the crack and face above to the top. 115 feet. FA: Andrew Barry & Mike Artz, June 1986.

442 The Upheaval 5.9 ☆☆ 🄿

First done as an R rated ground up effort, the original line used a 10c direct start to the right. Prior to being retrobolted it had seen only one repeat ascent in five years. Ironically it has became the most popular route on the the Endless Wall since then. Scramble up to the ledge, then begin from the right side and follow the line of five bolts to a pair of cold shuts. 85 feet. Note: In order to lower the leader using a 165-foot rope, the belayer must to be on the ledge. There have been a number of accidents resulting in broken ankles because inattentive belayers have allowed to end of the rope to pass through the belay device. FA: Rick Thompson, Glenn Thomas, & Bob Rentka, June 1986.

443 Newd Scientist 5.4

Climbs the face to the right of Kaymoor Slab. P1: Begin in the gully immediately right of the *The Upheaval* and climb the short face of the opposing wall, then move around to the right. Wander up and right to gain the center of the face, then cruise directly to a ledge with a good pine and belay. 50 feet. P2: Follow the left-facing corner to the top. 40 feet. FA: Andrew Barry & Suellen de Waard, June 1986.

444 ...with a Little Help From my Friends 5.10a/b ☆☆ 🄿

I was able to put up this route. Another of the all too popular routes. Start a few meters left of the arête and follow the line of eight bolts to a pair of cold shuts beside a large pine. 75 feet. FA: Mark Van Cura, Carl Samples, Rick Thompson, Tom Clancy, Ron Kampas, et al., September 1992.

445 Que's Jook Joint 5.11b ☆

Start at the low roof at the base of the arête and follow the line of four bolts on the left face. Finish on *Wimpy, Wimpy, Wimpy* or *Pocket Pool*. It's also possible to traverse left and join *With a Little Help From my Friends*. Length varies according to link up. FA: Unknown.

446 Wimpy, Wimpy, Wimpy 5.9 ☆

Start in the orange and black right-facing corner and cower up the crack to a flaring chimney that is followed to a large pine on a ledge. Rappel from cold shuts at the top of *With a Little Help From my Friends*. 65 feet. FA: Tondeleyo Dale & Bill Moore, June 1986.

Ken McLain groping the second slabby
ascent of *A Date With Dissapointment.*

photo: Rick Thompson

Doug Reed on the first
ascent of *Pudd's Pretty Dress.*

photo: Carl Samples

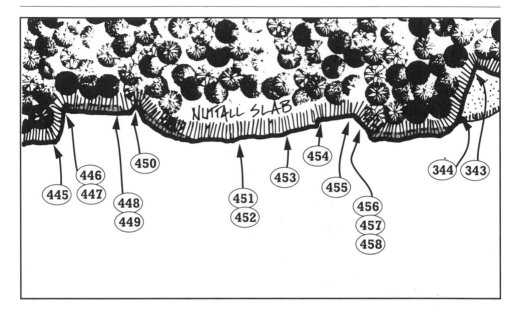

447   Pocket Pool 5.12c ☆☆

Start by either climbing the first part of *Wimpy, Wimpy, Wimpy* or *Que's Jook Joint* until it's possible to step onto right wall, then move up the face staying on the left side of overhanging arête . At the last good horizontal step right to the arête and power past a bolt to reach a left-leaning crack that is followed to a ledge with rap anchors. 85 feet. FA: Eddie Begoon & Bob Rentka, March 1990.

448   Pudd's Pretty Dress 5.12c/d ☆☆☆☆ 🄿

It's rumored Pudd was a cross dresser. Wow, this is one fine route! Start in the chimney just left of *Hefty, Hefty, Hefty* and climb to the first bolt, then follow the left-hand line of bolts to a station on the ledge at top. 85 feet. FA: Doug Reed, April 1990.

449   Villian's Course 5.13b ☆☆ 🄿

Using the same start as *Pudd's Pretty Dress* move up and clip the first bolt, then follow the right-hand line of bolts to cold shuts. 80 feet. FA: Doug Reed, September 1990.

450   Hefty, Hefty, Hefty 5.10a ☆

Start in the yawning chimney and follow the ever-tapering crack past a fist-size section in a corner. Belay on the ledge. 75 feet. FA: Stanley Todd, Bill Moore, & Tondeleyo Dale, June 1986.

451   Rotating Heads 5.10a R ☆

Climb *Walking in Your Footsteps* for about 30 feet to a good horizontal, then traverse left 20 feet to a small maple tree on the ledge. Climb straight up the face aiming for a short left-facing corner and the top. 85 feet. Note: Protection on this pitch may have you shaking in your britches. FA: Eddie Begoon & Jim MacAuther, September 1986.

452   Walking in Your Footsteps   5.10a R ☆☆
Start in the center of Nuttall Slab atop a small block. Climb a short left-facing flake to gain the face, then move up and right following the line of least resistance to reach a good horizontal at mid-height. Move left and up past a small flake and a ledge and continue straight up until it's possible to step right into a corner which leads to the top. 80 feet. FA: Mike Artz & Kenny Hummel, November 1985.

453   Totally-Clipse   5.8 ☆ (P)
Commence about 15 feet left of *Easy Street* and scramble up to a ledge, then climb the clean streak following the line of bolts to a pair of cold shuts at the top. 75 feet. FA: Rick Thompson & Lauren Garofalo, September 1990.

454   Easy Street   5.4
Start at the right edge of the Nuttall Slab and follow the dirty and heavily vegetated groove to a ledge and rappel. 60 feet. Note: It's possible to scramble up and left to the top. FA: Kenny Hummel & Stanley Todd, April 1986.

455   Rat's Alley   5.7
Begin in the corner and follow a right-facing flake to a ledge with a pine and rappel. 60 feet. FA: Kenny Hummel & Stanley Todd, April 1986.

456   The Meaty-Urologist   5.12c ☆ (P)
A nineties kind of twist to the weather forecasting profession. Commence on the right wall of the corner (the same start as *Fat'n Happy*) and follow four bolts directly to cold shuts. 45 feet. FA: Eric Hörst, November 1990.

457   Fat'n Happy   5.11c ☆☆
Start just right of *Rats Alley* and climb the short right-facing corner to a bush, then undercling right to a bolt. Climb directly past two more bolts, then step around to the right side of the arête and up to the top. 60 feet. FA: Eddie Begoon & Bob Rentka, March 1990.

458   Rhythm of Movement   5.12a ☆☆
Using the same start as *Fat'n Happy* traverse beyond the first bolt to reach a second bolt at the arête. Move up the left side of arête past a couple good horizontals, then step around to the right side and follow the lower angle face to the top. 65 feet. FA: Eddie Begoon & Bob Rentka, March 1990.

Rhythm of Movement is the last route described in an upstream direction from the Fern Point Ladder access point.

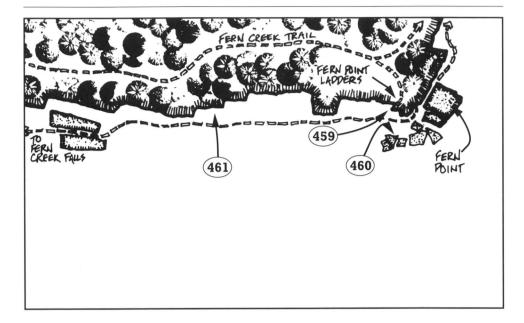

The route descriptions will now begin a downstream direction from the Fern Point Ladders along the Fern Creek North Wall.

459   Seeing Stars   5.11d ☆☆ 👌

Located in a nice shady spot, this route will make for a fine escape on a steamy day. Get started with a stick clip and crank up and slightly right, then back left to the arête on the left edge of the face which is followed to cold shuts at the top. 60 feet. FA: Carl Samples & Rick Thompson, May 1992.

460   Poochie Gets a Face Lift   5.12b TR

Climbs the center of the diamond shaped boulder about 100 feet downhill from *Seeing Stars*. In order to rig a toprope one must approach from the downhill side of the boulder and make an exposed scramble up and over the top of the boulder which forms a narrow ridge. 35 feet. Note: Equipped with cold shuts. FA TR: Rick Thompson, Bob Rentka, & Carl Samples, May 1992.

461   Vulcan Mind Funk 5.12b ☆

About two-thirds of the way along the trail to Fern Creek Falls you will come to a relatively clean right-arching double dihedral among a lot of greeness. Follow it past three bolts, then head directly past a roof to the top. 50 feet. FA: Harry Brealman, Jim Damon, Barry Rugo, & Tony Troochi, June 1990.

The following routes continue to be listed in a downriver direction and can be accessed via three means. If your goal is to do routes on the upriver end of Fern Buttress, the latter two options will probably provide the most efficient approach.

The following routes continue to be listed in a downriver direction and can be accessed via three means. If your goal is to do routes on the upstream end of Fern Buttress, the latter two options will probably provide the most efficient approach. The first method is to use the Fern Point Ladders and continue past *Vulcan Mind Funk* until you reach Fern Creek Falls. The only time this routine seems to be popular is when a climber who is already doing routes at Fern Point wants to climb around Fern Creek Falls.

The second option is the traditional Fox Hunter's Crack. If you' re coming in from the clifftop and want to do routes around Fern Creek Falls this downclimb provides quick access. However, the final section of the downclimb can be a bit of a squeeze with a pack on.

The last option is to use the Fern Creek Rappel, which deposits you a few hundred feet down the wall from Fern Creek Falls. For routes between the falls and *Stoat's Escape* this seems the most efficient access method. For routes beyond *Stoat's Escape* it's best to hike in from the downtream end of Fern Buttress.

Marc LeMenestrel on *The Land Before Time.*

photo: Rick Thompson

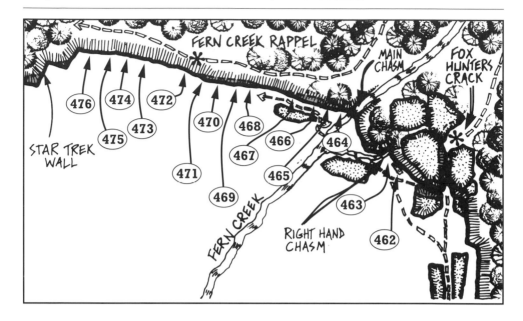

462   Water Power 5.11c ☆
Start six feet right of *Fern Creek Direct* and climb a flake to a ledge, then continue up the clean white face past a left-facing flake to the top. 50 feet. FA: Phil Heller & Alex Karr, April 1986.

463   Fern Creek Direct 5.11a ☆☆
Begin immediately right of the right-hand water spout of Fern Creek Falls and climb a thin crack in a steep white face to its end, then step left and ascend the face and arête to the top. 50 feet. FA: Phil Heller & Alex Karr, April 1986.

464   Fall Line 5.12b ☆☆ 🎣
Commence a short distance left of Fern Creek Falls and follow the line of seven bolts to a pair of cold shuts. 65 feet. FA: Doug Reed, fall 1991.

465   The Land Before Time 5.12c/d ☆☆ 🎣
Start from a block about 20 feet left of the previous route and follow the line of six bolts up the overhanging wall to an anchor just below the top. 55 feet. FA: Paul Pomeroy, October 1989.

466   Colors 5.13a ☆☆ 🎣
The next route follows a line of five bolts past a series of reachy bulges to a pair of cold shuts. 55 feet. FA: Doug Reed, fall 1991.

467   Roar of the Crowd 5.9- ☆
Step off blocks a short distance left of *Colors* and follow discontinuous cracks in a scooped-looking right-facing corner directly through a pair of roofs to the top. 70 feet. FA: Rick Fairtrace, Ron Walsh, & Jack Nard, April 1986.

468 Levitation 5.10d ☆
Begin three feet right of *Smoke on the Water* and levitate up and right through a cleft in the overhang, then continue to a second roof, which is passed to the left. Wander up a short face to the top. 75 feet. FA: Rick Fairtrace & Cal Swoager, May 1986.

469 Smoke on the Water 5.8- ☆
Locate a charred tree trunk beside a low roof. Start directly behind the trunk and pull the overhang, then angle up and left to a small pine. Cruise up the face directly to the top. 75 feet. FA: Rick Fairtrace & Bob Rentka, April 1986.

470 Blues Brothers 5.9 R ☆
Start about 10 feet left of the charred trunk and surmount the bulging face via juggy horizontals to gain a scooped-out area, then head directly for the top on crisp holds (5.6 R). 75 feet. FA: Eddie Begoon & Mike Cote, July 1986.

471 Lethargical Lion 5.8 ☆
Near the left end of the low roof band is a left-facing flake that's followed to its end. Continue past a short right-leaning roof and plod to the top finishing 10 feet right of the Fern Creek Rappel tree. 75 feet. FA: Rick Fairtrace & Bob Rentka, April 1986.

472 Rap-n-Go 5.9+
Start six feet left of *Lethargical Lion* and ascend the face past a small overhang, then continue straight up the face to the Fern Creek Rappel tree. 75 feet. FA: Rick Fairtrace & Bob Rentka, April 1986.

473 Stop the Presses, Mr. Thompson 5.11b ☆
Begin 50 feet left of the Fern Creek Rappel at some right-facing flakes in an orange wall that are followed to the start of a thin crack. Traverse five feet and climb directly to a good horizontal, then rail a few moves to the right and aim directly for the top passing a small roof and an awkward crack. 70 feet. FA: Cal Swoager, Rick Fairtrace, Bob Rentka, & Stuart Kuperstock, October 1986.

474 Common Ground 5.10c ☆
Commence 20 feet right of *Just Another Obscurity* and climb past two bolts, then step left and follow good holds directly to the top. 50 feet. Note: A selection of camming units will be helpful. FA: Eddie Begoon, June 1990.

475 Just Another Obscurity 5.12a ☆
Get going about 30 feet right of *Night Moves* and climb directly up the face past a lone bolt to the top. 50 feet. Note: Bring TCUs and medium size stoppers. FA: Eddie Begoon, June 1990.

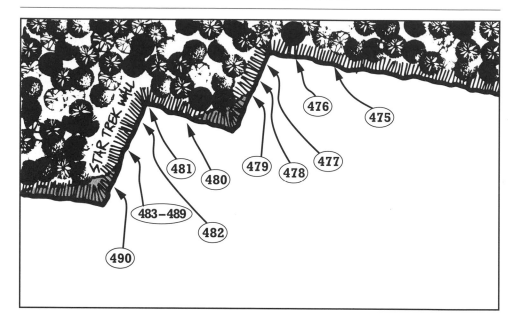

476   Night Moves 5.9 ☆
About 20 feet short of the downstream end of Fern Creek Wall is an obvious crack system, which is climbed to the top. 50 feet. FA: Rick Fairtrace & Scott Jones, March 1986.

477   Daughter of Dracula 5.10b R
Start 20 feet left of the corner and climb the clean streak past two pins to the top. 50 feet. FA: Eddie Begoon & Stanley Todd, March 1987

478   Subsidized Development 5.9 ☆
Begin 20 feet left of *Daughter of Dracula* and climb the face past four bolts finishing directly over the block at the top. 50 feet. Note: Tote Friends up to #3 and Tricams. FA: Jon Barker & Dan Stockwell, December 1991.

479   Holey Trinity 5.11a
Commence about 20 feet left of *Subsidized Development* and climb a direct line up the face passing two bolts en route to the top. 50 feet. Note: A selection of camming units is helpful. FA: Jon Barker & Dan Stockwell, December 1991.

480   Share the Earth 5.11d ☆☆
Begin immediately right of the corner and climb directly up the overhanging face past a good letter box aiming for the first of four bolts. Continue up the line of bolts and after clipping the last one step right and head for the top. 60 feet. Note: Carry TCUs and a #2 Camalot. FA: Eddie Begoon, June 1990.

The following nine routes are located on the Star Trek Wall, home to some of the best moderate grade climbs on Fern Buttress. With the exception of the first two routes listed all of the climbs are done in two short pitches as a result of the spacious belay ledge, known as the Bridge, which bisects the face. Because of the limited number of moderate routes available at the New River one can expect occasional overcrowding on these routes.

481   No Sign of Intelligent Life 5.7- ☆
Follow the right-facing dihedral to the top. 60 feet. FA: Rick Fairtrace, Hope & Jeff Uhl, & Scott Jones, October 1986.

482   Wrinkles and a Gold Card 5.8 ☆
Climb the face on the right margain of the Star Trek Wall. 65 feet. FA: Bill Wilson, Pierre Dairie, & Martin Paine, September 1988.

The following two routes provide access to the Bridge belay ledge.

483   Transporter Crack 5.6 ☆
Begin 25 feet uphill from the left edge of the face and transport yourself up the short, wide crack to the ledge. Traverse left and set up a belay where convenient. 40 feet. FA: Rick Fairtrace & Scott Jones, March 1986.

484   Three Dimensional Chess 5.8+ ☆
Climb a few meters up the *Transporter Crack* to a small tree, then traverse left on horizontals to a short crack. Advance up and left aiming for the *Impulse Power* crack and belay on the Bridge. 45 feet. FA: Markus Jucker & Pierre Lecavalier, November 1987.

The following five routes lead to the cliff top from the Bridge belay ledge.

485   Tractor Beam 5.8 R ☆
Begin just right of a giant hueco at the base of *Impulse Power* and climb directly to the of the face. 35 feet. Note: Bring small TCUs or a .5 Tricam. FA: Neil Ofsthun & Michael Stewart, March 1988.

486   Impulse Power 5.3 ☆
Warp your way up the right-hand crack. 35 feet. FA: Rick Fairtrace & Scott Jones, March 1986.

487   Beam Me Up, Scotty 5.6 ☆
Beam yourself up the middle crack. 35 feet. FA: Rick Fairtrace & Scott Jones, March 1986.

488   Crack of the Klingons 5.6 ☆☆
Thrust your way up the left-hand crack. 35 feet. FA: Rick Fairtrace & Scott Jones, March 1986.

489 The Wrath of Khan 5.8 ☆☆
Start at *Crack of the Klingons* and climb past the initial bulge, then transcend up and left to reach a small crack that angles left to meet to the arête. Balance around to the left side of the arête, then move up and left to the top. 55 feet. FA: Michael Stewart & Stuart Strickland, November 1987.

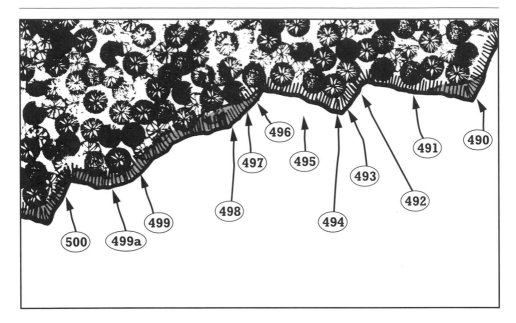

490 Project—In Progress—Panama
The roof crack with two bolts.

491 Berserker 5.11c ☆☆☆
This insanely fine climb features a pumpy finger crack. Begin 15 feet right of the
S and M dihedral and cruise the left-leaning crack to a pine at a ledge. Step right
and jam a strenuous finger crack, then reach left to the final finger crack, which
is followed it to the top. In the words of the first ascent party, "Drag yourself
over the lip, gasp for air, scream for joy!" 65 feet. FA: Phil Heller & Bob Burgher,
November 1985.

492 S and M 5.9 ☆☆
An aesthetic line that should prove to be painless. Follow the clean orange
dihedral to the top. 65 feet. FA: Stanley Todd, Mike Artz, & Andrew Barry, April
1986.

493 Pleasure and Pain 5.11b ☆☆☆
The abbreviated version of *It's a Fine Line Between Pleasure and Pain*. This
classic route should provide an adequate dose of cool and unusual punishment.
On the wall left of *S and M* is a discontinuous crack system on the lower third of
the face which is followed past several horizontals to a short right-facing corner.
Move up and left to a pin at the top of the corner, then angle right and up, then
back left to a second pin. Finish directly to the top. 70 feet. FA: Andrew Barry,
Mike Artz, & Stanley Todd, April 1986.

494 Sweet Dreams 5.11b ☆☆
Start by climbing the face just right of the arête until you reach a good horizontal, then move left and follow the arête to a ledge. Finish by cranking the flake system on the left side of the arête to the top. 80 feet. FA: Mike Artz, Andrew Barry, & Stanley Todd, May 1986.

495 Surge Complex 5.11a ☆☆☆
Surges of lactic acid and a complex crux are the protocol of this stunning route. Jam the left-leaning hand crack that splits the center of the wall past a bulge to a small roof. Pull the roof, then step left and follow a short crack until it's possible to step left again to gain a short, right-facing flake. Move up and pass a roof to the right finishing directly to the top. 85 feet. FA: Mike Artz, Andrew Barry, & Stanley Todd, May 1986.

496 Beech, Beeech, Beeeech! 5.6
Nothing worth beeching about here except trees! Downstream from *Surge Complex* is a right-facing dihedral with a large beech tree growing at its base. Climb it. 45 feet. FA: Tom Howard & Gaye Black, December 1985.

497 The Weight 5.11d ☆☆☆
Get started about 20 feet left of *Beech, Beeech, Beeeech* and climb directly past two bolts to gain a good rest below the overhanging orange headwall. Crank through the bulges to a hueco and a bolt, then follow a right angling flake to the top. 80 feet. Note: Bring small to medium stoppers and a full set of camming units. FA: Kenny Parker, January 1989.

498 The Scoop 5.11a ☆☆
Starting ten feet left of the previous route follow horizontals up and left to gain a right-angling ramp that leads to an orange corner. Dispense with the corner and the bulge above to gain the "Scoop", then clip the bolt and head straight for the top. 80 feet. Note: Bring lots of camming units and small Sliders. FA: Gene Kistler & Kenny Parker, January 1989.

499 Cresenta 5.10a ☆☆☆
This novel line ranks among the Fern Buttress classics. The initial arch stays dry during rain. Locate the prolific left-arching flake below the overhanging wall and follow it up and left to a stance at the end of the arch. Continue up the flake, then angle up and right to a ledge. Climb directly through a profusion of jugs and conclude with a short left-facing corner. 85 feet. FA: Tom Howard & Rick Thompson, December 1985.

499a Cresenta Direct Start—Fire and Waste 5.10b ☆
Start left of *Cresenta* and pull a low roof to reach a right-facing flake, which is followed to its end, then move up to a pin. Crank left to a horizontal crack, then hand traverse left and move up and back right to join *Cresenta* at the top of the arch. Finish as normal. FA: Eddie Begoon, Howard Clark, Kenny Parker, & Kelly Faust, February 1989.

Mark Van Cura on *Crack of the Kingons.*

photo: Rick Thompson

Eric Hörst on the spectacular *Just Send It.*

photo: Carl Samples

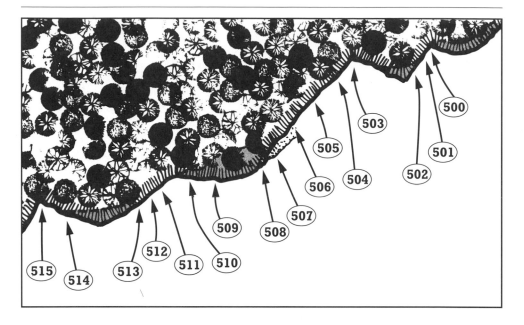

500 A Wild Hair 5.6

Climb the dihedral to a ledge, then move onto the right wall and follow a wide right-facing flake up to a ledge below a roof. Traverse left into the corner and up to the top. 75 feet. FA: Glenn Thomas & Carl Samples, September 1986.

501 Wampus Cat Blues 5.10c/d ☆☆

Commence immediately left of *A Wild Hair* and follow a seam to a roof, then scratch your way up the white face past a bolt to the top. 70 feet. FA: Kenny Parker, Kelly Faust, & Kevin Parker, March 1989.

502 Look, Me Awesome! 5.9

Begin about 40 downstream from *A Wild Hair* and climb the obvious crack identified by the large hueco. 70 feet. FA: John Eichenberger & Markus Jucker, March 1989.

503 Cowabunga 5.6

A hot contender for negative stars status. The next dihedral downstream starts as a flake. Slime your way to the top of the corner through the sea of mud and greenbriers. 55 feet. FA: Stanley Todd, Andrew Barry, & Mike Artz, May 1986.

504 The Monster 5.11a ☆

Start six feet left of *Cowabunga* and follow a thin left-facing flake to its end, then traverse left and pull down a series of solution pockets. Finish directly to a bent pine at the top. 80 feet. FA: Andrew Barry, Mike Artz, and Stanley Todd, May 1986.

505   Attack of Eddie Muenster 5.12a ☆☆
Start 15 feet right of *Constant Velocity* and climb the face past two bolts to a gain a good horizontal, then continue up the face passing more horizontals and a bolt in a bulge to the top. 80 feet. FA: Kenny Parker & Steve Downes, September 1989.

506   Constant Velocity 5.10b ☆☆☆
You'll most likely decelerate when you reach the overhanging wall at the top. Climb the attractive left-facing flake to its end at ledges, then continue directly up the overhanging wall past a roof to the top. 80 feet. FA: Mike Artz, Stanley Todd, & Andrew Barry , May 1986.

507   C-Section 5.11c ☆☆ 🄟
Begin a few paces right of the start to *Breach Birth* and climb directly past a bolt to gain the ledge. Step left crossing *Breach Birth* and follow the line of five bolts up the clean orange face to a pair of cold shuts. 70 feet. FA: Kenny Parker & Bill Burgos, September 1992.

508   Breach Birth 5.10c ☆
P1: Begin on a ledge at the upstream end of the roof and climb the left-facing white corner to the roof. Move right, pull it, and wander up to several ledges and belay. 35 feet. P2: Follow a beautiful open book to its end and traverse left to a ledge and belay. Rappel or follow a short pitch to the top. 55 feet. FA: Mike Artz, Stanley Todd, & Andrew Barry, April 1986.

509   Intimidation 5.10a ☆
One glance at this burly-looking roof will leave no question where the name came from. Climb a right-facing corner to the roof and follow the major weakness past the lip, then move up to some ledges. Follow a short crack to its end and finish up and left. 75 feet. FA: Mike Artz, Rick Fairtrace, & Andrew Barry, May 1986.

510   Anticipation 5.9
Climb the gently overhanging face ten feet right of *Sandy's Sweet Bottom* until it's possible to traverse right to the base of a crack, which is followed to the top. 60 feet. FA: Rick Fairtrace & Mike Artz, May 1986.

511   Sandy's Sweet Bottom 5.9
Begin directly below the hanging open book and climb the profusion of jugs past a bulge to reach a stance at the start of the dihedral, which is climbed to its end. Part up and right to the top. 60 feet. FA: Carl Samples & Ed McCarthy, March 1986.

512   New Tricks for the Old Dog 5.10c ☆ 🄱

The combined age of the first ascent party was more than 125 years and they're crankin'! Start 15 feet left of *Sandy's Sweet Bottom* on brilliant orange rock and follow the line of seven bolts stepping left at the finish to the cold shuts at the top of *Morning Dew*. 60 feet. FA: Tom Isaacson, Jeanette Helfrich, & John Raynor, June 1991.

513   Morning Dew 5.12a/b ☆ 🄱

A few paces downstream from the previous route is a line of six bolts that leads through some overhangs and a bulge to a pair of cold shuts. 60 feet. FA: Tom Isaacson & Tom Jones, September 1992.

514   Contemplation 5.10a

Twenty-five feet right of the *Stoats Escape* dihedral is a crack that is followed to the top. 40 feet. FA: Kenny Parker & Steve Lancaster, May 1986.

515   Stoats Escape 5.4

Inside this grungy chimney is an old ladder nailed to a tree trunk that provided access for miners during the coal boom. And although the ladder has long since deteriorated beyond usefulness the outside of the chimney can be stemmed to the top. 40 feet. FA: Andrew Barry, solo, 1985.

Stoats Escape is the last route described in a downstream direction from the access points near Fern Creek Falls.

Mark Van Cura on the elegant *Biohazard*, Fern Point.

photo: Rick Thompson

Scott Garso on the first ascent of *Baptism by Fire.*

photo: Rick Thompson

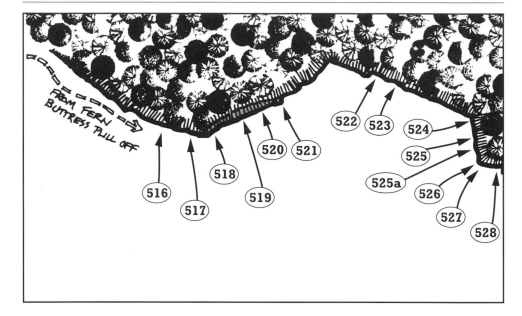

The following routes are described in an upstream direction using the Fern Buttress Trail, which provides direct access to the downstream end of the Endless Wall. See the Endless Wall Overview map for additional details.

516 Cow in a China Shop 5.8 ☆
No need for getting bullish here. Start six feet left of a tree and move directly up on plated incuts to reach the left side of a roof band at two-thirds height. Pull over the roof, then slightly right to a short right-facing corner. Finish up and left. 60 feet. FA: Carl Samples, Rick Thompson, Bob Rentka, Bob Cenk, Ron Kampas, & Jason Brooks, September 1988.

517 The No-zone 5.10a ☆
Begin at the right edge of the face and follow the clean streak to the top. 60 feet. FA: Rick Thompson & Jon McCue, October 1988.

518 Naked Potatoes 5.10b ☆
Start near the left side of the overhanging face and climb the right-leaning obtuse dihedral to its end at a bulging roof. Pull up and left, then hand traverse left until it's possible to climb straight to the top. 70 feet. FA: Eddie Begoon & Mike Artz, August 1987.

519 Ron Kauk Gets a Perm 5.12a ☆☆ 🄿
Attribute to Kauk's late 1980s transition from trad to sport climbing. Get started a short distance right of Naked Potatoes, just right of a mature oak and follow the line bolts up a bulging orange crack to a roof, then arc up and left past a brief slab to cold shuts. 60 feet. FA: Eric Hörst, Rick Thompson & Jason Brooks, September 1988.

520   Arm Forces 5.11c/d ☆ 🎧
The next line to the right is a four-bolt sport climb with cold shuts. 50 feet. FA: Eric Hörst & Mark Guider, November 1991.

521   Dead Beat Club 5.11c/d
Begin five feet right of *Arm Forces* and climb past a short right-facing flake to a pin, then continue slightly left and up to the next horizontal. Step right and head for the top. 50 feet. FA: Eddie Begoon & Mike Artz, November 1989.

522   The Mega Jug 5.11b ☆ 🎧
Begin on the left side of a tree and follow the line of four bolts to a cold-shut station. 45 feet. FA: Eric & Lisa Hörst, September 1990.

523   October Surprise 5.10d ☆ 🎧
Start at the left end of the low roof and climb past four bolts to cold shuts. 45 feet. FA: FA: Eric & Lisa Hörst, October 1991.

524   Dog Day Afternoon II 5.12a ☆ 🎧
A few paces right of the corner is an easy left-rising ramp, which is climbed to its end, then head directly up the face past four bolts to a pair of cold shuts. 70 feet. FA: Mark Robinson & Eric Hörst, October 1991.

525   Teleconnections 5.11d ☆☆ 🎧
Begin near the center of the face and follow a bolted seam to its end, then make a tricky traverse right and up to a station at the top. 70 feet. FA: Eric Hörst, Bob Rentka, Mike Artz, & Eddie Begoon, August 1987.

525a Teleconnections Direct Start—Power Talk 5.12b ☆ 🎧
Commence right of the start to *Teleconnections* and follow the line of bolts directly up the face and join *Teleconnections* just below the fifth bolt. 70 feet. FA: Eric Hörst, 1991.

526   Wings and a Prayer 5.12a ☆☆
A spicey companion climb to *Dixie Chicken.* Begin on the left side of the arête and climb a short right-facing flake and the face above past two bolts, then head slightly left for a short crack and straight for the top. 70 feet FA: Eddie Begoon, August 1990.

527   Dixie Chicken 5.11c ☆☆☆
Artz and Begoon's recipe for southern style crankin'. Begin on the right side of the tasty arête and strut directly to the top. 70 feet. FA: Mike Artz & Eddie Begoon, August 1987.

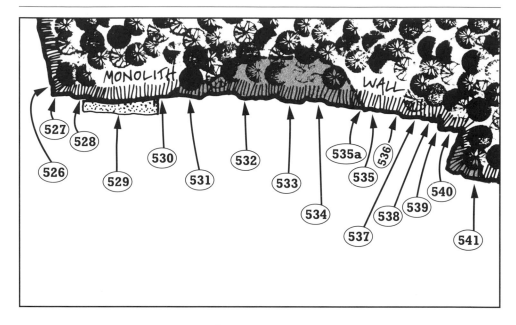

528 First Person 5.10c ☆ 🅟
Start a few feet right of the arête, just left of the block, and follow four bolts up the shallow corner to a pair of cold shuts. 50 feet. FA: Lisa & Eric Hörst, & Mark Robinson, October 1991.

529 Close to the Edge 5.12b ☆ 🅟
From atop the block follow five bolts to a pair of cold shuts. 50 feet. FA: Brian McCray, 1992.

530 Spiderwalk 5.10c ☆☆
Just left of the Monolith amphitheater lies a right-leaning broken crack system. Waltz up the cracks past several horizontals to a roof at the top and exit right to a belay. 60 feet. FA: Phil Heller & Alex Karr, November 1985.

531 Hummingbird 5.10c ☆
Start at the extreme left end of the amphitheater and follow a right-facing dihedral to a roof. Pull it at the point of least resistance and follow the face and crack to the top. 60 feet. FA: Gene Kistler & Bill Moore, July 1986.

532 My Stinking Brain 5.13a ☆☆ 🅟
Follow the left-hand line of six bolts in the amphitheater to a pair of cold shuts. 60 feet. FA: Doug Reed, fall 1993.

533 Project—In Progress—Unnamed
Climbs the line of bolts in the center of the amphitheater.

534   The Monolith 5.11d C1 ☆☆☆
This amazing roof still awaits that coveted first free ascent. In the center of the amphitheater is a painfully obvious bolt protection crack line. Climb it! 60 feet. FA: With aid Phil Heller & Alex Karr, November 1985.

535   Over the Edge 5.11c ☆☆☆ 👐
Begin at extreme right side of the amphitheater, on the face immediately right of the arête and follow the leftward angling line of bolts to a cold shut station. 50 feet. FA: Eric Hörst, September 1991.

535a Over the Edge Direct Start—Air Apparent 5.12c ☆☆ 👐
Start on the left side of the arête and follow three bolts up the overhanging wall, then power up and right joining *Over the Edge* below the fourth bolt. 50 feet. FA: Eric Hörst, October 1991.

536   Fried Mush 5.8
Begin about 35 feet right of *Over the Edge* and wander up the face to the top. 60 feet. FA: Bill Moore & Tondeleyo Dale, July 1986.

537   Chew Electric Death You Snarling Cur 5.8+
Begin to the right of the previous route at a small right-facing corner and wander up the jugular face to the top. 60 feet. FA: Roger Coit & Tiny Elliott, September 1990.

538   McStumpy's Sandwich Crack 5.6
Locate the small left-facing corner near the right side of the face and climb it to the top. 60 feet. FA: Carl Samples & Ed McCarthy, April 1986.

539   Devil's Arête 5.10a R
Climb the arête just right of *McStumpy's Sandwich Crack* past a pin to gain a flake that is followed to the top. 65 feet. FA: Dwight Atkinson & Randy Boush, March 1989.

540   The Puddy System 5.11a ☆
Get started immediately right of the arête and climb the parallel cracks in the narrow overhanging wall following the longest one to a flakey roof. Move right over the roof, then left past a short seam to gain a thin crack that leads to the finish. Engage in a desperate vegetative battle to stand on terra firma! 60 feet. FA: Eddie Begoon, Bob Rentka, & Carl Samples, September 1988.

541   The Yert Yak Crack 5.9+ ☆
Right of *The Puddy System* is a cluster of hemlocks that shroud an appealing roofy-corner. P1: A boulder problem start leads to the roof crack that is followed up and right to a ledge. Belay at a tree. 45 feet. P2: Begin directly behind the belay and climb the face to a large horizontal, then traverse right, jam a short crack, and finish directly up. 30 feet. FA: Ed McCarthy & Carl Samples, April 1986.

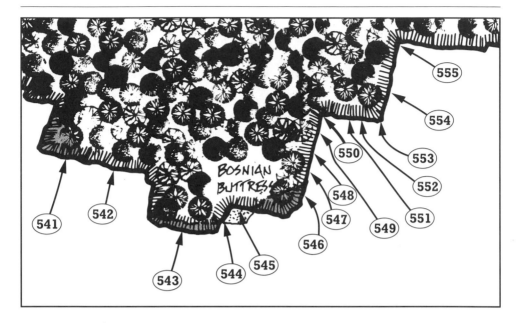

542   Wondering 5.10c

Begin on the left edge of the face at a left-facing corner and follow a wandering line to the top. 70 feet. FA: Mike Artz & partner, 1989.

543   Preservation of the Wild Life 5.11d ☆☆☆

Seldom done, this hair-raising climb is anything but tame. Embark 15 feet left of *Two Bag Face* at short crack near the center of face that is followed until it's possible to traverse left to a bolt, then move right under a bulge and pull a cruxy roof. Traverse left to gain a series of killer cracks which lead to the top. 100 feet. FA: Doug Reed & Rick Thompson, October 1988.

544   Two Bag Face 5.9 R ☆☆

A bit more enticing than the name implies. Struggle up the unprotected offwidth flake and climb the face on the right side of the arête for a short distance. Move left around the arête and follow perfect rock to the top. 80 feet. Note: The R-rated start can be avoided by traversing in on the ledge. FA: Phil Heller & Alex Karr, March 1986.

545   The Lichen in Me 5.10d ☆

Begin in the large dihedral and follow the left side of the pillar to its top, then crank left and up a left-facing corner pulling a small roof to gain the top. 70 feet. FA: Carl Samples & Bob Rentka, November 1988.

546   Bosnian Vacation 5.12d ☆☆☆ ⌐

Start your rock holiday just right of the arête and take the clip tour along the line of 10 bolts to a pair of cold shuts. 85 feet. FA: Kenny Parker, 1994.

547 Wall Drug 5.12c ☆☆ (p)
A short distance right of *Bosnian Vacation* is another trippy sport climb equipped with six bolts and a cold shut station. 75 feet. FA: Kenny Parker & Steve Downes, July 1990.

548 Mr. Workman's Crack 5.11b ☆☆
This laborious undertaking is named after a resident who lives atop the crag. Begin at a crack that splits the right side of the face and follow it, then move left to a thinner crack. Continue up the thinner crack until it peters out and finish up and right. 70 feet. FA: Phil Heller & Alex Karr, March 1986.

549 Workman's Comp 5.11a ☆☆ (p)
Start immediately right of *Mr. Workman's Crack* and toil past five bolts to a pair of cold shuts. 70 feet. FA: Eric Hörst & Mark Guider, October 1991.

550 Mrs. Workman's Corner 5.9+ ☆
Begin in the corner and crank the left edge of the twin-sided flake, then follow a crack and small left-facing corner on the left wall to its end at a tiny roof. Finish directly up. 70 feet. FA: Pete Absolon & Topper Wilson, July 1986.

551 Climb-max 5.11d ☆ (p)
A few meters right of the dihedral is a line of five bolts equipped with cold shuts. 70 feet. FA: Mark Guider & Eric Hörst, November 1991.

552 Graceland 5.11a ☆☆
Start a short distance left of the arête and boulder up the face to the start of a short crack. Climb the crack and continue straight up until it's possible to move left below a small roof to a stance at a hueco. Traverse right along the roof until you're almost to the arête (good pro here), then angle up slightly left to the top. 80 feet. FA: Eddie Begoon & Mike Artz, November 1986.

553 Toss That Beat in the Garbage Can 5.10d ☆☆☆
A bouldery start and perfectly timed rests make this route worthy. Climb the arête past a bolt and several small ledges to the top. 80 feet. FA: Mike Artz & Eddie Begoon, November 1986.

554 Hole in the Wall 5.11b
Start from the left end of the ledge and follow the dihedral to a large hueco. Pull directly over the top of the hole and aim for the top. 70 feet. FA: Alex Karr & Mike Kehoe, 1988.

555 Beat Me Daddy, Eight to the Bar 5.8
Climb the obvious right-facing slimy corner. 40 feet. FA: Tom Howard & Bruce Burgin, October 1985.

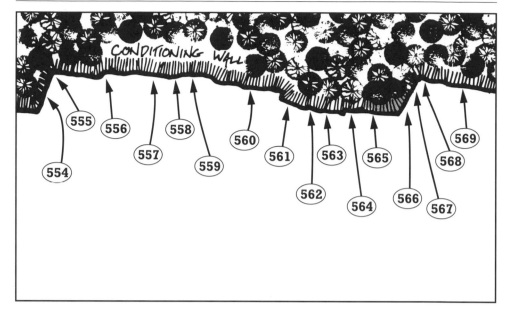

556 Mud and Guts 5.10b ☆☆
Despite its charismatic appearance this climb is a seep most of the time. Follow the right-facing dihedral that ramps leftward to the top. 70 feet. FA: Doug Reed & Tom Howard, September 1984.

557 Just Send It 5.13a/b ☆☆☆☆ 🄫
Another Hörst tester. Using the same start as *Welcome to Conditioning* make a few moves and immediately traverse left, then follow the line of bolts along the opposite facing dihedrals to cold shuts. FA: Eric Hörst, October 1992.

558 Welcome to Conditioning 5.12d/13a ☆☆☆ 🄫
The first 5.13 established on the Endless Wall. Start 25 feet right of *Mud and Guts* and lunge to a horizontal, then follow bolts up and slightly left to a jug. Rail right and power over the awkward roof, then follow the crack to a station. 60 feet. FA: Eric Hörst & Rick Thompson, March 1988.

559 Stab Me, I Don't Matter 5.13a/b ☆☆ 🄫
The moment you turn your back, the dagger goes in. Get started six feet right of the previous route at an obvious short crack in the overhanging orange wall and move up to a jug. Pump right and follow the line of bolts to a station below the roof. 60 feet. FA: Eric Hörst & Rick Thompson, October 1988.

560 Hold the Dog 5.11d ☆☆ 🄫
One of the earliest clip ups on the Endless Wall. Begin a few paces left of *Party Out of Bounds* at low right-facing flake and follow the line of fixed gear to a station at a medium-sized pine. 45 feet. FA: Rick Thompson, Eric Hörst, & Bob Rentka, September 1988.

561   Party Out of Bounds 5.11d ☆
Don't let this festive climb get out of hand! Locate the pair of cracks on the left side of the face and follow the left one until it's possible to traverse right along the ledge to the station at the top of *The Udderling*. 45 feet. Note: Bring plenty of small brass and TCUs. FA: Mike Artz & Eddie Begoon, November 1986.

562   The Udderling 5.12a ☆
Ten feet right of *Party Out of Bounds* is a sibling crack that's followed to a station on the ledge. 40 feet. FA: Eric Hörst & Rick Thompson, October 1988.

563   Toxic Waste 5.7
The loose rock on this pitch could be hazardous to your health! Begin 20 feet right of the previous route at a large flake leaning against the wall. Climb the left side of it past a small tree and continue up to a roof, then shift left and up to a ledge with some rhodies. Climb right and up to gain a left-diagonaling crack that is followed until it's possible to exit up and right to the top. 80 feet. FA: Mike Artz & Eddie Begoon, November 1986.

564   One of My Many Smells 5.9-
And not a pretty one, I might add. Climb the right-facing flake and face above to the top. 80 feet. FA: Carl Samples & Mark Van Cura, 1990.

565   Quickie in the Molars 5.12a ☆☆
P1: Start the action on the left side of arête and follow the line of bolts up the friable-looking face and belay at a ledge. 40 feet. P2: Traverse left 20 feet to left-facing flake which is followed over roof, then zigzag left, then right to the top. 40 feet. Note: The first pitch is entirely bolt protected but the second pitch will require a light rack. FA: Mike Artz & Eddie Begoon, December 1988.

565a Quickie in the Molars—Direct Finish 5.12a ☆
From top of first pitch, continue directly up headwall past another 5.12 crux to the top. 40 feet. FA: Jonny Woodward, April 1989.

566   Muscle Belly 5.12a ☆ 🄿
On the right face of the arête is a line of five bolts that lead to a pair of cold shuts below the roof. 60 feet. FA: Eric Hörst & Mark Guider, September 1991.

567   Wild Seed 5.11b ☆☆☆ 🄿
Start from a ledge in the center of the face and follow six bolts directly up and over the roof to a pair of cold shuts. 75 feet. FA: Eric Hörst , Lisa Hörst, & Mark Robinson, October 1991.

568   Lies and Propaganda 5.9+
Grovel up the dirty right-facing dihedral, then step right 20 feet short of the top and climb the face to avoid the filth. 80 feet. FA: Eddie Begoon & Mike Artz, December 1988.

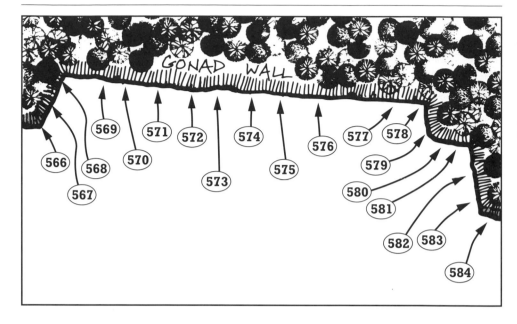

Upstream from the dihedral is a long nondescript face split by an occasional crack.

569 Gonad the Bavarian 5.11d ☆ ⓟ
Since its retro bolting, this route doesn't quite take the nads it used to. Begin 15 feet right of *Lies and Propaganda* and follow the bulging bolted crack and brief face to a pair of cold shuts. 50 feet. FA: Phil Heller & Alex Karr, March 1986.

570 Foutre la Doigt 5.12b ☆☆ ⓟ
The next line of bolts upstream from *Gonad the Bavarian* provides a fingery workout. 50 feet. FA: Eric Hörst & Mark Guider, May 1990.

571 No Kiss, No Lubrication 5.11d ☆
One of the most classic of the Karr and Heller names. To the right of the of the previous sport route is a bulging crack. Lube up and wham it! 50 feet. FA: Alex Karr & Phil Heller, March 1986.

572 Salvador Dali's Car 5.12b ☆☆ ⓟ
Ride the not-so surrealistic line of four bolts to a pair of cold shuts. 50 feet. FA: Eric Hörst, May 1990.

573 Chameleon 5.10d ☆☆ ⓟ
Who can name the star of this classic flick? The next route is a five-bolt sport climb that climbs a juggy face. 50 feet. FA: Mark Guider, Eric Hörst, & Rick Thompson, October 1991.

574   Old and in the Way   5.11b ☆
The name says it all. Boulder past a bolt to gain a small ledge, then continue through a bulging pocketed wall past a second bolt to an eye bolt station. 50 feet. FA: Kenny Parker & Blaze Davies, March 1989.

575   Fly Girls   5.12a ☆☆☆ 🄲
Commence immediately left of the large tree and fire off the line of five bolts. 50 feet. FA: Eric Hörst & Mark Guider, October 1991.

576   Doer, Not a Critic   5.11c ☆☆ 🄲
Start a short distance right of the tree and follow the line of six bolts to a pair of cold shuts. 50 feet. FA: Eric & Lisa Hörst, October 1991.

577   Aquatic Ecstasy   5.11b
A wet suit might make this one more do-able during the rainy season. Begin slightly right of the thin crack and climb directly to a horizontal, then step left and follow the crack to the top. 40 feet. FA: Kenny Parker & Steve Lancaster, June 1986.

578   Far Fletched   5.9
Climb the encrusted corner that lies 25 feet right of *Aquatic Ecstasy*. 45 feet. FA: John Gill & Fletch Taylor, July 1989.

579   Arbor Day   5.12a ☆☆☆
Classic! Commence on the blunt arête and climb to a bolt, then angle left past pin to a jug. Traverse right to a second bolt, then power directly past a third bolt to ledge and branch up and right to the finish. 60 feet. FA: Kenny Parker, Kelly Faust, Eric Hörst, & Travis Eisman, March 1989.

580   Fragile Egosystem   5.10b ☆☆ 🄲
Oh, the delicacy of some climber egos. Start five feet left of *Stoat goes to Joshua Tree*...and follow the line of bolts to a pair of cold shuts. 60 feet. FA: Rick Thompson & Eric Hörst, March 1989.

581   Stoat Goes to Joshua Tree and Tears a Flapper on Baby Apes   5.7
A contender for the longest route name at the New. Climb the vegetated crack system past a tree and a small roof in an alcove to the top. 60 feet. FA: Mike Artz, solo, July 1986.

582   Use Your Power   5.12d/13a ☆☆ 🄲
Why waste it when it can be put to good use on this route? Force your way up the line of six bolts to a cold-shut station. 60 feet. FA: Eric Hörst, October 1992.

583   Project—In Progress
The line of bolts on the left side of the arête.

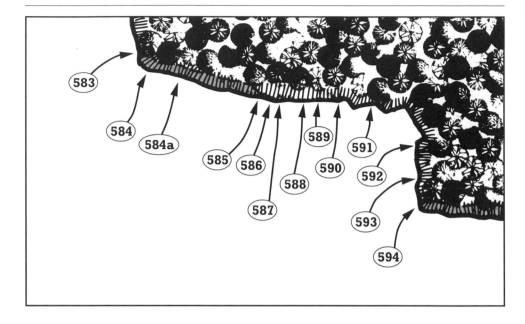

584   The Brawn Wall 5.12b ☆☆
P1: Begin a few paces right of the arête and follow the arching crack in the white dihedral past three pins to reach the roof. Traverse right across the overhanging wall and around corner to reach a small left-facing corner and set up a hanging belay. 40 feet. P2: Follow a right-facing corner to the top. 45 feet. FA: Chick Holtcamp & Bernard Nypaver, July 1988.

584a The Brawn Wall Direct Start — Project
A short distance right of the regular start is a line of three bolts.

584b The Brawn Wall Direct Finish 5.10c ☆☆
From the hanging belay climb directly through the roof and jam the overhanging crack to the top. 45 feet. FA: Chick Holtcamp & Bernard Nypaver, September 1988.

585   Pop Top 5.11c/d ☆
Start at a thin orange crack near the right end of the roofs and pull the low roof to the left to gain a short face. Climb up and left into a right-facing corner capped by a roof, then reach left and pull onto the face. Move straight up past a pin to a belay ledge with a bolt. 40 feet. FA: Bernard Nypaver, Chick Holtcamp, & Ed Parks, July 1988.

586   Eye of Zen 5.10b ☆
Using the same start as *Pop Top* pull directly onto the face and climb past a second overhang aiming directly for a pine at the top. 65 feet. FA: Chick Holtcamp & Bernard Nypaver, June 1988.

587   Rolling Rock   5.9 ☆

The fabled brew from Latrobe, Pennsylvania. Get started at the right end of the low roof, which is pulled to gain a small right-facing corner. Follow the corner to a fallen pine. 60 feet. FA: Bill Moore & Gene Kistler, July 1986.

588   Bolt Rookies 5.11a ☆

Start just right of *Rolling Rock* and move up to a bolt, then continue up and left over a roof and past a pin to the top. 60 feet. FA: John Burcham & Charlie Rafferty, June 1989.

589   Prepare to Succeed   5.11c/d ☆

Commence about 20 feet left of *Baptism by Fire* and crank directly through an inverted V and past a small right-facing corner. Continue past two small overlaps and follow the clean swath to the top. 65 feet. FA: Bernard Nypaver & Chick Holtcamp, September 1988.

590   Baptism by Fire   5.9 ☆☆

This popular outing should not be confused with a born-again lieback. Follow the left-facing flake into an apex slot avoiding any assistance from the inauspicious tree. Undercling a short roof and continue along the prime lieback flake to the top. 60 feet. FA: Scott Garso & Rick Thompson, April 1986.

591   Mean, Mean Girl   5.11d ☆☆

Begin about 20 feet right of the previous route and follow a right-facing, then left-facing flake system to its end. Crank up and traverse right to the end of a narrow roof band and snarl directly to the top. 60 feet. FA: Alex Karr & Phil Heller, April 1986.

592   Two Tone Arête   5.10b ☆ ℗

Begin on the right side of the arête and follow the line of six bolts to the top. 70 feet. FA: Paul Sullivan, 1992.

593   Emerald Dance   5.9 ☆☆☆

Climbing of a semi-precious nature. Locate the pair of cracks in the center of the face and follow the left one to a small roof, then traverse right to the start of another crack that is followed to a roof. Traverse right to a ledge with a small pine (possible belay), then ramble up and right merging with an arête that is followed to the top. 90 feet. FA: Mike Artz, Don Blume, & Gary Womont, March 1986.

593a Emerald Dance Direct Finish—Cold Turkey 5.11c ☆

Follow the normal route to the end of the second crack at the roof and pull it directly. FA TR: Alex Karr, April 1986.

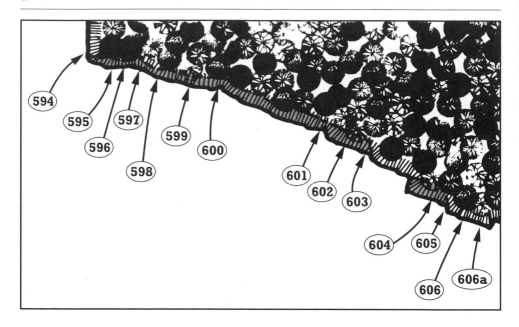

594   Thieves in the Temple 5.12a ☆☆☆ 🄿

Don't rob yourself of the opportunity to experience this great route! Start just left of the arête, pull the low roof and follow eight bolts up and left to cold shuts. 80 feet. FA: Doug Reed, 1993

595   Project—Unnamed

Identified by the rusting lone bolt in the center of the face. This line was mistakenly identified as *Rolling Rock* in the 1987 edition of New River Rock. The many who tried it (thinking they were getting on a 5.9) quickly found it to be seemingly impossible.

596   Grand Larceny 5.11c ☆☆☆

Begin on the right edge of the face and move past a bolt to gain a ramp. Continue past a two more bolts to the ledge and rappel. 60 feet. FA: Kenny & Kevin Parker, March 1989.

597   Presto 5.10a

No magic here, just awkward climbing. Begin in the chimney and squirm up the bombay to a rest below a huge roof. Pull it and continue the squirm to the top. 70 feet. FA: Doug Reed, solo, September 1984.

598   Wounded in Action 5.12b/c ☆☆ ℛ

Begin about 15 feet right of *Presto* and climb the right side of the arête past two bolts and a pin to gain a shallow corner that leads to a ledge equipped with a two bolt rap anchor. 40 feet. FA: Eddie Begoon & Mike Artz, December 1988.

599   Project—Abandoned
To the right of *Wounded in Action* is a single bolt that marks the current high point of this ground up attempt.

600   The Fourgasm 5.9 ☆
Start at the first crack to the right of *Presto,* below some large roofs and jam past the first roof to gain a left-facing corner. The corner leads to a second roof that is conquered directly out the wild-looking slot. Easier climbing leads to the top. 70 feet. FA: Tom Howard & Nick Brash, September 1984.

601   Bushong 5.9 ☆
Approximately 80 feet right of *The Fourgasm* is a wide crack in a flared open book that is jammed to a stance below the massive roof. Turn the roof by climbing out the left wall and follow easier climbing to the top. 70 feet. FA: Tom Howard & Doug Reed, September 1984.

602   Tongue-in-Groove 5.12a ☆☆ ⓟ ⓡ
Begin atop a leaning block and fire off the line of five bolts to a station below the final roof band. 50 feet. FA: Doug Reed & Rick Thompson, November 1988.

603   Sometimes a Great Notion 5.11a ☆☆
Get started in the rust-colored left-facing dihedral and follow it past three roofs, then move right to a ledge and belay. 70 feet. FA: John Harlin, Nico Mailander, & Liz Klobusicky, October 1988.

604   Portly Gentleman's Route 5.12c ☆☆☆☆
Immaculately stout! Start by jamming the short crack to reach the superb white, left-facing dihedral that is followed to the black roof. Pull it and follow the splitter tips crack to the top. 60 feet. FA: Greg Collins, 1988.

605   Beowulf 5.12a ☆☆
Start at the left edge of the *Sun Viking* face and follow crisp edges past three bolts to a pin. Make a strenuous hand traverse to the right, then follow a right-facing dihedral to a short crack and the top. 70 feet. FA: Eddie Begoon, February 1990.

606   Sun Viking 5.11d R ☆☆☆
The flexy edges at the start of this powerfully elegant route may give you second thoughts. Begin in the center of the face and crimp directly past a bolt and two pins, then hand traverse right to a flared crack that is followed to its end. Move up and left past a short fingercrack to the top. 80 feet. FA: Phil Heller & Alex Karr, November 1985.

606a Sun Viking Direct Start—Thor 5.12d ☆☆
Immediately right of the regular start is a short crack that leads to a thin face protected by two bolts. Finish on the upper cracks of the regular route. FA: Phil Heller, April 1988

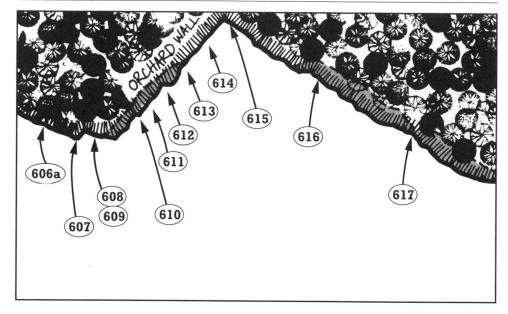

607 Loki 5.12b ☆☆☆
Sporty, but not a sport route. Begin at the arête 25 feet right of *Sun Viking* and climb past a bolt and through a bulge to reach a second bolt. Stand above the second bulge and traverse right to a devious blunt arête that is followed past another bolt. An easy right-facing corner leads to cold shuts. Note: Bring a #1 TCU in addition to your draws. 65 feet. FA: Eddie Begoon, August 1990.

608 White Out 5.12a ☆☆☆
Start at a short right-facing corner and climb past a pin and a bolt to reach a stance at the second pin. Move directly onto a beautiful white face to another bolt, then left past the final bolt and up to a cold shut station. 70 feet. Note: The first ascent only used fixed gear; however, it is possible to get a #2 or #3 TCU above the last bolt. FA: Eddie Begoon, March 1990.

609 God of Fire 5.11c ☆☆
Using the same start a *White Out* climb to the stance at the second pin, then step right around the arête and climb past another bolt en route to the top. 75 feet. Note: Bring small nuts and TCUs. FA: Mike Artz & Mike Cote, March 1990.

Around the corner and right of the *God of Fire* lies the greatest concentration of classic 5.10 cracks on Fern Buttress. This face is known as the Orchard Wall. Splitting the left-hand side of the wall are a pair of flared cracks below a large roof. The left-hand climb is....

610   Bisect 5.10c ☆☆

The original finish traversed right at the top of the crack below the large roof; however, most parties now step left at the crack's end and belay on the ledge. Begin at a left-facing corner capped by a low roof and pull it, then follow the crack to its end. Step left and belay. 60 feet. FA: Doug Reed, solo, September 1984.

611   Anal Clenching Adventures 5.10a ☆☆

The first route to be established on the Endless Wall and a fine one indeed. The first ascent party used one spot of aid. Begin 15 feet right of *Bisect* and jam the striking flared crack for 50 feet, then step left, crossing *Bisect* to the belay ledge. 65 feet. FA with aid: Rick Skidmore, Hobart Parks, & Steve Erskine, 1979. FA: Mike Artz, solo, February 1986.

612   Triple Treat 5.10a ☆☆☆☆

If ever there were a three-fer deal, this would be it. Tape up and begin about 20 feet uphill from the previous route and pull a low roof to gain a flared left-facing corner that leads past two more roofs and the top. 70 feet. FA: Tom Howard, Nick Brash, & Doug Reed, September 1984.

613   Springboard 5.10b ☆☆☆☆

This popular hand crack epitomizes the word plumline. Begin 15 feet right of *Triple Treat* and follow the hand crack to the top of the wall passing the "springboard" at about two-thirds height. 70 feet. FA: Nick Brash & Bruce Burgin, summer 1981.

614   Lewd Operator 5.10c ☆☆

A route for the rude and lascivious. Begin just uphill from *Springboard* and jam the curving crack its end, then make a move right and follow a short right-facing flake to a stance. Tiptoe leftward across an airy traverse to a reach a right-facing corner (just right of *Springboard)* and follow it to the top. 70 feet. FA: Rick Thompson & Scott Garso, April 1986.

615   The Awesome Flossom Corner 5.7

Climb the dihedral. 60 feet. FA: Mark Van Cura & Dave Sippel, 1986.

616   The Mighty Stoat 5.11c ☆

This short, yet stiff climb will put a pump in your earlobes. Thirty feet right of the Orchard Wall is a low roof split by cracks at either end. Follow the left-hand crack to the ledge. 40 feet. FA: Andrew Barry & Mike Artz, September 1985.

617   Shiny Faces 5.10d ☆☆

A few steps right of *The Mighty Stoat* is an overhanging crack that starts off-width and finishes fingers. 60 feet. FA: Tom Howard & Doug Reed, September 1984.

618 Hysteria 5.8+ ☆☆☆
This Gunks-like route may not cause uncontrollable laughter, but will most likely put a smile on your face. Begin around the corner from *Shiny Faces* at the extreme right end of the low roof and move up the left-hand margin of the face to a ledge. Continue up aiming for the tallest prow of rock and the top. 85 feet. FA: Mike Artz, Andrew Barry, & Rick Fairtrace, September 1985.

619 Mellow Drama 5.9+ ☆
Commence a few paces right of *Hysteria* by climbing up and slightly right to a narrow overlap. Step over the center of the overlap to the face above and merge with a right-facing dihedral that is followed to its end. Finish up and right. 75 feet. FA: Andrew Barry, Rick Fairtrace, & Mike Artz, September 1985.

620 Furry Nerd 5.10c R
Don't let this poorly protected route lodge a fur ball in your throat. Begin uphill from *Mellow Drama* and climb the blunt arête to its end, then move right and follow a line parallel to the right-facing corner of *Mellow Drama* to the top. 70 feet. FA: Andrew Barry, September 1985.

621 Wishbone Left 5.10b ☆
Right of *Furry Nurd* is a distinct open book capped by a triangular roof. Begin in the corner and diverge left following a wishbone-shaped crack past the left edge of the roof. Continue a few moves left, then climb directly to the top finishing at the same spot as *Furry Nerd*. 70 feet. FA: Rick Fairtrace & Scott Jones, October 1985.

622 Wishbone Right 5.9+
Follow the first 20 feet of *Wishbone Left,* then move onto the right wall and make

a rightward traverse under the roof. Pull the roof into a shallow groove that is followed to the top. 70 feet. FA: Andrew Barry, Mike Artz & Steve Lancaster, May 1986.

623   Total Sex Package   5.12a ☆☆☆ (β)
Start on the blunt arête to the right of the *Wishbone* routes and follow the line of seven bolts to a pair of cold shuts. 70 feet. FA: Kenny Parker & Bill Burgos, October 1992.

624   Project—In Progress—Give Me the Strap-On
The line of bolts to the right of *Total Sex Package.*

625   No Static at All   5.10a ☆☆
Another one of those Steely Dan things. Begin ten feet right of the dirty dihedral and climb the short crack to its end, then traverse right and follow the broken crack to the top (shares the finish with *Parsimony*). 70 feet. FA: Mike Artz, Gary Womont, & Don Blume, March 1986.

626   Parsimony   5.10c R ☆
Sparse protection at the onset mandates more effort than frugality. Begin 15 feet downhill from *No Static at All* and ascend the blank-looking face trending left to the start of a discontinuous crack (four feet to the right of the upper broken crack on *No Static at All*). Climb this crack to its end, then traverse a few moves left to the shared crack finish with *No Static at All*. 70 feet. FA: Andrew Barry & Mike Artz, September 1985.

627   Really Gotta Boogie   5.11c/d ☆☆
You may want to don your flight jacket for this one. Start five feet left of the arête and follow flakes to a bolt, then move up to flakes at the left end of the roof. Traverse right out of roof and lieback to good letterbox, then head directly for the top. 70 feet. FA: Eddie Begoon & Don Wood, January 1989.

628   Rumors of War   5.12c/d ☆☆ (β) ℛ
Begin the battle immediately left of *The Undulator* and fire off the line of fixed gear to a hidden double bolt rap station under the roof. 40 feet. FA: Eddie Begoon, March 1989.

629   The Undulator   5.7 ☆☆
A requisite course in New River off-widths. Chimney past the squeeze slot, then move up and right following the crack to the roof. Traverse right under the roof to a ledge. You can belay here or continue up a right-facing dihedral to the top. 80 feet. FA: Scott Garso & Rick Thompson, April 1986.

630   Optical Illusion   5.11c ☆☆☆
One of Fern Buttress' most imposing roof cracks. Just right of *The Undulator* is a low roof split by an amazing handcrack. Employ the necessary levitation to gain the ledge above. Rappel from here. 40 feet. FA: Mike Artz, September 1985.

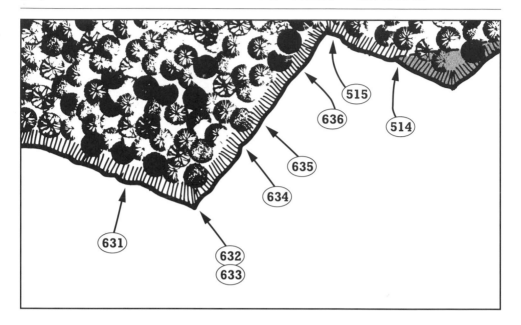

631   Grand Space 5.11b ☆☆☆
This celestial experience packs a lot of climbing into one pitch. Begin about 100 feet upstream from *Optical Illusion* and blast up the short overhanging finger crack to a ledge. Shuttle leftward and thrust up the left-facing dihedral, then pull the roof and ride the right-facing corner to a series of roofs. Take off, up, and left through the roofs and finish with a short finger crack. 100 feet. FA: Phil Heller & Alex Karr, March 1986.

632   Nervous Bachelor 5.11d ☆☆
Begin at the left edge of the face from atop a boulder and step onto the wall (same start as *Bill and Ken's Excellent Adventure)* and climb up to the first bolt, then move up and left following bolts to a ledge. Power left and out the roof to cold shuts. 85 feet. Note: Carry a handful of TCUs. FA: Kenny Parker & Bill Burgos, September 1992.

633   Bill and Ken's Excellent Adventure 5.11b ☆☆
Using the same start as the previous route climb directly up the face past three bolts to the top, using the same station as *Nervous Bachelor.* 85 feet. FA: Bill Burgos & Kenny Parker, July 1990.

634   Goofer's Retreat 5.9- ☆☆
The first 15 feet of this route is shared with *Ritz Cracker.* Jam the crack to the ledge, then step left into a left-facing dihedral which is followed to a ledge. Step left and doddle up the snaking crack system to gain the crest of the cliff. 90 feet. Note: It's also possible to climb the fist crack that lies left of the dihedral. FA: Dan Perry, Gaye Black & Tom Howard, November 1985.

635 Ritz Cracker 5.9 ☆☆☆☆
A premier route of its grade featuring a tasty handcrack, a spicy corner, and a meaty roof. Jam the sharp-edged crack directly to a good ledge with a small pine (possible belay), then step right and consume the left-facing dihedral and roof. Finish up and right. 85 feet. FA: Rick Fairtrace & Scott Jones, October 1985.

636 Jacuzzi Bop 5.11a ☆☆
Commence right of *Ritz Cracker* and bop up the face past a bolt, then move up and right past a second bolt to the top. 75 feet. FA: Blaze Davies & Bill Wilson, July 1990.

Jacuzzi Bop is the last route described in an upstream direction. Immediately to its right route is the chimney known as *Stoats Escape,* which was the last route previously described in a downstream direction.

Pete Absolon on *Triple Treat.*

photo: Carl Samples

Dave Sippel transcending the heady finish on *Brainteasers* in 1985.

photo: Rick Thompson

BEAUTY MOUNTAIN

This choice crag, which first became popular in the early '80s, was one of the original climbing destinations at the New River. Located in the upper gorge, this southwest-facing escarpment is approximately ¾ mile long and averages 60 to 120 feet. More than 110 routes have been established here. Though Beauty is best known for its collection of stunning cracks, in recent years it has also relinquished an impressive line up of sport climbs. The cliff is named after the town of Beauty which lies a few miles to the northeast. A scenic overlook, which is situated a short distance upstream from the main cliff, has been a long time favorite amongst visitors and locals alike.

In 1978 Beauty's first climb was done when Hobart Parks led the initial section of *Where the Big Boys Begin* (5.8). Two short routes, *Potato Chip* (5.6) and *Beginner's Luck* (5.5) were also done that summer. The following season saw an ascent of the first of the classic cracks when Nick Brash led the awful-width *Screamer Crack* (5.8+). Later that summer Steve Erskine established an aid line, complete with a hanging bivy, called *The Butler Done It* (5.9 A1). Parks and Erskine also teamed up that year for another aid route, *Wandering Souls* (5.8 A2). 1980 heralded the first ascent of one of Beauty's truly ultimate routes when Brash led *Super Crack* (5.9+).

During the next two seasons climber attention continued at a heightened level. September of '81 delivered Beauty's first 5.10 when Tom Howard established *Brain Teasers* (10a). Other memorable routes from this period were *Rod Serling Crack* (10b) and *Fat Man's Folly* (5.9). By '83 things were on a roll. Seneca Rocks guide Pete Absolon established the crag's first 5.11 when he freed *The Butler Done It*, renaming it *Welcome to Beauty* (11b). Other landmark cracks were also ticked. East coast offerings like *Burning Calves* (10b), *Spider Wand* (10b), *Wham, Bam, Thanks for the Jam* (10b) and *Mushrooms* (10a) all were climbed that year. The standards, as well as the selection of routes, were on a steady rise.

By '85 things were smokin' as the 5.11 grade became well entrenched. Cal Swoager added the dynamic duo routes, the *Left* and *Right Sons of Thunder* (11d & 11c), Mike Artz jammed out the splitter crack *Chasin' the Wind* (11b) and

Andrew Barry revealed his vision for severe face climbs with *Transcendence* (11c/d). In 1986 the 5.12 grade was unleashed with *The Beast in Me* (12a) and *Chorus Line* 12c). Although both of these routes are spectacular they're rarely repeated, most likely because they're not equipped in modern sport climbing style.

The first sport routes were done by visiting French climbers in the fall of '88. *Sleeping Beauty* (12a) and two shorter lines, *Mongoloid* (12d) and *Hot Bip* (12a) were climbed during that trip, but their most notable ascent was Beauty's first 5.13, *Stabat Mater* (13b). Other sport routes soon followed. *Grace Note* (12b), *Concertina* (12a), *Sportster* (13b), *Chunky Monkey* (12b) and *Ewe Can't Touch This* (12c/d) are all reflective of the superb quality rock that Beauty offers. In 1991 the crag's most difficult line was added when Harrison Dekker climbed *The Travisty* (13c/d), a route with an intriguing history. And though Beauty Mountain has matured into a dynamic and diverse crag, it will always be best recognized for its collection of stellar cracks.

ACCESS & ETIQUETTE

Currently, Beauty Mountain remains under the private ownership of the John Nuttall Estate. However, the parcel is slated for NPS acquisition. Of all the area crags Beauty has the most volatile access history. Even today the situation remains tenuous.

Until a few years ago the primary approach was from the upstream end of the cliff, but residents who disliked the parking area's location directly across from their homes eventually barricaded access to it. Since that time the primary approach has been relocated to the downstream end of the crag. However, there are a handful of parking spots near the former upstream parking area. These are the same spots used for Keeneys Buttress and are identified by a Nuttall Estate sign - see the Beauty Mountain Overview map for location. To approach from this direction follow the trail under the power lines past the second dip, then follow the trail that angles to the left and into the woods. After a few minutes you'll rejoin the powerline cut. Continue past a marshy section until you reach another low point and take the first trail to the left, following it down the drainage. The cliff will appear on your right. You'll have to use the route descriptions in reverse order if you use this approach.

The standard Beauty access is via the Short Creek drainage, which is situated at the downstream end of the crag. Parking and the initial part of the trail are the same ones used to access Upper Endless. The parking sites, which are limited to about half a dozen, are identified on the Beauty Mountain Overview Map. Park only at the small triangle of grass directly in front of the Nuttall Estate Cemetery sign. There are three or four spaces here. Pull straight in and please, no parallel parking and leave room for other cars. If these spots are filled, an alternative is to park along the side of the road to the cemetery, which angles off to the right (see map). Pull well off to the side and do not park at the cemetery. Also, do not park in front of any houses or along the narrow gravel road. If these parking sites are taken, please climb elsewhere.

A short stroll along the trail will lead you past two residences and some old cars. Please be courteous to these neighbors and respect their barking dogs, which will hopefully be chained. Remember, good relations with these folks are crucial to future access. After passing the houses the trail will begin a gentle descent and you'll pass the Intestinal Wall on the left. A short outcrop will develop on the right. Keep your eyes peeled for the Beauty Mountain trail that drops off to the left. A five minute hike will bring you to the Brain.

John Harlin on the 1985 first ascent of *Hot Flash*.

photo: Glenn Thomas

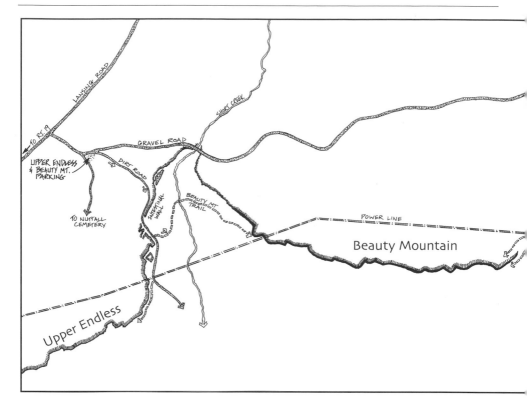

Upper Endless

Beauty Mountain

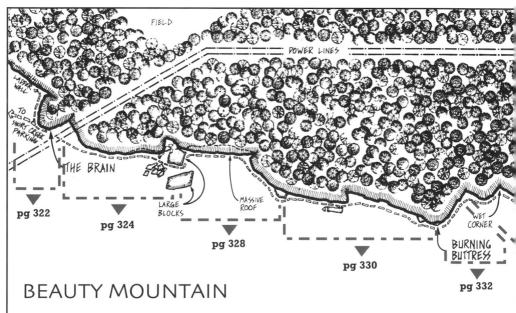

BEAUTY MOUNTAIN

pg 322
pg 324
pg 328
pg 330
pg 332

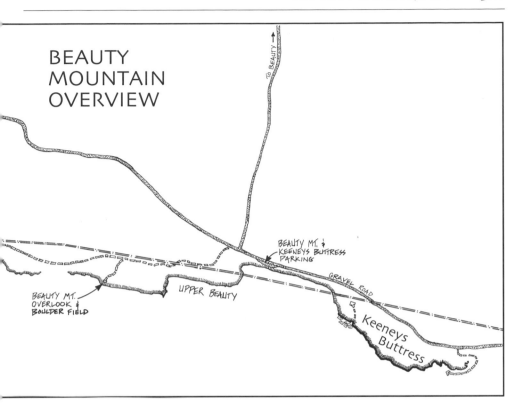

BEAUTY MOUNTAIN OVERVIEW

To BEAUTY

BEAUTY MT. & KEENEYS BUTTRESS PARKING

GRAVEL ROAD

BEAUTY MT. OVERLOOK & BOULDER FIELD

UPPER BEAUTY

Keeneys Buttress

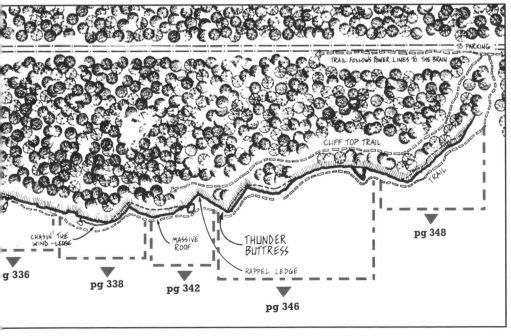

TO PARKING

TRAIL FOLLOWS POWER LINES TO THE BRAIN

CLIFF TOP TRAIL

TRAIL

CHASIN' THE WIND -LEDGE

MASSIVE ROOF

THUNDER BUTTRESS

RAPPEL LEDGE

pg 348

g 336

pg 338

pg 342

pg 346

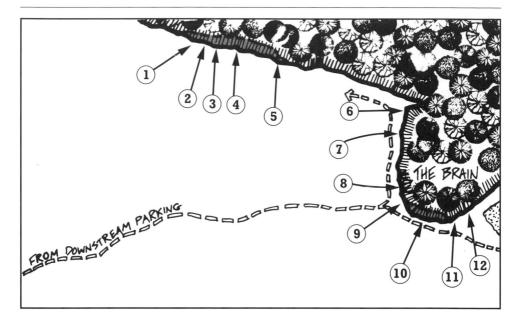

The first group of routes breach a tiered, overhanging wall with a seep along its base. The primitive and rapidly deteriorating ladders which grace the start of some of these routes are the traditional method of getting past the typically wet, blank rock. They're easily moved from route to route as required. In their absence, stick clip the first bolt and batman to the start.

1 Night Train 5.12b
The left-hand line features a variety of fixed gear; pins, bolts and wires. 40 feet. Note: Take a light rack. FA: Jordy Morgan, May 1989.

2 It's a Fine Line 5.12d ☆☆
Definitely fine, steep and pumpy too! The next line to the right is equipped with five bolts and cold shuts. 40 feet. FA: Doug Cosby, July 1990.

3 Smokin' Guns 5.12a ☆
The next route to the right is prone to having a dirty finish. Five bolts lead to a cold shut station. 40 feet. FA: Doug Cosby & Brian Kelleher, July 1990.

4 Choke it Up 5.12d ☆
As the conversation went one evening, I was pressing Doug to name this new route. After laughing over some hilarious possibilities he still couldn't settle on a name that really stuck. Finally I insisted it was time to "choke it up." That one seemed perfect. The fourth line of bolts that breaches the roofs. 40 feet. FA: Doug Reed, October 1991.

5 Heller Route 5.12d ☆
When first climbed this route was protected exclusively with fixed wires. It was later retrobolted. Near the right side of the roofs is a distinct, left-facing corner

system. Follow the line of bolts up the corner to the headwall and cold shuts. 40 feet. Note: Normally climbed from the ground, if a ladder is used the grade is more like 5.12a/b. FA: Phil Heller, May 1989.

The following eight routes are located on The Brain. Its main face is uniquely textured with wild flutes and runnels which present some rather insecure climbing. Recently bolt hangers were stolen from some of these routes and the anchors at the top of *Journey to the Center of the Brain* and *Brain Teasers* were also stripped of hangers. It's likely local climbers have replaced them by now, however, check the situation out before attempting them.

6   Way Cerebral 5.11b
Climbs the arête just right of the chimney. Start ten feet right and move up and left to arête, then follow it to the top. Three bolts. 60 feet. Gear: #0 TCU, Qds. FA: Glenn Ritter & Rick Templeton, August 1989.

7   Green Thing 5.9
Commence at a thin crack and follow it until it dies out. Finish directly to the top. 60 feet. FA: John Burcham & Paul Sobelesky, May 1986.

8   You Want it, You Got it 5.9 ☆ 🅑
Give the public what it demands. Near the right side of the face is an obvious line of five bolts to an anchor. 65 feet. FA: Brian Kelleher & Doug Cosby, June 1990.

9   Brain Wave 5.7
Start just left of the low roof and surge up jugs and horizontals staying on the left side of the outside corner. 65 feet. FA: Unknown.

10   Out of Mind 5.10a
Begin in the center of a low roof. Crank past the boulder start and climb the left edge of the face to the top. 65 feet. FA: John Burcham & Andrew Barry, June 1986.

11   Journey to the Center of the Brain 5.7 ☆☆
A classic voyage filled with adventure. Start just left of *Brain Teasers* at the left edge of the face and move up and left to get established at the start of the main face of *The Brain. Climb* directly up the center of the cerebral wall to the top. 65 feet. Note: A few different variations are possible. There are belay bolts on top. FA: Stuart Kuperstock & Cal Swoager, November 1983.

12   Brain Teasers 5.10a ☆☆☆
No time for a mental block on this crux. One of Beauty Mountain's early classics. Start at the obvious, broken crack and climb up and right into a small, right-facing corner capped by a roof. Traverse right six feet past a pin to a second, right-facing corner. Climb up and out of the corner and finish directly up the pocket-riddled face past two pins to the top. 65 feet. Note: There are belay bolts on top. FA: Tom Howard & Bill Newman, September 1981.

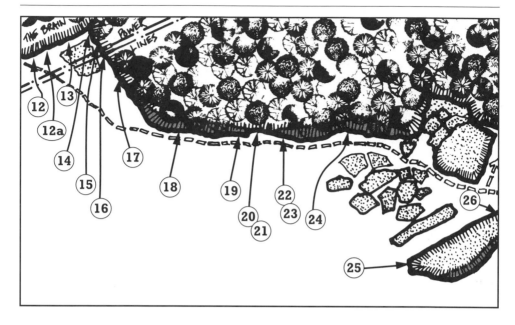

12a   Brain Teasers Direct Start — Brain Child 5.11b
Start right of the crack and follow the tricky face directly to the second right-facing corner. Finish as normal. FA: Andrew Barry & John Burcham, June 1986.

12b   Brain Teasers Direct Finish — Brain Storm 5.8 ☆
Follow the route as normal to the roof in the first right-facing corner. Climb directly over the roof and aim straight for the top. FA: Andrew Barry & John Burcham, June 1986.

13   Brain Tweezers 5.10b ☆☆ 🄟
In the center of the face is a line of five bolts to a cold shut station. 65 feet. FA: Carl Samples, Rick Thompson, Ron Kampas & Bob Rentka, July 1990.

14   Bearpaw Crack 5.8
Claw your way up the green, lichen choked, obviously filthy flare. 55 feet. FA: Nick & Doug Brash, August 1984.

15   M.E.N.S.A. 5.11d/12a ☆☆ 🄟
Just right of *Bearpaw Crack,* climb the gently overhanging grey face past four bolts to an anchor. 50 feet. FA: Porter Jarrard & Joe Crocker, August 1989.

16   Toadstool 5.8+
Start about 15 feet right of *Bearpaw Crack* and follow the flake up and left to the top. 60 feet. FA: Cal Swoager & Stuart Kuperstock, November 1983.

17   Hot Flash 5.10c/d ☆☆
Don't get caught in the heat of the moment. Start at the left end of a small, low roof and pull it then follow a thin, right-facing flake to a horizontal. Move right

and pull the second roof to gain a stance below the overhanging, right-arching flake. Move up the flake until it ends, then angle left on wild solution pockets at the top. 60 feet. Note: Large camming units are helpful for protecting the finishing moves. FA: Rick Thompson & John Harlin, September 1985.

18   Chunky Monkey 5.12b/c ☆☆☆☆ ௰
Hyper-Mega-Classic! Even Ben & Jerry's version may not be as sweet as this one. Start about 25 feet right of *Hot Flash* and follow the line of fixed gear up the overhanging face and bulging roof to the victory headwall. 65 feet. Note: Climbable in a light rain. FA: Harrison Dekker & Porter Jarrard, May 1990.

19   Project – Abandoned
Line of bolts left of *The Travisty* that end about two-thirds of the way up the wall.

20   The Travisty 5.13c/d ☆☆☆ ௰
The history of this route is as controversial as any at the New. A visiting climber who was working on the first ascent, drilled two pockets at the crux, of course making the route easier. Because local climbing ethics are firmly opposed to the creation of holds, the pockets were artfully filled-in, restoring the route to its natural, more difficult state. Harrison Dekker later redpointed this testpiece "au natural," and today it remains one of the most difficult routes in the region. The spelling of the route name is a pun on the name of the driller. Begin below the hanging, right-facing dihedral and follow bolts up and left until just below the dihedral's start. Power up and right, then directly to the top. 70 feet. FA: Harrison Dekker, October 1991.

21   Project — In Progress
Begins at *The Travisty*, moves right after the first bolt. Continues up line of bolts.

22   Whiney Bugs 5.12b ☆ ௰
Start on the right side of a short, blunt arête and climb up, moving right after the second bolt. Continue up and right past five more bolts to an anchor. 75 feet. FA: Scotty Greenway, 1992.

23   Project — Abandoned — Super Whiney Bugs
Using the same start as *Whiney Bugs*, continue left after the second bolt following the line of bolts to the top.

24   Komatose 5.12c ☆ ௰
Begin at a small, rust colored corner and follow four bolts to a cold shut station. 40 feet. FA: Koma Shuichi, May 1992.

The following four routes are located on the Beauty Mountain Boulder.

25   The Greenway 5.10b ௰
Obvious line of three bolts with anchor. 35 feet. FA: Scotty Greenway, Spring 1992.

26   Where's Gus? 5.9 ௰
Line of bolts on the mellow arête. 35 feet. FA: Gus Glitch, Spring 1992.

Kenny Parker on *Chunky Monkey.*

photo: Dennis Cole

Chick Holtkamp on the first ascent of the roof start to *Genocide.*

photo: Carl Samples

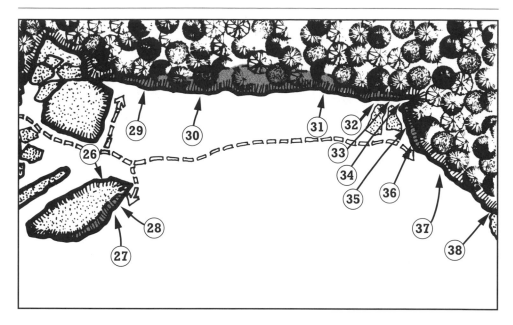

27   Hot Bip 5.12a ☆ ௫

The left-hand route is protected by three bolts. 25 feet. FA: Nicholas Richard, Pierre Deliage in September, 1988.

28   Mongoloid 5.12d ☆ ௫

Mutant bouldering. The obvious right-hand line of five bolts. 25 feet. FA: Pierre Deliage, September 1988.

29   Genocide 5.12a R ☆☆☆

This sensational crack may annihilate your finger strength! Originally done by rappelling to a hanging belay at the base of the crack, the roof start was freed a few years later. Begin at the left end of the huge alcove below the left-hand crack. Climb up to a pin under the roof (5.11d R) and exit left to gain the start of the crack. Jam it to the top. 85 feet. FA of crack: Phil Wilt & Mike Artz, July 1983. FA of roof: Chick Holtkamp & Ed Park, October 1987.

30   Project — In Progress

Right of *Genocide* is a line of bolts that leads to a fingercrack.

31   Chick's Roof 5.11d

Another one of those routes that is almost always seeping. The right end of the huge, roofed alcove is breached by a spectacular crack/corner. Follow it to the top. 85 feet. FA: Chick Holtcamp, et al., 1988.

32   Green Envy   5.12b/c ☆☆ 🅑

Notoriously pumpy and intricate. Twenty feet left of *Disturbance*, follow the path of six bolts to a cold shut station. 70 feet. Note: The second clip is difficult. Many opt to stick clip it. FA: Doug Reed, May 1990.

33   Disturbance   5.11d ☆☆☆ 🅑

A classic shady day outing. Begin a short distance left of the chimney and follow the line of seven bolts along the striking, hair-line crack to a cold shut station. 70 feet. FA: Doug Reed, May 1990.

34   Stay Tuned   5.8

Begin in the wide chimney and climb the first ten feet of it then step onto the right wall. Follow the enjoyable face up the clean streak to the top. 80 feet. Gear: TCUs helpful. FA: John Gill, Glenn Ritter & Bernie Nypaver, July 1989.

35   Screams in the Woods   5.11b

Begin by pulling a low overhang and move up to a ledge. Pull the second overhang at a right-facing flake and follow a crack for 20 feet. Traverse left onto a slab and head for the top, passing a pin. 65 feet. Note: Bring several .5 size Friends. FA: Bernard Nypaver, Chick Holtcamp, Ed Kowalski & Pete Timoch, September 1987.

36   Garden Club   5.11d/12a ☆ 🅑

Twenty feet left of *Warp Factor III*, behind a tree, is a line of seven bolts and a cold shut station. 60 feet. FA: Doug Reed & Bob Rentka, July 1990.

37   Warp Factor III   5.9 ☆

Don't let the mediocre start fool you, the roof on this route can be loads of fun. Start just right of the obvious right-facing dihedral and boulder the easy face to a ledge. Shift into warp drive and fly up the corner to the roof. Pull the roof and continue up a short crack. Move left and follow the ramp to the top. 60 feet. FA: Ed McCarthy & Cal Swoager, May 1985.

37a   Warp Factor III Variation Finish — Aye, Aye Captain   5.10b

Follow *Warp Factor III* to the roof then traverse right, under the roof, to its end. Head directly to the top. 60 feet. FA: Bernard Nypaver & Peter Timoch, August 1986.

38   Baby Cakes   5.12a ☆☆

A technical tips crack with a cute little name. Originally 5.11c A0, this was one of the first aid eliminates done by Hörst. Begin atop the left side of the block, below a small roof. Pull the roof and follow the thin crack past a pin to the top. 60 feet. FA with aid: Rick Fairtrace & Scott Jones, March 1986. FA: Eric Hörst & Alex Karr, May 1987.

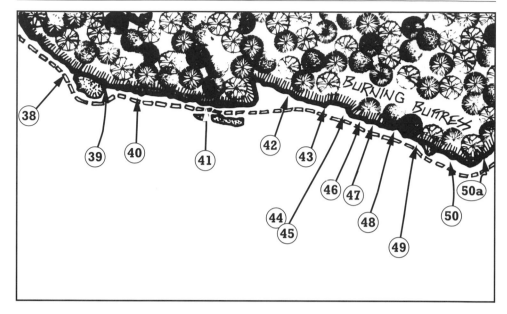

39 Hallelujah Crack 5.11c ☆☆

Fingercracks this divine can cause a religious experience. Small fingers are a definite advantage. Begin just right of the block. Face climb up and right and jam the outstanding crack to the top. 60 feet. FA: Cal Swoager & Ed McCarthy, May 1985.

40 Project — Abandoned

Overhanging face with bolts to crack with pins.

41 Project — In Progress

Roof to corner. Cold shuts at top.

42 Happy Hands 5.9 ☆☆

Last time I did this route my hands weren't smiling. One of the Burning Buttress classics, and a fine one indeed! Follow the handcrack to the top. 70 feet. Note: This route was climbed by different parties about the same time in 1983. It remains unclear which actually did the first ascent. FA: Bob Value, Jack Nard & Keith Biearman or Ed McCarthy & Phil Wilt, May 1983.

43 Broken Sling 5.10a R ☆☆

A mysterious, broken red sling was visible near the top of this route for a couple of years before it was completed. Begin just left of *Spider Wand* and climb the right-facing flake system until it ends. Continue directly up the poorly protected face to the top. 70 feet. FA: Cal Swoager & Ed McCarthy, April 1985.

44 Spider Wand 5.10b ☆☆☆

Named after a traditional New River climber's tool; any long, dead branch used to remove the gigantic spider webs that entangle many routes. Get ready for fist jammin'! Climb the obvious flared, left-facing dihedral and pull the roof on the right side. Move right and follow the crack to the top. 70 feet. FA: Doug Reed, Tom Howard & Vernon Scarborough, May 1983.

45   Wham, Bam, Thanks for the Jam 5.10b ☆☆☆☆
Right out of the New River Rock Hall of Fame. Dandy! Climb the initial 20 feet of *Spider Wand*, then hand traverse right around the corner to gain the start of a supremo handcrack. Follow it to the top (Joins *Spider Wand* above the roof). 70 feet. FA: Phil Wilt & Ed McCarthy, May 1983.

46   The Ruchert Motion 5.13a ☆☆☆ 🖝
More like the crimping motion, an overabundance of tiny holds can be enjoyed on this one. About ten feet left of *Fade to Black*, follow the line of bolts to a cold shut station. 75 feet. FA: Rick Thompson & Carl Samples, November 1994.

47   Fade to Black 5.12b ☆ 🖝
In the spring of 1988 visiting climber Greg Collum equipped this route but returned home before getting the redpoint. Start 20 feet left of *Burning Calves* at a left-facing flake. Climb the flake then follow a line of seven bolts up the face. 75 feet. FA: Doug Reed, September 1988.

48   Burning Calves 5.10b ☆☆☆☆
A Burning Buttress sensation, this is one of the sweetest 5.10 fingercracks at the New. Begin almost directly behind a mature oak and follow a thin crack in a tiny left-facing corner to a stance below a roof. This resting spot is affectionately named "the calf-burn." Continue up the crack to the top. 75 feet. FA: Doug Reed, Tom Howard & Vernon Scarborough, May 1983.

48a   Burning Calves Direct Finish 5.9+
Instead of traversing off below the final roof, pull it directly. FA: Alex Karr, October 1989.

49   Bubbaheads 5.11c ☆
Start left of a large block and crank bouldery moves up the right side of an arête to a stance below a roof. Move up and right past the roof and follow the steep crack to the top. 80 feet. FA: Eric Zschiesche, July 1985.

50   East Meets West 5.9 ☆
Named in remembrance of the random reunion of these three old friends who stumbled on to one another, climbing in the backwoods of West Virginia. Begin at the low point in the trail, on the left side of the prow. P1: Climb a short, thin fingercrack to a roof, then traverse right to the ledge and belay. 25 feet. P2: Climb directly to the top of the dihedral above (be gentle with the detached blocks in the corner — a 150-pounder was pulled off on the first ascent), then follow the ramp to the top. 110 feet. FA: Eugene Genay, Rich Pleiss & Jack Nard, April 1983.

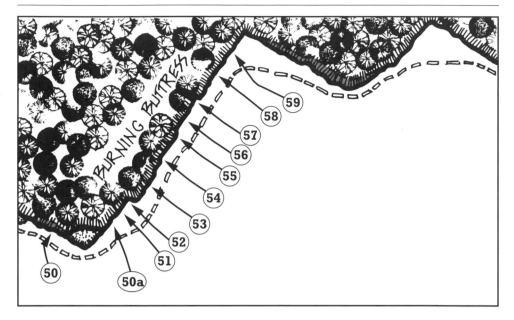

50a East Meets West Direct Start — Exposing the Pink 5.11a ☆

Fingery! A fine alternative for getting to the ledge. Begin on the right side of the prow at a shoulder-height roof with a thin crack above it. Follow it to the roof and rail left to the ledge. Belay. 25 feet. FA: Rick Thompson, Scott Garso & Bob Rentka, August 1985.

50b East Meets West Variation Finish — Bourbon Street 5.10d ☆☆

This intoxicating finish is a recommended complement to the *Exposing the Pink* start. Climb the second pitch to the top of the dihedral then undercling the long flake to the left. Finesse the left-facing dihedral and face above to the top. FA: Mike Artz, Cal Swoager, September 1985.

51 Sportster 5.13b ☆☆☆ 🄡

One of Doug Reed's most spectacular face climbs. Throttle up! About 20 feet left of *The Will to Power*, a flake leads to a line of eight bolts and a cold shut station. 80 feet. FA: Doug Reed, May 1990

52 The Will to Power 5.11c R ☆☆☆

A climb tailor-made for the lunger in all of us. The question is, are you willing to commit? Begin in a small dihedral which is followed to a small roof (bolt), then traverse left and up to a stance. Move right onto the arête and climb it via lunges to good holds. Angle left to the top. 90 feet. Note: It's an excellent idea to have a hook along to protect the moves above the stance. FA: Andrew Barry, Mike Artz & Stanley Todd, June 1986.

53   Chorus Line 5.12c ☆☆☆
This impressive line was one of New River's first 5.12s and was done at a time when the focus on fixed gear was quite different than today. There are a number of high clips and some committing moves on rusty, ¼" bolts. Nonetheless, it's an exceptional route worthy of the effort. Start just right of *The Will to Power* and climb a right-facing flake, then traverse right on small holds and lunge for a bucket. Move up to a stance below a bulge and a bolt, then power another long lunge. Trend up and right past a small roof to another bolt. Traverse right moving past a third bolt, then angle left to a pin. Power directly to the top. 85 feet. Note: It's prudent to protect the traverse off of the initial flake by moving up onto a small ledge in the dihedral of *The Will to Power* where it is possible to get protection on the face above the traverse. FA: Mike Artz & Andrew Barry, June 1986.

53a   Chorus Line Direct Start 5.12c ☆☆☆
Begin about 15 feet right of the standard start and crank directly up the face past two pins to join the regular route. FA: Doug Reed, October 1988.

54   Ad Lib 5.12d ☆☆☆ 🎵
This one will test your ability to improvise. Using the same start as *Steve Martin's Face*, climb up and left following the line of fixed gear to the top. 75 feet. FA: Porter Jarrard, September 1989.

55   Steve Martin's Face 5.11c ☆
Get serious! If you're looking for comic relief you've got the wrong route. This one's intricate and committing. Begin from a small ledge and climb past the left side of a large flake then traverse right to gain the next flake. Follow it to a bolt which is clipped with a keyhole hanger or a wire nut (one of Barry's Aussie bolts!). Staying below the bolt, traverse right six feet and move directly up then left above the bolt to reach a small alcove. Exit the alcove to the right and follow a short face to the top. 80 feet. FA: Andrew Barry, Mike Artz, & Rick Fairtrace, September 1985.

56   Grace Note 5.12b ☆☆☆ 🎵
A bouldery tempo graces this popular sport climb. Follows the line of six bolts just left of *Rod Serling Crack*. 75 feet. FA: Doug Reed, November 1989.

57   Rod Serling Crack 5.10b ☆☆☆☆
This sci-fi climb is beyond the "Twilight Zone" of crack climbing. Don't miss it! Begin in the obvious, left-facing dihedral which leads to a triangular roof. Move out the roof crack to a stance and follow the fingercrack to the top. 75 feet. Note: Beware of the potential rope jam in the roof. FA: Jim Okel, Tom Howard & Dan Perry, October 1981.

58   Dark Shadows 5.12a ☆☆ 🎵
Begin just right of *Rod Serling Crack* and follow six bolts to a cold shut station. 75 feet. FA: Gary Beil, July 1994.

Porter Jarrard on the first ascent of *Ad Lib*.

photo: Peter Noebels

John Eichenberger on the stellar *Supercrack*.

photo: Andrew Barry

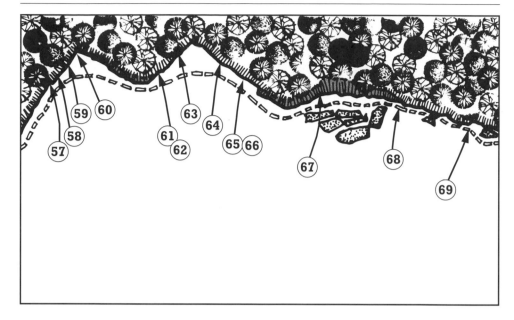

59   Broken Dreams 5.13a? ☆ 🅑

Currently unrepeated, the crux hold snapped off when Carl Samples was following the first ascent. It's most likely more difficult now. Start 20 feet right of Rod Serling Crack and follow the line of seven bolts to a cold shut station. 75 feet. FA: Porter Jarrard, June 1990.

60   Point in Question 5.10a ☆

Rod Serling's oft-used line on the "Twilight Zone." Climb the crack in the large, right-facing dihedral to a small roof with diverging cracks above it. Follow the left-hand crack to the top. 75 feet. FA: Tom Howard, Jim Okel & Dan Perry, October 1981.

61   Quick Robin, to the Bat Crack! 5.10a ☆☆☆
aka The Bat Crack

If only Batman and Robin knew they'd been immortalized in a rock climb. Boulder up to a left-facing dihedral which is followed to a stance ten feet below a roof. Move right onto the blunt arête and continue up a flake on the arête past a small roof. Finish up a tiny left-facing corner. 70 feet. FA: Phil Wilt, Carl Samples & Ed McCarthy, August 1983.

61a   Bat Crack Direct Finish 5.10b R

From the stance below the roof move left and up to gain a small ledge then finish on unprotected moves. FA: John Burcham & Andrew Barry, May 1986.

62   Hilti as Charged 5.11d ☆

Climb the first ten feet of *The Bat Crack,* then move onto the left wall and follow five bolts to a cold shut station. 65 feet. Gear: Carry a small rack for the start. FA: Doug Cosby, July 1990.

63   Wild Dogs 5.10c
Like a rabid mongrel, this route can bite. Start a short distance left of the grungy dihedral at a shallow, left-facing corner. Follow it to a ledge and move to the right. Crank the crack up to a small roof, then traverse left and up to a flake then back right to the crux finishing moves. 70 feet. FA: Andrew Barry, May 1986.

64   Sleeping Beauty 5.12a ℗
Weeping Beauty would be a more appropriate name considering it's a seep most of the year. Unbeknownst to the visiting French climbers who established this route, the face is only dry a couple months of the year. Starts 35 feet left of *The Zoomin' Human* near the start of a right-rising crack. Seven bolts lead to a bolt belay just below the top. 75 feet. FA: Nicolas Richard & Pierre Deliage, September, 1988.

65   West Virginia Water Torture 5.13a ☆☆ ℗
An apt description of the mental anguish one endures when climbing at the New during the rainy season. Some say it lasts most of the year. Using the same start as *The Zoomin' Human* climb the line of bolts directly above to a cold shut station. 75 feet. FA: Doug Cosby, September 1990.

66   The Zoomin' Human 5.10a ☆
A free variation of a former aid route called *Wandering Souls*, 5.8 A2. The original line nailed the rising, horizontal crack that starts about 20 feet left of the free start. Begin about 15 feet left of the hanging, left-facing dihedral and climb a few moves straight up, then angle right past flakes and a pin to reach the start of the dihedral which is climbed to the top. FA with aid: Hobart Parks & Steve Erskine, August 1979. FA: Ed McCarthy & Carl Samples, September 1985.

67   Tetelestai 5.11d/12a ☆
Greek meaning: "paid in full." Ascend the crack in the right-facing corner, past a roof and a fixed doll, to a stance below a huge roof split by an impressive crack. Jam it to the top. 85 feet. FA: Cal Swoager & Mike Artz, September 1985.

68   Quaking Flakes 5.8
Not exactly a breakfast cereal. In fact, if not handled with a gentle touch, these flakes could be harmful to your health. Begin about 70 feet left of *Mononuclear* at a high point in the trail. Start the climb just right of a dirty crack, and follow the right-leaning flake system to its end. Traverse left and belay at the tree. 70 feet. FA: Tom Howard & Fred Young, July 1985.

69   Mononuclear Knows It 5.8 ☆
Start at a right-facing groove that lies about 100 feet downstream from *Fat Man's Folly*. Follow the groove to the top. 75 feet. FA: Tom Howard & Bill Newman, September 1981.

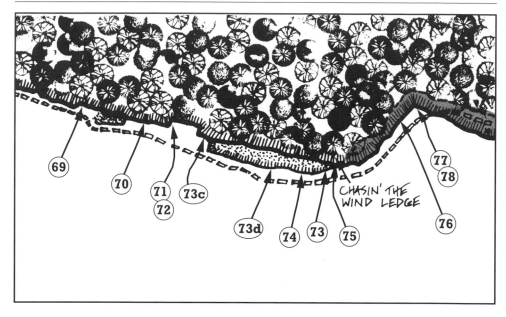

70   Ewe Can't Touch This 5.12c/d ☆☆☆ 🎯

The thought of this multi-cruxed, slabathon brings a sheepish grin to my face.
About 30 feet left of *Fat Man's Folly* is a line of ten bolts that leads to a cold shut
station. 95 feet. WARNING: This route is longer than half a rope length. Tie a
knot in the end of your rope so your belayer can't let it pass through the belay
device. FA: Rick Thompson, Carl Samples & Bob Rentka, July 1990.

71   Fat Man's Folly 5.9 ☆☆☆

A requisite Beauty Mountain climb, it offers a grab bag of textbook climbing
situations. One of the early Beauty Mountain classics. At the left end of the
Chasin' the Wind ledge is a squarish alcove. Follow the left-hand dihedral to the
roof and move left to gain the squeezer crack. Inch your way up it until it chokes
down to hand size and jam to the top. 80 feet. Note: Beware of rope drag. FA:
Tom Howard, Nick Brash & Bill Newman, September 1981.

72   Gimme, Gimme Shock Treatment 5.12b ☆☆

Is this Eddie's idea of some sort of twisted therapy? A spanking is more likely
what you'll get. Follow *Fat Man's Folly* to the roof, pull it directly and move up
past two bolts. Angle up and right toward the third bolt then back left past the
final bolt finishing up to a small ledge with a tree. 75 feet. Gear: Bring your
TCUs. FA: Eddie Begoon & Peter Noebels, September 1989.

73   Chasin' the Wind 5.11b ☆☆☆☆

As sweet a fingercrack as you'll find in the Mountain State. To locate this route
you'll need to step away from the cliff and eye the splitter crack in the wall
above the ledge. There are four different lines leading to the ledge. The one
described here was followed by the first ascent party. P1:(5.11a) Start about 30
feet right of the upper crack and climb the corner or face just to the left to gain

some laybacks. Move up the laybacks to a flakey roof then traverse left to the ledge and belay at the base of the crack. 40 feet. P2:(5.11b) Jam the crack to its end then step left and wander up the face to the top. 75 feet. FA: Mike Artz & Cal Swoager, September 1985.

73a Chasin' the Wind Direct Finish 5.11b ☆☆☆☆
From the end of the crack make two steps right and climb directly to the top. FA: Doug Reed & Tim Fisher, March 1988.

73b Chasin' the Wind Variation — Into the Wind 5.11b ☆☆☆
More virtuous crack climbing! Climb the first 20 feet of the second pitch, then move right and up across the face to the start of another gorgeous crack. Follow it to the top. FA: Cal Swoager & Stuart Kuperstock, September 1985.

The following three route descriptions each provide alternate methods for reaching the *Chasin' the Wind* ledge.

73c Chasin' the Wind Indirect Start 5.9 X
Begin below the left end of the ledge and boulder up the unprotected open book until it's possible to move right onto the ledge. 30 feet. FA: Doug Reed, 1985.

73d Chasin' the Wind Direct Start 5.12a R
Begin below the rappel pins at the left end of the ledge and crank directly up past a bolt and a short crack to the ledge. 30 feet. Gear: Small-medium wires. FA: Alex Karr, September 1988.

74 Nazz, Nazz 5.12b ☆ 🖐
P1:(5.12a) Begin about ten feet left of the regular start to *Chasin' the Wind* and follow three bolts in the overhanging brown face and belay on the ledge. 30 feet. P2:(5.12b) Follow the line of fixed gear ten feet right of the second pitch of *Chasin' the Wind* to a rap anchor. 85 feet. FA: Porter Jarrard, August 1989.

The following route begins from the *Chasin' the Wind* ledge.

75 Echo 5.11d R ☆☆
Commence at the extreme right side of the ledge and climb up and right, then follow the beautiful face directly to the top. 75 ft. FA: Doug Reed & Tim Fisher, March 1988.

76 Rainy Daze 5.9+ ☆
Climbs the cracks in the wall left of *Lone Rhinoceros* to pins at the roof. Rappel. Be sure to check the solidness of the pins! 35 feet. FA: Rick Fairtrace & Scott Jones, August 1985.

77 Lone Rhinoceros 5.10c
This beastly route will give you a wild ride. Begins directly below the looming offwidth roof crack. P1: Follow cracks in the wall right of the corner to gain the bomb bay. Ride it past the lip and set up a hanging belay. 50 feet. P2: Follow cracks to the top. 45 feet. FA: Eric Anderson & Andrew Barry, August 1985.

The photo that brought New River into the national limelight.
Tom Howard on *Photo Finish.*

photo: Bruce Burgin

Andrew Barry on *The Beast in Me*, one of the first 5.12s at the New.

photo: John Burcham

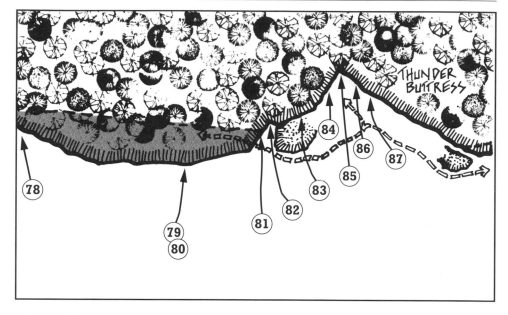

78   This Won't Hurt a Bit 5.10 A2

Climb *Lone Rhinoceros* to the roof then aid right, following flakes to reach a striking, 20 foot roof crack. Follow the crack to the lip, pull it and step or pendulum left to *Lone Rhinoceros*. 60 feet. Note: The first ascent team employed clean aid with the exception of three carefully placed knifeblades. Please employ only clean aid if you choose to do this route. FA: Fletch Taylor & John Gill, January 1989.

79   The Perfect View 5.11d ☆☆

Unique position and perfect rock! Left of *Super Crack* is a huge roof. This route climbs the face above the roof. Begin from the top by rappelling to the double bolt belay just above the lip of the roof. From the hanging belay, step right and up the white streak following cracks and horizontals to a pin. Finish straight up past a bolt. 75 feet. FA: John Burcham & Bob Rentka, August 1989.

80   Air 5.11a ☆☆☆

Begin from the hanging belay start of *The Perfect View* and head up and right past a fixed nut to the killer arête which is followed to the top. 75 feet. FA: John Burcham & Bob Rentka, August 1989.

81   Gun Club 5.12c ☆☆ 👊

Believe it or not, this desperate pitch was soloed by visiting climber Dan Osman in 1991. Start five feet left of *Super Crack* and follow the line of nine bolts to the top. 100 feet. FA: Brook Sandahl, April 1989.

82   Super Crack 5.9+ ☆☆☆☆

Super crack, super corner, whatever you want to call it, this pitch is simply outrageous! Start about 40 feet left of and downhill from *Screamer Crack* at a blocky-looking corner. Awkward moves up a flake lead to a roof. Move left to gain the crack proper which is followed past a pin to the ledge. 100 feet. FA: Nick Brash & Chuck Basham, July 1980.

82a Super Crack Variation — Photo Finish 5.9 ☆
A photogenic finish to a super route. Just say cheese! From the ledge at the top of *Super Crack*, make a rising, leftward traverse to reach a stance below a roof on the arête. Pull the roof directly. 40 feet. FA: Tom Howard, Ben Fowler, Chuck Basham & Bruce Burgin, June 1984.

83 The Beast in Me 5.12a ☆☆
More overpowered than climbed, *Transcendence*'s companion route will prove enjoyable for the steep face connoisseur. May The Beast be with you. Start left of *Transcendence* on deceptively easy ground. A dazzling series of cranks leads past a fixed wire and the bolt-protected crux. Finish directly up. Note: The original keyhole-hanger bolt has been replaced. 75 feet. FA: Andrew Barry & John Burcham, May 1986.

84 Transcendence 5.11c/d ☆☆☆ 👂
This was one of Andrew Barry's masterpiece, ground-up first ascents. Unfortunately in 1991 some visiting climbers mistakenly bolted it, under the misconception they were establishing a new route. Had they checked the guidebook or asked local climbers before they acted, the route could have been spared such bastardization. Follow the line of bolts just left of *Screamer Crack* to a cold shut station. 75 feet. FA: Andrew Barry & Phil Heller, September 1985.

85 Screamer Crack 5.8+ ☆☆
Named to honor the incredible screamer Bruce Burgin logged while attempting the first ascent. His partner promptly took over the lead and ran it out to the top! Bring your big gear, it's all you'll need. Follow the corner to the ledge. 75 feet. FA: Nick Brash & Bruce Burgin, August 1979.

86 Mushrooms 5.10a ☆☆☆
A mind expanding crack that suffers from dirt constantly washing down it. You may want to rap and brush the dirt off prior to climbing it. About 15 feet right of *Screamer Crack*, follow the crack system to the top. 80 feet. FA: Phil Wilt & Ed McCarthy, June 1983.

87 L.S.D. 5.12a
Did Jerry Garcia really visit the New River or was it just a vision of climbs to come? Just right of *Mushrooms*, boulder up to a bolt then move straight up the face aiming for a pin at mid-height. Follow flakes and corners to the top. 75 feet. Gear: Friends and TCUs. FA: Blaze Davies, Kenny Parker & Jon Reggelbruge, August 1988.

Andrew Barry venturing
onto the headwall of
Welcome to Beauty.

photo: John Burcham

Andrew Barry eyeing the crucial traverse on
Right Son of Thunder.

photo: John Harlin

Porter Jarrard soloing *Mushrooms.*

photo: Peter Noebels

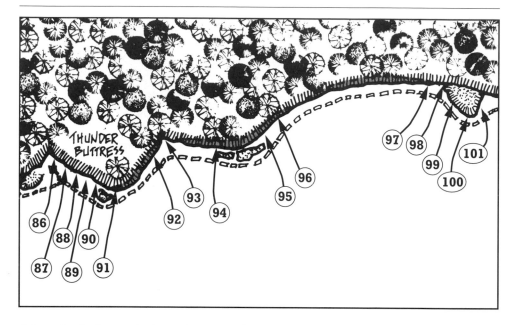

88   Left Son of Thunder 5.11d ☆☆☆
This Siamese twin of *Right Son of Thunder* features a thin fingers crux. This route and its twin were established on the same day! Start 20 feet left of *Right Son of Thunder* at a discontinuous crack which is followed to its end at a horizontal. Climb directly up a couple more moves then rail right to join the finish of *Right Son of Thunder*. 80 feet. FA: Cal Swoager & Ed McCarthy, August 1985.

89   Right Son of Thunder 5.11c ☆☆☆☆
An ultimate route with all the attributes one could dream of. One of Cal Swoager's most remarkable first ascents at the New. Begin just left of *Momma's Squeeze Box* and storm up the obvious crack past a pin, then move right and clip a bolt. Power directly up to a horizontal and rail left about ten feet. Finish directly up the face and belay on the ledge below the last roof. 80 feet. FA: Cal Swoager, August 1985.

90   Momma's Squeeze Box 5.8 ☆☆
This textbook offwidth squeezefest has better than expected protection. Don't overlook the small cracks inside the yawning abyss. Follow the obvious chimney to the top. 70 feet. FA: Tom Howard & Bill Newman, September 1981.

91   Concertina 5.12a ☆☆☆ 🎵
A symphony of moves that Mozart would find exquisite. Begin from the top of the block and step across the void following six bolts to a cold shut station. 75 feet. FA: Doug Reed & Bob Rentka, June 1990.

92   Stabat Mater 5.13b ☆☆☆ 𝄢

This splendid climb was Beauty Mountain's first 5.13. The eye-bolts define the line. P1:(5.13b) Start off of a block and begin a series of bouldery moves past five bolts to a hanging two-bolt belay. 40 feet. P2:(5.12b) Continue past eight bolts to the top. 60 feet. FA: Pierre Deliage, September 1988.

93   Beauty and the Beast 5.10d

More beast than beauty, this route is often wet and when it's not, it's just plain grungy. Climbs the obvious, wide dihedral. 100 feet. FA: Doug Reed & Tom Howard, May 1983.

94   Backlash 5.12a 𝄢

Begin under a roof and follow four bolts to a cold shut station. 40 feet. FA: Doug Reed & Bob Rentka, June 1990.

95   Loud Noise 5.12b/c ☆☆☆ 𝄢

Just left of *Let's Make A Deal*, step off the top of the block and follow eight bolts to a cold shut station. 95 feet. WARNING: This route is longer than half a rope and many parties lower from the last bolt. FA: Doug Reed, November 1989.

96   Let's Make a Deal 5.11c ☆☆ 𝄢

Be prepared to deal with some widely spaced bolts on the easier, upper half of this pitch. Left of the major, grungy corner, step proudly onto the wall from top of the block and follow the line of six bolts to a cold shut station. 80 feet. FA: Kenny Parker, Steve Downes, Porter Jarrard, Pep Boixados & Joan Caban, June 1990.

97   Clairvoyance 5.9+

Begins with the obvious crack 20 feet left of *Death of a Salesman* and continues up the face to the top. 60 feet. FA: Andrew Barry, July 1986.

98   Death of a Salesman 5.9

Squirm up the flared corner. Rappel from the top of the block. 40 feet. FA: Jack Nard & Bob Value, June 1983.

99   Beginner's Luck 5.5

Follow the obvious left-facing flake to the top of the block. 40 feet. FA: T.A. Horton & Rick Skidmore, July 1978.

100   Potato Chip 5.6

Climbs the right-facing flake to the top of the block. 40 feet. FA: Hobart Parks & Steve Erskine, July 1978.

101   Short'n Sweet 5.7 ☆

Climb the obvious line of weakness that splits the center of the upstream side of the block. Rappel from the top of the block or scramble to the top of the wall. 45 feet. FA: Bruce Burgin & Nick Brash, May 1984.

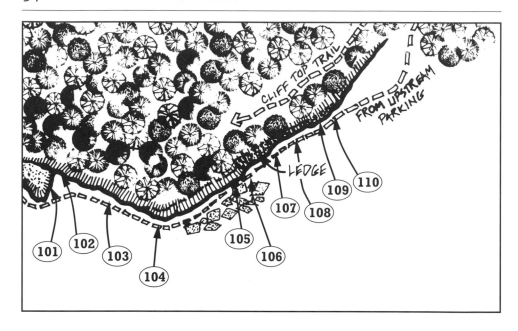

102 Pulp 5.12a ☆

Begin just right of the corner, about 30 left of *Welcome to Beauty*, and scramble up to the ledge then traverse right until below a bolt. Climb straight up to the bolt and continue past two small roofs and two more bolts. Wander up the face to the top. 60 feet. Gear: TCUs, medium wires & small camming units. FA: Porter Jarrard & Steve Cater, September 1989.

103 Welcome to Beauty 5.11b ☆☆☆

Fingercrack aficionados rejoice, this route is fabulous! Another of the historic Beauty Mountain routes, it was the second climb completed here, though the first to reach the top of the cliff. It was put up in a two day, aid ascent and named *The Butler Done It*, 5.9 A1. The pair of bolts were placed on the first ascent to enable an overnight, hanging bivy to be set up as big wall training. Begin by following either of the two handcracks in the center of the face to the roof about 30 feet up. Jam over the roof and crank the graceful, left-curving fingercrack to the top. 90 feet. FA with aid: Steve Erskine, Hobart Parks, & T.A. Horton, August 1979. FA: Pete Absolon & Chris Guenther, July 1983.

103a Welcome to Beauty — Right Hand Variation 5.11c ☆☆

Follow *Welcome to Beauty* past the roof, then continue directly up the right-hand crack till it peters out. Traverse left across the face and rejoin the regular route. FA: Cal Swoager & Greg Phillips, August 1983.

104 Simple Harmonic Motion 5.10a ☆

Stout for its grade, the second pitch is a real thriller! Begins at a blunt arête with a "beak-like" protrusion at its base. P1: Climb up the right side of the nose to small, right-facing flakes. Diagonal up to the crest of the nose, then up to a long ledge under a roof. Belay at the left end of the ledge. 75 feet. P2: Move left around the end of the roof and pull into the overhanging corner. Rad stemming leads to the top. 45 feet. FA: Rich Pleiss & Ron Augustino, June 1983.

105 Where the Big Boys Begin 5.10b ☆☆
aka Sojourners
Historically significant, pitch one of this route was the first climb established at Beauty Mountain. When Swoager climbed it in 1985 he was unaware of the earlier ascent of the first pitch, naming the route *Sojourners*. P1: Climb the crumbly face to the left of the wide crack up to a roof, then move right and lieback up the right-facing corner to a ledge. 60 feet. P2: Walk 50 feet right and climb the striking, orange corner to a roof. Pull it and finish up the reversing corners. 40 feet. FA P1: Hobart Parks & Steve Erskine, July 1978. FA P2 and first complete ascent: Cal Swoager & Stuart Kuperstock, September 1985.

106 Plastic Attraction 5.12a ☆☆ 𝄞
Attractive indeed. However, this fine little climb is the REAL thing. Climb the blunt orange arête past four bolts to a cold shut station on the ledge. 45 feet. FA: Doug Reed & Bob Rentka, June 1990.

107 Brooks Route 5.11d 𝄞
Right of *Plastic Attraction* is a line of three bolts that lead to the ledge. As of press time hangers were missing from the rap station so you may need to walk off the ledge or rap from the top of *Plastic Attraction*. 45 feet. FA: Greg Brooks, May 1990.

108 Sharkey's Day 5.11d ☆
P1:(5.11b) Begin about 20 feet right of the *Brooks Route* at an obvious flake leaning against the wall. Climb the flake then up and right past two bolts to a very short fingercrack. Move back left to a short corner below a tiny roof (#3 RP), and finish directly up the corner to the belay ledge. 45 feet. P2: (5.11d bolted) Follow the line of fixed gear to the top. This pitch is known as "Sharkey's Night." 45 feet. FA P1: Rich Pleiss & Jim Nonemaker, April 1988. FA P2: Alex Karr, June 1988.

109 Ergodicity 5.8
To reach the start of this pitch, either climb *Throw Down Those Childish Toys* or walk along the mid-height ledge that starts at the beginning of the cliff. Start left of the large tree and follow a right-facing corner up to a roof. Traverse right to easier ground, then head for the top. 35 feet. FA: Andrew Barry, July 1986.

110 Throw Down Those Childish Toys 5.7
A rack of camming units will provide sufficient protection on this short pitch. Begin about 20 feet upstream from *Sharkey's Day*. Follow the right-curving flake system to a ledge with a large tree and belay. Walk off right or climb *Ergodicity*. 40 feet. FA: Rick Thompson, Nick Brash & Tom Howard, August 1985.

Andrew Barry on *Right Son of Thunder.*

photo: John Harlin

KEENEYS BUTTRESS

This little-known crag, which lies a half mile upstream from Beauty Mountain, remained virgin to the hands of climbers until 1987. Most of the routes were done during the following two seasons. Since then the crag has remained shrouded in obscurity and for the most part unvisited. For some this sparse climbing activity, not surprisingly, is one of the biggest reasons to come here. And the lack of crowds ensures that a backwoods character can experienced, one reminiscent of the New in the early 1980s when the crags had a far more untamed atmosphere. This is the first time information has been published on this crag.

Keeneys can be an ideal midsummer destination. Here you can find relief from the scorching sun under a canopy of hemlock and oak. Of course, there are standard effects of the shade like the additional time it takes to dry after rain, and the generally clammier feel of the rock. But if you're searching for the full-on trad experience, the absence of any sport climbs will make this crag particularly appealing. By minimizing your impacts Keeneys' more natural state can be preserved for future generations.

ACCESS & ETIQUETTE

This crag suffers from the same limited parking dilemma as Beauty Mountain. Currently, the only available parking is at the upstream parking area for Beauty Mountain, which is limited to three or four cars max. If the parking spots are taken, climb somewhere else. Do not park anywhere but in spots designated by the Nuttall Estate signs.

Like Beauty Mountain and most of the Endless Wall, Keeneys is located on Nuttall Estate property which is targeted for acquisition by the National Park Service. When climbing here, it's crucial that you obey the Nuttall Estate's "Dusk to Dawn—No Trespassing" rule. In addition, maintain a low profile and always respect local residents and their privacy. By following these simple suggestions you will be supporting efforts to preserve long-term access.

The hike from the parking area takes less than 10 minutes; approach details are shown on the area map. Instead of using the access trail to return to your car, an alternate exit uses a short, fifth-class climb-out up the chimney just right of *Happiness is a Pair of Warm Gums*. Beware of poison ivy.

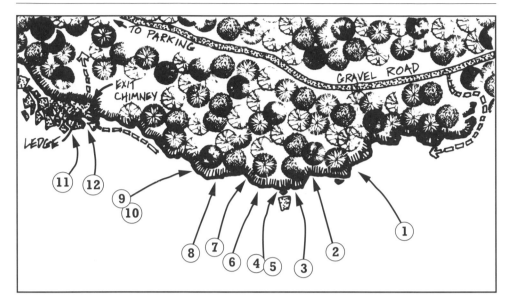

1   Voyage to Uranus 5.11a ☆☆☆
Keeneys' most distinctive route is well worth the walk. It takes on the definitive orange dihedral capped by a huge roof. Begin in a small, left-facing corner and move up to the top of a pedestal, then continue up the magnificent right-facing dihedral which ends at the roof. Undercling right to the roof's end and follow a right-facing corner to the top. 90 feet. FA: Carl Samples & Ed McCarthy, July 1988.

2   Eminent Domain 5.11c ☆☆
Commence in the offwidth, right-facing corner and squeeze your way up to the roof. Pull it and master the awkward finger crack in the corner. 70 feet. FA: Ed McCarthy & Brent Banks, August 1988.

3   It's a Honker! 5.10b
Follow the obvious flare to a ledge then step left and climb the crack and small left-facing corner to the top. 60 feet. FA: Carl Samples & Ed McCarthy, August 1988.

4   Right Son of Lichen 5.9 ☆
Start at a short crack and move up to the ledge then continue directly into a corner. Exit right and finish up the right-arching crack. 50 feet. FA: Carl Samples & Ed McCarthy, August 1988.

5   Left Son of Lichen 5.9+ ☆
Using the same start as *Right Son of Lichen,* step left along the ledge and crank the wide crack in a small right-facing corner to the top. 50 feet. FA: Ed McCarthy & Carl Samples, August 1988.

6   Frozen in the Big Position 5.10b

An offwidth identifies the start of this one. Assume the position and squirm to the ledge, then continue directly up the orange face to an angling flake. From a stance atop the flake, step left and fire up the clean streak. 60 feet. FA: Ed McCarthy & Brent Banks, August 1988.

7   We'll Have to Whisk It 5.10b

"If I wanted to clean I'd have stayed home and done the house" —Harrison Dekker. Begin a couple of paces right of the left-facing corner and move straight up to a ledge. Proceed past a bolt to a crack that is followed to the top. 60 feet. FA: Ed McCarthy & Carl Samples, July 1988.

8   Meat Puppets 5.11b ☆☆☆

Suggestive of what your hands may feel like when you're done with this one. Starts at a striking, thin crack which is followed to the roof. Traverse right a short distance and pull the roof, following the crack and face to the top. 75 feet. FA: Bill Moore & Mike Cote, February 1987.

9   Honker Heaven 5.8

Climb fractured rock to a ledge with a tree, then move straight up the left-hand flake to the top. 50 feet. FA: Carl Samples & Ed McCarthy, summer 1988.

10   Honker Hell 5.9

Using the same ugly start as *Honker Heaven,* step right along the ledge and climb the right-hand flake. Traverse right to the top. 50 feet. FA: Ed McCarthy & Carl Samples, July 1988.

The next 2 routes will require a bit of scrambling and route finding to locate. Though certainly on the short side, they're both worth the effort.

11   Diet Hard 5.11d ☆☆

Unless you've also got power, it's unlikely a weight-loss program alone will get you up this techno corner. Start at the distinctive right-facing white corner that is followed up to the first roof. Undercling right past a pin, then up a second right-facing corner and crank directly over the roof, finishing up the crack. 50 feet. FA: Rob Turan, September 1988.

12   Happiness is a Pair of Warm Gums 5.10a ☆

Start at the arête in the alcove and pucker up and left to the obvious crack that is followed to the top. 30 feet. FA: Mark Van Cura & Carl Samples, June 1989.

Beyond these routes, the rock deteriorates significantly. The cliff line, however, continues with a few minor breaks almost the entire way to Beauty Mountain. A few routes have recently been done on this section of cliff. The stand-out route is Doug Reed's spectacular 12b arête, which is located directly below the parking area.

Dave Sippel on the 1985 second ascent of *Diversity in Microcosym*, Endless Wall.

SUNSHINE WALL

Positioned directly across the canyon from the Bridge Buttress is the brilliantly hued Sunshine Buttress. This attractive face is the cornerstone of the Sunshine Wall, which rambles upstream for over a mile. Routes on Sunshine Buttress proper and a few others in the immediate vicinity are of fine quality, but for the most part the balance of the cliff is a chossy low-grade formation that contains few quality routes. Sunshine Buttress has a south east orientation and therefore, catches good sun exposure. This can make it a desirable place to hang in cooler weather—as long as it's sunny.

ACCESS & ETIQUETTE

Sunshine Wall was acquired by the National Park Service in December, 1989 in a 296-acre purchase from the Berwind Land Company. This is the only other crag with access as convenient as the Bridge Buttress. Park at the pulloff on the bend directly below the Sunshine Buttress.

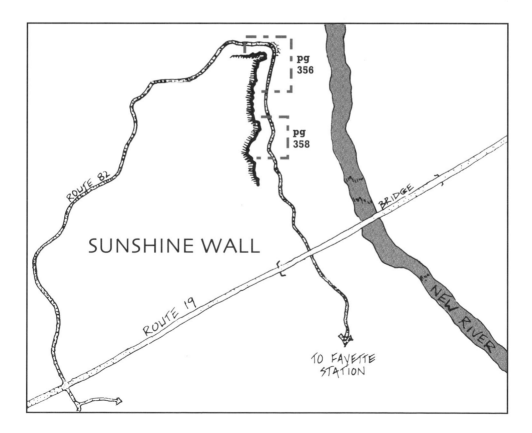

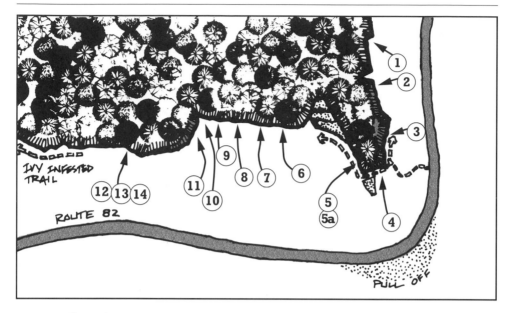

1   Afro-Sheener 5.9 ☆
Begin from a ledge and climb the left side of the arête. 50 feet. FA: Pat Crotty & Scott Bishop, 1991.

2   Love Puppy 5.11c ☆
Pull the crack out the low roof and head directly up the face past two bolts to the top. 70 feet. FA: Lee Munson, 1992.

3   Mother's Milk 5.12c/d ☆ ℗
Follow twin flake/cracks to a line of 11 clips that lead out the tiered roof and face above to cold shuts. 75 feet. FA: Paul Harmon, summer 1991.

4   Project - Abandoned ℗
The line of bolts up the bookend.

5   Unbroken Chain 5.12a ☆☆☆ ℗
Climb the line of bolts that moves right to the arête, then directly to the top. Eight clips total. 80 feet. FA: Tom Cooper & Paul Harmon, summer 1991.

5a   Unbroken Chain Variation Finish - Unnamed 5.12a ☆ ℗
Follow *Unbroken Chain* to the sixth bolt, then diverge to the left following three more bolts to an anchor. 85 feet. FA: Paul Harmon, summer 1991.

6   Unnamed 5.11d ℗
Begin at a small right-facing corner and fire off the four bolt line to cold shuts below the roof. 40 feet. Note: As of press time the first bolt was vandalized, hence a long stick clip to the second bolt is required. FA: Paul Harmon, 1991.

7   Rich Mixture 5.11c ℗
Start three feet left of the previous route and follow a line of six clips that lead

up, then left to cold shuts. 55 feet. Note: The first bolt has been vandalized on this one too. FA: Paul Harmon, 1991.

8   Original Crankster 5.13a ☆☆ (b)

Crank up your equipment one pace to the left of *Rich Mixture* and climb the line of bolts up a steep face and through a bulge. 55 feet. FA: Paul Harmon, 1991.

9   Syndicate Fool 5.12b (b)

Start three feet left *Original Crankster* and follow the most left-hand line of eight bolts. 65 feet. FA: Paul Harmon, 1991.

10   Just Say Yo to Jugs 5.10c ☆

To the left of the previous route is a wide corner and crack system that is followed past a roof and a loose block (high the route) to the top. 75 feet. FA: Rick Mix & Mark Shissler, 1991.

11   Necromancer 5.10c ☆ (b)

Immediately left of the corner is a three bolt mini clip up that leads to a set of anchors under the roof. 35 feet. FA: Paul Harmon & Tom Cooper, 1991.

11a   Necromancer Finish - Popeye Syndrome 5.11d ☆☆ (b)

From the *Necromancer* anchors continue up the line of six bolts through the triangular roofs to a second set of anchors. 75 feet including the start. FA: Paul Harmon, 1991.

12   He Man Adhesive 5.11c/d (b)

Around the corner are three routes that share a common start. Begin at a left-facing flake and move right after clipping the second bolt and follow three more bolts to the ledge. Step left and lower from the *Mango Boingo* anchors or do the direct finish. 50 feet to ledge. FA: Paul Harmon, 1991.

12a   He Man Adhesive Direct Finish - Head Like a Hole 5.11c ☆ (b)

Follow *He Man Adhesive* to the ledge, then step across the ledge and follow five more bolts up the colorful headwall to cold shuts. 45 feet. FA: Paul Harmon & Rick Mix, 1991.

13   Mango Boingo 5.12b ☆☆ (b)

Commencing at the same start, climb directly up the line of six bolts to anchors beside the small pine. 50 feet. FA: Paul Harmon & Mark Shissler, 1991.

14   Mango Boingo Variation Finish - Disco Apocalypse 5.12c ☆ (b)

Follow *Mango Boingo* to the fourth bolt, then move left and continue past four more bolts to cold shuts. 65 feet. FA: Paul Harmon, 1991.

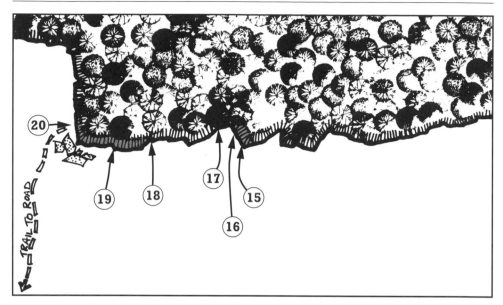

A 15 to 20 minute hike upstream along the base of the mostly grungy wall will bring you to a small collection of routes. But considering the sea of poison ivy you'll have to traipse through, it probably makes more sense to approach directly up the slope above the road.

15   Unnamed 5.12b
Begin under the large roof and follow five bolts to cold shuts. 50 feet. FA: Unknown.

16   Brash-Burgin Route 5.9
Climb the flake to the roof, skirt to the left, and continue up the dihedral to the top. 70 feet. FA: Nick Brash & Bruce Burgin, about 1980.

17   Flaming Asshole Resistant Material 5.9 ☆
Left of the roof is a seven-bolt clip-up. 65 feet. FA: Unknown.

18   Path of the Elders 5.10
Climb the flake past the large bird nest. 70 feet. Note: Be very careful to not disturb the nest during spring and early summer nesting season. FA: Unknown.

19   Unnamed 5.10
Begin in under the roof and struggle up the wide flake to a sling anchor. 40 feet. FA: Unknown.

20   South Rimjob 5.12b ☆
Follow the line of five bolts to anchors. 50 feet. FA: Unknown, 1992.

20a   South Rimjob Variation—Rimshot 5.12a
Using the same start follow the leftward diverging line of bolts. 40 feet. FA: Unknown, 1992.

Russ Clune does *Techman*, Endless Wall.

photo: Rick Thompson

Doug Cosby on *Yowsah.*

photo: Tom Isaacson

KAYMOOR

On the rim opposite Diamond Point lies Kaymoor, New River's most popular sport climbing crag. Its fashionable status is well deserved and is primarily attributed to the steep routes, big holds, and preponderance of mid-grade clip-ups. But buyer beware. On weekends and holidays this place can be overrun with climbers giving it a sort-of lollapalooza atmosphere. Arguably, Kaymoor's most spectacular feature is the Glory Hole, the swell of tiers where some of New River's steeper routes are found. And the great rock doesn't stop there. Primo routes can be on nearly every buttress.

Because the majority of Kaymoor is north facing it is an ideal place to hang in hot temps. However, in cooler weather you'll have to play it by ear, it can be a real chiller.

Kaymoor's climbing history is perhaps the most condensed of any crag at the New. Through the end of 1986 virtually every established route was on the north rim. Spring of 1987 found local activists hungry to explore new crags. While the majority of those activists had become mesmerized with the boom at Bubba City, one had something different in mind. Rick Fairtrace had gazed at the miles of virgin rock on the south rim for years. A warm March weekend found him searching the crag for unclimbed cracks. On that first trip he christened Kaymoor with *Raiders of the Lost Crag*, a climb that today is still recognized as one of Kaymoor's better trad offerings.

Fairtrace returned on a number of other occasions that season, leaving a little legacy of routes. Trad showcase climbs like *Searching for Sanctuary*, *Malfunction Junction*, and *The Shining*. Sadly, a nagging bout with tendinitis kept him from returning during the following years. With the exception of a December 1987 letter in which he described his new routes to me, their existence was not mentioned to any other climbers. Kaymoor slipped back into hibernation.

By 1990 the north rim crags had ripened with routes and once again the thirst for new crags grew strong. This time it was Doug Reed who succumbed to the lure of Kaymoor. In November, as the climbing season was nearing its end and he readied to head south for the winter, Reed decided to have a quick look. Ironically, he approached the crag from the railroad tracks at the bottom of the canyon, nearly a thousand feet below! He had no idea that a road provided access just above the crag, and was also unaware of the previous visits by Fairtrace. As he walked the base of the cliff that November afternoon his mind wandered ahead to the coming spring when he would return to explore the treasures of Kaymoor.

When the following April arrived Reed returned for another season of New River cragging. He hadn't been in Fayetteville more than a few days when he made a bee line for Kaymoor, but this time he used the rim top approach. Exhibiting his 20/20 new route vision, Reed zoomed in on *Magnitude*, Kaymoor's first sport climb. That same afternoon he began working on the first of the Glory Hole routes and yep, this one turned out to be quite a classic as well; the all-time favorite *Lactic Acid Bath*. The following weekend more classics went in like *Out of the Bag* and *The Rico Suavé Arête*. In no time at all the secret was "out of bag" as Kaymoor became the latest New River rage. Two other prominent activists played a significant role in shaping Kaymoor's climbing, Doug Cosby and Porter Jarrard. Some of their best include *Thunderstruck*, *White Lightening*, *Sanctified*, and *Dining at the Altar*.

The two seasons that followed were action packed. On occasion the fresh rock feeding frenzy resembled the floor of the New York Stock Exchange as climbers vied for the dwindling opportunity to establish new routes. By the end the 1992 season first ascent activity tapered off. Since then, Kaymoor's chic status has continually grown as the sport climbering ranks across the United States have exploded.

ACCESS & ETIQUETTE

In 1989 the National Park Service acquired a 1,375-acre Berwind Land Company parcel. This crucial acquisition secured a pivotal section of the south rim. Included were the South Nuttall Wall, Kaymoor, Butcher Branch, the Seven-Eleven Wall, and Long Point. Combined, they make up the majority of quality rock on the south rim, a total of more than six miles of cliff line. The historic remains of the once thriving coal town of Kaymoor were also part of that acquisition. This intriguing spot is one of the most visited attractions in the park and is well worth the short hike. Climbers are also encouraged to stop at the Canyon Rim Visitor Center to view the various National Park Service displays on the mining era when coal, not whitewater and rock, was king. You'll be surprised at how extensively developed the town of Kaymoor was.

Kaymoor is approached from Fayetteville by bearing left at the signs at Gatewood Road (across from Sherrie's Beer Store and Charlie's Pub). Proceed approximately two miles, turn left at the sign for Kaymoor #1 and continue on the rugged road for about a mile. The parking area is on the right just beyond the remains of the tipple house. The trailhead is a stone's throw in an upstream direction and is clearly marked. A short descent will bring you to the Glory Hole. To reach the First Buttress continue on the Kaymoor Miner's Trail until a well-worn path angles up a bank on the left.

Climbers are reminded that Kaymoor is a designated historic site. DO NOT disturb any natural or cultural objects such as the tipple remains. If you're wandering around any of the historic remains do not enter any structures, mines, or coke ovens.

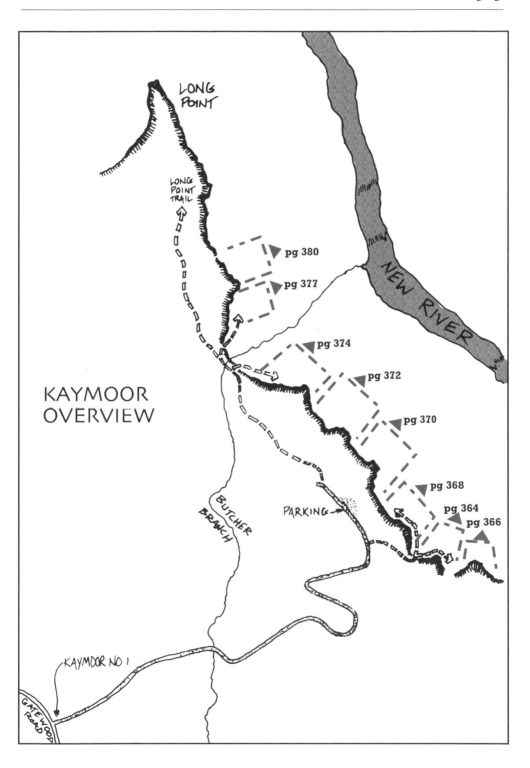

LONG
POINT

LONG
POINT
TRAIL

pg 380

pg 377

NEW RIVER

pg 374

pg 372

KAYMOOR
OVERVIEW

pg 370

pg 368

pg 364

pg 366

BUTCHER
BRANCH

PARKING

KAYMOOR NO 1

GATEWOOD ROAD

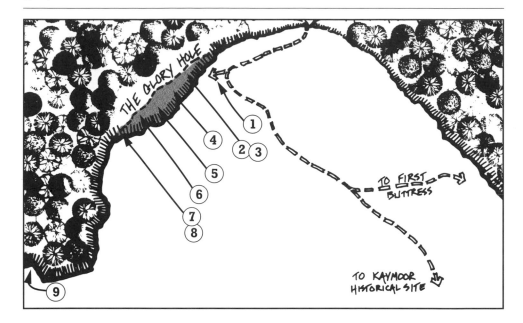

THE GLORY HOLE

These routes are directly adjacent to the Kaymoor Miner's Trail. Maintain a particularly low profile when climbing here and please, no vulgar explicatives or shouting. Also, leave all fixed draws in place. The Glory Hole is also known as The Hole.

1   Final Exit 5.12c ☆ 🐾
Start right of the massively tiered section of The Glory Hole and follow seven bolts to cold shuts. 60 feet. Note: Originally 5.12a, the crux hold recently broke resulting in the grade change. FA: Doug Reed, May 1991.

2   Scar Lover 5.12c 🐾
The next route starts at a right-facing corner that is climbed to the second bolt, then move right and carve your way up the most right-hand line of five more bolts to cold shuts. 70 feet. FA: Doug Reed, May 1991.

3   Burning Cross 5.13a ☆☆ 🐾 ⌒
Using the same start as *Scar Lover* move left after the second bolt and fire through the roofs to cold shuts at the top of the crag. 75 feet. FA: Doug Reed, June 1991.

3a   Burning Cross—Skull Poke Link Up—Yowsah 5.12b ☆☆ 🐾 ⌒
This entertaining link-up is a real scream. Climb *Burning Cross* to the sixth bolt and move left to the last bolt on *Skull Poke*. FA: Doug Reed, June 1991.

4   Skull Poke 5.12b/c ☆☆ 🎣 ↺

Begin a few paces left of *Scar Lover* at a chossy right-facing flake and crank directly past six bolts to cold shuts. 60 feet. FA: Doug Reed, April 1991.

4a   Skull Poke Direct Finish 5.13a 🎣 ↺

Continue past the *Skull Poke* cold shuts and power directly to the cold shuts on *Burning Cross*. FA: Doug Reed, summer 1992.

5   Blood Raid 5.13a ☆☆ 🎣 ↺

Get going in the chossy flake to the left of *Skull Poke* and follow the line of bolts past the velcro draw until it's possible to move right to finish at the *Skull Poke* cold shuts. 60 feet. FA: Doug Reed, June 1991.

6   Lactic Acid Bath 5.12d ☆☆☆☆ 🎣 ↺

Why take a shower when you can bathe in this route's glory? This spanking line was the first in The Glory Hole and the second sport climb at Kaymoor. Begin left of the previous start and climb the chossy face past a bolt to a second bolt in a short right-facing facet, then pump your way out the right-hand line of clips to cold shuts near the top. Nine clips in all. 75 feet. FA: Doug Reed, April 1991.

6a   L.A.B. Direct Finish - Massacre 5.13a 🎣 ↺

Tackle the *Lactic Acid Bath* to the last bolt, then continue to the left past an additional bolt and top out. 80 feet. Note: No cold shuts on this one. FA: Doug Reed, fall 1991.

6b   L.A.B. Variation—In the Flat Field 5.13b/c 🎣

Take the *Lactic Acid Bath* to the seventh bolt and shift left following additional bolts to cold shuts. 65 feet. FA: Porter Jarrard, September 1991.

6c   L.A.B.—Mojo Hand Link Up—Devil Doll 5.12d ☆☆☆ 🎣

Follow *Lactic Acid Bath.* past the fifth bolt and move left along bolts leading to a connection with *Mojo Hand*. FA: Porter Jarrard, September 1991.

7   Mojo Hand 5.12d ☆ 🎣

Start under the left margin of the massive roof and scramble up easy terrain to the roof, then follow the line of clips diverging to the right to pair of cold shuts. 60 feet. FA: Doug Reed, May 1991.

8   Project—In Progress 🎣

Using the same start and first bolt as *Mojo Hand* follow the left-hand line of bolts to cold shuts.

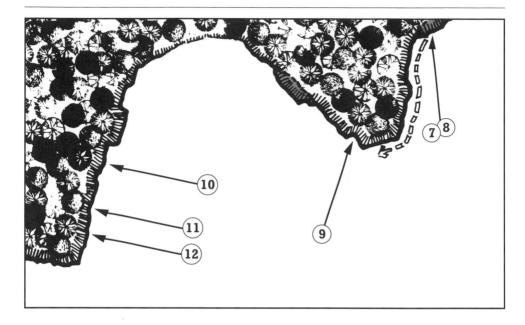

UPPER KAYMOOR

9   Smell the Glove 5.11c
Start on the upstream side of the buttress and follow seven clips to cold shuts. 60 feet. FA: Matt Kelly & Phil Schreiber, May 1991.

10   Flat Motor'n 5.11b/c ☆
Speed your way up the line of six bolts to a pair of cold shuts. 60 feet. FA: Steve Cater & Eric Anderson, 1993.

11   Ooops, It's a Trad Route 5.10b
Originally established as a trad route, it subsequently got a sport climbing face lift. Commence about 20 feet right of *Clock's On* and follow five bolts to a cold-shut station. 50 feet. FA: Mark Stevenson & John Plumb, August 1991.

12   Clock's On 5.11b ☆
Follow the most left-hand line of seven bolts to cold shuts. 65 feet. Note: Optional gear may give you added peace of mind between the third and fourth bolts. FA: Steve Cater, August 1991.

Tom Isaacson immersed in the *Lactic Acid Bath.*

photo: Doug Cosby

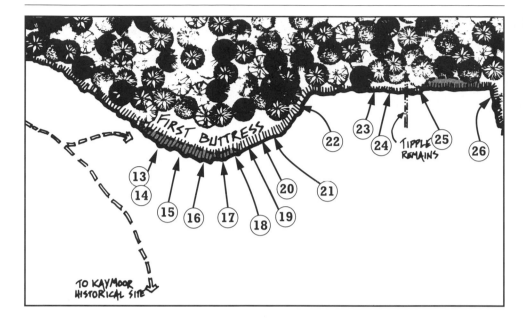

FIRST BUTTRESS

13   The World's Hardest Five Twelve 5.12a ☆☆☆ 🕭

Based on the name, you'll know what to expect. Start at the first line of clips you come to and fire off the power draining line of eight bolts to cold shuts. 65 feet. FA: Doug Reed, April 1991.

14   The World's Hardest Variation—The Haulage 5.12c/d ☆☆☆ 🕭

Begin at the same start, then move left at the third bolt following four more bolts to a cold-shut station. 65 feet. FA: Porter Jarrard, April 1991.

15   The Tantrum 5.12d ☆ 🕭

A few paces right of *The World's Hardest Five Twelve* are seven cranky clips that lead to cold shuts. 50 feet. FA: Doug Reed, summer 1992.

16   Sanctified 5.13a ☆☆☆ 🕭

There's nothing sacred about this spectacular climb. Start about 15 feet to the right of *The Tantrum* and pull through a series of roofs, then continue up the stellar arête to a pair of cold shuts at the top. Ten bolts in all. 85 feet. FA: Porter Jarrard, April 1991.

17   Tarbaby 5.12b ☆ 🕭

Begin on the right side of the arête and pull the low roof, then follow five bolts to a pair of cold shuts. 50 feet. FA: Porter Jarrard, April 1991.

18   Oh, It's You Bob 5.11b ☆ ⑤
It's Bob Rentka, of course! Start at the right edge of the roof and fire off the line of eight bolts that lead to cold shuts. 70 feet. FA: Steve Jones & Doug Cosby, 1992.

19   Magnitude 5.11d ☆☆☆☆ ⑤
Webster's says: Relative brightness of a celestial body designated on a numerical scale. Any way you size this one up it's stellar! But beware, the final moves can be a real show stopper. The next line to the right follows seven bolts to cold shuts. 75 feet. Doug Reed, April 1991.

20   The Leather Nun 5.13a A0 ☆ ⑤
Time for a little discipline. The last sport route on this buttress climbs past a super smooth crux and a spot of aid to reach the easier climbing above and the cold shuts. Eight bolts total. 75 feet. FA: Porter Jarrard, April 1991.

21   Wienie From the Past 5.10c ☆☆
If you can imagine, a trad route amongst a sea of silver snails! Climb the crack system on the right side of the wall to a pair of cold shuts. 75 feet. FA: Glenn Thomas & Mark Guider, May 1991.

22   The Rubber Glove Test 5.12d ☆ ⑤
Climb the multi-tiered inverted slab protected by six bolts to a pair of cold shuts. 55 feet. FA: Doug Reed, fall 1991.

23   100% Real Cheese 5.11c/d ⑤
Be ready for one really hard move. Begin about 50 feet left of the tipple and follow the line of four bolts to a pair of cold shuts. 40 feet. FA: Gary Beil & Angie McGinnus, September 1991.

24   Attack of the Moss Clods 5.10a ⑤
Commence about 10 feet right of the previous route and follow four bolts to cold shuts. 40 feet. FA: Angie McGinnus & Gary Beil, September 1991.

25   The Pocket Petting Zoo 5.12c ☆ ⑤
On the left side of the cave is a severely overhung tiered feature protected by bolts. 45 feet. FA: Doug Reed, April 1991.

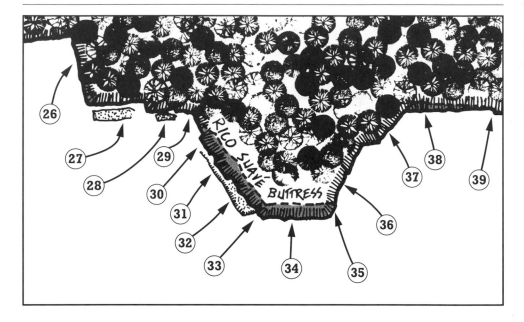

RICO SUAVÉ BUTTRESS

26   Project—In Progress 🄿
The line protected by five bolts on the upstream facing wall.

27   The Uninflatable Ewe 5.12b ☆☆☆ 🄿
This one is worth getting blowed up over. And where else would one find an inflatable sheep but in the mountin' state. Begin on the left side of the colorful face and follow the line of seven bolts past a roof to a pair of cold shuts. 65 feet. FA: Rick Thompson & Bob Value, April 1993.

28   Totally Tammy 5.10a ☆☆ 🄿
As in Tammy Faye Baker. Start a few paces left of the corner from atop a block and follow intriguing moves along five bolts to a cold-shut station below the roof. 60 feet. Doug Cosby, August 1991.

29   Second Thoughts 5.10b
One look at this pile and you'll know what inspired the name. Begin in the corner and follow the right-facing flake to the roof band, then bail left 15 feet to a pair of cold shuts. 55 feet. FA: Bernard Nypaver, August 1991.

30   Grit and Bear It 5.11a 🄿 ⌇
Get started a few feet right of the corner and grit and bear your way up the sandy rock (crosses over *Sand in My Crack* after the second bolt) past five bolts to a pair of cold shuts. 55 feet. FA: Greg Flerx & Gary Beil, August 1991.

31   Sand in My Crack 5.7 ℞

A few feet to the right of *Grit and Bear It* is a right-facing flake that's followed to the roof band. Traverse right to the cold shuts at the top of *Grit and Bear It*. 55 feet. FA: Gary Beil, August 1991.

32   Not on the First Date 5.11a ℞

And sometimes not on the second one either. Start near the right side of the ledge and follow four bolts on the left side of the arête to a pair of cold shuts. 55 feet. FA: Diane Connelly & Ken McLain, September 1991.

33   The Rico Suavé Arête 5.10a ☆☆☆☆ 🎣 ℞

This chic route suffers from a scourge of popularity. The revelation behind the name can be learned by querying Reed. Begin from the extreme right end of the ledge (or from the ground below) and follow the line of seven bolts up the right side of the blunt arête to a pair of cold shuts below the roof. 65 feet. FA: Rick Thompson & Doug Reed, April 1991.

33a   The Rico Suavé Arête Finish—Coal Miner's Tale 5.12b ☆ 🎣

From the *Rico Suavé* cold shuts follow the line of bolts out the roof and make a long leftward traverse to a pair of cold shuts. 35 feet. FA: Doug Reed, summer 1992.

34   Out of the Bag 5.11d ☆☆☆☆ 🎣 ℞

Ultimate classico! The first route done on this section of Kaymoor, this one delivers a grab bag of sustained face climbing. Climb the center of the face past seven bolts to a pair of cold shuts. 75 feet. FA: Doug Reed & Rick Thompson, April 1991.

35   Preparation H 5.12a ☆☆ 🎣

An impeccable arête romp. Finesse your way up the perfect arête moving to the right side at about half height. Power directly past the crux and finish back to the left. 65 feet. Note: It's also possible to finish directly up the left side at 5.11d. FA: Harrison Dekker & Rick Thompson, April 1992.

36   Pockets of Resistance 5.12a ☆☆ 🎣

This one sports some sweet little pockets, but if only it were longer. Start a short distance right of the arête and fire off the line of four bolts to cold shuts. 60 feet. FA: Doug Cosby, Brian Kelleher, & Ken McLain, August 1991.

37   Nude Brute 5.13a/b ☆ 🎣

Start just left of the corner and follow the line of bolts up and left to a pair of cold shuts. 60 feet. FA: Doug Reed, May 1991.

38   The Good Old Days 5.9 ☆

Climb the corner to the right of *Nude Brute*. 75 feet. FA: Doug Cosby, Brian Kelleher, & Ken McLain, May 1991.

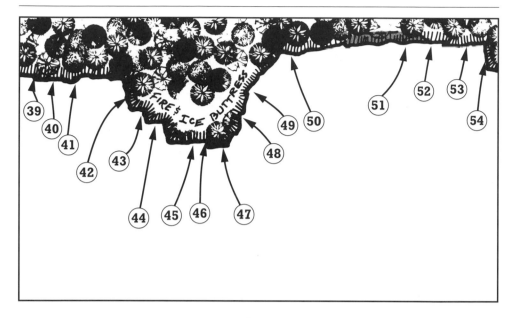

39   Collateral Damage 5.11a 🅟

A short stroll downstream will bring you to the next sport route. Climb the face and shallow chimney past four bolts to an anchor. 50 feet. FA: Doug Cosby & Brian Kelleher, April 1991.

40   Consumer Liability 5.10a

Start 15 feet right of *Collateral Damage* and jam and lieback the crack to a pair of cold shuts. 60 feet. FA: Gary Beil & Tom Isaacson, fall 1992.

41   Buried Treasure 5.11c ☆

Begin by climbing the thin crack, then follow the face past three bolts to cold shuts at the top. 75 feet. FA: Bernard Nypaver, John Plumb, & Jim Kozak, September 1991.

FIRE AND ICE BUTTRESS

42   Albatross 5.13b ☆ 🅟

Climb the overhanging bolt-protected crack immediately right of the cave. 35 feet. FA: Jim Woodruff, summer 1992.

43   Bovine Seduction 5.10d

Climb the left-hand crack and pull through the roofs to reach cold shuts near the top. 70 feet. FA: Gary Beil, April 1993.

44   S.L.A.P. 5.12a ☆ 🅟
aka Squeal Like a Pig

Begin on the right side of the next arête and follow four bolts to cold shuts. 40 feet. FA: Doug Cosby & Brian Kelleher, July 1991.

45   Carolina Crocker and the Tipple of Doom 5.12a ☆☆☆ ⬧
A Kaymoor Klassic and perfectly named companion route to Kaymoor's first climb. Begin around the corner from *S.L.A.P.* and embark on the 10-bolt adventure that ends at a pair of cold shuts. 85 feet. FA: Joe Crocker, May 1991.

46   Raiders of the Lost Crag 5.10b ☆☆☆
The first route to go up at Kaymoor. Could there be a more appropriate name? Start to the right of the low roof and follow the crack in the orange and black wall past the roof and angle up and right to gain a large alcove. Exit via the large crack to the right and head for the top. 90 feet. FA: Rick Fairtrace, Rick Fairtrace Jr. & Scott Jones, March 1987.

47   Malfunction Junction 5.10c ☆☆
The higher you climb on this one, the better it gets. Criss-crosses *Raiders of the Lost Crag.* To the right of the previous route is a shallow left-facing dihedral that is climbed to an overhang, then jam the angling cracks to the *Raiders of the Lost Crag* alcove. Exit the left side of the alcove and climb the thin crack to a pine. 90 feet. FA: Rick Fairtrace & Scott Jones, June 1987.

The next two routes are New River's scaled down answer to the famous Seneca Rocks routes *Castor* and *Pollux.*

48   Ice 5.11c ☆
A big chill could be yours if you don't have the umph to overcome this power-dependant crux. Climb the left-hand crack to ledges and rappel. 50 feet. FA: Rick Fairtrace & Scott Jones, April 1987.

49   Fire 5.10c ☆
Begin a few paces right of *Ice* and follow the overhanging crack to a rap station at two pins. 40 feet. FA: Rick Fairtrace & Scott Jones, April 1987.

50   The Sound and the Slurry 5.11d ⬧
Start in the dihedral and move up and right to an arête following the line of five bolts to a pair of cold shuts. 50 feet. FA: Doug Reed, May 1991.

51   The Shining 5.11a ☆☆ ⬅
First done in a driving rain on the Fourth of July. This radiant route overhangs the entire way. Begin under the low roof and follow the slot to the overhanging crack that is jammed to a rap station. 90 feet. FA: Rick Fairtrace & Scott Jones, July 1987.

52   White Lightning 5.13b ☆☆☆ ⬧
You'll need some real spark to get past this crux. Get started a short distance right of the low roof and arc directly up the clean face to a pair of cold shuts. 80 feet. FA: Doug Cosby, summer 1993.

53   Thunder Struck 5.12b ☆☆☆☆ ⬧
One of Kaymoor's finest offerings. Start at a large flake and ascend the line of seven bolts to a cold shut station. 65 feet. FA: Doug Cosby, May 1991.

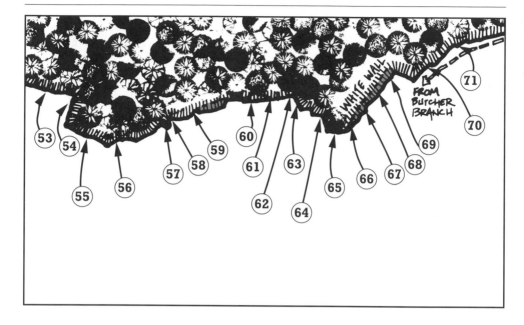

54   Almost Heaven 5.10b ☆ 🎣

Maybe not a perfectly descriptive name, the route is nonetheless located in the "almost heaven" state. On the right wall of the dihedral is a four bolt line that leads to cold shuts. 40 feet. FA: Ken McLain & Doug Cosby, May 1991.

55   I'll Be-Gooned 5.10b R

Follow a nebulous line up the face and be prepared to once again find yourself in a puckered pose. 75 feet. FA: Eddie Begoon, summer 1991.

56   Ride'm Cowboy 5.12a 🎣

Definitely more exciting than those 25-cent versions at the grocery store. Start on the right side of the arête and follow the line of nine bolts to a cold-shut station. 70 feet. FA: Doug Cosby, July 1991.

57   The Cow Girl 5.12b/c 🎣

Ride the line of bolts up the overhanging fin to cold shuts. 35 feet. FA: Komaba Shuichi, May 1991.

58   Damn the Lieback, Full Stem Ahead! 5.10b ☆

Start on the right side of the fin and struggle out the offwidth roof to gain a left-facing corner that leads to the top. 75 feet. FA: George Muehleim, Giuliano Maddamma, & John Gill, September 1991.

59   Swinging Udders 5.12a ☆☆ 🎣

Milk the line of six bolts to a pair cold shuts. 60 feet. FA: Doug Reed & Rick Thompson, May 1991.

60   Boss Cocky 5.12c ☆☆ ℗
Likely to leave you with a lasting impression. Follow the line of eight bolts up the shallow corner to the roof. 70 feet. FA: Porter Jarrard, May 1991.

61   Searching For Sanctuary 5.9+ ☆☆☆
To the right of the roof is a leftward-rising flake that leads to a crack that is followed to the top. 80 feet. Note: An alternate start is to climb the seam directly to the crack. FA: Rick Fairtrace, Scott Jones & Rick Fairtrace Jr., April 1987.

62   Hidden Pleasures 5.9 ☆☆
A dandy little trad route. Follow the corner past the large jutting flake near the top. 80 feet. FA: Scott Jones & Rick Fairtrace, May 1987.

63   Jane Fonda's Total Body Workout 5.11b
An offwidth of the most perverse nature. To the right of the previous route is an overhanging offwidth in a right-facing corner that leads to a left-facing dihedral. Pull the roof and squeeze the chimney to the top. 80 feet. FA: John Gill & George Muelheim, August 1991.

64   Moon Child Posse 5.11c ☆☆ ℗
This one's way fine! Start left of the low roof and follow the line of eight bolts (some equipped with homer-made hangers) to cold shuts. 85 feet. FA: Steve Cater, May 1991.

65   Half & Half 5.11b ☆
Begin in the corner and follow it to the line of five bolts that leads to the top. 70 feet. FA: Bernard Nypaver & Glenn Ritter, fall 1991.

WHITE WALL

66   I Smell A-rête 5.11c ☆ ℗
Start on the right side of the arête and follow the line of seven bolts to cold shuts. 75 feet. FA: Glenn Ritter, August 1991.

67   Dining at the Altar 5.12a ☆☆☆ ℗ ⌐
Guaranteed to serve you a healthy portion of crimping cuisine. The first route established on the White Wall. Climb the line of seven bolts to a pair of cold shuts. 75 feet. FA: Porter Jarrard, May 1991.

68   Project—Abandoned ℗ ⌐
Immediately right of *Dining at the Altar* is another line of bolts. 5.12a to the existing high point at the roof.

69   Pettifogger 5.12c ☆☆☆ ℗ ⌐
Webster's says: A petty, quibbling unscrupulous lawyer. Hmmmm.... Start just left of the corner and follow the line of bolts on the right side of the face through a bulge to cold shuts. 75 feet. FA: Doug Reed, 1992.

70   New Clear Potato Meltdown 5.11b ☆

Climb the left leaning wide flake to a bulge, then slab your way to the cold shuts at the top. Four bolts total. FA: Doug Cosby, July 1991.

71   J Tree Route 5.10a ☆

Begin at a left-facing corner and follow it to a ledge, then continue up a second left-facing dihedral and belay at the J-shaped tree. 45 feet. FA: Rick Fairtrace, Scott Jones, & Rick Fairtrace Jr., May 1987.

Mike Freeman on *Control.*

photo: Tom Isaacson

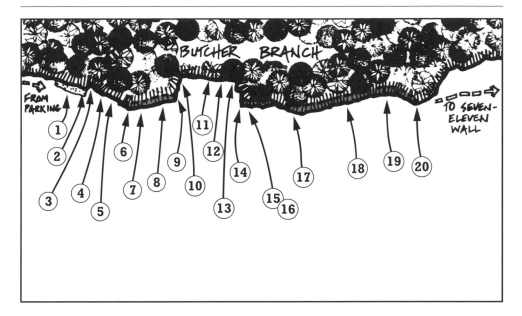

BUTCHER BRANCH

To reach Butcher Branch and the Seven-Eleven Wall from the parking area walk along the road in a downstream direction until a well worn trail forks off to the right. Continue until you cross Butcher Branch (it's actually the name of the stream). Just beyond the stream the trail angles down to the base of the cliff. Do not cut to the right before you get to the stream. This fork will lead you to the downstream end of Kaymoor.

1   Stop Pulling My Ear 5.10d
Begin ten feet left of the dihedral and climb the six-bolt line to a pair of cold shuts. 65 feet. FA: Gary Beil & Angie Faulkner, May 1993.

2   Play it by Ear 5.10a
Start just left of the dihedral and scramble to the top of the block, then follow six bolts to the cold shut station. 65 feet. FA: Gary Beil & Angie Faulkner, May 1993.

3   Just Another Glitch 5.6
Follow the often wet right-facing corner to the top. 70 feet. FA: Lieb Yrag & Nialcm Nek, August 1991.

4   The Green Piece 5.10b ☆☆
A celebrated sport climb. Start a few paces right of *Just Another Glitch* and follow six bolts. 70 feet. FA: Scotty Greenway, June 1991.

5 Low Voltage 5.10b

Begin immediately right of *The Green Piece* and follow seven clips to cold shuts. 70 feet. FA: Bill Webster, Ed Pavelcvhek, & Brian Payst, September 1991.

6 Ministry 5.12b ☆

At the left end of the low roof is a line of four bolts that lead to a lone cold shut. 40 feet. FA: Doug Reed, June 1991.

7 Sancho Belige 5.11c ☆☆☆

Schteeep and schweeet. Start a few paces right of *Ministry* and pull the low roof, then crank the line of seven bolts to cold shuts. 75 feet. FA: Shannon Langely, June 1991.

8 The Bicycle Club 5.11d ☆

A short distance to the right is a line of five bolts with a cold-shut station. 55 feet. FA: Doug Reed, June 1991.

9 Boing 5.10d

Start just right of the arête and six clips will lead you to a pair of cold shuts. 70 feet. FA: Gary Beil, 1993.

10 Springer 5.10b ☆

Jump into action just left of the dihedral and slab climb the line of six bolts to a pair of cold shuts below the huge roof. 75 feet. FA: Glenn Ritter, August 1991.

11 The Bag 5.10d ☆☆

In the center of the wall is a striking crack that is jammed to the top. 75 feet. FA: Rick Fairtrace & Scott Jones, fall 1987.

12 Lost Souls 5.12a ☆☆

Dyno, dyno, dyno! Begin left of the dihedral and follow six clips to cold shuts. 65 feet. FA: Steve Cater, May 1991.

13 Jumpin' Ring Snakes 5.9

Follow the crack system in the left facing dihedral to the top. 65 feet. FA: Lieb Yrag & Nialcm Nek, August 1991.`

14 Flight of the Gumbie 5.9 ☆☆☆

A fashionable flight plan for the neophyte sport pilot. Begin on the left side of the arête and climb past eight bolts to a cold-shut station. 65 feet. FA: Gary Beil & Doug Cosby, May 1991.

15 Bourbon Sauce 5.11d ☆☆

Climb the line of bolts to the roof, then move left and up to cold shuts. 65 feet. FA: Doug Reed, May 1991.

16 Control 5.12a ☆ (b)

Using the same start as the previous route move up to the roof, then shift right to the anchor at the top of *Kaos*. Cruise back left past three more bolts to anchors. 65 feet. FA: Doug Cosby, May 1991.

17 Kaos 5.12c (b)

A short distance to the right is a line of four bolts equipped with cold shuts. 45 feet. FA: Doug Cosby, May 1991.

18 Mo' Betta' Holds 5.11c/d ☆☆☆ (b)

Mo' a dat bigga' fun on mongo jugs thang! Another few paces down the wall is a six-clip line that mounts a major roof. 70 feet. FA: Doug Reed, June 1991.

19 All the Right Moves 5.11d ☆ (b)

Near the right side of the roof band is an eight-bolt route with cold shuts. 80 feet. FA: Doug Reed, May 1991.

20 Hard Core Female Thrash 5.11c ☆☆ (b)

Start at the right edge of the roof band and thrash your way up the prominent left-facing dihedral past six bolts to a cold-shut station. 70 feet. FA: Doug Reed, June 1991.

Doug Cosby on *Slash and Burn*.

photo: Tom Isaacson

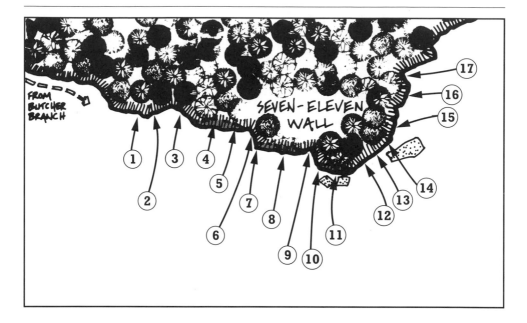

SEVEN-ELEVEN WALL

A short walk beyond the end of Butcher Branch will bring you to the Seven-Eleven Wall.

1   Squirrely Adventure 5.10a 🅟
The first route follows good holds along the line of eight bolts to a pair of cold shuts. Note: Beware of wasps and loose rock. 75 feet. FA: Dave Surber, April 1993.

2   Fearless Symmetry 5.11d ☆ 🅟
Begin a short distance right of the corner and climb thin cracks and a flake system along a line of six clips to cold shuts. 75 feet. Note: Easier if you detour left at the second bolt. FA: Doug Reed, July 1991.

3   The Sting 5.11d ☆☆ 🅟
Start below a shallow left-facing corner and climb past seven bolts and a piercing crux to a cold shut station. 70 feet. FA: Doug Reed, June 1991.

4   Tit Speed 5.11c ☆☆ 🅟
Start below a white face with a high first bolt and wander along seven clips to cold shuts. 75 feet. FA: Doug Reed, June 1991.

5   Tony the Tiger 5.11c ☆☆ 🅟
Commence ten feet left of the dihedral and climb up, then step left onto the face following clips past the roofs to shuts below the top. Nine bolts in all. 80 feet. FA: Doug Reed, July 1991.

6   Enigma 5.10a
Normally done as a toprope from the *Scenic Adult* anchors. Climb the corner to the top. 80 feet. FA: A total mystery.

7   Scenic Adult 5.11d ☆☆☆ 🎣
Not exactly a pastoral scene, the graphic exposure at the top will leave you breathless. Climb along the face to the right of the arête, then back left to the arête proper at the crux. Fire off the exposed traverse to the right and finish back left to the shuts. 90 feet. Ten bolts. WARNING: The belayer must be careful not to drop the leader; a 50-meter rope will barely get you to the ground. FA: Doug Reed, summer 1991.

8   Bimbo Shrine 5.11b ☆ 🎣
Start behind a huge hemlock with a stick clip and follow eight bolts to the station at the top. 75 feet. FA: Doug Reed, spring 1992.

9   Broken Foot 5.8
Begin in the corner and grovel up the dirty crack to the roof, then traverse right to the cold shuts at the top of *Mr. Hollywood*. 80 feet. FA: Dave Surber, November 1992.

10   Mr. Hollywood 5.12a 🎣
Mr. look-so-good doesn't turn out to be Mr. climb-so-good. Start just left of the outside corner and move up and around the corner to the right and strut up the shallow crack to the top. 65 feet. FA: Steve Cater & Doug Cosby, July 1991.

11   Slash and Burn 5.12d ☆☆☆☆ 🎣
This stellar outing is sure to kindle a blistering pump. Start below the flat wall and smoke past nine bolts to a pair of cold shuts. 75 feet. FA: Doug Reed, May 1991.

12   Buzz Kill 5.12c 🎣
Power past the slabby crux and whir your way up the line of 10 bolts to a pair of cold shuts. FA: Eric Anderson, 1992.

13   Fairtracer 5.10d ☆☆☆
Another one of those plucky cracks. Start immediately left of the boulder and jam the divine hand crack to the top. 85 feet. FA: Rick Fairtrace & Scott Jones, June 1987.

14   First Steps 5.10c ☆☆☆ 🎣
Exemplary face climbing every step of the way. Scramble to the top of the boulder and follow six bolts to a pair of cold shuts. FA: Doug Reed, June 1991.

15   Fuel Injector 5.13b ☆☆ 🎣
To date the scene of many attempts, but no repeats. Start right of the hefty boulder and climb up the face and through the overhang to cold shuts. Eight bolts in all. FA: Doug Reed, fall 1993.

16   The Butcher Man 5.11a

Follow four bolts up the short arête to a station. FA: Scotty Greenway & Mike Emelinoff, June 1991.

17   Ed and Bill's Excellent Adventure 5.10a ☆☆

Climb the crack in the dihedral to the top. FA: Ed Pavelchek & Bill Webster, September 1991.

Elizabeth Erskine doing the *Hardcore Female Thrash.*

photo: Tom Isaacson

ROUTES BY RATING

Route names, (Chapter), rating, (page number)

5.1-5.5

5.6

5.7

5.7 (continued)

- ☐ Crescent Moon (Endless) (234)
- ☐ Ducks Unlimited (Bridge) (70)
- ☐ Easily Flakey (Bridge) (52)
- ☐ Eating Bimbo Pie (Bubba) (129)
- ☐ Garden Weasel (Endless) (187)
- ☐ Gaye Belayed (Bridge) (77)
- ☐ Gone with the Bubba (Bubba) (145)
- ☐ Gut Feeling (Endless) (212)
- ☐ Helmeted Warrior of Love (Bubba) (161)
- ☐ Hopfenperle Special, The (Bridge) (74)
- ☐ Horton's Tree (Bridge) (45)
- ☐ In the Palm of His Hand (Endless) (182)
- ☐ In Tribute to Skid (Bridge) (63)
- ☐ It Comes In Spurts (Bubba) (131)
- ☐ Journey to the Center of the Brain (Beauty) (323)
- ☐ Jumpin' Jack Flash (Junkyard) (99)
- ☐ Lollipop (Bridge) (65)
- ☐ Lucky Pierre Direct Start —This One Is for Vicki (Bridge) (81)
- ☐ Midnight Moonlight (Bridge) (73)
- ☐ Nasty Body O'Dour (Bubba) (153)
- ☐ New River Gunks (Junkyard) (99)
- ☐ No Sign of Intelligent Life (Endless) (287)
- ☐ Purity Made (Endless) (204)
- ☐ Rat's Alley (Endless) (281)
- ☐ Ratz Holm (Bubba) (163)
- ☐ Rock, The (Endless) (182)
- ☐ Romper Room (Bridge) (75)
- ☐ Sand in My Crack (Kaymoor) (371)
- ☐ Seventh Sign (Endless) (262)
- ☐ Short'n Sweet (Beauty) (347)
- ☐ Spamling, The (Bridge) (80)
- ☐ Stalking the Wild Toad (Bubba) (161)
- ☐ Stoat Goes to Joshua Tree and Tears a Flapper on Baby Apes (Endless) (305)
- ☐ Supersymmetry (Endless) (245)
- ☐ Thought Crime (Endless) (251)
- ☐ Throw in the Rack (Bridge) (75)
- ☐ Toxic Waste (Endless) (303)
- ☐ Two Step Arête Variation Finish— Steppin' Out (Endless) (213)
- ☐ Undulator, The (Endless) (313)
- ☐ Up to Disneyland (Bridge) (39)
- ☐ Walking on the Moon Direct Start— Moonraker (Endless) (220)
- ☐ Wasted Woute (Bubba) (138)
- ☐ Who Knows? (Junkyard) (104)
- ☐ Wong Woute, The (Bubba) (130)

5.8

- ☐ Air Wailing (Bubba) (145)
- ☐ Ambiance (Endless) (255)
- ☐ Ann's Revenge (Junkyard) (96)
- ☐ Barefoot Alley (Bridge) (38)
- ☐ Bat Cave (Endless) (187)
- ☐ Bearpaw Crack (Beauty) (324)
- ☐ Beat Me Daddy, Eight to the Bar (Endless) (301)
- ☐ Betty's Boop (Bubba) (140)
- ☐ Black Dog (Animal) (115)
- ☐ Brain Teasers Direct Finish — Brain Storm (Beauty) (324)
- ☐ Bubba Safari (Bubba) (125)
- ☐ Bubbalicious (Bubba) (145)
- ☐ C.T. Crack (Bubba) (164)
- ☐ Carcus Tunnel Syndrome (Endless) (250)
- ☐ Chew Electric Death You Snarling Cur (Endless) (299)
- ☐ Chinese Style (Bridge) (68)
- ☐ Cow in a China Shop (Endless) (296)
- ☐ Creamy (Bubba) (128)
- ☐ Dark Hollow (Bridge) (75)
- ☐ El Routo de los Contrivadores (Bubba) (127)
- ☐ Ergodicity (Beauty) (349)
- ☐ Exhaust Pipe (Bubba) (128)
- ☐ Exit If You Can (Bubba) (127)
- ☐ Face Lift — Direct Start (Bubba) (160)
- ☐ Fantasy (Endless) (214)
- ☐ Food For Thought (Bridge) (81)
- ☐ Fossilized Faggits (Bubba) (127)
- ☐ Fried Mush (Endless) (299)
- ☐ Hall Effect, The (Bridge) (39)

5.8 (continued)

- ☐ Happy Head (Bridge) (68)
- ☐ Honker Heaven (Keeneys) (353)
- ☐ Hysteria (Endless) 5.8+ 312)
- ☐ I Just Eight (Junkyard) (110)
- ☐ Labrador Reliever (Animal) (118)
- ☐ Lavender Chockstone (Bubba) (144)
- ☐ Ledge City (Bridge) (40)
- ☐ Lethargical Lion (Endless) (285)
- ☐ Midway (Bridge) (76)
- ☐ Mixed Emotions (Bubba) (165)
- ☐ Momma's Squeeze Box (Beauty) (346)
- ☐ Mononuclear Knows It (Beauty) (337)
- ☐ Mounting Madness (Bridge) (43)
- ☐ Mr. Ed (Junkyard) (101)
- ☐ Never Alone (Junkyard) (110)
- ☐ Out to Lunch (Bridge) (39)
- ☐ Peanut Bubba and Jam (Bubba) (130)
- ☐ Pink Eye (Endless) (225)
- ☐ Porcupine Crack (Bridge) (78)
- ☐ Pound of Prevention, A (Bubba) (127)
- ☐ Prowesse Direct Finish, The—The Repossessed (Endless) (265)
- ☐ Quaking Flakes (Beauty) (337)
- ☐ Reception, The (Endless) (261)
- ☐ Robin (Endless) (180)
- ☐ Rocky Roads (Bridge) (39)
- ☐ Screamer Crack (Beauty) (343)
- ☐ Smoke on the Water (Endless) (285)
- ☐ Sphagnum Dopus (Bridge) (75)
- ☐ Stay Tuned (Beauty) (329)
- ☐ Tasty Flake (Bubba) (145)
- ☐ Thank God I'm Bubbafied! (Bubba) (127)
- ☐ Thought Crime Variation Finish—Stroke Victim (Endless) (251)
- ☐ Three Dimensional Chess (Endless) (287)
- ☐ Tide, The (Endless) (209)
- ☐ Til' Tuesday (Bubba) (147)
- ☐ Toadstool (Beauty) (324)
- ☐ Totally-Clipse (Endless) (281)
- ☐ Tractor Beam (Endless) (287)
- ☐ Trial, The (Bubba) (163)
- ☐ Trashed Again Variation Finish — Rock 'n Roll Hours (Bubba) (140)
- ☐ Two Step Arête (Endless) (212)
- ☐ Two Step Arête Variation—The One Step (Endless) (213)
- ☐ Unnamed (Endless) (184)
- ☐ Walk in the Park (Junkyard) (104)
- ☐ Weenie Roast (Endless) (195)
- ☐ Where Real Men Dare (Bridge) (59)
- ☐ White Bubbas On Dope (Bubba) (140)
- ☐ Wrath of Khan, The (Endless) (287)
- ☐ Wrinkles and a Gold Card (Endless) (287)
- ☐ Zag (Bridge) (49)

5.9

- ☐ Afro-Sheener (Sunshine) (356)
- ☐ Afternoon Delight Direct Start — Pinnacle Flats (Bridge) (79)
- ☐ Anticipation (Endless) (293)
- ☐ Aquaman (Endless) (180)
- ☐ Artful Dreamer, The (Bridge) (77)
- ☐ Axis Bold As Bubba (Bubba) (136)
- ☐ Baptism by Fire (Endless) (307)
- ☐ Basic Bubba Crack (Bubba) (125)
- ☐ Batman (Endless) (180)
- ☐ Bedtime for Bubba (Bubba) (134)
- ☐ Beef Boy Field Day (Bubba) (165)
- ☐ Beer Belly Roof (Bridge) (42)
- ☐ Big Al's (Bridge) (74)
- ☐ Big Gulp (Endless) (200)
- ☐ Black Noise (Endless) (227)
- ☐ Blackberry Blossom (Bridge) (64)
- ☐ Bloodtest (Bubba) (160)
- ☐ Blues Brothers (Endless) (285)
- ☐ Brash-Burgin Route (Sunshine) (358)
- ☐ Bubba Bath (Bubba) (133)
- ☐ Bubba Shitty (Bubba) (151)
- ☐ Bubba's Lament (Bubba) (141)
- ☐ Burning Calves Direct Finish (Beauty) (331)
- ☐ Bushong (Endless) (309)
- ☐ Butler, The (Bridge) (40)
- ☐ Contortionist, The (Junkyard) (100)
- ☐ Caffeine Free (Endless) (200)
- ☐ Celluloid Vipers (Endless) (230)

5.9 (continued)

- [ ] Chasing Spiders...Variation Finish — Chased by Spiders to the Left (Junkyard) (111)
- [ ] Chasin' the Wind Indirect Start (Beauty) (339)
- [ ] Chattasuga Choo-Choo (Bridge) (77)
- [ ] Chockstone (Bridge) (54)
- [ ] Clairvoyance (Beauty) (347)
- [ ] Closer to the Heart (Endless) (230)
- [ ] Crack Sap (Junkyard) (97)
- [ ] Dead Animal Crackers (Endless) (275)
- [ ] Death of a Salesman (Beauty) (347)
- [ ] Diversity in Microcosm (Endless)(269)
- [ ] Diversity in Microcosm Variation Finish (Endless) (269)
- [ ] Doce Doe (Endless) (232)
- [ ] Double Flat (Endless) (217)
- [ ] Double Negative (Endless) (205)
- [ ] Dreamtime (Animal) (114)
- [ ] East Meets West (Beauty) (331)
- [ ] Emerald Dance (Endless) (307)
- [ ] Far Fletched (Endless) (305)
- [ ] Fat Man's Folly (Beauty) (338)
- [ ] Fist Fodder (Endless) (274)
- [ ] Flaming Asshole Resistant Material (Sunshine) (358)
- [ ] Flight of the Gumbie (Kaymoor) (378)
- [ ] Flirting With VMC (Endless) (209)
- [ ] Fly'n Hawaiian, The (Endless) (264)
- [ ] Flying Sideways (Endless) (251)
- [ ] Fool Effect (Endless) (277)
- [ ] Fourgasm, The (Endless) (309)
- [ ] Four Sheets to the Wind (Junkyard) (97)
- [ ] Gang Bang (Endless) (224)
- [ ] Gaye's Gaze (Bridge) (44)
- [ ] George, George, George of the Gorge, Watch Out For That Tree (Endless) (257)
- [ ] Good Book, The (Endless) (196)
- [ ] Good Old Days, The (Kaymoor) (371)
- [ ] Goofer's Retreat (Endless) (314)
- [ ] Grafenberg Crack, The (Endless) (229)
- [ ] Green Thing (Beauty) (323)
- [ ] Happy Hands (Beauty) (330)
- [ ] Hey Woody, Hinckley's Not the Center of the Universe Any More! (Bridge) (76)
- [ ] Hidden Pleasures (Kaymoor) (375)
- [ ] Honker Hell (Keeneys) (353)
- [ ] Hubba Bubba (Bubba) (153)
- [ ] Jackie Gleason Flake, The (Endless) (216)
- [ ] Jane (Endless) (274)
- [ ] Jaws (Bridge) (53)
- [ ] Jumpin' Ring Snakes (Kaymoor) (378)
- [ ] Just Another Crack (Bubba) (164)
- [ ] La Bumba (Bubba) (143)
- [ ] Lapping the Sap Variation — The Hornet (Junkyard) (96)
- [ ] Law of Diminishing Returns, The (Bubba) (152)
- [ ] Layback, The (Bridge) aka Zig (48)
- [ ] Leave it to Bubba (Bubba) (127)
- [ ] Leave it to Bubba Variation Finish - Fred Sandstone Flake (Bubba) (128)
- [ ] Left Son of Lichen (Keeneys) (352)
- [ ] Lies and Propaganda (Endless) (303)
- [ ] Long John Jam (Endless) (185)
- [ ] Long Reach (Junkyard) (96)
- [ ] Look, Me Awesome! (Endless) (292)
- [ ] Lucky Pierre at L.A.S.W.A. (Bridge) (81)
- [ ] Lunar Debris (Endless) (234)
- [ ] Macho Man (Bridge) (44)
- [ ] Mankey Monkey, The (Bridge) (42)
- [ ] Mayfly, The (Bridge) (47)
- [ ] Mayfly, The, Variation Finish—The Gayfly (Bridge) (47)
- [ ] Metamorphosis, The (Bubba) (164)
- [ ] Mellow Drama (Endless) (312)
- [ ] Milk Run (Bridge) (73)
- [ ] Mr. Peanut Head (Bridge) (79)
- [ ] Nasty Groove (Endless) (263)
- [ ] New Yosemite aka Climbing Under the Influence (Junkyard) (98)
- [ ] Night Moves (Endless) (286)
- [ ] No Bubbas Allowed (Bubba) (149)
- [ ] Nookie Monster (Ambass.) (86)
- [ ] One of My Many Smells (Endless) (303)
- [ ] Palladium (Bridge) (43)
- [ ] Pink Pooka Party (Endless) (215)

5.9 (continued)

- [ ] Pre-Marital Bliss (Endless) (272)
- [ ] Princess Diana (Junkyard) (97)
- [ ] Prowesse, The (Endless) (264)
- [ ] Rainy Daze (Beauty) (339)
- [ ] Rap-n-Go (Endless) (285)
- [ ] Recreation (Junkyard) (105)
- [ ] Reverse Traverse, The (Bridge) (79)
- [ ] Riding the Crest of a Wave (Endless) (276)
- [ ] Right Son of Lichen (Keeneys) (352)
- [ ] Ritz Cracker (Endless) (315)
- [ ] Roar of the Crowd (Endless) (284)
- [ ] Rolling Rock (Endless) (307)
- [ ] Roy's Lament (Endless) (206)
- [ ] Roy's Lament Direct Start (Endless) (206)
- [ ] S and M (Endless) (288)
- [ ] Sandy's Sweet Bottom (Endless) (293)
- [ ] Scarey (Bridge) (44)
- [ ] Scrubbing Bubbas (Bubba) (147)
- [ ] Searching For Sanctuary (Kaymoor) (375)
- [ ] Share the Faith (Bridge) (76)
- [ ] Smooth Operator (Endless) (268)
- [ ] Sneak Preview Variation Start—Ray-Hauls Redemption Round (Endless) (225)
- [ ] Spoon Fed (Junkyard) (111)
- [ ] Squids in Bondage (Junkyard) (109)
- [ ] Statistical Reminder (Endless) (212)
- [ ] Stolen Kisses (Endless) (222)
- [ ] Subsidized Development (Endless) (286)
- [ ] Super Crack (Beauty) (342)
- [ ] Super Crack Variation — Photo Finish (Beauty) (343)
- [ ] Sweet Potatoe (Endless) (185)
- [ ] Third Dimension, The (Bridge) (65)
- [ ] Tree in Your Face (Bridge) (39)
- [ ] Trashed Again Variation Finish—Arch Bubba (Bubba) (140)
- [ ] Two Bag Face (Endless) (300)
- [ ] Unnamed (Endless) (180, 184, 256)
- [ ] Upheaval, The (Endless) (278)
- [ ] Video Waves (Endless) (275)
- [ ] Warp Factor III (Beauty) (329)
- [ ] What a Jamb (Endless) (225)
- [ ] Where's Bulimia? (Endless) (191)
- [ ] Where's Gus? (Beauty) (328)
- [ ] Wienie Roast (Ambass.) (89)
- [ ] Wimpy, Wimpy, Wimpy (Endless) (278)
- [ ] Wishbone Right (Endless) (312)
- [ ] You Want it, You Got it (Beauty) (323)
- [ ] Your Mother.... (Bridge) (59)
- [ ] Yert Yak Crack, The (Endless) (299)
- [ ] V-Slot aka Ride A Rock Horse (Junkyard) (101)

5.10a

- [ ] Amigo Bandito (Endless) (227)
- [ ] Anal Clenching Adventures (Endless) (311)
- [ ] Angel's Arête (Bridge) (49)
- [ ] Anomalous Propagation (Junkyard) (104)
- [ ] Apostrophe (Bubba) (161)
- [ ] Attack of the Moss Clods (Kaymoor) (369)
- [ ] Bad Head of Lettuce (Endless) (230)
- [ ] Bhopal West (Bridge) (74)
- [ ] Biohazard (Endless) (265)
- [ ] Black and Tan (Endless) (231)
- [ ] Brain Teasers (Beauty) (323)
- [ ] Broken Sling (Beauty) (330)
- [ ] Bubba Does Debbie (Bubba) (145)
- [ ] Bubba Has Balls (Bubba) (139)
- [ ] Bubba Meets She-Ra (Bubba) (137)
- [ ] Bubba's Big Adventure (Bubba) (163)
- [ ] Bumbling Bubbas (Bubba) (139)
- [ ] Butterbeans (Bridge) (55)
- [ ] Chasing Rainbows (Ambass.) (88)
- [ ] Consumer Liability (Kaymoor) (372)
- [ ] Contemplation (Endless) (294)
- [ ] Cool Crack (Bubba) (165)
- [ ] Crack a Smile (Endless) (248)
- [ ] Cresenta (Endless) (289)
- [ ] Cruise Slut (Bubba) (161)
- [ ] Crystal Vision (Endless) (230)
- [ ] Devil's Arête (Endless) (299)

5.10a (continued)

- [ ] Diddler, The (Endless) (229)
- [ ] Dust Bowl (Endless) (241)
- [ ] Ed and Bill's Excellent Adventure (Kaymoor) (382)
- [ ] Enigma (Kaymoor) (381)
- [ ] Entertainer, The (Junkyard) (101)
- [ ] Enteruptus (Junkyard) (98)
- [ ] Face Lift (Bubba) (160)
- [ ] Farewell to Bubba (Bubba) (149)
- [ ] Fat Chicks (Bubba) (140)
- [ ] First Strike (Bridge) (74)
- [ ] Frictional Heat Experiment, The (Endless) (241)
- [ ] Gemini Crack — Right (Bridge) (65)
- [ ] Gloom Index, The (Bridge) (77)
- [ ] Golden Olmpics (Endless) (275)
- [ ] Happiness is a Pair of Warm Gums (Keeneys) (353)
- [ ] Hefty, Hefty, Hefty (Endless) (280)
- [ ] Hideosity, The (Bubba) (166)
- [ ] Highlander (Bridge) (68)
- [ ] House of Cards (Bridge) (39)
- [ ] If Frogs Had Wings (Bubba) (162)
- [ ] Imperial Strut (Endless) (203)
- [ ] Intimidation (Endless) (293)
- [ ] J Tree Route (Kaymoor) (376)
- [ ] Keep it Tight but Don't Give Me Aids (Junkyard) (99)
- [ ] Keep it Tight....Variation Finish (Junkyard) (99)
- [ ] Kidspeak (Ambass.) (86)
- [ ] Lapping the Sap (Junkyard) (96)
- [ ] Lobster in Cleavage Probe (Endless) (225)
- [ ] Lunar Tunes (Ambass.) (86)
- [ ] Men Under Water (Endless) (232)
- [ ] Meth-iso-cyinate (Bridge) (75)
- [ ] Mid-Height Crisis (Bubba) (164)
- [ ] Mongrels (Animal) (117)
- [ ] Monster in My Pants (Endless) (226)
- [ ] Mushrooms (Beauty) (343)
- [ ] Nestle Krunch Roof Direct Start (Endless) (240)
- [ ] No Static at All (Endless) (313)
- [ ] No-zone, The (Endless) (296)
- [ ] Nutrasweet (Endless) (200)
- [ ] Out of Mind (Beauty) (323)
- [ ] Oyster Cracker (Endless) (204)
- [ ] Permission Granted (Endless) (231)
- [ ] Pig Pen (Bubba) (135)
- [ ] Play it by Ear (Kaymoor) (377)
- [ ] Point in Question (Beauty) (336)
- [ ] Presto (Endless) (308)
- [ ] Quick Robin, to the Bat Crack! aka The Bat Crack (Beauty) (336)
- [ ] Rhododenema (Junkyard) (101)
- [ ] Rico Suavé Arête, The (Kaymoor) (371)
- [ ] Rotating Heads (Endless) (280)
- [ ] Sandman, The (Bridge) (38)
- [ ] Senility Variation Finish—Captain Chaos (Endless) (197)
- [ ] Separator, The (Endless) (226)
- [ ] Simple Harmonic Motion (Beauty) (348)
- [ ] Skinny Boys (Bubba) (140)
- [ ] Southern Hospitality (Endless) (239)
- [ ] Spineless Perpetrator, The (Ambass.) (87)
- [ ] Squirrely Adventure (Kaymoor) (380)
- [ ] Sunshine Daydream (Endless) (195)
- [ ] Synaptic Lapse (Bridge) (69)
- [ ] Take Me to the River (Bubba) (153)
- [ ] Tarzan (Endless) (275)
- [ ] Technarête (Endless) (228)
- [ ] Terminus (Endless) (261)
- [ ] Totally Tammy (Kaymoor) (370)
- [ ] Tree Route (Bridge) (53)
- [ ] Triple Treat (Endless) (311)
- [ ] Unnamed (Endless) (187)
- [ ] Walking in Your Footsteps (Endless) (281)
- [ ] Walrus, The (Bridge) (77)
- [ ] Werewolf (Bubba) (128)
- [ ] Whales in Drag (Junkyard) (97)
- [ ] Zee Crack, The (Endless) (185)
- [ ] Zoomin' Human, The (Beauty) (337)

5.10a/b

☐ Euro Nation (Endless) (254)
☐ Perserverence (Endless) (217)

☐ Team Jesus (Junkyard) (100)
☐ With a Little Help From my Friends (Endless) (278)

5.10b

☐ Almost Heaven (Kaymoor) (374)
☐ Autumn Fire (Endless) (272)
☐ Bat Crack Direct Finish (Beauty) R (336)
☐ Beach, The (Endless) (209)
☐ Berlin Wall (Bridge) (65)
☐ Big Cheese, The (Bridge) (73)
☐ Blind Sight (Endless) (195)
☐ Blunder and Frightening (Bridge) (48)
☐ Brain Tweezers (Beauty) (324)
☐ Brass Monkey (Endless) (239)
☐ Bubbarête (Bubba) (125)
☐ Burning Calves (Beauty) (331)
☐ Camalot (Bubba) (147)
☐ Can I Do It 'Til I Need Glasses? (Endless) (249)
☐ Catatonic Conflicts (Bridge) (65)
☐ Clumsy Club Crack (Ambass.) (87)
☐ Command Performance (Endless) (277)
☐ Consenting Clips (Ambass.) (89)
☐ Constant Velocity (Endless) (293)
☐ Crazy Ambulance Driver (Bubba) (162)
☐ Crazy Ambulance Driver Variation — Emergency Room Exit (Bubba) (162)
☐ Cresenta Direct Start—Fire and Waste (Endless) (289)
☐ D.S.B. (Deadly Sperm Build-up) (Bubba) (138)
☐ Dab Hand (Endless) (204)
☐ Daily Waste (Bubba) (164)
☐ Damn the Lieback, Full Stem Ahead! (Kaymoor) (374)
☐ Danger in Paradise (Junkyard) (97)
☐ Daughter of Dracula (Endless) (286)
☐ Dementing Situations (Bubba) (157)
☐ Dog Fight (Bridge) (45)
☐ Dumbolt County (Bubba) (126)
☐ Durometer 64 (Endless) (249)
☐ Eat at the Wye (Bubba) (139)

☐ Enteruptus Variation Start — Scott's Turf Builder (Junkyard) (98)
☐ Eye of Zen (Endless) (306)
☐ Fantasy Direct Finish (Endless) (214)
☐ Fragile Egosystem (Endless) (305)
☐ Frigidator (Junkyard) (99)
☐ Frozen in the Big Position (Keeneys) (353)
☐ Gift from the Mayor (Bubba) (166)
☐ Glass Onion, The (Endless) (241)
☐ Green Piece, The (Kaymoor) (377)
☐ Greenway, The (Beauty) (325)
☐ Grin Reaper (Endless) (275)
☐ High and Lively (Endless) (188)
☐ Hunger Artist, The (Bubba) (162)
☐ I'll Be-Gooned (Kaymoor) (374)
☐ Impaled (Bridge) (75)
☐ Inexorably Delicious Variation Start - Exquisite Lace (Endless) (266)
☐ Insertum Outcome (Endless) (229)
☐ It's a Honker! (Keeneys) (352)
☐ Jams Across America (Bridge) (79)
☐ Jimmy's Swagger (Bridge) (70)
☐ Joey's Face (Bridge) (75)
☐ Junk Food (Bridge) (64)
☐ Liddlebiddanuthin' (Ambass.) (89)
☐ Life's a Bitch and Then You Climb (Endless) (273)
☐ Lotus Land (Bridge) (47)
☐ Low Voltage (Kaymoor) (378)
☐ Men Who Love Sheep (Bubba) (160)
☐ Mud and Guts (Endless) (302)
☐ Naked Potatoes (Endless) (296)
☐ Night Gallery (Endless) (225)
☐ Ode to Stoat (Bridge) (78)
☐ One-Eyed Viper (Animal) (115)
☐ Ooops, It's a Trad Route (Kaymoor) (366)
☐ Pancake Ledge (Bridge) (70)
☐ Party All the Time, Party All the Time (Endless) (266)
☐ Party in My Mind (Endless) (266)

5.10b (continued)

- [ ] Party Till Yer Blind (Endless) (266)
- [ ] Permission Granted Direct Finish (Endless) (231)
- [ ] Pit Bull Terror (Animal) (115)
- [ ] Plastic Sturgeons (Bubba) (160)
- [ ] Promised (Bridge) (68)
- [ ] Promised Direct Start (Bridge) (68)
- [ ] Raiders of the Lost Crag (Kaymoor) (373)
- [ ] Remission (Endless) (249)
- [ ] Rod Serling Crack (Beauty) (333)
- [ ] Roy's Lament Direct Finish (Endless) (207)
- [ ] S.T.A.N.C. (Endless) (223)
- [ ] Second Thoughts (Kaymoor) (370)
- [ ] Skiggle Von Wiggle (Endless) (187)
- [ ] Sneak Preview (Endless) (225)
- [ ] Solitude Standing (Bubba) (163)
- [ ] Spider Wand (Beauty) (330)
- [ ] Springboard (Endless) (311)
- [ ] Springer (Kaymoor) (378)
- [ ] Strike a Scowl (Endless) (248)

- [ ] Sundowner (Bridge) (63)
- [ ] Thing Foot (Bubba) (166)
- [ ] 'Til the Cows Come Home (Bridge) (72)
- [ ] Timberline (Endless) (268)
- [ ] Two Tone Arête (Endless) (307)
- [ ] Underfling (Bridge) (54)
- [ ] Warp Factor III Variation Finish — Aye, Aye Captain (Beauty) (329)
- [ ] Wasted Weeblewobble, The (Endless) (227)
- [ ] We'll Have to Whisk It (Keeneys) (353)
- [ ] We're Having Some Fun Now (Bubba) (148)
- [ ] Wedgie (Endless) (188)
- [ ] Wham, Bam, Thanks for the Jam (Beauty) (331)
- [ ] Where the Big Boys Begin (Beauty) aka Sojourners (349)
- [ ] Wishbone Left (Endless) (312)
- [ ] Women Who Won't Wear Wool (Bubba) (160)

5.10 or 5.10b/c

- [ ] Mo (Endless) 5.10 (181)
- [ ] Path of the Elders (Sunshine) 5.10 (358)
- [ ] Turan-ocaurus Wrecks (Endless) 5.10 (181)
- [ ] Unnamed (Endless) 5.10 (181, 185)
- [ ] Unnamed (Sunshine) 5.10 (358)

- [ ] This Won't Hurt a Bit (Beauty) 5.10 A2 (342)
- [ ] Almost Heaven (Endless) 5.10b/c (198)
- [ ] Exoduster (Endless) 5.10b/c (272)
- [ ] F.U.B. (Bubba) 5.10b/c (147)

5.10c

- [ ] A Dog Always Returns to Its Vomit (Animal) (116)
- [ ] Airwaves (Bubba) (131)
- [ ] Americans, Baby, The (Endless) (255)
- [ ] Aquarian Conspiracy (Endless) (274)
- [ ] Back in the Saddle (Endless) (269)
- [ ] Between Coming and Going (Endless) (229)
- [ ] Bisect (Endless) (311)
- [ ] Boltus Prohibitus (Bridge) (43)
- [ ] Born Under a Bad Smell (Animal) (115)
- [ ] Brain Death (Endless) (205)

- [ ] Brawn Wall Direct Finish, The (Endless) (306)
- [ ] Breach Birth (Endless) (293)
- [ ] Brown Dirt Cowboy (Junkyard) (108)
- [ ] Bubba Meets She-Ra Direct Start — Psychotic Turnbuckles (Bubba) (137)
- [ ] Celibate Mallard (Endless) (206)
- [ ] Churning in the Huecos (Junkyard) (104)
- [ ] Common Ground (Endless) (285)
- [ ] Crimes of Fashion (Endless) (235)
- [ ] Double Twouble (Bubba) (165)

5.10c (continued)

- [ ] Dr. Rosenbud's Nose (Bridge) (76)
- [ ] Enemy Line (Junkyard) (108)
- [ ] Esse Crack (Bridge) (69)
- [ ] Erogenous Zone, The (Endless) (208)
- [ ] Eurobubba (Bubba) (151)
- [ ] F.A.B. (Bubba) (147)
- [ ] Faith Crack (Junkyard) (109)
- [ ] Fire (Kaymoor) (373)
- [ ] First Person (Endless) (298)
- [ ] First Steps (Kaymoor) (381)
- [ ] Furry Nerd (Endless) (312)
- [ ] Gemini Crack — Left (Bridge) (65)
- [ ] Good Life, The (Animal) (119)
- [ ] High Octane (Endless) (195)
- [ ] Hummingbird (Endless) (298)
- [ ] Ikon of Control, The (Bubba) (130)
- [ ] Just Say Yo to Jugs (Sunshine) (357)
- [ ] Kansas Shitty (Junkyard) (105)
- [ ] Labor Day (Bridge) (46)
- [ ] Le Brief (Bridge) (74)
- [ ] Lewd Operator (Endless) (311)
- [ ] Lone Rhinoceros (Beauty) (339)
- [ ] Lying Egyptian (Endless) (203)
- [ ] Malfunction Junction (Kaymoor) (373)
- [ ] Maranatha (Bridge) (62)
- [ ] Meto Power (Bridge) (78)
- [ ] Necromancer (Sunshine) (357)
- [ ] Nestle Krunch Roof (Endless) (240)
- [ ] New Tricks for the Old Dog (Endless) (294)
- [ ] Nutcrafter Suite, The (Endless) (251)
- [ ] Parsimony (Endless) (313)
- [ ] Petrified Pink Puke (Endless) (200)
- [ ] Pipe Dreams (Bridge) (58)
- [ ] Poison Ivy (Junkyard) (110)
- [ ] Race Among the Ruins (Bridge) (43)
- [ ] Rapscallion's Blues (Junkyard) (97)
- [ ] Rock Lobster (Endless) (222)
- [ ] Sixteenth Rung (Endless) (183)
- [ ] Snake Patrol (Endless) (221)
- [ ] Spiderwalk (Endless) (298)
- [ ] Taming the Shrewd (Bubba) (131)
- [ ] Tools For Mutant Women (Endless) (181)
- [ ] Translate Slowly (Endless) (225)
- [ ] Underdiddled, The (Ambass.) (86)
- [ ] Undeserved, The (Endless) (207)
- [ ] Unnamed (Endless) (183)
- [ ] Wienie From the Past (Kaymoor) (369)
- [ ] Wild Dogs (Beauty) (337)
- [ ] Wire Train (Endless) (217)
- [ ] Wondering (Endless) (300)

5.10c/d

- [ ] Arthur Murray Crack (Bubba) (145)
- [ ] Endangered Species (Endless) (197)
- [ ] Hot Flash (Beauty) (324)
- [ ] Insistent Irony (Bubba) (138)
- [ ] Perpendiculus (Bubba) (127)
- [ ] Rival (Endless) (183)
- [ ] Wampus Cat Blues (Endless) (292)
- [ ] One Life at a Time, Please (Bridge) (73)
- [ ] The Vertex (Bridge) (79)

5.10d

- [ ] Aimless Wanderers (Junkyard) (109)
- [ ] Android (Endless) (202)
- [ ] Bag, The (Kaymoor) (378)
- [ ] Beauty and the Beast (Beauty) (347)
- [ ] Blood Donors (Endless) (195)
- [ ] Boing (Kaymoor) (378)
- [ ] Bovine Seduction (Kaymoor) (372)
- [ ] Bye Bye Bow Wow (Bridge) (63)
- [ ] Can I Do It....Variation - Straight Up and Stiff (Endless) (249)
- [ ] Chameleon (Endless) (304)
- [ ] Comfortably Numb (Ambass.) (86)
- [ ] Dingo (Animal) (116)
- [ ] Do the Funky Evan (Endless) (224)
- [ ] East Meets West Variation Finish — Bourbon Street (Beauty) (332)

5.10d (continued)

- ☐ Emotional Barbecue (Junkyard) (108)
- ☐ Entertainer Direct Finish, The — Realignment (Junkyard) (101)
- ☐ Fairtracer (Kaymoor) (381)
- ☐ Hog Wollor (Endless) (244)
- ☐ Immaculate Combustion (Bubba) (125)
- ☐ Incredible Overhanging Wall, The (Bridge) (39)
- ☐ Inexorably Delicious (Endless) (266)
- ☐ Kiss of the Spider Woman (Bridge) (42)
- ☐ Levitation (Endless) (285)
- ☐ Lichen in Me, The (Endless) (300)
- ☐ Liddlebiddariddum (Endless) (212)
- ☐ Little Creatures (Bubba) (156)
- ☐ Little Wing (Bubba) (136)
- ☐ Live Wire (Endless) (263)
- ☐ Magnum Gropus (Bridge) (75)
- ☐ Manute Bol (Endless) (273)
- ☐ More Bum, More Fun (Animal) (118)
- ☐ Motivation (Endless) (196)
- ☐ My Wife is a Dog (Bridge) (65)
- ☐ Newvana (Bubba) (150)
- ☐ New Speedway Boogie (Endless) (224)
- ☐ October Surprise (Endless) (297)
- ☐ Off Like a Prom Dress (Endless) (220)
- ☐ Orgasmatron, The (Endless) (213)
- ☐ Paralleling (Endless) (277)
- ☐ Pinkney Route, The (Endless) (183)
- ☐ Pride of Cucamunga (Endless) (229)
- ☐ Puppylove (Animal) (115)
- ☐ Radial Rimmed (Bubba) (146)
- ☐ Raging Tiger, The (Bubba) (133)
- ☐ Raptilian, The (Bubba) (136)
- ☐ She's Too Fat For Me (Endless) (184)
- ☐ Shiny Faces (Endless) (311)
- ☐ Slick Olives (Endless) (263)
- ☐ Solitaire (Endless) (199)
- ☐ Stiff but Not Hard (Bubba) (145)
- ☐ Stop Pulling My Ear (Kaymoor) (377)
- ☐ Tentative Decision (Bridge) (53)
- ☐ Thilly Puddy (Endless) (254)
- ☐ Toss That Beat in the Garbage Can (Endless) (301)
- ☐ Trashed Again (Bubba) (139)
- ☐ Trick or Treat Variation Start — Dynamite Crack (Bridge) (59)
- ☐ Tworgasaminimum (Bubba) (156)
- ☐ Under a Blood Red Sky (Bridge) (39)
- ☐ Unnamed (Ambass.) (87)
- ☐ You Snooze, You Lose (Bridge) (43)
- ☐ Veil of Addiction (Endless) (232)
- ☐ Zealous (Junkyard) (105)

5.11a

- ☐ Isotope Cemetery (Bubba) (146)
- ☐ Adam Ant (Endless) (222)
- ☐ Air (Beauty) (342)
- ☐ All Things Considered (Bubba) (152)
- ☐ Amarillo Dawn (Animal) (119)
- ☐ Are You Asparagus? (Bridge) (62)
- ☐ Attacktician, The (Bubba) (146)
- ☐ Australian Whore (Animal) (118)
- ☐ Big Mac Attack (Bridge) (70)
- ☐ Bitch in Heat (Animal) (116)
- ☐ Bolt Rookies (Endless) (307)
- ☐ Bubba Meets Jesus (Junkyard) (100)
- ☐ Butcher Man, The (Kaymoor) (382)
- ☐ Cal n' Hobbes (Junkyard) (100)
- ☐ Can't Find My Way Home (Bridge) (59)
- ☐ Chicks in the Woods (Bubba) (142)
- ☐ Collateral Damage (Kaymoor) (372)
- ☐ Commuter Flight (Junkyard) (111)
- ☐ Crankenstein (Bubba) (151)
- ☐ Desperados Under the Eaves (Bridge) (58)
- ☐ Deviated Septum (Junkyard) (111)
- ☐ Deviated Septum Variation — Direct Deviation (Junkyard) (111)
- ☐ Discombobulated (Endless) (221)
- ☐ Diving Swan, The (Endless) (251)
- ☐ Dog Day Afternoon (Animal) (116)
- ☐ Dreams of White Toilet Paper (Endless) (214)
- ☐ East Meets West Direct Start — Exposing the Pink (Beauty) (332)

5.11a (continued)

- [ ] Face It Bubba (Bubba) (125)
- [ ] Face Value (Bubba) (164)
- [ ] Fern Creek Direct (Endless) (284)
- [ ] Frilled Dog Winkle (Bubba) (166)
- [ ] Fun With Jello (Endless) (205)
- [ ] Golden Escalator, The (Bubba) (133)
- [ ] Graceland (Endless) (301)
- [ ] Grapefruit Wine (Bridge) (55)
- [ ] Grit and Bear It (Kaymoor) (370)
- [ ] Handsome and Well Hung aka Blood and Guts (Bridge) (49)
- [ ] Happy Campers (Bubba) (134)
- [ ] Happy Hooker, The (Ambass.) (89)
- [ ] High Times (Bridge) (46)
- [ ] Holey Trinity (Endless) (286)
- [ ] I Don't Want Her (Endless) (183)
- [ ] Jacuzzi Bop (Endless) (315)
- [ ] Just Say No (Junkyard) (98)
- [ ] King of Swing (Bubba) (163)
- [ ] Life-O-Suction (Bubba) (124)
- [ ] Linear Encounters (Endless) (260)
- [ ] Lycrascopic (Bubba) (144)
- [ ] Man from Planet Zog, The (Bubba) (126)
- [ ] Mellifluus (Endless) (263)
- [ ] White Powderête (Endless) (184)
- [ ] Midas Touch, The (Bridge) (47)
- [ ] Min-arête (Bridge) (63)
- [ ] Monster, The (Endless) (292)
- [ ] Morning Glory (Animal) (118)
- [ ] Mortimer (Bridge) (42)
- [ ] Muckraker (Endless) (11a (216)
- [ ] Name It and Claim It (Junkyard) (109)
- [ ] New Fangled Dangle (Endless) (208)
- [ ] New Wave (Endless) (278)
- [ ] Not Bosched Up (Bridge) (59)
- [ ] Not on the First Date (Kaymoor) (371)
- [ ] Ook Ook Kachook (Bridge) (77)
- [ ] Open Mouths (Endless) (239)
- [ ] Ovine Seduction (Endless) (245)
- [ ] Parental Guidance Suggested (Bubba) (146)
- [ ] Penalty for Early Withdrawal (Bridge) (43)
- [ ] Plastic Man (Endless) (181)
- [ ] Pleasure Principles (Ambass.) (89)
- [ ] Point the Bone (Animal) (115)
- [ ] Puddy System, The (Endless) (299)
- [ ] Puddsucker (Bubba) (136)
- [ ] Raging Waters (Endless) (248)
- [ ] Raptured (Bridge) (53)
- [ ] Risky Business (Bubba) (165)
- [ ] Rock Rash (Junkyard) (97)
- [ ] Scoop, The (Endless) (289)
- [ ] Scream Seam (Endless) (226)
- [ ] Senility (Endless) (197)
- [ ] Sheena is a Punk Rocker (Endless) (186)
- [ ] Shining, The (Kaymoor) (373)
- [ ] Sometimes a Great Notion (Endless) (309)
- [ ] Stratowienie, The (Endless) (254)
- [ ] Stuck in Another Dimension (Junkyard) (101)
- [ ] Suck Face (Junkyard) (105)
- [ ] Sufficiently Wasted (Endless) (227)
- [ ] Sugar Bubbas (Endless) (221)
- [ ] Surge Complex (Endless) (289)
- [ ] To Bubba or Not to Be (Bubba) (165)
- [ ] Tongulation Variation — Slip of the Tongue (Bubba) (143)
- [ ] Translate Slowly Direct Start (Endless) (225)
- [ ] Trick or Treat (Bridge) (59)
- [ ] Underdog (Animal) (117)
- [ ] Voyage to Uranus (Keeneys) (352)
- [ ] Waka Jawaka (Bubba) (166)
- [ ] Walking on the Moon (Endless) (217)
- [ ] Wedgie Direct Start—Out of Hand (Endless) (188)
- [ ] Workman's Comp (Endless) (301)
- [ ] Undeserved, The, Variation—Mig Squadron (Endless) (207)

5.11b

☐ Anxiety Neurosis (Junkyard) (104)
☐ Aquatic Ecstasy (Endless) (305)
☐ Arms Control (Endless) (228)
☐ Ba Boschka (Bubba) (145)
☐ Basket Case (Endless) (187)
☐ Be Bold and Be Strong (Bridge) (40)
☐ Bill and Ken's Excellent Adventure (Endless) (314)
☐ Bimbo Shrine (Kaymoor) (381)
☐ Brain Teasers Direct Start — Brain Child (Beauty) (324)
☐ Bubba's Big Adventure — Direct Start (Bubba) (163)
☐ Bunny Hop of Death, The (Endless) (183)
☐ Chasin' the Wind (Beauty) (338)
☐ Chasin' the Wind Direct Finish (Beauty) (339)
☐ Chasin' the Wind Variation — Into the Wind (Beauty) (339)
☐ Childbirth (Junkyard) (109)
☐ China Crisis (Bubba) (153)
☐ Churning in the Butter (Endless) (198)
☐ Clock's On (Kaymoor) (366)
☐ Cumberland Blues (Bubba) (127)
☐ Dispose of Properly (Endless) (181)
☐ Dog Fight Direct Finish — Bailing Wire (Bridge) (45)
☐ Egg Man, The (Bridge) (77)
☐ Englishman's Crack (Bridge) (52)
☐ Even Cowgirls Get the Blues (Endless) (187)
☐ Exoduster Direct Finish—Eat My Dust (Endless) (272)
☐ Fierce Face (Bubba) (125)
☐ Fingers in da Dyke (Bubba) (144)
☐ Five-Eight (Junkyard) (108)
☐ Four Star (Endless) (209)
☐ Golden Summer (Bridge) (44)
☐ Grand Space (Endless) (314)
☐ Hah! (Bubba) (137)
☐ Hah! — Direct Start (Bubba) (137)
☐ Half & Half (Kaymoor) (375)
☐ Head with No Hands (Bubba) (156)
☐ Hole in the Wall (Endless) (301)
☐ Idiotsyncracies (Endless) (229)
☐ Jane Fonda's Total Body Workout (Kaymoor) (375)
☐ King of Swing — Direct Finish (Bubba) (163)

☐ Kline The Billy Goat (Endless) (203)
☐ Last Tango, The (Bridge) (64)
☐ Ledge Lips (Bridge) (62)
☐ Legacy, The (Endless) (222)
☐ Meat Puppets (Keeneys) (353)
☐ Mega Jug, The (Endless) (297)
☐ Mr. Workman's Crack (Endless) (301)
☐ My Sister Makes Cluster Bombs (Bubba) (129)
☐ Neuva Vida (Animal) (119)
☐ New Clear Potato Meltdown (Kaymoor) (376)
☐ New Life (Endless) (193)
☐ Oh, It's You Bob (Kaymoor) (369)
☐ Old and in the Way (Endless) (305)
☐ Pearly Gates (Bridge) (49)
☐ Perpetual Motion (Bubba) (152)
☐ Pleasure and Pain (Endless) (288)
☐ Que's Jook Joint (Endless) (278)
☐ Rattle and Hum (Bubba) (133)
☐ Razor Sharp (Endless) (221)
☐ Reachers of Habit (Junkyard) (100)
☐ Recondite (Endless) (228)
☐ Rob's Route (Bridge) (65)
☐ Route 66 (Endless) (198)
☐ Screams in the Woods (Beauty) (329)
☐ Shear Strength (Bubba) (135)
☐ Sheer Energy (Bubba) (134)
☐ Skinhead Grin (Bubba) (151)
☐ Smore Energy (Endless) (273)
☐ Somethin' Fierce (Endless) (206)
☐ Sooner or Ladder (Endless) (234)
☐ Spurtual Reality (Endless) (190)
☐ Stop and I'll Shoot (Endless) (255)
☐ Stop the Presses, Mr. Thompson (Endless) (285)
☐ Suggestions (Bubba) (147)
☐ Sweet Dreams (Endless) (289)
☐ Tour de Bubba (Bubba) (156)
☐ Two-Edged Sword (Bridge) (58)
☐ Unnamed (Ambass.) (89)
☐ Unnamed (Endless) (183)
☐ Way Cerebral (Beauty) (323)
☐ Welcome to Beauty (Beauty) (348)
☐ Wild Seed (Endless) (303)
☐ Squids in Bondage — Childbirth Linkup (Junkyard) (109)
☐ Young Whippersnapper's Route (Endless) (207)

5.11b/c

- [ ] A Touch of Tango (Bridge) (54)
- [ ] Bonemaster Gear Fling, The (Endless) (234)
- [ ] Dragon in Your Dreams (Ambass.) (88)
- [ ] Flat Motor'n (Kaymoor) (366)
- [ ] Height of Flashin', The (Endless) (240)
- [ ] Homer Erectus (Endless) (250)
- [ ] Look Who's Pulling (Bubba) (137)
- [ ] Reaching New Heights (Junkyard) (99)
- [ ] Slabbers of Habit (Endless) (262)
- [ ] Square Pegs (Bridge) (63)
- [ ] State of the Artz (Endless) (187)
- [ ] Stupendid Animation (Endless) (245)

5.11c

- [ ] Aesthetica (Endless) (231)
- [ ] Alpha and the Omega, The (Endless) (199)
- [ ] Andropov's Cold (Junkyard) (99)
- [ ] April Fools (Endless) (254)
- [ ] Berserker (Endless) (288)
- [ ] Bodyphobic (Endless) (250)
- [ ] Boschtardized (Bubba) (144)
- [ ] Bubbaheads (Beauty) (331)
- [ ] Buried Treasure (Kaymoor) (372)
- [ ] Burning Bungee (Bridge) (73)
- [ ] C-Section (Endless) (293)
- [ ] Call of the Wild (Animal) (116)
- [ ] Centurion, The (Endless) (202)
- [ ] Channel Zero (Endless) (217)
- [ ] Dark Side, The (Endless) (244)
- [ ] Dixie Chicken (Endless) (297)
- [ ] Doer, Not a Critic (Endless) (305)
- [ ] Doggy Style (Animal) (117)
- [ ] Driven to the Edge (Endless) (263)
- [ ] Dubious Young Lizards (Bubba) (126)
- [ ] Dyno Pleas — First Pitch (Bubba) (139)
- [ ] Ed Sullivan Show, The (Endless) (254)
- [ ] Emerald Dance Direct Finish—Cold Turkey (Endless) (307)
- [ ] Eminent Domain (Keeneys) (352)
- [ ] Ex-Puddition, The (Endless) (251)
- [ ] Fat 'n Happy (Endless) (281)
- [ ] Fidget (Endless) (257)
- [ ] Force, The (Bridge) (64)
- [ ] Freeman Route, The (Bridge) (63)
- [ ] Give a Boy a Gun (Endless) (205)
- [ ] God of Fire (Endless) (310)
- [ ] Grand Larceny (Endless) (308)
- [ ] Hairy Canary (Bridge) (73)
- [ ] Hallelujah Crack (Beauty) (330)
- [ ] Hangdog (Animal) (115)
- [ ] Hard Core Female Thrash (Kaymoor) (379)
- [ ] He Man Adhesive Direct Finish - Head Like a Hole (Sunshine) (357)
- [ ] Hooked on Bionics (Endless) (273)
- [ ] Hydroman (Bubba) (134)
- [ ] I Smell A-rête (Kaymoor) (375)
- [ ] Ice (Kaymoor) (373)
- [ ] J.Y.D. (Junkyard) (99)
- [ ] Kentucky Whore (Animal) (119)
- [ ] Lactic Weekend (Endless) (186)
- [ ] Leave Me Bee (Endless) (227)
- [ ] Let's Make a Deal (Beauty) (347)
- [ ] Love Puppy (Sunshine) (356)
- [ ] Marionette (Bridge) (54)
- [ ] Meniscus Burning (Endless) (277)
- [ ] Mighty Stoat, The (Endless) (311)
- [ ] Modern Lovers (Junkyard) (105)
- [ ] Moon Child Posse (Kaymoor) (375)
- [ ] Mr. Fantasy (Endless) (215)
- [ ] Needful Things (Bridge) (75)
- [ ] Never Cry Tuna (Endless) (205)
- [ ] New Age Equippers (Endless) (257)
- [ ] New-veau Reach (Ambass.) (87)
- [ ] Nine Lives (Junkyard) (96)
- [ ] Optical Illusion (Endless) (313)
- [ ] Over the Edge (Endless) (299)
- [ ] Power Line, The (Bubba) (131)
- [ ] Power Lung (Endless) (190)
- [ ] Redemption (Junkyard) (105)
- [ ] Rich Mixture (Sunshine) (356)
- [ ] Right Son of Thunder (Beauty) (346)
- [ ] Sancho Belige (Kaymoor) (378)
- [ ] Slave to the Past (Bridge) (74)
- [ ] Slip Trip (Junkyard) (101)
- [ ] Smell the Glove (Kaymoor) (366)

5.11c (continued)

- ☐ Space Truck'n Bubbas (Bubba) (143)
- ☐ Spectre, The (Endless) (276)
- ☐ Steve Martin's Face (Beauty) (333)
- ☐ Stim-o-Stam (Endless) (265)
- ☐ Strange Duck (Endless) (244)
- ☐ Stretch Armstrong (Bridge) (53)
- ☐ Super Face (Endless) (214)
- ☐ Texas Wine (Endless) (260)
- ☐ Tit Speed (Kaymoor) (380)
- ☐ Tony the Tiger (Kaymoor) (380)
- ☐ Unnamed (Endless) (224)
- ☐ Wasted Armenian, The (Endless) (227)
- ☐ Water Power (Endless) (284)
- ☐ Welcome to Beauty — Right Hand Variation (Beauty) (348)
- ☐ Will to Power, The (Beauty) (332)
- ☐ Zygomatic (Endless) (249)

5.11c/d

- ☐ 100% Real Cheese (Kaymoor) (369)
- ☐ Arm Forces (Endless) (297)
- ☐ Back With My Kind (Endless) (207)
- ☐ Dead Beat Club (Endless) (297)
- ☐ Free Flow (Endless) (217)
- ☐ He Man Adhesive (Sunshine) (357)
- ☐ Luck of the Draw (Endless) (244)
- ☐ Mo' Betta' Holds (Kaymoor) (379)
- ☐ Pop Top (Endless) (306)
- ☐ Prepare to Succeed (Endless) (307)
- ☐ Really Gotta Boogie (Endless) (313)
- ☐ Transcendence (Beauty) (343)

5.11d

- ☐ Agent Orange (Bridge) (59)
- ☐ All the Right Moves (Kaymoor) (379)
- ☐ Beware of Eurodog (Junkyard) (105)
- ☐ Bicycle Club, The (Kaymoor) (378)
- ☐ Bourbon Sauce (Kaymoor) (378)
- ☐ Brooks Route (Beauty) (349)
- ☐ Brown Out (Bubba) (134)
- ☐ Bubbas on a Landscape (Bubba) (138)
- ☐ Chick's Roof (Beauty) (328)
- ☐ Climb-max (Endless) (301)
- ☐ Crank to Power (Bubba) (130)
- ☐ Darwin's Dangle (Bubba) (143)
- ☐ Destination Unknown (Bridge) (80)
- ☐ Destination Unknown Direct Start — The Texas Bolt Massacre (Bridge) (80)
- ☐ Diet Hard (Keeneys) (353)
- ☐ Disturbance (Beauty) (329)
- ☐ Double Feature (Endless) (234)
- ☐ Dresden Corner (Bridge) (54)
- ☐ Drug Virgin (Endless) (226)
- ☐ Echo (Beauty) (339)
- ☐ Fattburger (Endless) (266)
- ☐ Favorite Challenge (Endless) (220)
- ☐ Fearless Symmetry (Kaymoor) (380)
- ☐ Geneva Convention, The (Ambass.) (89)
- ☐ Giant Steps (Endless) (230)
- ☐ Gonad the Bavarian (Endless) (304)
- ☐ Guns of Sassoun (Endless) (274)
- ☐ Hilti as Charged (Beauty) (336)
- ☐ Hold the Dog (Endless) (302)
- ☐ Inventing Situations (Bubba) (157)
- ☐ Keine Kraft (Bubba) (148)
- ☐ Leave It to Jesus (Endless) (244)
- ☐ Leave It to Jesus Direct Finish (Endless) (245)
- ☐ Left Son of Thunder (Beauty) (346)
- ☐ Mack the Knife (Bubba) (139)
- ☐ Magnitude (Kaymoor) (369)
- ☐ Mean, Mean Girl (Endless) (307)
- ☐ Monolith, The (Endless) (299)
- ☐ Motor King (Endless) (217)
- ☐ Necromancer Finish - Popeye Syndrome (Sunshine) (357)
- ☐ Nervous Bachelor (Endless) (314)
- ☐ No Kiss, No Lubrication (Endless) (304)
- ☐ Out of the Bag (Kaymoor) (371)
- ☐ Party Out of Bounds (Endless) (303)
- ☐ Perfect View, The (Beauty) (342)
- ☐ Preferred Dynamics (Bridge) (53)

5.11d (continued)

- ☐ Preservation of the Wild Life (Endless) (300)
- ☐ Progresso (Endless) (213)
- ☐ Radford Rockers (Endless) (275)
- ☐ Reaches from Hell (Bubba) (151)
- ☐ Ribbon, The (Endless) (256)
- ☐ River Heart (Endless) (203)
- ☐ Roll it Over in Your Mind (Endless) (263)
- ☐ Salvation Salesman (Bridge) (69)
- ☐ Scenic Adult (Kaymoor) (381)
- ☐ Seeing Stars (Endless) (282)
- ☐ Sepultura (Bridge) (59)
- ☐ Share the Earth (Endless) (286)
- ☐ Sharkey's Day (Beauty) (349)
- ☐ Slab-o-Meat (Endless) (277)
- ☐ Smore Energy-Mental Wings Link Up-Chouinard-Steck Variation (Endless) (273)
- ☐ Soft Torture (Endless) (275)
- ☐ Son of Frankenstein (Endless) (262)
- ☐ Sound and the Slurry, The (Kaymoor) (373)
- ☐ Staticline (Endless) (239)
- ☐ Stick, The (Endless) (231)
- ☐ Sting, The (Kaymoor) (380)
- ☐ Struck by Lichening (Endless) (239)
- ☐ Sun Viking (Endless) (309)
- ☐ Teleconnections (Endless) (297)
- ☐ Tongulation (Bubba) (143)
- ☐ Tuna Fish Roof (Endless) (206)
- ☐ Unnamed (Ambass.) (87)
- ☐ Unnamed (Sunshine) (356)
- ☐ Vidassana (Endless) (213)
- ☐ Wonderwoman (Endless) (181)
- ☐ Welcome to Huecool (Bridge) (69)
- ☐ Whamawete (Bubba) (137)
- ☐ Whetterbox, The (Endless) (261)
- ☐ Weight, The (Endless) (289)

5.11d/5.12a

- ☐ Flash Point (Endless) (255)
- ☐ Garden Club (Beauty) (329)
- ☐ Golden Years (Endless) (203)
- ☐ Is It Safe? (Endless) (261)
- ☐ M.E.N.S.A. (Beauty) (324)
- ☐ Metabolic Optimizer (Bubba) (166)
- ☐ Rockin' Robyn (Bridge) (73)
- ☐ Tetelestai (Beauty) (337)

5.12a

- ☐ Acid Atomizer, The (Endless) (263)
- ☐ Arbor Day (Endless) (305)
- ☐ Attack of Eddie Muenster (Endless) (293)
- ☐ Baby Cakes (Beauty) (329)
- ☐ Back With My Chyme (Endless) (209)
- ☐ Backlash (Beauty) (347)
- ☐ Beast in Me, The (Beauty) (343)
- ☐ Beowulf (Endless) (309)
- ☐ Bubba Meats Savannah (Bubba) (137)
- ☐ Bubbatism by Fire (Bubba) (157)
- ☐ Burnin' Down the House (Bubba) (153)
- ☐ Carolina Crocker and the Tipple of Doom (Kaymoor) (373)
- ☐ Chasin' the Wind Direct Start (Beauty) (339)
- ☐ Cheez Boys (Endless) (196)
- ☐ Concertina (Beauty) (346)
- ☐ Control (Kaymoor) (379)
- ☐ Crimes of Flashin' (Endless) (269)
- ☐ Dark Shadows (Beauty) (333)
- ☐ Dead Painters Society (Endless) (262)
- ☐ Dining at the Altar (Kaymoor) (375)
- ☐ Dog Day Afternoon II (Endless) (297)
- ☐ Dueling Banjos (Endless) (181)
- ☐ Exqueetion, The (Endless) (257)
- ☐ Erotica (Endless) (231)
- ☐ Espresso Yourself (Endless) (195)
- ☐ Fantasy Face (Endless) (214)
- ☐ Fast Asleep in a Dangerous World (Bridge) (64)
- ☐ Fine Motor Control (Endless) (248)
- ☐ Flirting With Apollo Reed (Endless) (209)

5.12a (continued)

- ☐ Fly Girls (Endless) (305)
- ☐ Freakly Stylee (Endless) (265)
- ☐ Frenzyed (Bridge) (48)
- ☐ Galapagos (Bubba) (143)
- ☐ Genocide (Beauty) (328)
- ☐ Growing Hole, The (Endless) (230)
- ☐ Harvest (Endless) (221   )
- ☐ Hell Bound for Glory (Endless) (241)
- ☐ Hot Bip (Beauty) (328)
- ☐ Idol Point Arête (Endless) (276)
- ☐ In Real Life (Endless) (227)
- ☐ Iron Cross (Bubba) (162)
- ☐ Jack the Tripper (Endless) (183)
- ☐ Jet Cap (Endless) (212)
- ☐ Just Another Obscurity (Endless) (285)
- ☐ L.S.D. (Beauty) (343)
- ☐ Lap Child (Junkyard) (109)
- ☐ Leechate (Bridge) (81)
- ☐ Let the Wind Blow (Bridge) (45)
- ☐ Let's Get Physical (Bridge) (55)
- ☐ Likmé (Bubba) (143)
- ☐ Little Head Logic (Bridge) (62)
- ☐ Lord of the Jungle (Bubba) (165)
- ☐ Lost Souls (Kaymoor) (378)
- ☐ Magnificent Puddcasso, The (Endless) (262)
- ☐ Mercenary Territory (Bubba) (166)
- ☐ Michelin Man (Bubba) (146)
- ☐ More Studly Than Puddly (Bubba) (139)
- ☐ Mr. Hollywood (Kaymoor) (381)
- ☐ Mr. Pudd's Wild Ride (Bubba) (132)
- ☐ Muscle Belly (Endless) (303)
- ☐ New World Order aka Masoko Tango (Endless) (223)
- ☐ Overlooked, The (Bridge) (39)
- ☐ Plastic Attraction (Beauty) (349)
- ☐ Pockets of Resistance (Kaymoor) (371)
- ☐ Positron (Endless) (257)
- ☐ Pounded Puppies (Bubba) (148)
- ☐ Preparation H (Kaymoor) (371)
- ☐ Pulp (Beauty) (348)
- ☐ Quickie in the Molars (Endless) (303)
- ☐ Quickie in the Molars—Direct Finish (Endless) (303)
- ☐ Rabbit Almost Died, The (Endless) (235)
- ☐ Reason over Might (Bubba) (126)
- ☐ Regatta de Blank (Bubba) (153)
- ☐ Rhythm of Movement (Endless) (281)
- ☐ Ride'm Cowboy (Kaymoor) (374)
- ☐ Rites of Summer (Bubba) (157)
- ☐ Roadcutt Manor (Bridge) (81)
- ☐ Ron Kauk Gets a Perm (Endless) (296)
- ☐ S.L.A.P. aka Squeal Like a Pig (Kaymoor) (372)
- ☐ Sleeping Beauty (Beauty) (337)
- ☐ Smokin' Guns (Beauty) (322)
- ☐ South Rimjob Variation—Rimshot (Sunshine) (359)
- ☐ Spurtin' Fer Certain (Endless) (186)
- ☐ Stratagem, The (Bridge) (47)
- ☐ Strongly Stationary (Bridge) (69)
- ☐ Sultans of Swing (Bridge) (69)
- ☐ Swinging Udders (Kaymoor) (374)
- ☐ Tatoo (Endless) (207)
- ☐ Team Machine (Bridge) (53)
- ☐ Thieves in the Temple (Endless) (308)
- ☐ Tongue in Groove (Endless) (309)
- ☐ Total Sex Package (Endless) (313)
- ☐ Truth or Contra-Expenses (Bubba) (126)
- ☐ Udderling, The (Endless) (303)
- ☐ Unbroken Chain (Sunshine) (356)
- ☐ Unbroken Chain Variation Finish - Unnamed (Sunshine) (356)
- ☐ Veni, Vedi, Veci (Bubba) (125)
- ☐ Virgin Thing (Endless) (231)
- ☐ White Out (Endless) (310)
- ☐ Wings and a Prayer (Endless) (297)
- ☐ World's Hardest Five Twelve, The (Kaymoor) (368)

5.12a/b

- ☐ Baby Rage (Endless) (199)
- ☐ Bubbas at Arapiles (Endless) (204)
- ☐ Cutting Edge, The (Bubba) (133)
- ☐ Hourglass (Endless) (190)
- ☐ Midnight Moonlight Direct Finish — Akron Motor Speedway (Bridge) (73)
- ☐ Mind Shaft (Bridge) (69)
- ☐ Morning Dew (Endless) (294)
- ☐ Pilots of Bekaa (Junkyard) (109)
- ☐ Two Fish Limit (Endless) (226)
- ☐ Wad Cutter (Endless) (205)

5.12b

A Date With Disappointment (Endless) (277)

Auld Lang Syne (Ambass.) (88)

Barbecued Babies aka Zeno's Route (Endless) (186)

Berlin Wall Direct Start — Reunification (Bridge) (65)

Blackhappy (Endless) (231)

Bolting Blowfish, The (Ambass.) (87)

Bouldergiest (Endless) (220)

Brawn Wall, The (Endless) (306)

Bubba Black Sheep (Bubba) (145)

Bullet the New Sky (Endless) (223)

Burning (Bubba) (147)

Can't Find My Guernsey Cow (Endless) (240)

Civilizing Mission (Endless) (257)

Close to the Edge (Endless) (298)

Critical Path (Bubba) (151)

Dangerous Liasions (Endless) (257)

De-Funked (Endless) (261)

Desperate but Not Serious (Bubba) (136)

Dragon in Your Dreams Direct Start — Enter the Dragon (Ambass.) (88)

Dyno Pleas — Second Pitch (Bubba) (139)

European Vacation (Endless) (182)

Eyes of the Mind (Bridge) (69)

Fade to Black (Beauty) (331)

Fall Line (Endless) (284)

Fearful Symmetry (Endless) (199)

Fish Out of Water (Endless) (188)

Foutre la Doigt (Endless) (304)

Gift of Grace, The (Endless) (245)

Gimme, Gimme Shock Treatment (Beauty) (338)

Grace Note (Beauty) (333)

Green Room (Bridge) (52)

Harlequin (Endless) (239)

Harmonic Jello (Bubba) (124)

Horton's Tree Direct Finish — Mean Old Mr. Gravity (Bridge) (45)

Hot Tuna (Endless) (205)

I Advanced Masked (Endless) (220)

I Feel Like a Wog (Endless) (217)

Into the Fire (Bubba) (135)

Jesus and Tequila (Endless) (238)

Just Forget It (Endless) (197)

Le Futuriste (Endless) (260)

Live and Let Live (Endless) (193)

Loki (Endless) (310)

Man-0-War (Endless) (204)

Mango Boingo (Sunshine) (357)

Meat Is Murder (Endless) (266)

Ministry (Kaymoor) (378)

Mississippi Burning (Endless) (221)

Nazz, Nazz (Beauty) (339)

Night Train (Beauty) (322)

No Mas (Endless) (207)

Not 'til Verdon (Bubba) (163)

Old Duffer's Route (Endless) (209)

Overkill Variation Finish—Future Proof (Endless) (194)

Pearl River (Endless) (203)

Pocket Pussy (Endless) (269)

Poochie Gets a Face Lift (Endless) (282)

Power Source (Endless) (228)

Pump and Circumstance (Bubba) (157)

Rainy Day Route (Endless) (235)

Rebel Spade (Endless) (208)

Rico Suavé Arête Finish, The—Coal Miner's Tale (Kaymoor) (371)

Rock Waves (Bubba) (144)

Sacrilege (Endless) (238)

Salvador Raleigh's Blow Up Dolly (Endless) (256)

Shotgun (Endless) (199)

Slide Rule (Endless) (194)

South Rimjob (Sunshine) (359)

Stories Without Words (Bubba) (157)

Syndicate Fool (Sunshine) (357)

Tarbaby (Kaymoor) (368)

Teleconnections Direct Start—Power Talk (Endless) (297)

Through the Never (Endless) (273)

Thunder Struck (Kaymoor) (373)

Uniflatable Ewe, The (Kaymoor) (370)

Unnamed (Sunshine) (358)

Veni, Vedi, Veci Direct Start — Flexible Strategies (Bubba) (125)

Vulcan Mind Funk (Endless) (282)

West Virginia Highway aka Coal Miner's Daughter (Bridge) (46)

5.12b (continued)

- ☐ Whiney Bugs (Beauty) (325)
- ☐ Whip It (Endless) (256)
- ☐ Yew Nosemite (Junkyard) (98)
- ☐ Verge, The (Bridge) (58)

5.12b/c

- ☐ Arapiles Please (Bubba) (137)
- ☐ Blacklist (Endless) (193)
- ☐ Brother Sun (Junkyard) 5.12 b/c (110)
- ☐ Bubba Down Under (Bubba) (151)
- ☐ Bubbacide (Bubba) (135)
- ☐ Caption (Endless) (208)
- ☐ Chunky Monkey (Beauty) (325)
- ☐ Finders Keepers (Endless) (192)
- ☐ French Tickler (Endless) (276)
- ☐ Green Envy (Beauty) (329)
- ☐ How Hard Is That Thang? (Endless) (245)
- ☐ Lisa's Lunge Time (Endless) (255)
- ☐ Loud Noise (Beauty) (347)
- ☐ Mega Magic (Bridge) (49)
- ☐ Modern Primitive (Endless) (268)
- ☐ Mystery Dance (Junkyard) (101)
- ☐ Pigtail (Endless) (194)
- ☐ Salvador Dali's Car (Endless) (304)
- ☐ Shudder Bugger (Endless) (251)
- ☐ Stubble (Endless) (198)
- ☐ The Cow Girl (Kaymoor) (374)
- ☐ This Sport Needs an Enema (Endless) (250)
- ☐ Where's Bohemia? (Bubba) (147)
- ☐ Wounded in Action (Endless) (308)

5.12c

- ☐ American Sportsman, The (Bubba) (143)
- ☐ Are You Experienced? (Bridge) (53)
- ☐ Be-Attitudes (Endless) (261)
- ☐ Belly Up (Endless) (190)
- ☐ Best Little Road Cut Out of Texas, The (Bridge) (81)
- ☐ Boss Cocky (Kaymoor) (375)
- ☐ Bubba Lou (Bubba) (135)
- ☐ Bubbacide Direct Finish — Lean Productions (Bubba) (135)
- ☐ Buzz Kill (Kaymoor) (381)
- ☐ Chorus Line (Beauty) (333)
- ☐ Chorus Line Direct Start (Beauty) (333)
- ☐ Clean Sweep (Endless) (241)
- ☐ Fat Back (Endless) (199)
- ☐ Fat Factor (Bridge) aka Luv Jugs (45)
- ☐ Fiesta Grande (Endless) (187)
- ☐ Final Exit (Kaymoor) (364)
- ☐ Fortitude (Bubba) (163)
- ☐ Great White Shark, The (Bubba) (152)
- ☐ Gun Club (Beauty) (342)
- ☐ Harbinger Scarab (Endless) (269)
- ☐ Incredarête (Bubba) (151)
- ☐ Innocence Mission, The (Bubba) (131)
- ☐ It's Brutal Bubba (Bubba) (133)
- ☐ Kaos (Kaymoor) (379)
- ☐ Kiss My Fingers (Bridge) (63)
- ☐ Meaty-Urologist, The (Endless) (281)
- ☐ Noelle (Endless) (235)
- ☐ Komatose (Beauty) (325)
- ☐ Love Shack (Bridge) (47)
- ☐ Mango Boingo Variation Finish - Disco Apocalypse (Sunshine) (357)
- ☐ Martini Face (Endless) (224)
- ☐ Maximum Leader (Endless) (241)
- ☐ Mental Wings (Endless) (273)
- ☐ Over the Edge Direct Start—Air Apparent (Endless) (299)
- ☐ Pettifogger (Kaymoor) (375)
- ☐ Pocket Petting Zoo, The (Kaymoor) (369)
- ☐ Pocket Pool (Endless) (280)
- ☐ Portly Gentleman's Route (Endless) (309)
- ☐ Ramrod (Endless) (184)
- ☐ Reefer Derby (Ambass.) (88)
- ☐ Scar Lover (Kaymoor) (364)
- ☐ Sloth (Endless) (191)

5.12c (continued)

- ☐ Sparks (Endless) (208)
- ☐ Standing Up in the Big Tent (Endless) (256)
- ☐ Stink Bug (Endless) (217)
- ☐ Stop the Presses Rico Suavé! (Bubba) (135)
- ☐ Success Through Deception (Ambass.) (89)
- ☐ Suspended Sentence (Endless) (202)
- ☐ Techman (Endless) (265)
- ☐ Tip Terror (Endless) (185)
- ☐ Vidassana Direct Start—Wu Wei (Endless) (213)
- ☐ Voyeur's Hand (Endless) (241)
- ☐ Vulcan Block (Endless) (223)
- ☐ Wall Drug (Endless) (301)

5.12c/d

- ☐ Ewe Can't Touch This (Beauty) (338)
- ☐ Fascist Architecture (Endless) (265)
- ☐ Gin and Bulls (Endless) (203)
- ☐ Holier Than Thou (Endless) (193)
- ☐ Hubba Bubba Direct Start - Skewered (Bubba) (153)
- ☐ Kama Futra (Bubba) (148)
- ☐ Land Before Time, The (Endless) (284)
- ☐ Mother's Milk (Sunshine) (356)
- ☐ Plyometrics (Endless) (268)
- ☐ Pudd's Pretty Dress (Endless) (280)
- ☐ Rumors of War (Endless) (313)
- ☐ Stealth' n Magic (Endless) (265)
- ☐ What Will People Think? (Endless) (277)

5.12d

- ☐ Absolute Reality (Bubba) (139)
- ☐ Ad Lib (Beauty) (333)
- ☐ Bosnian Vacation (Endless) (300)
- ☐ Choke it Up (Beauty) (322)
- ☐ Express Yourself (Endless) (257)
- ☐ Gag Reflex (Bridge) (49)
- ☐ Heller Route (Beauty) (322)
- ☐ It's a Fine Line (Beauty) (322)
- ☐ Jesus Wept (Bubba) (133)
- ☐ L.A.B.—Mojo Hand Link Up—Devil Doll (Kaymoor) (365)
- ☐ Lactic Acid Bath (Kaymoor) (365)
- ☐ Mojo Hand (Kaymoor) (365)
- ☐ Mongoloid (Beauty) (328)
- ☐ Oblivion (Endless) (239)
- ☐ Pirouette (Bridge) (48)
- ☐ Plug, The (Endless) (272)
- ☐ Rainy Day Route Variation Finish - Big Boss Man (Endless) (235)
- ☐ Rubber Glove Test, The (Kaymoor) (369)
- ☐ Slash and Burn (Kaymoor) (381)
- ☐ Sun Viking Direct Start—Thor (Endless) (309)
- ☐ Superstition (Endless) (191)
- ☐ Saint, The (Endless) (276)
- ☐ Tantrum, The (Kaymoor) (368)
- ☐ Vertical Wench, The (Endless) (261)

5.12d/5.13a

- ☐ Eurobics (Endless) (260)
- ☐ Masterpiece Theater (Bubba) (152)
- ☐ Use Your Power (Endless) (305)
- ☐ Welcome to Conditioning (Endless) (302)

5.13a

- [ ] A-Pocket-Leaps Now (Bubba) (148)
- [ ] Blood Raid (Kaymoor) (365)
- [ ] Bloodshot (Endless) (223)
- [ ] Broken Dreams (Beauty) (336)
- [ ] Burning Cross (Kaymoor) (364)
- [ ] Colors (Endless) (284)
- [ ] Dial 911 (Endless) (221)
- [ ] Diamond Life (Bubba) (135)
- [ ] Dissonance (Endless) (223)
- [ ] Dreams of White Hörsts (Bubba) (153)
- [ ] Fat Cat (Bridge) (78)
- [ ] Gymtonic (Bridge) (52)
- [ ] Idols of the Tribe (Endless) (273)
- [ ] L.A.B. Direct Finish - Massacre (Kaymoor) (365)
- [ ] Leather Nun, The (Kaymoor) (369)
- [ ] Libertine (Endless) (238)
- [ ] Locked on Target (Bridge) (55)
- [ ] Mind's Eye (Bubba) (133)
- [ ] My Stinking Brain (Endless) (298)
- [ ] Original Crankster (Sunshine) (357)
- [ ] Overkill (Endless) (194)
- [ ] Pocket Route, The (Endless) (223)
- [ ] Quinsana Plus (Endless) (235)
- [ ] Ruchert Motion, The (Beauty) (331)
- [ ] Sanctified (Kaymoor) (368)
- [ ] Silent But Deadly (Endless) (223)
- [ ] Skull Poke Direct Finish (Kaymoor) (365)
- [ ] Stab Me, I Don't Matter (Endless) (302)
- [ ] Super Mario (Endless) (182)
- [ ] Unnamed (Endless) (202)
- [ ] Weatherman's Thumb, The (Endless) (249)
- [ ] West Virginia Water Torture (Beauty) (337)
- [ ] Whammy (Bridge) (47)
- [ ] Wicca (Bridge) (44)

5.13a/b

- [ ] Jesus and Tequila Variation Finish—Get Thee Behind Me Satan (Endless) (238)
- [ ] Just Send It (Endless) (302)
- [ ] Nude Brute (Kaymoor) (371)

5.13b

- [ ] Albatross (Kaymoor) (372)
- [ ] 'Bout Time (Endless) (269)
- [ ] Cosmic Thing (Endless) (226)
- [ ] Fuel Injector (Kaymoor) (381)
- [ ] Racist, The (Endless) (221)
- [ ] Ragnarock (Endless) (193)
- [ ] Ride the Lightening (Endless) (192)
- [ ] Shovel Jerk (Endless) (223)
- [ ] Sportster (Beauty) (332)
- [ ] Stabat Mater (Beauty) (347)
- [ ] Sweetest Taboo, The (Endless) (269)
- [ ] Titan's Dice (Endless) (231)
- [ ] Tubin' Dudes (Endless) (183)
- [ ] Villian's Course (Endless) (280)
- [ ] White Lightning (Kaymoor) (373)
- [ ] Xanth (Endless) (191)

5.13b/c, 5.13c/d

- [ ] L.A.B. Variation—In the Flat Field (Kaymoor) 5.13b/c (365)
- [ ] Satanic Verses (Endless) 5.13b/c (235)
- [ ] Travisty, The (Beauty) 5.13c/d (325)

NEW ROUTE ADDENDUM

BEAUTY MOUNTAIN

Dancing in the Flesh 5.12b ☆ 🅟 aka D.E.N.S.A.
Immediately right of *M.E.N.S.A.* is a line of four bolts that lead to cold shuts. 55 feet. FA: Michael Stewart & Jim Suffecool, July 1996.

ENDLESS WALL

The following new routes are located in the Cirque:

Unnamed 5.11b ☆ 🅟
Begin immediately left of *Spurtual Reality* and follow four bolts to shared anchors with *Spurtual Reality*. 50 feet. FA: Roxanna Brock, December 1996.

Satanic Traverses 5.12c ☆☆☆ 🅟 ℛ
The classic traverse from hell. Begin by climbing *Powerlung* to the anchors, then move down on big holds and continue along the seemingly endless traverse past the second bolt on *Pooh's Corner* and the fourth bolt on route #65 (currently a project) until you reach a pair of anchors. Bring enough draws to clip 19 bolts. 165 feet. Note: requires a 60 meter rope. FA: Brian McCray, December 1996.

New Testament 5.12d ☆☆ 🅟 ℛ
Begin 15 feet right of *Pooh's Corner* and climb directly past three bolts, then traverse right past seven more bolts to anchors. 90 feet. FA: Brian McCray, December 1996.

Unnamed 5.12d ☆☆ 🅟 ℛ
Start 30 feet right of *New Testament* and climb past six bolts to a station at a horizontal slot. 50 feet. FA: Brian McCray, December 1996.

Graffiti 5.12a/b ☆ 🅟 ℛ
Climb the initial left-facing flake of *Where's Bulimia?*, then continue directly up the thin face to anchors at a ledge. 50 feet. FA: Brian McCray, November 1996.

High Yeller 5.13a ☆ 🅟 ℛ
Begin immediately left of *Finders Keepers* and follow eight bolts up and left to anchors at a large hueco. 70 feet. FA: Brian McCray, November 1996.

Mr. McGoo 5.12c ☆ 🅟 ℛ
Described in the Endless Wall chapter as project/route #79, this line was recently completed. 60 feet. FA: Brian McCray, October 1996.

Hasta La Vista, Baby 5.12b ☆☆ 𝄞 ℛ
Described in the Endless Wall chapter as project/route #82, this one was also recently completed. Now has eight bolts. 60 feet. FA: Brian McCray, October 1996.

The following two routes are located on the downstream corner of the pillar that stands in front of the Cirque Ladder. See the map on page 194 for reference.

Topiary 5.12b ☆ 𝄞
Climb the center of the narrow orange face past a short right angling crack and a technical finish to cold shuts. Seven bolts. 60 feet. FA TR: Rick Thompson, November 1994. FA: Angie McGinnis, December 1996.

Spree 5.11a ☆ 𝄞
Begin about ten feet left of *Topiary*, on the left side of the arête, and follow six bolts to cold shuts. 65 feet. FA: Angie McGinnis, October 1996.

The following two routes are located on the upstream end of the Mungolian Wall.

Project - In Progress
Currently the most right-hand route on the Mungolian Wall. Begin about 40 feet right of the *Stalactite* and crank the line of seven bolts to cold shuts.

Welcome to Mungolia 5.11a ☆ 𝄞
Begin 30 feet right of the *Stalactite*, just right of the large tree and follow eight bolts to cold shuts. 60 feet. FA: Doug Reed, October 1996.

Stuart Pregnall on the first ascent of *Frenzied,* at the Bridge Buttress.

photo: Rick Thompson

Karen Pregnall on the second ascent of *Insistent Irony,* at Central Bubba.

photo: Rick Thompson

ACCESS: It's every climber's concern

The Access Fund, a national, non-profit climbers organization, works to keep climbing areas open and to conserve the climbing environment. Need help with closures? land acquisition? legal or land management issues? funding for trails and other projects? starting a local climbers' group? CALL US!

Climbers can help preserve access by being committed to Leave No Trace (minimum-impact) practices. Here are some simple guidelines:

- **ASPIRE TO "LEAVE NO TRACE"** especially in environmentally sensitive areas like caves. Chalk can be a significant impact on dark and porous rock – don't use it around historic rock art. Pick up litter, and leave trees and plants intact.

- **DISPOSE OF HUMAN WASTE PROPERLY** Use toilets whenever possible. If toilets are not available, dig a "cat hole" at least six inches deep and 200 feet from any water, trails, campsites, or the base of climbs. *Always pack out toilet paper.* On big wall routes, use a "poop tube" and carry waste up and off with you (the old "bag toss" is now illegal in many areas).

- **USE EXISTING TRAILS** Cutting switchbacks causes erosion. When walking off-trail, tread lightly, especially in the desert where cryptogamic soils (usually a dark crust) take thousands of years to form and are easily damaged. Be aware that "rim ecologies" (the clifftop) are often highly sensitive to disturbance.

- **BE DISCRETE WITH FIXED ANCHORS** *Bolts are controversial and are not a convenience* – don't place 'em unless they are *really* necessary. Camouflage all anchors. Remove unsightly slings from rappel stations (better to use steel chain or welded cold shuts). Bolts sometimes can be used proactively to protect fragile resources – consult with your local land manager.

- **RESPECT THE RULES** and speak up when other climbers don't. Expect restrictions in designated wilderness areas, rock art sites, caves, and to protect wildlife, especially nesting birds of prey. *Power drills are illegal in wilderness and all national parks.*

- **PARK AND CAMP IN DESIGNATED AREAS** Some climbing areas require a permit for overnight camping.

- **MAINTAIN A LOW PROFILE** Leave the boom box and day-glo clothing at home – the less climbers are heard and seen, the better.

- **RESPECT PRIVATE PROPERTY** Be courteous to land owners. Don't climb where you're not wanted.

- **JOIN THE ACCESS FUND** To become a member, make a tax-deductible donation of $25.

The Access Fund
Preserving America's Diverse Climbing Resources
PO Box 17010
Boulder, CO 80308
303.545.6772 • www.accessfund.org